D1320817

ROYAL HISTORICAL SOCIETY GUIDES AND HANDBOOKS

No. 18

HISTORIANS' GUIDE TO EARLY BRITISH MAPS

ROYAL HISTORICAL SOCIETY
GUIDES AND HANDBOOKS
ISSN 0080–4398

MAIN SERIES

1. *Guide to English Commercial Statistics, 1696–1782.* By G. N. Clark and Barbara M. Franks. 1938.
2. *Handbook of British Chronology.* Edited by F. M. Powicke, Charles Johnson and W. J. Harte. 1939. 2nd edition, edited by F. M. Powicke and E. B. Fryde, 1961. 3rd edition, edited by E. B. Fryde, D. E. Greenway, S. Porter and I. Roy, 1986.
3. *Medieval Libraries of Great Britain. A list of surviving books.* Edited by N. R. Ker. 1941. 2nd edition, 1964.
4. *Handbook of Dates for Students of English History.* Edited by C. R. Cheney. 1945. Reprinted, 1991.
5. *Guide to the National and Provincial Directories of England and Wales, excluding London, published before 1856.* By Jane E. Norton, 1950.
6. *Handbook of Oriental History.* Edited by C. H. Philips. 1951.
7. *Texts and Calendars. An analytical guide to serial publications.* By E. L. C. Mullins. 1958. Reprinted (with corrections), 1978.
8. *Anglo-Saxon Charters. An annotated list and bibliography.* By P. H. Sawyer. 1968.
9. *A Centenary Guide to the publications of the Royal Historical Society 1868–1968 and of the former Camden Society 1838–1897.* By Alexander Taylor Milne. 1968.
10. *Guide to the Local Administrative Units of England.* Volume I. *Southern England.* By Frederic A. Youngs, Jr. 1980. Reprinted, 1981.
11. *Guide to Bishops' Registers of England and Wales. A survey from the middle ages to the abolition of episcopacy in 1646.* By David M. Smith. 1981.
12. *Texts and Calendars II. An analytical guide to serial publications 1957–1982.* By E. L. C. Mullins. 1983.
13. *Handbook of Medieval Exchange.* By Peter Spufford, with the assistance of Wendy Wilkinson and Sarah Tolley. 1986.
14. *Scottish Texts and Calendars. An analytical guide to serial publications.* By David and Wendy Stevenson. 1987.
15. *Medieval Libraries of Great Britain.* Edited by N. R. Ker. *Supplement to the second edition.* Edited by Andrew G. Watson. 1987.
16. *A Handlist of British Diplomatic Representatives 1509–1688.* By Gary M. Bell. 1990.
17. *Guide to the Local Administrative Units of England. Volume II. Northern England.* By Frederic A. Youngs, Jr. 1991.

SUPPLEMENTARY SERIES

1. *A Guide to the papers of British Cabinet Ministers, 1900–1951.* Compiled by Cameron Hazlehurst and Christine Woodland. 1974.
2. *A Guide to the reports of the U.S. Strategic Bombing Survey.* I *Europe.* II *The Pacific.* Edited by Gordon Daniels. 1981.

HISTORIANS' GUIDE TO EARLY BRITISH MAPS

A GUIDE TO THE LOCATION OF PRE-1900 MAPS OF THE BRITISH ISLES
PRESERVED IN THE UNITED KINGDOM AND IRELAND

General Editor   Helen Wallis

Assisted by Anita McConnell

LONDON

OFFICES OF THE ROYAL HISTORICAL SOCIETY

UNIVERSITY COLLEGE LONDON, GOWER STREET
LONDON WC1E 6BT
1994

ISBN 0 86193 141 6

Printed and bound in Great Britain by
Butler & Tanner Ltd, Frome and London

'To the antiquarian of the 25th century, I hope it will be found useful, should a single copy of it have the singular good fortune to be preserved till that period, as affording them an opportunity, by consulting the angular measurement, of determining the position of many places in the County with a tolerable degree of accuracy, of which the devouring hand of time may not, perhaps, have left the least vestige remaining.'

John Lindley, Surrey Place, 15 April 1793.

(From his *Memoir of a map of the County of Surrey; from a survey made in the years 1789 and 1790,* London, 1793).

Contents

Preface and Acknowledgements

Great Britain and Ireland enjoy a rich cartographic heritage, yet historians have not made full use of early maps in their writings and research. This has been partly due to lack of adequate information about what maps are available. The Royal Historical Society took action some years ago to remedy the situation, in planning to add maps to their series of Guides. Their Literary Director accordingly invited me to undertake the editing of an Historians' Guide to British Maps.

The project reflects the growing interest in maps since the end of the Second World War. Various national and international societies responded to this interest and saw the compilation of directories of map collections as a priority. By the 1970s many scholars were working on the history of British cartography, amongst whom I was able to recruit an expert team of assistants.

In consultation with the literary directors of the Royal Historical Society we decided to divide the Guide into two parts. Part I describes 'the history and purpose of maps' in a series of short essays on the early mapping of the British Isles. Part II comprises a guide to the collections, national and regional, based in the first instance on the completion of over 200 questionnaires and on follow-up visits as required. The British Library provided a generous grant to cover the main costs and the British Academy supplemented this with a grant to meet postage and other out-of-pocket expenses.

Thus funded, the work was well advanced by 1984, when various changes in the Map Library of the British Library and pressure of other work forced me to hold the project in suspense. My retirement as Map Librarian of the British Library in 1986 made it necessary for me to review our plans.

It was then clear that a full time professionally qualified and properly funded project assistant with computer facilities was essential for the completion of the task. In the later months of 1992 we recruited to this post Dr Anita McConnell, an historian of science.

An Executive Committee comprising Tony Campbell, my successor as Map Librarian of the British Library, Ralph Hyde, Keeper of Prints and Maps at the Guildhall Library, London, Anita McConnell and myself, organised the planning of the project, thus resuscitated. We recruited some new members to the team of authors for Part I. For Part II, the old returns were sent out again for updating and many new questionnaires were distributed, bringing the total to nearly 450.

This final period of work was completed in about 18 months. The many people who have helped are acknowledged below. To Anita McConnell I give special thanks, for without her indefatigable services the Guide would not have seen the light of day. We also thank Tony Campbell, Peter Barber and Geoff Armitage, of the Map Library in the British Library, for their valuable advice and assistance.

We hope that this Guide will enable maps to gain their place as a national resource, and that historians in particular will discover the wealth of our cartographic heritage.

For major contributions to the earlier stages of this work special thanks are due to Sarah Tyacke, then Deputy Map Librarian of the British Library, now Keeper of the Records at the Public Record Office. Her activities as my project assistant were invaluable. Our team then comprised, in addition to Sarah Tyacke and myself, John Andrews, Professor of Geography at Trinity College, Dublin, Michael Francis, Keeper of Prints, National Library of Wales, J. B. (Brian) Harley, Montefiore Reader in Geography of the University of Exeter, Joe Hegarty of the Map Room, National Library of Scotland, Donald Hodson, expert in county bibliography, Yolande Hodson, Senior Research Assistant in the Map Library of the British Library, P. D. A. (Paul) Harvey, Professor of Medieval History at the University of Durham, Ralph Hyde, Peter Penfold, recently retired Curator of Maps at the Public Record Office and Christopher Terrell of the National Maritime Museum, Greenwich. Ken Newton, County Archivist of Essex, advised on local records. Peter Penfold made follow-up visits to many archives in London and southern England. The deaths of Ken Newton (1978), Brian Harley (1991) and Peter Penfold (1993) are recorded with deep regret. Our thanks are also due of course to the many county archivists, local librarians and their assistants who patiently completed the forms and then checked our edited version of their returns.

In the last period of work, 1992–4, Anita McConnell acted as my fulltime project assistant, and as stated above, made possible the completion of the project. Paul Ferguson, Map Librarian of Trinity College, Dublin, completed for Ireland the work begun by John Andrews who has continued to advise us. Robert Davies, Assistant Keeper, Department of Pictures and Maps in the National Library of Wales, has supervised the returns for Wales. Paul Harvey co-ordinated the returns for the University of Durham. Elizabeth Baigent of St Hugh's College, Oxford, dealt with the colleges of Oxford University; Sarah Bendall of Emmanuel College, Cambridge, supervised the returns of the Cambridge colleges. Tony Campbell has been a most helpful adviser in overall editorial matters.

The grants of the British Library and British Academy in the early 1980s and of the Leverhulme Trust in 1993–94 have provided us with the means to undertake the work, and are gratefully acknowledged.

Finally I must thank the literary directors of the Royal Historical Society for their advice and encouragement throughout.

Helen Wallis
May 1994

PART I

THE HISTORY AND PURPOSE OF MAPS

	Editor's Introduction	Helen Wallis.
1	General maps of Great Britain and the British Isles.	Rodney Shirley.
2	Medieval maps, to 1500.	Paul Harvey.
3	County maps.	Donald Hodson.
4	Cartobibliographies of county maps, local maps and town plans of England and Wales.	Geoff Armitage
5	County surveys.	Elizabeth M. Rodger.
6	Military surveys of Great Britain and Ireland. c.1290–1700.	Peter Barber.
7	Military surveys, 1700–1900.	Yolande Hodson.
8	Ordnance Survey maps.	Geoff Armitage and Helen Wallis.
9	Town plans.	Geoff Armitage and Helen Wallis.
10	Estate maps.	Sarah Bendall.
11	Tithe, parish and enclosure maps.	Roger Kain.
12	Archaeological maps.	William Ravenhill.
13	Geological maps.	Karen S. Cook.
14	Thematic and statistical maps.	Helen Wallis.
15	Road maps	Tony Campbell.
16	Fire insurance plans.	Gwyn Rowley.
17	Navigable waterways and railway maps.	David Smith.
18	Metal mining maps.	Roger Burt.
19	Maps in Parliamentary papers.	Susan Gole.
20	Maritime Surveys.	Christopher Terrell and Helen Wallis
21	Agriculture and land use maps.	Elizabeth Baigent.
22	Maps of Ireland.	John Andrews and Paul Ferguson.
23	Maps of Scotland.	Jeffrey Stone.
24	Maps of Wales.	Robert Davies.
25	Place names and gazetteers.	Francis Herbert.
26	Map collecting.	Peter Barber and Tony Campbell.

1

Editor's Introduction   Helen Wallis

Although map making was one of the new crafts of the European Renaissance in the late 15th and early 16th centuries, surveying had its origins before 2000 BC in ancient Egypt and Babylon. The achievements of Greek geography and astronomy from *c*.500 BC onwards, and of Roman surveying and mapping from 200 BC, laid the foundations of European map making in later centuries, but without establishing a continuous tradition. Thus the two great medieval mappae mundi, the Ebsdorf map *c*.1239–40, destroyed in World War II but preserved in facsimile, and the Hereford world map, *c*.1280, in Hereford Cathedral, are derivations from a Roman original, Agrippa's survey of the Roman empire *c*.AD 14, but the intervening series of maps is lost. Both maps were inspired by Englishmen: the Ebsdorf map is attributed to Gervase of Tilbury (*c*.1160–1235?), and the Hereford map was devised by Richard of Haldingham, also known as Richard de Bello.

In medieval England maps were normally made as an adjunct to other activities, for example, as illustrations to medieval chronicles. The first separate map of Great Britain, *c*.1250, was designed by Matthew Paris (d.1259), the monk of St Albans, to illustrate his *Chronica Majora* and his *Historia Anglorum*. A few local plans are known, such as that of the water works of Christ Church Priory, Canterbury, *c*.1165, and others drawn as aids to settle legal disputes. The earliest known treatise on surveying written in English dates from the 14th century.[1] It describes the use of the quadrant and plane-table in measuring first heights, then distances, then depths. Diagrams illustrate the instruments. However, surveys at this date were not necessarily rendered in the form of maps.

Printed works on surveying were first published in the early 16th century. Anthony Fitzherbert's treatise on surveying, 1523, explains how a lordship or manor should be surveyed. The earliest general text book on geometrical survey was that of Richard Benese, an Augustinian canon of Merton Priory, *This boke sheweth the maner of measurynge of all maner of lande*, Southwark, ?1537.

The new profession of surveying took some time, however, to gain acceptance. In *The Surveyors Dialogue*, London, 1607, pp. 2–4, 6, John Norden (1548–1626), an attorney, map maker and surveyor, practising in Middlesex, sets out the advantages of surveying, and deems it necessary

---

[1] BL, Sloane ms. 213 ff.121–123.

to defend the surveyor against suspicious farmers: 'And often times you are the cause that men lose their land', the Farmer complains. The Surveyor replies, not perhaps entirely convincingly, 'the faulty are afraid to be seen ... the innocent need not fear to be looked into.' Norden's book became a standard work and was reprinted as late as 1738.

The 'Mathematicall Clients' of the 16th century surveyors, as Ralph Agas called them, included the great landowners, such as the ninth earl of Northumberland, who employed the Yorkshire surveyor Christopher Saxton, and William Cecil, Lord Burghley, who employed Norden. As surveyor of Crown Lands for James I, Norden executed two of his masterpieces, his manuscript survey of the Duchy of Cornwall, c.1609, now in Trinity College, Cambridge (and available in facsimile since 1972), and the Honor of Windsor, 1607. This is preserved in two examples, one manuscript in the British Library, Harleian ms. 3749, the other in the archives of Windsor Castle (a photocopy of the latter is in the BL Map Library).

The estate survey in its many forms was one of the great achievements of British map making. Most plans are in manuscript and, as private property, many have entered the public domain through deposit in local Record Offices or through acquisition by the national and copyright libraries. Other works remain in private hands. We have been able to present a full survey of the rich holdings of Oxford and Cambridge colleges, but have attempted or secured only selective returns from the great private houses. Thus Longleat is included but the maps of Hatfield House must be sought in the returns of the Historical Manuscripts Commission or in the fine Roxburghe Club volume edited by R. A. Skelton and J. N. Summerson, *A description of the maps and architectural drawings in the collection ... now at Hatfield House* (Oxford, 1971).

An overall listing of surveyors and their works is recorded in *Peter Eden's Dictionary of Land Surveyors of Great Britain and Ireland c.1540– 1850*, edited by Sarah Bendall (London, British Library forthcoming). This expanded edition will replace that edited by Peter Eden, published in 1976.

The development of the map maker's craft in the 16th century was contemporary with the early advances in surveying. As R. A. Skelton

4

observed, the early printer and the early map maker grew up together.[1] The invention of wood-cut and copper-plate engraving made it possible to provide multiple copies. This provision of the 'exactly repeatable pictorial statement', as W. M. Ivins Jr. calls it, was as revolutionary for map-making as was printing from moveable type for the history of the book.[2] For the first time scholars and men of affairs could consult the same maps. The first printed map of the British Isles was 'Prima tabula', the first of ten maps of Europe found in Ptolemy's *Cosmographia*, first published with maps at Bologna in 1477. The map shows the country as it was known in about AD 150, with Scotland tilted towards the east.

Although the English map trade in the 16th century lagged behind that of Italy and the Netherlands, England made notable advances in regional mapping, or chorography, as Ptolemy called it. Christopher Saxton, known as the 'father of English cartography', produced what is sometimes claimed to be the first national atlas of any country when he issued his county maps as an atlas of England and Wales in 1579. (Atlases of Switzerland, 1552, and of the hereditary Austrian Crown lands, 1561, predate it.)

The county map became henceforward one of the most popular types of map. It was a genre in which England excelled. The first atlas of the British Isles, *The Theatre of the Empire of Great Britaine*, London, 1611–12, by John Speed, was even more popular than Saxton's atlas. The inset town plans and the decorative features have made Speed's maps the most sought after of all county maps. Joan Blaeu's atlas of Scotland, 1654, which formed volume V of the *Atlas Novus* (Amsterdam, 1654), is equally outstanding as the first atlas of Scotland, with maps based on the surveys and maps of Timothy Pont and Robert and James Gordon. The holdings of Speed's maps in English repositories and of Blaeu's in Scottish collections indicate the outstanding place of these atlases in our cartographic heritage.

The disadvantage of copper-plate engraving was its conservative influence, which controlled the market. Copper-plates were a form of capital. Stocks of old plates were sold and resold. Plates were refurbished and revisions made, such as the addition of roads, but the basic survey remained unchanged. The original date '1610' remained on many of the Speed plates until 1743, when Henry Overton removed it.

[1] R. A. Skelton, 'The early map printer and his problems'. *The Penrose Annual. A review of the Graphic arts* (ed. Herbert Spencer), **57**, London 1964, p.171.
[2] William M. Ivins, Jr., *Prints and visual communication*, London, 1953, pp.23–4.

In 1770 Cluer Dicey and Co. reissued collections of maps derived from the copper-plates of Speed and Saxton, and so the Elizabethan picture of the countryside was perpetuated. The date of an impression taken from the plate may thus be many years later than the date of engraving. Maps described by archivists as 'Speed 1610' need further investigation to ascertain their date of printing. Saxton's wall-map of England and Wales, engraved on 20 plates in 1583, also had a long life. The plates were still on sale, extensively revised, in 1795.

In the period of the Restoration, from 1660, map publishing once again became a major enterprise, and various projects for new surveys were put in hand. John Bagford's collections for a history of printing contain many advertisements for these schemes.[1] John Ogilby, from 1671 His Majesty's Cosmographer, planned an 'English Atlas', to be supported by subscriptions and lotteries, but only three county maps were printed, Kent, Middlesex and Essex, together with his plan of London and Westminster, 1677, and his road atlas, the *Britannia*, 1675. John Seller, also a Royal Cosmographer, attempted an *Atlas Anglicanus*, for which he completed six counties (1676–80). The remapping of England to which these and other entrepreneurs aspired proved beyond their means.

Despite these limitations, the map trade flourished. To meet the demands of the market, map sellers such as Peter Stent and chart sellers such as Joseph Moxon would assemble maps of various authors to form what is now known as an *atlas factice* or composite atlas. The contents of these and all other atlases published before 1800 in the British Library, as well as maps in books if nine or more in number, are being recorded on computer by Rodney W. Shirley. For the map trade itself, Sarah Tyacke's *London Map-sellers 1660–1720* (Tring, 1978), is a standard work, comprising the advertisements for maps in the *London Gazette*, 1668–1719, with biographical notes on the map sellers.

These aspects of the history of British county mapping explain why carto-bibliographies of county atlases by the late R. A. Skelton and Donald Hodson, among others, are an essential guide to the assessment of early maps as evidence. The terms used by late 17th and early 18th century cartographers, such as 'from the best authorities' or 'from the latest authorities', indicate that the maps were compiled from other men's

---

[1] BL, Harleian mss., volumes 5906b-5997, 5935, 5946, 5947, 5956.

work. The artist and printmaker William Hogarth was responsible for an important change in practice when he secured in 1734 the passing of an Act of Parliament protecting copyright. The term 'Published as the Act directs', followed by the day of first publishing, appears henceforward on separate sheet maps and atlases.

Other terms commonly found on engraved printed maps distinguish, in Latin, author, engraver and publisher. They are listed by R. A. Skelton as follows: with reference to the cartographer, *delineavit, descripsit, invenit, auctore*; with reference to the engraver, *sculpsit* (*sculp., sc.*), *fecit, caelavit, incidit* or *incidente*; with reference to the printer or publisher, *excudit* (*excud., exc.*), *formis, sumptibus, apud, ex officina.*[1]

The great improvements in county surveying in the second half of the 18th century resulted partly from the encouragement given by the Royal Society of Arts, which in 1759 offered a premium of £100 for any original county survey on a scale of one inch to a mile. By 1775 nearly half of the country had been covered by one inch to a mile mapping. Many estate surveyors now turned to county surveying. The antiquary Richard Gough (1735–1809) assessed their achievements as follows: 'Surveys on large scales were reserved for the labours of a Rocque, a Jefferies, and a Taylor, and a Chapman. – I invert the chronological order for the climax of merit'.[2] John Rocque, Thomas Jefferys, Isaac Taylor and John Chapman were the surveyors singled out for special mention.

R. V. Tooley, followed by Elizabeth M. Rodger, has compiled lists of the large scale county maps and plans of cities not printed in atlases, to a total of 800. The numerous entries were then expanded, county by county, in *The Map Collector* from 1978 to 1987 by Tooley, and Rodger is continuing the series.

Even the best of the 18th century surveys, however, fell short of the standards to be observed by the Ordnance Survey, for they lacked trigonometrical control. When Charles Lennox, 3rd Duke of Richmond, took up his duties as Master-General of the Board of Ordnance in the Tower of London, he brought in his own surveyors as draughtsmen. His initiatives and those of General William Roy, who died in 1790, led to

---

[1] R. A. Skelton, *Decorative printed maps of the 15th to 18th centuries*, London, 1952, p.4.
[2] [Richard Gough], *British topography, Or, an historical account of what has been done for illustrating the topographical antiquities of Great Britain and Ireland*, London, 1780, vol.I, p.xvi.

the establishment of the Ordnance Survey in 1791, the agency for the National Survey of Great Britain and Ireland.

The original Ordnance Surveyors Drawings, which are now preserved in the Map Library of the British Library, are drawn at a scale of 2 inches, 3 inches and 6 inches to the mile, and cover the southern and central areas of England, together with Wales, dating from 1791 to around 1840. They formed the basis for the First Edition one inch to the mile Ordnance Survey map. As the most accurate map of the country to that date, the drawings have been subpoenaed on various occasions in evidence in courts of law in cases to determine public highways when evidence turns on the status of roads at the time of the Public Highway Act of 1835.

The First Edition 25 inches to the mile Ordnance Survey plans issued in the 1870s onwards set another record for accuracy. Even individual trees are located in their true position (a practice later abandoned). The 'Area Books' which accompany the sheets give information on aspects of land use, thus enhancing the value of the record. The First Edition 25 inch OS ranks as the most frequently consulted material in the Map Library of the British Library, which has almost complete holdings.

At the same time, economic changes were transforming the landscape, and a host of special purpose maps such as plans of railways and mining projects was produced. In urban mapping the Goad Fire Insurance Plans, published from 1886, became a major documentary source.

Another 19th century cartographic development was the scientific or thematic map. The new science of 'moral statistics' emerging in the 1820s and 1830s in the works of French and Belgian pioneers such as Charles Dupin and Adolphe Quetelet had its impact in Great Britain. The marriage commissioner Joseph Fletcher (1813–52), encouraged by Albert, the Prince Consort, mapped and published in 1849, the statistics of literacy, debt, etc., from marriage registers. Augustus Petermann came to Edinburgh in 1845 after training in the workshop of the physical geographer Heinrich Berghaus in Berlin, and used census data to compile maps of population and industrial employment. Henry Harness made maps of Ireland showing population by shading and traffic flow to accompany the Report of the Commissioners for Railways, 1837. The invention of lithographic printing, in general use from about 1860, gave much greater flexibility to the techniques of graphic depiction, especially through the facility of colour printing.

Map collectors have their place in this guide as preservers of the records. Sir Robert Cotton the antiquary (1571–1631) collected maps, many of them official state papers, in the course of building up what is reckoned to have been the richest library of 17th century England. His collection became one of the three foundation collections of the British Museum in 1753, and passed to the newly-founded British Library in 1973.

In 1780 another great collector, Richard Gough, presented in his *British Topography* the earliest survey of British maps and charts. He ventured the opinion, 'A public library is the safest port; and of all public libraries the British Museum is on the most liberal plan ...'[1]. He promised his collections to the Museum but later changed his mind and redirected them to the Bodleian Library at Oxford. The Museum, however, was to gain what may rank as the greatest 18th century map collection in the world with the acquisition of King George III's Topographical Collection in 1828. The King's Maritime Collection followed, in part, in 1844, with further transfers in 1952 and 1988. These collections are now in the Map Library of the British Library.

Map makers, map publishers, map sellers and their clients, together with collectors, curators and scholars, have all contributed to our cartographic heritage. The essays which follow in Part I give an account of the many types of map which have their place in the repositories recorded in Part II. They are intended also to help historians and others assess the value of maps as evidence.

[1] [Gough], vol.I, p.xlvii.

1 General maps of Great Britain and the British Isles   Rodney Shirley

We can trace three main streams of influence that shaped the earliest maps of Britain: Ptolemaic maps, Roman itinerary maps and portolan charts. The oldest extant manuscript maps based on the conceptions of the second century AD Alexandrine geographer Claudius Ptolemy date from the late thirteenth century. A map of the British Isles, with Scotland characteristically mis-aligned east-west, was one of 26 maps in Ptolemy's *Geographia* when it was first printed in 1477 and different versions were printed in subsequent Ptolemaic atlases up to the 1730s.

The next most ancient source is the Roman itinerary, of which the best known surviving example is the Peutinger Table, a late 12th or 13th century copy of a route map of the Roman Empire originally drawn 350-400 AD. Other lost Roman maps undoubtedly influenced pilgrim route maps, and Matthew Paris's map of Great Britain of about 1250 could well have been based on some earlier itinerary. A late successor of a Roman-type map was probably consulted by the author of the remarkable map of Great Britain of *c*.1360 known as the Gough Map. This large map on vellum portrays England, Wales and Scotland, including a network of roads, with an accuracy so far in advance of any other medieval maps as to present a cartographic puzzle.

The third stream of development was the portolan chart, emanating from Mediterranean sources in the late thirteenth century. Sea-faring traders brought back information about the coastal waters of the British Isles, to be incorporated in such charts. The southern coasts of England and Ireland are relatively well-marked with place names, whereas the rest of England and Scotland are poorly represented. The 'modern' map of the British Isles prepared by Martin Waldseemüller for his 1513 edition of Ptolemy's *Geographia* is clearly derived from a portolan chart.

In the 1540s, new general maps of England or the British Isles drawn by Sebastian Münster (1540) and George Lily (1546) suggest reliance on some intermediary based on the Gough Map of two centuries earlier. Lily's map, a relatively sophisticated copperplate engraving produced in Italy, influenced several later map-makers north and south of the Alps. In 1564 the Flemish cartographer Gerard Mercator produced an exceptionally fine printed map of the British Isles on eight sheets based on information sent to him by an unidentified correspondent, probably John

Elder. In about the same year Laurence Nowell drew a small but distinctive rendering, possibly based in part on official maps (now lost) in the hands of Sir William Cecil, later Lord Burghley. Nowell's coloured manuscript map was acquired by the British Library in 1982.

It was not, however, until the surveys of Christopher Saxton in the 1570s that there was a reasonably accurate depiction of England and Wales as a whole. His general map of 1579, a summation of his county surveys, was complemented by his twenty-sheet map of 1583, the latter on the scale of about seven miles to the inch. Saxton's outline remained the authoritative model for nearly 200 years, and was copied by successor British, Dutch, French and German cartographers. Peripheral improvements took place through the better mapping of the Isle of Man (Thomas Durham, 1595), of Scotland (initially by Timothy Pont in the late sixteenth century and then by Robert Gordon in the 1640s), of Ireland (William Petty's surveys of 1655–56) and of Cornwall (not correctly oriented until about 1700).

Two important general maps of the later seventeenth century were by John Ogilby and John Adams. Ogilby's map of the roads of England and Wales appeared in his *Britannia* of 1675 and was one of the first maps to show the roads throughout the realm, apart from Richard Carr's post-road map of 1688 and a few earlier isolated county maps. In 1677 Adams published his large distance map engraved on twelve sheets. Here the motivation was explicitly rational and economic: a specifically thematic map of the country based on distance measurements between localities rather than essential geographic features. As such, it proved highly popular, with large and reduced-size derivatives in print for over 100 years.

The eighteenth century was not noted for innovative mapping until, towards its end, the advent of the Ordnance Survey. General maps of England by map-makers such as John Rocque, Thomas Kitchin, Thomas Jefferys and John Andrews still largely relied on the outline established by Saxton, although they often incorporated greater topographical detail based on recent individual county surveys, and depicted a more extensive road network. The maps often claimed that they were 'based on the astronomical observations of the Royal Society', but this did not reflect any integrated national survey. No greater initiative was displayed by Continental cartographers who tended to copy what was locally available.

In the early nineteenth century several interesting 'thematic' maps may be noted, among them those by Charles Smith (1806, canals and navigable rivers); William Smith (1815, geological structures); John Walker of

11

Wakefield (1830, inland navigation, mineral production, railways); and George Bradshaw (1839, railways of Great Britain). Other general maps, printed both in school atlases and separately, reflected the growing demand for educational and missionary purposes. Novelty general maps forming jigsaws, children's instructive games, humorous cartoons or political broadsheets were also popular.

The progress of the Ordnance Survey throughout the nineteenth century, although uneven, gradually yielded properly triangulated positional data. This allowed general maps to be constructed to a much greater accuracy than hitherto, and one of the first such maps based specifically on the Ordnance Survey results to date was Wyld's map of England, 1826. The Ordnance Survey itself did not publish a smaller scale general map of the whole of the British Isles until the 1:1,000,000 map of 1905. Commercial firms, meanwhile, had been making use of data available nationally for many years.

Further reading

Crone, G. R. (1961) *Early Maps of the British Isles* AD *1000–1597*. London: Royal Geographical Society. [For pre-Saxton maps.]

Dilke, O. A. W. (1985) *Greek and Roman maps*. London: Thames and Hudson. [For classical cartography.]

Parsons, E. J. S. (1958) *Introduction to the Facsimile ... the Gough Map*. Oxford: Bodleian Library. [For the Gough map.]

Shirley, Rodney W. (1972, repr. 1991) *Early Printed Maps of the British Isles 1477–1650*. London: Antique Atlas Publications.

Shirley, Rodney W. (1988) *Printed Maps of the British Isles 1650–1750*. London: The Map Collector Publications and The British Library.

Smith, David. (1985) *Victorian Maps of the British Isles*. London: Batsford.

Thrower, Norman J. W. (ed.) (1978) *The Compleat Plattmaker*. Berkeley: University of California Press. [For the 17th and 18th centuries generally.]

For references to the cartography of Ireland, Scotland and Wales, see citations to Essays 22, 23 and 24.

2 Medieval maps to 1500   Paul Harvey

In the Roman Empire maps seem to have been widely understood and used. Knowledge of cartography, however, did not survive the barbarian invasions, and in medieval Europe maps were few in number and were used only for limited purposes among particular groups of people. In the British Isles hardly any maps at all were drawn in the middle ages outside England; in medieval England there were probably more maps than in most parts of Europe, but even so the number produced must have been very small. None was drawn to a consistent scale.

One legacy of Roman cartography that appeared in medieval England was a succession of copies – at many removes and greatly distorted – of a world map; it included an outline of the British Isles and their rivers which in the archetype had probably been carefully constructed and accurate. The earliest English copy to survive, and perhaps the best, is the tenth- or eleventh-century Anglo-Saxon or Cotton Map (in British Library Cotton MS Tiberius B.V.), but it also lies behind the group of detailed world maps, all drawn in England or with likely English associations, produced in the twelfth to fourteenth centuries. The group included the giant Ebsdorf Map (destroyed in 1943 but reconstructed in replica) and the Hereford Map, the largest survivor. The same world map contributed at least the outline to the remarkable map of Britain drawn, in four versions, by Matthew Paris in the mid-thirteenth century. The only thirteenth-century map of any single region of Europe, it takes as its centre-line an itinerary from Dover to Durham or beyond and each version includes many inland features drawn from the map-maker's own knowledge at first or second hand. The Roman world map perhaps contributed also to the fifteenth-century maps of Scotland (which await detailed study) in manuscripts of John Harding's chronicle.

The portolan charts produced for Mediterranean navigation from the thirteenth century onwards had little influence on English maps, though from the earliest known, drawn about 1300, they extended along the Atlantic coast to include the British Isles. By the 1320s, knowledge gained from the 'Flanders voyages' of Italian galleys had given these charts a tolerably good outline of the south and east coasts of England, but until the late fifteenth century the rest of their outline of Britain and Ireland remained rudimentary. However, the portolan charts contributed to one recently discovered English world map, the Aslake Map, and to the most remarkable cartographic monument of medieval England, the Gough Map of Britain.

The Gough Map (Bodleian Library MS Gough Gen.Top.16) takes the east and south coasts of England from portolan charts, the rest of its outline from the tradition of the Roman world map. Drawn about 1360, it shows an extensive river system, many towns and villages and a partial road system, with mileages entered between staging-points. How or why it was drawn is not known; it has no surviving antecedent or successor and the only comparable fourteenth-century regional map is one of Italy in about 1320.

Remarkable too are the thirty-five maps (or closely-related groups of maps) of small areas of England: few other parts of medieval Europe can produce such a concentration. There are none at all from Wales or Scotland, and probably none from Ireland. They are, however, of widely differing styles, from sketched diagrams to elaborate picture-maps, and seem mostly to have been drawn independently of one another. One dates from the mid-twelfth century, two from the thirteenth, then some ten or twelve from each half century between 1350 and 1500. They come from all parts of England, but there is a slight concentration in the general area of the Wash. It is fairly certain that very few maps of this kind were produced: they are not merely the survivors of a widespread genre of local maps. Their modest growth in the late middle ages may perhaps be connected with the plans of projected buildings that master masons showed their clients.

References

Miller, K. (1895–8) *Mappaemundi: die ältesten Weltkarten*. Stuttgart: J. Roth.

J. P. Gilson, and H. Poole. (eds.) (1928) *Four maps of Great Britain designed by Matthew Paris about AD 1250*. London: British Museum.

Parsons, E. J. S. (1958) *The map of Great Britain circa AD 1360 known as the Gough Map*. Oxford: Bodleian Library.

Skelton, R. A. and P. D. A. Harvey. (1986) *Local maps and plans from Medieval England*. Oxford: Clarendon Press.

Harley, J. B. and D. Woodward. (1987) *The history of Cartography*. Chicago and London: University of Chicago Press. Vol 1, 283–500.

Barber, P. (1989) Old encounters new: the Aslake World Map, in M. Pelletier (ed.) *Géographie du monde au moyen âge et à la renaissance*,

Paris: Éditions du Comité des travaux historiques et scientifiques, pp. 69–88.

Haslam, G. (1989) The Duchy of Cornwall map fragment, in M. Pelletier (ed.) *Géographie du monde au moyen âge et à la renaissance*, pp. 33–44.

Wolf, A. (1989) News on the Ebsdorf World Map: date, origin, authorship, in M. Pelletier (ed.) *Géographie du monde au moyen âge et à la renaissance*, pp. 51–68.

Harvey, P. D. A. (1991) *Medieval maps*. London: British Library.

Harvey, P. D. A. (1992) Matthew Paris's maps of Britain, in P. R. Coss and S. D. Lloyd (eds.) *Thirteenth Century England, IV*, pp. 109–121. Woodbridge: Boydell Press.

3 County maps   Donald Hodson

The printed county atlas of the British Isles has always been a distinctive cartographic publication, not exactly paralleled in other countries. Until the adoption of national sheetlines, with the coming of the Ordnance Survey at the beginning of the nineteenth century, the county was seen as the basic unit of mapping: neither too large nor too small to be depicted as an individual map, despite the considerable variation in size of the counties. The largest, Yorkshire, was often divided into its Ridings, while tiny Rutland frequently had to share a plate with neighbouring Leicestershire.

The value of the county map to historians is largely determined by two factors: the accuracy and the scale. County maps on a scale of one inch to a mile, or larger, are a product of the eighteenth century and are dealt with in this publication as a separate chapter: similarly Irish, Scottish and Welsh maps have their own sections. Described here are the more important smaller-scale maps of English counties.

The first survey of England and Wales was carried out by Christopher Saxton between about 1570 and 1578, and his atlas of thirty-four county maps appeared in 1579. Towards the end of the same century John Norden produced county maps based on original surveys, some intended for his *Speculum Britanniae*. These, unlike the Saxton equivalents, showed the main roads. The counties of Hampshire, Hertfordshire, Middlesex, Surrey and Sussex were published in the 1590s, and the others remained in manuscript until the eighteenth and nineteenth centuries. It appears that the maps of Norden were more highly regarded than those of Saxton since the herald, William Smith, who drew twelve maps (1602–3) and the historian John Speed, who published the imposing and well-known atlas *The theatre of the empire of Great Britaine* (1612), both compiled their maps from Saxton only where a map by Norden was not available. Much of the story of maps is the story of plagiarism and, over the years as the trade developed, the London publishers of county maps and atlases elevated this practice to a high art.

During the seventeenth century (and even later for many counties) the maps of Saxton and Norden remained, for the most part, and often at second or third hand, the basis for the English county atlas. A few counties were resurveyed and this new information ultimately became incorporated into the atlas maps. In 1695 a newly edited Camden's

Britannia appeared, illustrated by a set of county maps by Robert Morden. As usual these were not based on original surveys, but a real effort was made to plunder all the latest material, and to update the place-names, though the maps were severely criticised by contemporaries.

This set of maps has some value in providing a snap-shot of the topographical knowledge available at the end of the seventeenth century, immediately before the new large-scale surveys began to appear.

The only other publications worth mentioning are the *Large English Atlas* (1760) and *Cary's new and correct English Atlas* (1787). As with the Morden set of maps these incorporated much new data, notably that now becoming available from the large-scale surveys.

Detailed information on county atlases published from 1579 to 1703 can be found in Skelton (1970). For atlases first published from 1704 to 1763, together with their subsequent editions, see Hodson. Chubb covers the years 1579 to 1870 but has been superseded for the period before 1763 by Skelton and Hodson.

References

Chubb, T. (1927) *The printed maps in the atlases of Great Britain and Ireland, a bibliography, 1579–1870.* London: the Homeland Association.

Skelton, R. A. (1970) *County atlases of the British Isles, 1579–1850.* London: Carta Press.

Hodson, D. (1984, 1989) *County atlases of the British Isles published after 1703.* 2 vols. Tewin: The Tewin Press. [Atlases published up to 1763 and their subsequent editions].

4. Cartobibliographies of county maps, local maps and town plans of England and Wales
Geoff Armitage

Cartobibliographies, which are detailed listings of maps, are a major source of information about maps for a particular area. They should be distinguished from catalogues, which are usually listings of an institution's holdings, or exhibitions. A good cartobibliography should list every map known of the area and enable the enquirer to identify an individual map. It should also name the map-maker and engraver, establish the date and mention the work, if any, from which it derives. Apart from cartobibliographies, there exist other listings, monographs or reproductions with notes, which, although not as detailed or complete, may still prove useful, especially if no cartobibliography is available. The notes given below are a very brief survey of the types of cartobibliography available.

For a listing of the best cartobibliographies, and other useful material on county maps and local maps, see Geoff Armitage, 'County cartobibliographies of England and Wales: a select list', *The Map Collector* **52** (1990), 16–24. A similar listing of cartobibliographies of town plans will appear in *The Map Collector* in 1994, together with an update of the county listing. Many of the works listed can be consulted in the British Library Map Library, as can all the works mentioned below. The major cartobibliographies for counties and town plans should also be obtainable at the relevant reference library.

Cartobibliographies and other listings broadly fall into three main categories: i) county maps; ii) local maps within a county (these would include manuscript material such as estate maps and enclosure maps) and iii) town plans.

i) County maps

There are good cartobibliographies for many, but not all of the English and Welsh counties. A number, such as those by Thomas Chubb (Gloucestershire, 1913; Norfolk, 1928; Somerset, 1914; Wiltshire, 1911), Sir George Fordham (Cambridgeshire, 1908; Lancashire, 1938; Northamptonshire, 1948; Northumberland, 1949; Yorkshire 1933) are inevitably somewhat dated but are often still standard works. There have been several recently-published cartobibliographies of county maps, notably by Donald Hodson (Hertfordshire, 1974), David Kingsley (Sussex, 1984) and Eugene Burden (Berkshire, 1988, a typescript with limited circulation.) Burden's Berkshire has the added advantage of giving the institution's shelfmarks for the items described, whereas some of the early cartobibliographies do not even give locations.

Rather than listing each map in strict chronological order, these more recent cartobibliographies list all editions of a map in conjunction with the first. This method was pioneered in P. D. A. Harvey and Harry Thorpe's Warwickshire (1959), and enables a map's printing history to be seen at a glance. Burden's cartobibliography is continuously revised and has reached a sixth edition.

A major advantage of good cartobibliographies of county maps is that they enable maps of other undocumented counties to be identified by analogy, as most were published as a series or in atlas form. Many cartobibliographies have excellent introductions on the subject of county maps in general, as well as of the particular county and constitute some of the best literature available on the subject.

The British Library Map Library has a policy of actively encouraging would-be cartobibliographers to produce one for their county of interest, especially if one does not already exist. Important forthcoming cartobibliographies are for Kent by Anthony Burgess, and for the printed maps of Lincolnshire, 1576–1900, by Raymond Carroll (to be published in the Lincoln Record Society series in 1995 or 1996).

ii) Local maps

Cartobibliographies of local maps within a particular county mainly consist of listings of manuscript estate maps, enclosure maps and tithe maps, together with such miscellaneous items as district maps, railway and other thematic maps.

Some cartobibliographies contain listings of all these types of maps, others concentrate on one type. Good cartobibliographies of local maps can be more difficult to locate than cartobibliographies of county maps, the best probably being those by Harold Nichols of Derbyshire (1980) and Nottinghamshire (1987), both of which contain detailed notes in the introduction. There is a forthcoming cartobibliography of printed local maps of Berkshire by Eugene Burden (1994–5, limited edition).

Catalogues of material in particular institutions, especially record offices, are more numerous than cartobibliographies. Particularly good examples of these are those for Kent (Felix Hull, 1973), Sussex (Francis Steer, 1962 and 1968) and Essex (F. W. Emmison, 1947–68), which also includes county maps.

iii) Town plans

In general there are fewer good cartobibliographies of town plans. Notable exceptions to this are Berkshire town plans by Eugene Burden (1992, limited edition), London 1553–1850 by James Howgego (2nd edition, 1978) and London, 1851–1900 by Ralph Hyde (1975), Portsmouth by Donald Hodson (1978), Leeds by Kenneth Bonser and Harold Nichols (1961), Norwich by George Stephen (1928) and an unpublished manuscript cartobibliography of Bath by Reginald Wright (1925).

As for county and local maps, there are many other less detailed listings of town plans, as well as collections of facsimiles and reproductions which can be used. It is often not possible to identify town plans by analogy because of their varied nature. However, many printed town plans were published as a series, in atlas form or as insets to county maps, and thus are identifiable by this method.

5 County surveys   Elizabeth M. Rodger

County surveys are large scale (one inch or more to the mile) maps of individual counties of the British Isles based upon actual surveys of the terrain, published from 1700 until the mid nineteenth century when the Ordnance Survey's one-inch series was well established.

This new era in British cartography began in 1700 with the publication of Joel Gascoyne's nine-sheet map of Cornwall on a scale of one inch to one mile; this was the ancestor of the familiar One Inch Map. It was a milestone from several points of view. It was the first printed map of a complete county on such a large scale, and was compiled from a new survey, rather than copied from earlier maps. It was an isolated initiative by a marine and estate surveyor supported by local land-owners and twenty years passed before the next one-inch map was published: Williams' Denbigh and Flint. A handful of further English and Scottish counties were surveyed and published by the middle of the eighteenth century. While they were superior to the smaller scale maps previously in existence they were inaccurate by modern standards.

The main impetus for more accurate county surveys came in 1762 when the Royal Society of Arts advertised a premium of up to £100 for "an accurate survey of any county upon the scale of one inch to one mile". Isaac Taylor, who had already published his surveys of Herefordshire (1754) and Hampshire (1759) was the first to submit a map, but his survey of Dorset (1765) was not considered sufficiently accurate by the local gentry to warrant an award. That honour and 100 guineas went to Benjamin Donn in 1765 for his twelve-sheet map of Devon, surveyed between 1759 and 1765. Nine other county surveys received awards between then and 1809. The accuracy of these eighteenth-century surveys varied considerably, but they were undoubtedly an improvement on earlier maps, and usually claimed to be based upon an actual trigonometrical survey of the county concerned.

One inch to the mile was the usual scale, but some of the English home counties were larger than that: for instance, John Rocque's maps of Berkshire (1752), Middlesex (1754) and Surrey (1768) are at two inches to the mile and even show parish boundaries and land use. This scale was also favoured by Thomas Jefferys for Bedfordshire (1765), John Andrews and Andrew Dury for Hertfordshire (1766), Kent (1769) and Wiltshire (1773), and John Chapman and Peter André for Essex (1777).

During the eighteenth century each county map was a separate venture usually sponsored by the local gentry who would take out subscriptions in advance to underwrite the project. By 1800 all English counties, except Cambridgeshire, had been surveyed at least once, likewise half of Scotland, two Welsh and ten Irish counties.

In the early nineteenth century two enterprises attempted to map all the English (and a few Scottish and Welsh) counties: the brothers Christopher and John Greenwood, and Andrew Bryant. The Greenwoods published surveys (nearly all one-inch) of 38 counties between 1817 and 1834, while Bryant covered eleven English counties on a slightly larger scale between 1822 and 1835. It appears that they were working at the same time as and competing with the earliest surveyors of the Board of Ordnance; sometimes three new maps appeared within a few years of one another. The Greenwoods produced an atlas of county maps of all England on smaller scales in 1834, but ultimately their business collapsed as they were not able to compete successfully with the national mapping agency.

References

Harley, J. B. (1962) *Christopher Greenwood, county map-maker and his Worcestershire map of 1822.* Worcestershire Historical Society.

Harley, J. B. (1963) The Society of Arts and the surveys of English counties 1759-1809. *Studies in the Society's archives,* **32**, 43–46; **33**, 119–124; **34**, 269–275; **35**, 538-542.

Harley, J. B. (1965) The re-mapping of England, 1750–1800, *Imago Mundi* **19**, 56–57.

Harley, J. B. (1972) *Maps for the local historian. A guide to the British sources.* London: Standing Conference for Local History. [Reprinted from *The Local Historian.*]

Laxton, P. (1976) The geodetic and topographical evaluation of English county maps 1740–1840, *Cartographic Journal* **12**, 37–54.

Rodger, Elizabeth M. (comp.) (1972) *The large scale county maps of the British Isles, 1596–1850, a union list.* 2nd revised edition, Oxford: Bodleian Library.

Smith, David. (1988) Chapter 9, on county maps, in *Maps and plans for the local historian and collector.* London: Batsford.

Tooley, R. V. and continued by Elizabeth M. Rodger (from 1978). Large scale English county maps and plans of cities not printed in atlases. *Map Collector.*

6 Military Surveys of Great Britain and Ireland
c. 1290–1700
Peter Barber

While medieval maps sometimes indicate the site of castles and military and invasion routes, the creation of specifically military maps and their use for planning as well as commemoration or education first started in the mid 1520s (Barber 1992; Barber, Mercator) and comprised plans of proposed or actual fortified harbour works and fortifications. Between 1539 and 1550, and again in the 1580s and 1590s, extensive surveys of English and Welsh coasts, which resulted in medium and small-scale regional maps, (including, in the 1580s, beacon maps) were undertaken in anticipation of foreign invasion (Colvin). Manuscript surveys of the Scottish coasts, associated with Alexander Lindsay and possibly captured from the Scots, were used for invasions of Scotland after 1542 (Moir). These were accompanied by selected medium and large-scale mapping of the Lowlands. In the intervening period, the provincial surveys undertaken in Ireland by Lythe, the Brownes, Jobson and later Bartlett are to be seen in part as an English military response to repeated native rebellions (Andrews 1970). All of these constitute the earliest detailed surveys of the British Isles and the emphasis on landing places, relief and settlement reflects their military purpose. All these surveys were accompanied by the creation of numerous plans of particular fortifications. They continued to be created in the reign of James I. Some pictorial maps of Irish skirmishes and battles, apparently intended for ministers, also survive (Dunlop; Gowen). Though some of these battle plans may derive from encampment plans, none is now known.

The seventeenth century saw little military mapping in England, Scotland or Ireland, due to the relative tranquillity over a period of years and the poverty of Stuart governments. Instead there are a series of plans of fortifications in strategic ports (D Hodson; Stuart) and forts in Ireland (Black) as well as London and Edinburgh. An exception is provided by the commemorative plans of Civil War engagements styled on contemporary Dutch broadsheets, often produced by commercial publishers such as Peter Stent, which may be based on operational surveys of encampments etc. by soldiers attached to the Quartermasters' staffs. No such plans are, however, known to have survived. At the same period, existing small-scale maps, such as Saxton's survey of England and William Petty's county maps of Ireland (1685), were re-engraved and advertised as being

23

useful for the strategic planning of campaigns and for quartering of troops (Shirley; Skelton 1978).

A decisive change in the production of military maps was associated with the emergence of Britain as a world power following the Glorious Revolution. Once again government became able to finance surveys of England's shores such as Edmund Dummer's of English ports along the South and South-West Coasts undertaken after 1697 (Barber 1989).

The earlier military maps had no fixed style, ranging from the pictorial to the earliest ichnographic (i.e., plan) surveys known in England, with no evidence for a gradual 'improvement' over time (Harvey). By the close of the seventeenth century, however, the French colouring and stylistic conventions, which were to become customary in the next century, were beginning to be imported into Britain (Barber 1989).

The earliest military mapmakers were foreign-born military engineers or native-born Englishmen trained in other fields, particularly masons (Shelby; Colvin; Merriman 1983). By the later years of Elizabeth I native-born military engineers were customary, and by the Stuart period fortification mapping was organised by the Surveyor-General's section of the Board of Ordnance (Porter), led in this respect by a handful of Engineers of Great Britain or Scotland (of varying grades) such as the foreign-born Bernard de Gomme, Martin Beckmann or (in Scotland), John Slezer or the English Thomas Phillips (Loeber) with civilian artists such as Wenceslas Hollar sometimes being involved. There were some signs of a more dedicated approach to military cartography in the early 1680s, during the period of Charles II's rule without parliament, such as the establishment of an archive for military maps in the Tower of London in 1683 (Porter; Y. Hodson). The continuous alliance between 1689 and 1713 with the Dutch Republic, whose map publishers still dominated the European map trade and whose military cartographers had had their skills honed by more than a century of almost continuous military conflict, however, lessened the pressures on Britain to organise its military mapping on larger and more efficient lines to match its new global responsibilities. Nevertheless, a few former officers from William III's short-lived private regiment of engineers, consisting largely of Dutchmen and Huguenots, provided military mapmakers and foreign skills from 1700 (Mason & Barber).

The largest repositories of early military mapping are the Public Record Office and the British Library (Department of Manuscripts, particularly the Cotton Collection, and the King's Topographical Collection, Map Library). Significant holdings are also owned by Trinity College, Dublin

(Carew maps); the National Maritime Museum (Dartmouth Papers); the Duke of Rutland (Belvoir Castle); the Marquess of Salisbury (Hatfield House).

References

Andrews, J. H. (1970) Geography and government in Elizabethan Ireland. In N. Stephens and R. Glasscock (eds.) *Irish Geographical Studies presented to E Estyn Evans*. Belfast: Institute for Irish Studies, pp. 178–191.

Barber, P. M. (1989) British Cartography, in R. P. Maccubin and M. Hamilton-Phillips (eds.) *The Age of William III and Mary II. Power, Politics and Patronage 1688–1702. A reference encyclopedia and exhibition catalogue*. Williamsburg: The College of William and Mary; New York: Grolier Club; Washington D.C.: The Folger Shakespeare Library, pp. 95–104.

Barber, P. M. (1992) England I: Pageantry, Defense and Government: Maps at Court to 1550; England II: Monarchs, Maps and Ministers, 1550–1625, in D. Buisseret (ed.) *Monarchs, Ministers and Maps. The Emergence of Cartography as a tool of Government in Early Modern Europe*. Chicago: University of Chicago Press, pp. 26–98.

Barber, P. M. (forthcoming) Mercator and the Mapping of the British Isles. In M. Watelet (ed.) *Mercator, l'homme et son temps*.

Black, E. (1990) *Kings in conflict. Ireland in the 1690s*. Exhibition Catalogue. Belfast: Ulster Museum.

Colvin, H. M. (1975, 1982) *The History of the King's Works*. vol **4**. London: H.M.S.O.

Dunlop, R. (1905) Sixteenth century maps of Ireland. *English Historical Review*, **20**, 309–37.

Gowen, M. (1981) A Bibliography of contemporary plans of late sixteenth and seventeenth century artillery fortifications in Ireland. *Irish Sword*, **14**, 230–6.

Harvey, P. D. A. (1981) The Portsmouth Map of 1545 and the Introduction of Scale Maps into England. *Hampshire Studies* (Portsmouth), 33–49.

Hodson, D. (1978) *Maps of Portsmouth before 1801*. (Portsmouth: Portsmouth Records Society).

Hodson, Y. (1991) *Map Making in the Tower of London. Ordnance Survey's early years. An Exhibition to celebrate the bicentenary of Ordnance Survey*. Portsmouth: Ordnance Survey.

Loeber, R. (1977–9) Biographical Dictionary of Engineers in Ireland, 1600-1730. *Irish Sword*, **13**, 30–44, 230–55, 283–314.

Mason, A. S. and P. M. Barber (1991) 'Captain Thomas, the French engineer' and the teaching of Vauban to the English. *Proceedings of the Huguenot Society* **25**, 279–87.

Merriman, M. (1983) Italian military engineers in Britain in the 1540s. In S. Tyacke (ed.) *English map-making 1500–1650, historical essays.* London: British Library, pp. 57–67.

7 Military Surveys, 1700–1900   Yolande Hodson

Military mapping for Great Britain and Ireland for the period 1700–1900 falls into four main categories: large-scale precise surveys of buildings and relatively small areas of territory associated with defence, such as a dockyard and its immediate hinterland; medium-scale mapping of areas designated for encampments; small-scale surveys of larger tracts of land for the purposes of military administration, such as the disposition of troops against a possible invasion; and fourthly, small-scale route reconnaissance surveys and manoeuvre mapping. In general, the medium and smaller-scale maps provided more detailed information on physical features, communications and land-use than did their civilian counterparts.

These groups of mapping were often the product of original surveys, but they also made use of existing material, such as the county maps and surveys noted in sections 3 and 4, and, in the nineteenth century, they were usually based on Ordnance Survey data (see section 6). Military surveys which were made before the introduction of the Ordnance Survey large-scale mapping programme (1824 for Ireland, 1841 for Great Britain), and which remain principally in manuscript, are an invaluable source of topographical information.

The different techniques of survey, which varied according to the purpose of the military mapping, are described in Jones (1974), which gives an account of the training of the nineteenth-century military surveyor, Harley and O'Donoghue (1975–81), which concentrates on the Ordnance Survey as a training ground for military mapping, and Hodson (1987), which covers the small-scale requirements of the military map in the eighteenth century. These sources also describe individual mapping exercises, and provide useful background information for the evaluation of the accuracy of military maps.

While there is no overall account of British military cartography of the British Isles, much has been written about some of the more notable mapping episodes, such as General Wade's mapping associated with military road building in Scotland from 1725–1740, by Moir (1973 and 1983), Roy's survey of the mainland of Scotland, 1747–1755, by Skelton (1967), and Charles Vallancey's survey of Ireland in the 1770s, by Andrews (1966), while an account of the military surveys of Kent, 1788–1799, appears in Hodson (1989). The only major military campaign on

27

British soil to produce battle plans and associated operational mapping was fought in Scotland by the Duke of Cumberland against Prince Charles Edward Stuart, the Young Pretender, from 1745 to 1746. Many of these maps are now preserved in King George III's Military Map Collection at Windsor Castle, which is available on microfiche (See 'Cumberland' in **References**) and are discussed in Hodson (1988). Much of the eighteenth-century military mapping was carried out by the Board of Ordnance, whose general mapping functions are described in Hodson (1991), and by Harley and O'Donoghue (1975). The Ordnance Survey one-inch map of Great Britain was begun as a military enterprise (see section 6), but by 1892 did not fulfil military requirements in many ways. A specifically designated military one-inch map was not authorised until about 1923.

Little has been written about the nineteenth-century military mapping of Great Britain and Ireland, independent of the Ordnance Survey, but the origins of the organisation and development of the separate survey and mapping responsibilities of the Quartermaster-General's Department, which eventually led to the formation of the Geographical Section, General Staff, is dealt with by Clark and Jones (1974), and a brief history is given in Frith (1906).

The principal repositories for military mapping are the Public Record Office, the National Library of Scotland (eighteenth-century Board of Ordnance mapping for Scotland), and the British Library Map Library (King George III's Topographical Collection) and Department of Manuscripts. Smaller collections of British material are preserved in the library of the Royal Engineers' Institution, and in the Staff College and Royal Military College, Sandhurst.

References

Andrews, J. H. (1966) Charles Vallancey and the map of Ireland. *Geographical Journal* **132**, 48–61.

Cumberland (William Augustus, Duke of Cumberland) (1987) *The Cumberland collection of military maps from the Royal Library, Windsor Castle.* London: Ormonde Publishing. Comprises introduction by Yolande Hodson, xii pp.; a set of 692 microfiches; geographical listing, 112pp.; and chronological listing, 69pp. (The Cumberland Collection is now known as King George III's Military Map Collection.)

Frith, G. R. (1906) *The Topographical Section of the General Staff.* Chatham: School of Military Engineering.

Harley, J. B. and Y. O'Donoghue (1975, 1977, 1981) Introductory essays to the first three volumes of facsimiles of the Old Series Ordnance Survey maps of England and Wales. Lympne Castle: Harry Margary.

Hodson, Y. (1987) The military influence on the official mapping of Britain in the eighteenth century. *IMCoS Journal* **27**, 21–31.

Hodson, Y. (1988) Prince William, Royal map collector. *The Map Collector* **44**, 2–12.

Hodson, Y. (1989) *Ordnance Surveyors' Drawings 1789–c.1840: the original manuscript maps of the Ordnance Survey of England and Wales from the British Library Map Library*. With an introduction, summary listing and indexes by Tony Campbell. Reading: Research Publications.

Hodson, Y. (1991) *Board of Ordnance Surveys 1683–1820. Ordnance Survey: past, present and future*. Chichester: Survey and Mapping Alliance.

Jones, Y. (1974) Aspects of relief portrayal on 19th century British military maps. *The Cartographic Journal* **11** (1), 1–15.

Moir, D. G., with a Committee of the Royal Scottish Geographical Society. (1973 and 1983) *The early maps of Scotland to 1850*. 2 vols. Third Edition. Edinburgh: The Royal Scottish Geographical Society.

Skelton, R. A. (1967) *The military survey of Scotland 1745–1755*. Edinburgh: The Royal Scottish Geographical Society. Special Publication No.1.

8 Ordnance Survey maps

Geoff Armitage and Helen Wallis

The Ordnance Survey, established in 1791, had its origins in both military and civilian mapping. The survey of Scotland by William Roy after the 1745 rebellion inspired General Roy and the Board of Ordnance with the idea of undertaking a trigonometrical survey of England. Roy's initial proposal was made in 1763, after the Peace of Paris, and a four mile baseline was measured on Hounslow Heath in 1784 as the first stage of the national survey. In the civilian initiatives Charles Lennox, 3rd Duke of Richmond, played a major role. As a Sussex landowner he was employing civilian surveyors and when he was appointed Major General of the Board of Ordnance in April 1782 and set up at the Tower of London, he brought to his survey Thomas Yeakell as a Chief Draftsman. Roy himself died in 1790, one year before the Ordnance Survey was initiated.

The survey work of the Ordnance engineers was undertaken at first at scales of two inches (1:31,680), three inches (1:21,120) and six inches to the mile (1:10,560), and over the years from 1791 to around 1840 covered the southern part of England and Wales as far north as a line through Hull and Preston. These manuscript maps, known as the Ordnance Surveyors' Drawings, are held in the Map Library of the British Library and have been catalogued by Hodson, (the later Revision Sketches are not included). They form the basis of the 1:63,360 printed one inch to a mile Ordnance Survey maps (Harley and O'Donoghue).

Between 1825 and 1842 the Ordnance Survey mapped Ireland at six inches to the mile, and between 1841 and 1855 they also mapped Lancashire, Yorkshire and seven Scottish counties at this scale. The six-inch has remained the largest scale of survey and publication for moorland districts (in practice much of Scotland and some upland parts of England and Wales). In 1854 it was replaced as the standard scale of survey for rural areas by the 1:2500 (approximately twenty-five inches to the mile), which was completed for Great Britain in 1896. Urban areas were also mapped at the twenty-five inch scale. From this twenty-five inch survey, maps at six inches and at one inch to the mile were published. Ireland (apart from certain mountain districts) was remapped at 1:2500, County Dublin in the 1860s and the remainder between 1891 and 1914.

After 1825 it was usual to map major towns at a much larger scale than that used for the surrounding countryside. In Ireland before 1842 scales ranged between 1:2640 and 1:1056 (between two feet and five feet feet to the mile), with the latter being adopted as standard in Great Britain between 1842 and 1855. In 1850–53, in response to the need to improve urban living conditions, about two dozen towns in England and Wales were mapped at 1:528 (ten feet to the mile) with sanitary information added for the benefit of the various Boards of Health. From 1855 the standard urban scale was 1:500 (approximately ten feet to the mile) in both Britain and Ireland but with some exceptions where scales of five feet or ten feet to the mile were retained.

Between 1844 and 1890 about half of England was revised at 1:10,560 and in 1891 a general revision of the 1:10,560 and 1:2500 surveys of Great Britain was begun, and completed in 1914. The one inch mapping of both Britain and Ireland was revised independently in the 1890s. With certain exceptions such as London, urban mapping at 1:1056 (five feet to the mile), 1:528 and 1:500 (exactly, and approximately, ten feet to the mile) was not revised after 1895, so that most towns have only one set of maps at a scale of larger than 25 inches. However more than one edition was published for some 90 towns including London.

Detailed information on survey and revision dates for counties and towns is given for Great Britain in Oliver (1993) and for Ireland in Andrews (1974). Oliver (1993) also includes a general bibliography of further reading. For ease of public access, the Map Library of the British Library has the most complete holdings of editions and is the main repository for the 25-inch and larger scales. National Libraries of Scotland and Wales have their own appropriate holdings and a good coverage for elsewhere in the British Isles.

References

Andrews, J. H. (1993) *History in the Ordnance Map.* 2nd edition, Kerry (Powys): David Archer.

Andrews, J. H. (1975) *A paper landscape: The Ordnance Survey in nineteenth-century Ireland.* Oxford University Press.

Harley, J. B. and Y. O'Donoghue (1975–87) *The Old Series Ordnance Survey maps of England and Wales.* 8 vols. Lympne Castle: Harry Margary. This includes reproductions of the maps, carto-bibliographies, and scholarly introductory essays.

Harley, J. B. (1975) *Ordnance Survey maps – a descriptive manual.* Southampton: Ordnance Survey.

Harley, J. B. (1979) *The Ordnance Survey and land-use mapping*. Norwich: Geo Books.

Harley, J. B. and C. W. Phillips (1964) *The historian's guide to Ordnance Survey maps*. London: National Council for Social Service.

Hodson, Y. (1989) *Ordnance Surveyors' Drawings 1789–c.1840*. Reading: Research Publications.

Oliver, R. (1993) *Ordnance Survey maps: a concise guide for historians*. London: Charles Close Society.

Owen, T. and E. Pilbeam. (1992) *Ordnance Survey, map makers to Britain since 1791*. Southampton: Ordnance Survey; and London: HMSO.

Seymour, W. A. (ed). (1980) *A history of the Ordnance Survey*. Folkestone: Dawson.

Reprinted Ordnance Survey maps

Ninety-seven sheets of the First Edition of the One-Inch Ordnance Survey of England and Wales were reprinted, with an introduction by J. B. Harley, by David and Charles, Newton Abbott, 1969–71.

Town maps, based on the Ordnance Survey plans at 25 inches (1:2500) and reduced to 15 inches to the mile, have been published by Alan Godfrey Maps, 57–58 Spoor Street, Dunston, Gateshead NE11 9BD. Over 600 maps have been issued to date, with further issues in hand. These maps are of various dates and generally include an essay on the history of the area and extracts from a contemporary directory.

9 Town plans   Helen Wallis and Geoff Armitage

Among English local maps from the medieval period there are three 15th century plans of towns and hamlets. The most striking is the plan-view of Bristol c.1480, in Robert Ricart's 'The Maire of Bristowe is Kalendar' (No. 28 in Skelton and Harvey). In medieval book illustrations strict topographical depiction of landscapes was rare (Croft-Murray and Hulton).

When the art and craft of mapmaking developed in the Renaissance, the town plan became one of the most accomplished of map forms. Practitioners devised a style for printed maps that appealed to civic pride and responded to the demands of the market. The town was drawn in perspective from an elevated viewpoint. The descriptive terms for these images vary according to the angle of the supposed viewpoint, and their usage is inconsistent (Smith 1991; Ravenhill). In the 'birds-eye view' the artist depicts the town seen from an angle, and the building profiles may obscure parts of the street layout whereas in 'plan-view' he draws it as if seen from above, the elevations of buildings being less prominent. Map makers and writers on optics in the 17th century called the technique 'scenographia' in contrast to the ground plan survey, known as 'ichnographia', and to the profile 'orthographia'. The advantage for the historian is that architectural features of buildings are revealed, and a three dimensional impression conveyed.

In the early years of the 16th century surveyors, engineers and artists working for officers of state were already employing this form of landscape drawing, which was derived from the Low Countries. A masterpiece of depiction is 'The large Plat of the Haven of Dover', showing harbour, town and castle, drawn in September 1538, and probably by Richard Lee (BL, Cotton Augustus I.i.22–23). This is one of many manuscript town plans in the collection assembled by the antiquary Sir Robert Cotton (1571–1631), now in the British Library.

William Cuningham, a physician at Norwich, made in 1558 the earliest dated town plan now known, a woodcut map of Norwich, published in the *Cosmographical Glasse*, London, 1559. A far more detailed and larger scale plan, of unknown date and perhaps earlier, is the map of London, c.1558, which was probably designed and engraved abroad. It is known from the only two copper plates surviving from what was probably a 12-sheet map. An idea of the whole plan can be gained from a derived

Elizabethan woodcut map, probably dating to *c*.1561–70 and popularly but wrongly known as the Agas map, after Ralph Agas who produced a plan of Oxford in 1578. Another map perhaps derived from the same source is the plan of London *c*.1570 in the great city atlas, *Civitates orbis terrarum*. volume I, by Georg Braun and Frans Hogenberg, Cologne, 1572.

William Smith, the herald and topographer, put together the first collection of plans and views of English towns in his 'Particular Description of England', 1588. (BL, Sloane manuscript 2596; printed in 1879) (Wheatley and Ashbee). Only Bristol and perhaps Bath and Canterbury are from original surveys (Smith, p.151; Smith 1991).

The Elizabethan surveyors Christopher Saxton and John Norden both made town plans as well as, or as part of, their county surveys. Norden's Middlesex, published as part of his popular geographical description of England, *Speculum Britanniae*, London, 1593, contains plans of London and Westminster. Saxton made surveys of Manchester in 1590 and Dewsbury in 1600. Some of the more detailed mapping of towns and hamlets at that time was the work of a family of Essex surveyors, the Walkers of Hanningfield, whose manuscript surveys are mainly preserved in Essex Record Office.

In the early 17th century John Speed's *Theatre of the Empire of Great Britaine*, 1611–12, the first atlas of the British Isles, provided the first comprehensive collection of town plans, displayed as insets on the county maps. Some are original surveys, indicated by their 'scale of paces'. Over seventy town plans are included. These are plan-views with features in relief. Braun and Hogenberg included eighteen towns in the British Isles in *Civitates orbis terrarum*, their city atlas, published in six volumes between 1572 and 1618.

Although the plan-view remained in vogue until the 1670s, as illustrated by James Millerd's Bristol, 1673, with later editions up to 1730, it became increasingly common for surveyors to make ground plans based on mathematically precise methods of survey and drawn to scale. In London the disaster of the great fire of 1666 hastened the need for a geometrical plan. John Ogilby (1600–1676), Cosmographer to Charles II, set about preparing 'A New and Accurate Description of the famous City of London, with the perfect Ichnography thereof'. He died before the survey was finished, and his step-grandson William Morgan completed the plan for publication. Drawn on a scale of 100 feet to one inch, it is the first linear ground plan of a British town. John Rocque, a French Huguenot resident in England, was the most celebrated urban map maker of the

18th century. His plan of London and Westminster, 1746, was done to a scale of 26 inches to the mile. In the same year he produced a survey of London, Westminster and the country ten miles round, at $5\frac{1}{2}$ inches to the mile. John Horwood's survey of London, on 32 sheets at 26 inches to the mile, with every house depicted, may be regarded as the supreme example of individual achievement in the 18th century. Examples of the Rocque and Horwood surveys of London are preserved in the British Library Map Library, the Guildhall Library, and in other major London repositories. They are reproduced in the publications of the London Topographical Society, founded in 1880.

Inset plans of towns or parts of town such as ports, military or industrial features were included on many large scale county or regional maps. They may provide a useful guide to the appearance of such features, but Smith (1992) has shown that frequently, for reasons of cheapness, these vignettes were based on earlier surveys than the large map which they accompany. His article provides a bibliography of these inset plans and their original dates. On a national scale John Wood's *Town Atlas* of Scotland, first edition 1828, provided the finest collection of 19th century town plans. Another notable Scottish work was the 12-sheet map of Edinburgh of 1891, made by the famous Edinburgh firm of Bartholomew. It is based on the Ordnance Survey's five foot scale town plan, 1876–77 (1:1056).

Both the development of thematic cartography and the introduction of lithography as a method of colour printing led to more elaborate kinds of urban mapping in the 19th century. The fire insurance plans of Charles E. Goad from 1885 and Charles Booth's 'poverty map' of London, 1889, illustrate the increasing preponderance of social and industrial factors in topographical mapping.

References

Armitage, G. (1994) 'Cartobibliographies of city and town plans of England and Wales: a select list', will be published in *The Map Collector*, 1994.

Croft-Murray, E. and P. Hulton (1960) *Catalogue of British Drawings.* Vol. I, Text, p.xxii. London: British Museum.

Elliot, James. (1987) *The City in Maps: urban mapping to 1900.* London: British Library.

Howgego, J. (1978) *Printed maps of London c.1553–1850.* Folkestone: Dawson.

Hyde, R. (1975) *Printed maps of Victorian London, 1851–1900*. Folkestone: Dawson.

Marks, S. P. (1964) *The map of mid-sixteenth century London*. London Topographical Society No. 100.

Ravenhill. W. (1986) 'Bird's-eye view and Birds-flight view', *The Map Collector* **35**, 36–7.

Skelton, R. A. and P. D. A. Harvey (1986) *Local maps and plans from medieval England*. Oxford: OUP. pp. 309–16.

Smith, D. (1988) *Maps and plans for the local historian and collector*. London: Batsford. See Chapters 15 to 18, pp. 148–93, which include his Town Bibliography for the British Isles, pp. 175–77.

Smith, D. (1991) 'The enduring image of early British townscapes', *Cartographic Journal* **28** (2), 163–75.

Smith, D. (1992) 'Inset town plans on large scale maps of Great Britain', *Cartographic Journal* **29** (2), 118–136.

Tooley, R. V. Cartobibliographies of town plans are printed in R. V. Tooley's series on 'Large scale English county maps and plans of cities not printed in atlases' which appeared in *The Map Collector* from 1978 and was continued by E. Rodger from 1989.

Wheatley, H. B. and E. W. Ashbee (ed). (1879) *The particular description of England 1588*. London: privately printed.

10 Estate maps   Sarah Bendall

From the late sixteenth to the mid-nineteenth centuries, estate maps were
made to show landowners' estates. These plans are usually manuscript,
large-scale (commonly at three or six chains to the inch, 1:3169 or 1:
6336), and depict rural, urban and industrial areas. A map can show a
particular field; or more extensive holdings such as enclosed plots or an
owner's strips of land scattered among open fields; or, in series of sheets
or an estate atlas, tracts of land covering many parishes. As a map was
drawn to show a particular owner's property, the surrounding landscape
is often shown only in summary form, if at all. The most detailed maps
include individual buildings in perspective drawings or in plan; field
names and acreages and many other features such as roads, hedges,
parks and gardens, orchards and woodland. The maps may be decorated
with vignettes of the manor house or church, heraldic devices, title
cartouches, elaborate scale bars and compass roses, and scenes of
contemporary agricultural activity.

Estate maps, therefore, often form parts of collections of estate papers;
many are deposited in county record offices. To locate the maps of an
estate, the first place to try is usually the local county office of the estate:
the office may have copies of maps if not the originals, or may know
where they are kept. The National Trust usually deposits family archives
of the houses in its care with local record offices and some corporate
landowners also do this. The records of the Charterhouse, for example,
are deposited in the Greater London Record Office; and the Durham
County Record Office holds the papers of the National Coal Board. If
an owner held land in more than one county, the estate papers could
either be distributed among a number of offices or kept together; thus it
may be necessary to make enquiries at more than one place.

Other collections of estate maps and papers are found in national
collections, whilst some remain in private hands or are in solicitors'
offices. The National Libraries of Ireland, Scotland and Wales; the British
Library; the Public Record Office, and those of Ireland, Northern Ireland
and Scotland; and other major libraries such as the Bodleian and those
of Cambridge University and Trinity College, Dublin, all hold maps of
estates of all areas of the British Isles. Maps of Crown Estates are either
deposited in the Public Record Office or are with the Crown Estates
Commissioners; ecclesiastical estate maps may be kept in diocesan record

offices or by the Church Commissioners. Other places to try are local studies libraries and local museums. Papers which are still in private hands can be harder to locate: some institutions, such as St Bartholomew's Hospital in London and the colleges of Oxford and Cambridge look after their own archives, as do some families. Diligent searching and enquiry may be needed to track down some of these records; the National Register of Archives may provide helpful leads. In a study of estate maps of Cambridgeshire, for example, maps were found in over 50 different repositories, from Warwickshire to Leeds.

Once the papers have been found, much depends on their sorting and indexing. Catalogues may be published of certain collections: the record offices of Kent, Essex, Sussex and Scotland are among those which have published lists of maps in their custody. Card catalogues may supplement these published volumes; other collections depend on unpublished guides. Calendars by the Historical Manuscripts Commission, both published and unpublished, can provide useful finding aids. Other collections may not have been fully catalogued or their maps not described separately, so it is always well worthwhile asking searchroom staff for their guidance. As with all historical sources, estate maps must be used with caution; they were produced for specific purposes by particular societies, and users today forget this at their peril.

References

Adams, I. H. (1966–) *Scottish Record Office: descriptive list of plans.* Edinburgh: HMSO.

Andrews, J. H. (1985) *Plantation acres: an historical study of the Irish land surveyor and his maps.* Belfast: Ulster Historical Foundation.

Bendall, A. S. (1992) *Maps, land and society: a history with a carto-bibliography of Cambridgeshire estate maps, c.1600–1836.* Cambridge: Cambridge University Press.

Davies, R. (1982) *Estate maps of Wales 1600–1836.* Aberystwyth: National Library of Wales.

Emmison, F. G. (ed.) (1947–68) *Catalogue of maps in the Essex Record Office 1566–1855* (with 3 supplements). Chelmsford: Essex County Council.

Fletcher, D. (forthcoming) *Estate maps of Christ Church, Oxford: the emergence of map consciousness c.1600 to 1840.* (Oxford, Christ Church).

Harley, J. B. (1972) *Maps for the local historian: a guide to the British sources.* London: Bedford Square Press for the Standing Conference for Local History.

Hindle, B. P. (1988) *Maps for local history*. London: Batsford.

Hull, F. (1973) *Catalogue of estate maps 1590–1840 in the Kent County Archives Office*. Maidstone: Kent County Council.

Smith, D. (1988) *Maps and plans for the local historian and collector: a guide to types of maps of the British Isles produced before 1914 valuable to local and other historians and mostly available to collectors*. London: Batsford.

Steer, F. W. (1962, 1968) *A catalogue of Sussex estate and tithe award maps*. Vols 1 and 2. Lewes: Sussex Record Society.

Thomas, H. M. (1992) *A catalogue of Glamorgan estate maps*. Cardiff: Glamorgan Record Office.

Walne, P. (1969) *A catalogue of manuscript maps in the Hertfordshire Record Office*. Hertford: Hertfordshire County Council.

11 Enclosure maps, tithe maps, parochial assessment maps, local Boards of Health maps
Roger Kain

These maps of the parishes and townships of England and Wales form one 'family' in the sense that they were almost all produced by private land surveyors in the course of implementing government legislation: namely private and general enclosure acts, the Tithe Commutation Act of 1836, the Parochial Assessment Act of 1836, and the Public Health Act of 1848. Though there are both earlier and later examples, these maps span about 100 years from the mid eighteenth to the mid nineteenth centuries. For many parishes and townships they are the earliest large-scale maps (from about 1:10,000 to 1:500) of local topography before the Ordnance Survey, while enclosure and tithe maps are the earliest systematic records of property ownership and occupation before the cadastral record generated by the 1910 Finance Act commonly known as the 'Lloyd George Domesday' (Kain and Baigent 1992). In total for England and Wales there are some 11,800 tithe maps and probably at least 6,500 enclosure and other parochial maps.

Enclosure is the process whereby land that was exploited collectively, or over which there was common rights, was divided into parcels owned in severalty with each proprietor exchanging his share of common rights over the wider area for exclusive rights in part of it. It is still largely unclear why by the eighteenth century enclosure by act, known as parliamentary enclosure, became the norm when in preceding centuries communities had found local agreements sufficient. At the most pragmatic of levels, an act enabled a majority of proprietors in a village community who advocated enclosure to constrain a minority who were opposed to it.

The number of private or public acts of enclosure and enclosures under the terms of General Enclosure Acts, passed by Parliament in 1801, 1836, 1840 and 1845 to obviate the need for a separate act for each community, totals some 5,250 covering more than 3m hectares or about a quarter of England (Chapman 1987). The period 1755–1780 saw 38 per cent of the total and the Napoleonic War years, some 43 per cent of all parliamentary enclosures.

Enclosure maps are attested by their surveyors on oath as true and

40

accurate. Parcels depicted on the plans are linked by reference numbers to the enclosure award. Not all enrolled (officially deposited) copies of awards have maps, as commissioners were in law required to enroll only the award and, probably for the sake of economy, sometimes adhered strictly to this limited requirement (Turner and Tate 1978; Turner 1980). Nor have all maps survived. For parliamentary enclosures before 1770 the survival rate is less than 33 per cent; for those enacted after 1810 it is more than 90 per cent; for the period as a whole it is just over 70 per cent (Turner 1984). Few maps are found accompanying parliamentary enclosure awards before the last quarter of the eighteenth century (Chapman 1978).

A rough estimate of the total number of enclosure maps for England can be made by reference to Tate and Turner's *Domesday of Enclosure Awards* (1978); counting entries in this source produces a figure of about 4125 places for which there is an enclosure map, a figure which is certainly an underestimate. Research suggests that enclosure maps exist for about 10 per cent more places than are listed in Tate and Turner. The documentation relating to Wales is more up-to-date as John Chapman (1992) has produced a detailed guide to the 227 enclosures of the principality.

When the British government passed its Tithe Commutation Act in 1836 to convert tithes into a monetary tithe rent-charge, it set in train a survey which was unprecedented in England and Wales in terms of area covered, detail of enquiry and exactness of the record (Kain and Prince 1985; Kain 1986). Three documents were prepared for each tithe district: a tithe apportionment; a tithe map and a tithe file. After a long debate about the nature of maps required for tithe commutation, the Tithe Act Amendment Act was passed in 1837 and established two classes of tithe map. First-class maps are those which the Commissioners considered sufficiently accurate to serve as legal evidence of boundaries and areas and can be identified by the certificate of accuracy which they bear and also by the Commission's official seal. The category of second-class maps includes both those maps which were intended to be first-class but which failed the stringent tests of accuracy applied by the Tithe commission, and also by a far larger number of maps which land owners elected to use but which were not submitted for first-class testing. Often these second-class tithe maps were based on existing surveys, perhaps estate or enclosure maps.

All tithe maps, whatever their origin, show the boundaries of the tithe district and its constituent tithe areas, the parcels of land on which tithe rent-charge was apportioned. These usually corresponded to fields, but in some instances they constituted whole farms or, more rarely, a whole township. On most tithe maps the boundaries of enclosed fields are represented by continuous lines and those of unenclosed fields by dotted lines. Occasionally, hedges, fences and gates are also portrayed. The amount of other detail shown on tithe maps varies considerably. Most maps mark the courses of streams, canals, ditches, drains, the outlines of lakes and ponds and lines of roads and paths. Some use conventional symbols as recommended by Lieutenant Robert Kearsley Dawson, an officer in the Royal Engineers seconded to the Tithe Commission to superintend the tithe surveys (Kain and Oliver forthcoming).

Whereas enclosure and tithe maps are well-known classes of local maps and have been frequently illustrated and consulted, other parochial maps are much less well-known. Parochial Assessment maps are the most numerous of these, though there is no agreement as to how many might be extant. David Smith (1988) and B. Paul Hindle (1988) suggest that there are 4,000–5,000 surveys but neither indicates how many were accompanied by maps. In 1853 Robert Dawson, then superintendent of enclosure and parochial assessment mapping in addition to tithe surveys, quoted a figure of about 1267 maps made under the 1836 Parochial Assessment Act, a figure which it is easier to reconcile with known survivals. Research has shown that these maps are more numerous in the urbanised and industrialised parts of the country, a fact which increases their value to historians as it is in these areas that the evidence of tithe and enclosure maps is weakest. The Parochial Assessment Act of 1862 also generated maps but the number of these is as yet quite unknown.

About 170 Local Boards of Health were set up under the 1848 Public Health Act; these were required to furnish large-scale maps but how many maps survive is uncertain. Again, this is an important category of local map as they cover towns for which, as noted above, enclosure and tithe maps are not usually extant.

References

Chapman, J. (1978) Some problems in the interpretation of enclosure awards, *Agricultural History Review* **26**, 108–14.

Chapman, J. (1987) The exent and nature of Parliamentary Enclosure, *Agricultural History Review* **35**, 25–35.

Evans, E. (1993) *Tithes: Maps, Apportionments and the 1836 Act*. Chichester: British Association for Local History, 1993.

Hindle, B. P. (1988) *Maps for local history*. London: Batsford.

Kain, R. J. P and H. C. Prince (1985) *The Tithe Surveys of England and Wales*. Cambridge: Cambridge University Press.

Kain, R. J. P. (1986) *An Atlas and Index of the Tithe Files of Mid Nineteenth-Century England and Wales*. Cambridge: Cambridge University Press.

Kain, R. J. P. and E. Baigent (1992) *Cadastral Maps in the Service of the State: a History of Property Mapping*. Chicago: University of Chicago Press.

Kain, R. J. P. and R. Oliver (forthcoming) *The Tithe Maps of England and Wales*. Cambridge: Cambridge University Press.

Smith, D. (1988) *Maps and Plans for the Local Historian and Collector*. London: Batsford.

Turner, M. (ed.) for W. E. Tate (1978) *A Domesday of English Enclosure Acts and Awards*. Reading: University of Reading.

Turner, M. (1980) *English Parliamentary Enclosure: Its Historical Geography and Economic History*. Folkestone: Dawson.

Turner, M. (1984) *Enclosures in Britain, 1750–1830*. London: Macmillan.

12 Archaeological maps   William Ravenhill

This category of thematic maps aims to locate ancient sites and monuments in order to relate them to one another and to their encompassing landscapes. Incorporated therefore within the ambit of an archaeological map are the two concepts of location and space relationships. Such maps provide an efficient and unique method of illustrating distributions of archaeological phenomena and when these are displayed as overlays to other environmental variables they aid analysis, stimulate ideas, and help in the formulation of working hypotheses. The technique has become one of the most powerful tools available to archaeologists and has been responsible for leading them to enunciate some of their most creative syntheses.

Although the first sign of an interest in mapping ancient sites and monuments may be detected in antiquity, it was the devoted interest of the Italian humanists not only in the monuments of their more glorious past but also in cartography after the re-discovery of Ptolemy's *Geographia*, that wove these two cultural strands into a developing symbiosis.

Diffusion of both the humanistic and cartographic contexts of the Renaissance spread to Britain in the sixteenth century and by its last decade British maps began to mark ancient sites. This purely locational phase continued into the eighteenth-century 're-mapping of England'. The new surveying field-work was undertaken by individuals, mostly on a subscription basis, the clientele being the gentry who occupied country seats, the clergy and the well-to-do who would have considered an interest in the antiquities of their region as one of their polite accomplishments, a propensity the map-makers endeavoured to satisfy.

Archaeology, among others, was one of the interests of Major General William Roy. For some years before his death in 1790 he had been advocating the creation of a national cartographic survey. When, a year later, the Master General of the Ordnance did order such a survey, there is no doubt that it was the archaeological interest bequeathed by Roy, plus the influence of the Royal Society, which led to the earlier and eighteenth-century tradition being maintained so that Ordnance maps would also bear indications of ancient sites and monuments. Their appearance, however, on the two, three and six-inch manuscript Surveyors' Drawings depended on the union of personal enthusiasm on the part of the individual surveyors and their ability to tap the resources of local antiquaries. The full impact of such contacts with expert local knowledge was felt when the surveyors combined with the antiquaries, Sir Richard Colt Hoare and William Cunnington, to produce the drawings for the area covering south Wiltshire and some adjacent parts of Hampshire. The subsequent engraving of these drawings to produce Sheet XIV of the One Inch Old Series so impressed William Mudge, the first effective director of the Ordnance Survey, and so extended his archaeological horizon by it that he encouraged his colleagues to study this sheet as a model for their practice elsewhere. After 1810 the manuscript drawings increasingly reveal that more careful attention was being paid to antiquities, and in 1816 specific instructions were included in the brief to surveyors to note antiquities wherever they occurred. This marked the official documented awareness towards field antiquities and in fact inaugurated almost 170 years of mapping of antiquities by the Ordnance Survey.

The discrete archaeological map, as distinct from those considered above, appeared half-way through the eighteenth century with William Roy's map of the Antonine Wall and his subsequent maps of Roman military antiquities in Northern Britain. Then in 1850 John Yonge Akerman plotted the find spots of indigenous coins in south-east England. This is claimed to be one of the first analytical archaeological distribution maps ever made and as such it may be regarded as the harbinger of what later became, under the inspiration of O. G. S. Crawford and Sir Cyril Fox, the essential tool in the study of countless problems in archaeology.

References

Akerman, J. Y. (1850) On the condition of Britain from the descent of Caesar to the coming of Claudius, accompanied by a map of Britain in its ancient state, showing the finding of indigenous coins, *Archaeologia* **33**, 177–90.

Close, C. (1926) *The early years of the Ordnance Survey*. London.

Crawford, O. G. S. (1912) The distribution of early bronze age settlements in Britain, *Geographical Journal* **40**, 184–203.

Fox, C. (1923) *The archaeology of the Cambridge region*. Cambridge.

Harley, J. B. (1965) The re-mapping of England, *Imago Mundi* **19**, 56–7.

Hodson, A. Y. (1989) *Ordnance Surveyors' Drawings, 1789-c.1840*. Reading: Research Publications.

Haverfield, F. (1906) The Ordnance Survey maps from the point of view of the antiquities shown on them, *The Geographical Journal* **27**, 165–76.

Phillips, C.W. (1980) *Archaeology in the Ordnance Survey.* Council for British Archaeology.

Ravenhill, W. (1990) Archaeology and cartography, *Devon Archaeological Society Proceedings,* **48**, 1–13.

Roy, W. (1793) The military antiquities of the Romans in Britain. *The Society of Antiquaries of London.*

Scaglia, G. (1964) The origin of an archaeological map of Rome by Alessandro Strozzi, *Journal of the Warburg and Courtauld Institutes* **27**, 137–63.

Seymour, W.A. (ed.) (1980) *A History of the Ordnance Survey.* Folkestone: Dawson.

13 Geological maps   Karen Severud Cook

The area symbols on modern geological maps show the extent of rocks
classified according to their composition, age and mode of origin.
Geologists employ explanatory text, maps and other types of graphics
to present their interpretations of the three-dimensional environment. In
addition to scientific research into the history of the earth, geological
maps find applications in land-use planning and construction projects,
as well as in extractive industries like mining.

Although advances towards geological mapping had been made throughout Europe in the eighteenth century, the first true geological map,
William Smith's 'A Delineation of the Strata of England and Wales',
was published in London in 1815. The subsequent development of
mapping as an integral part of geological science can be traced in the
proliferation of geological maps, but their cartographical precursors
should also be considered. Geology-related point symbols appeared first
on general maps, later on specialized mineralogical maps. In addition,
large-scale mining plans and sections sometimes showed geological features. During the 18th century advancing geological knowledge allowed
rock types underlying superficial deposits and vegetation to be interp-
olated and represented on maps by outline or area colours and patterns.
Types of maps and symbols varied. For example, petrographic maps
differentiated rocks by composition alone, while geognostic maps also
took the origins of the rocks into account.

The different types of geology-related maps appeared in a variety of
formats and contexts. Existing, general-purpose printed maps were used
as base maps onto which observers compiled geological information by
hand, both from field observations and other map sources. Finished
versions were shown informally to friends or presented at scientific
meetings. Writings about geology were published in scientific, mining,
and, from their founding in the early nineteenth century onward, geological journals; maps and other illustrations were usually submitted in
manuscript form and then specially reproduced. Books about geology,
as well as about related topics, such as topography, agriculture and
mineral springs, were similarly illustrated. Larger-format maps were also
published as sheets, often accompanied by explanatory text and other
illustrations. The Geological Survey of Britain, founded 1835, and that
of Ireland, founded 1848, became increasingly important as compilers

and publishers of maps, particularly of large-scale map series. From the 1840s onward geological maps became common in commercially-published thematic and general atlases.

John Challinor's bibliographical study of the history of British geology, and the relevant sections of W. A. S. Sarjeant's international bibliography of the history of geology, which also includes biographical sources, offer general introductions to the literature on the subject. More specific is D. A. Bassett's geological cartobibliography of Wales, a work whose detailed notes are helpfully broader in geographical scope than the title suggests. The introduction to V. A. Eyles's selected list of early geological maps of Scotland to 1850 is much briefer but apt. There are as yet no comparable geological cartobibliographies for England or Ireland, but there are other information sources. Literature on regional geology often traces the historical development of geological knowledge of the area concerned and cites older as well as current geological maps. Historical studies, which have tended to focus on the development of British geological science before 1850, frequently include information about mapping. In addition to area studies, individual biographical studies and histories of societies, government agencies and commercial publishers are useful sources. Also fairly common are studies of the publication history of a particular map or group of maps. Less numerous are historical studies of other aspects of geological cartography, such as compilation methods, symbol design and map reproduction. Recent literature on the history of geological cartography in Great Britain continues to appear in different fields of study and should be sought in current bibliographies of cartography, geology and the history of science.

A geological library will offer the easiest access to geological maps. The modern and historical holdings of the library and archives of the British Geological Survey (based at its Keyworth headquarters near Nottingham since 1987) are international in coverage but particularly strong for Britain. Other specialist collections are to be found in the libraries and archives of museums and geological societies. At institutions like the Natural History Museum and the Geological Society of London, however, various factors may limit public access. Some university libraries will also offer concentrations of geological maps and literature, but the amount of older material held will vary. The recent bequest of the collection of Victor and Joan Eyles, historians of geology, has given the University of Bristol Library particular strength in this area. The national and copyright libraries hold much relevant material in their general as well as their map libraries, but finding geological literature and maps in general library catalogues can be tedious. If the interest is in geological maps of a particular area, the holdings of county and local archives, as well as the local-history sections of public libraries, should also be explored.

References

Bassett, D. A. (1967) *A source-book of geological, geomorphological and soil maps for Wales and the Welsh borders (1800–1966)*. Cardiff: National Museum of Wales.

Bridson, G. D. R., V. C. Phillips and A. P. Harvey (1980) *Natural History manuscript resources in the British Isles*. London: Mansell; New York: R. R. Bowker.

Challinor, J. (1971) *The history of British geology: a bibliographical study*. Newton Abbott: David & Charles.

Eyles, V. A. (1983) 'Early geological maps', in D. G. Moir (ed.) *The early maps of Scotland to 1850*. 3rd edition. Vol 2, 126–137. Edinburgh: Royal Scottish Geographical Society.

Sarjeant, W. A. S. (1980) *Geologists and the history of geology: an international bibliography from the origins to 1978*. London: Macmillan.

14 Thematic and statistical maps   Helen Wallis

The object of thematic maps is to represent the character of a particular distribution, whereas general maps show the locations of a variety of phenomena. When N. Creutzberg applied the term 'thematic' to special purpose or scientific maps in 1953, it was quickly and widely adopted.

Although few thematic maps appeared before 1700, scientific developments in the later part of the 17th century laid the foundations of thematic cartography. The first true scientific maps made in England were by the astronomer and geographer Edmond Halley (1656–1742). His map of the trade winds in the *Philosophical Transactions* of the Royal Society, 1688, was the fore-runner of flow-line maps. His charts of magnetic variation were published in 1701 (the Atlantic Ocean) and 1702 (the World). In constructing these two charts he invented the line of equal value (the isoline), a device which in later years had a remarkable progeny.

The modern science of statistics also had its origins in the late 17th century, when John Graunt (1620–1674) and Sir William Petty (1623–1687) began to investigate demographic problems. Petty's first essay in the new art of 'Political Arithmetic' appeared in 1683. Graphical methods were not applied to statistics, however, until a century later. William Playfair in *The Commercial and Political Atlas*, London, 1786, was the first to use graphical methods, which he called 'lineal arithmetic'. The atlas contained graphs but no maps. Playfair's contemporary, the German A. F. W. Crome (1753–1833), is regarded as the inventor of the statistical map.

By the 1820s sociological phenomena began to be represented in map form. The term 'moral statistics', which was used for this type of mapping, first appeared in 1833 in André-Michel Guerry, *Essai sur la statistique morale de la France*. Guerry (1802–1866) included maps of crimes and other sociological phenomena in his *Statistique morale de l'Angleterre comparée avec la statistique morale de la France*, Paris, 1864, which was introduced by a brilliant essay on scientific and thematic cartography, pp.1–64.

In the British Isles, Henry Drury Harness in 1837 devised a set of five innovative maps for the *Atlas to Accompany Second Report of the Railway*

Commissioners, Ireland, Dublin, 1838. These include population and geological maps and two of traffic flow.

Another important cartographer was the German August Petermann (1822–1878), who worked in Edinburgh (1845–1847) and London (1847–1854). He was appointed in 1852 'Physical Geographer and Engraver on Stone' to Queen Victoria. Petermann had gained his early training at Potsdam in the Geographische Kunstschule of Heinrich Berghaus (1797–1884). Berghaus had applied the cartographic techniques of Alexander von Humboldt (derived from Halley) to a wide range of phenomena, and published his *Physikalischer Atlas* in two volumes in 1845 and 1848. A. K. Johnston's *The Physical Atlas*, Edinburgh, 1848, on which Petermann worked, was derived from, and improved on, the *Physikalischer Atlas*. It has been described as the first truly comprehensive thematic atlas.

In London, using census data, Petermann made maps of the British Isles showing population (1849, 1851 and 1852). His other productions included a cholera map of the British Isles, 1848, and 'Great Britain, Distribution of the Occupations of the People', published in Parliamentary Papers: *Accounts and Papers*, LXXXVIII 1852–3, vol 1 (2).

For statistical mapping, including moral statistics, a notable event was the formation of the Statistical Society of London in 1834 out of the British Association for the Advancement of Science, which added a Statistical Section at its third meeting. Its prospectus named four classes of statistics of concern to society: economic, political, medical, moral and intellectual. The statistician Joseph Fletcher (1813–1852) made the first map of population density in England to accompany eleven other maps of 'moral statistics', such as improvident marriages. His paper, which was illustrated with maps at the prompting of Albert, the Prince Consort, was published in the *Journal of the Statistical Society*, vol 12, 1849. That geographers and historians have somewhat neglected this remarkable field of sociological mapping probably results from its unfamiliar name.

Maps of the social environment dealt with such problems as epidemic cholera (Dublin 1841, Glasgow 1844, London 1855) and sanitary conditions in general (Sanitary Map of the Town of Leeds, in Henry Chadwick, *Report on the Sanitary Condition of the Labouring Population,* 1842). Henry Mayhew's *London Labour and the London Poor,* 1862, and Charles Booth's *Lives and Labour of the People of London,* 1889, are notable for their maps of criminality and poverty. Many thematic and statistical maps are to be found in state papers, medical reports and scholarly periodicals. Some have only recently come to light, for as A. H. Robinson remarks, the most certain way to bury a contribution is to publish it in a government document (Robinson, p. 229). For urban historians and geographers insurance plans rank as one of the most important classes of special purpose maps. The firm of Charles E. Goad, originally of Montreal, which set up in London in 1885, mapped many of the most important towns and cities in the British Isles.

National collections such as the British Library's are major repositories for thematic and statistical maps, but the maps have to be sought in a variety of places. Some are recorded in the British Library's *Catalogue of Printed Maps*, and the most notable have featured in the British Museum's and British Library's exhibition catalogues. Facsimiles of notable thematic maps of London, such as Thomas Milne's Land Use map of the London Region, 1800, Robert Mylne's 'Map of the Geology and Contours of London and its Environs', 1856, and Booth's poverty maps, 1889, have been published by the London Topographical Society.

References

Robinson, Arthur H. (1982) *Early Thematic Maps in the History of Cartography*. Chicago and London: Chicago University Press.

Wallis, Helen and A. H. Robinson. (1987) *Cartographical Innovations: An International Handbook of Mapping Terms to 1900*. Tring: Map Collector Publications, in association with the International Cartographic Association.

15 Road maps   Tony Campbell

The earliest appearance of Britain's roads on a map reflects the written itineraries that preceded it. Central to the four maps of Britain produced in the mid 13th century by Matthew Paris is an itinerary from Newcastle and London and on to Dover, passing through the author's monastery at St Alban's. Places were presented in a straight line, as they were on the separate itinerary map Matthew Paris drew for the route from London to Dover and thence to southern Italy (Harvey).

The first attempt to portray the network of Britain's roads, noting also the distance between towns, is represented by the unsigned 'Gough Map' of *c*.1360. This has no recognised antecedents and it would be 300 years before another map of Britain showed roads – Hollar's of 1667 (Shirley). Since Christopher Saxton's survey of England and Wales in the 1570s omitted roads so did the 'Quartermaster's Map' derived from it, which was used by both sides in the Civil War.

From the mid 1670s onwards printed maps started to mark post roads and crossroads. That same decade saw publication of John Ogilby's celebrated *Britannia* of 1675. Its 100 strip road maps traced 2519 miles of roads in England and Wales, and helped standardise the mile at 1760 yards (Harley). County maps that had hitherto excluded roads – except for those by John Norden and Philip Symonson in the 1590s and William Smith's of 1602–3 – would later display them as a matter of course. The large-scale county surveys of the second half of the 18th century traced roads with reasonable accuracy, prefiguring the careful work of the Ordnance Survey.

Ogilby's strip road maps were widely imitated throughout the 18th century. The first series of road maps to break away from his models were those produced in 1782 by Carrington Bowles in response to the spread of turnpike trusts. This was soon followed by two influential works: Daniel Patterson's *British Itinerary* (1785) and John Cary's *Survey of the high roads from London* (1790 onwards). For bibliographical details of road books see Chubb, and Kingsley. Cary's appointment by the Post Office to survey 9000 miles of roads led, in *Cary's new itinerary* (1798), to the first measured roads since Ogilby. George Taylor and Andrew Skinner issued the first collections of road maps for Scotland in 1776 and Ireland in 1778 (Andrews).

The building, diverting and turnpiking of roads led to the production of special maps. The 19th century Parliamentary 'deposited plans' are now in the House of Lords Record Office, with duplicates often preserved in the appropriate record office (Hindle).

The heyday of coach travel, roughly 1730–1830, created a great demand for published road maps in pocket format. The more specialised needs of Victorian England led to the introduction of cycling maps in the 1880s, the relevent information often being overprinted onto an older base map (Smith 1985). With the present century, attention has turned to motoring maps (Nicholson).

Distance tables are related to road maps. Pilgrim guides developed, in Tudor times, into distance books (with estimates along main roads) and thence into road books with written descriptions (Smith 1988). John Norden invented the triangular table in 1625 to show distances between English towns (Wallis & Robinson). Using Ogilby's data, John Adams produced a distance map of England and Wales in 1677, distinguishing 'computed and measured miles'. To counter abuses by Hansom cab drivers, a sequence of London maps after 1833 provided distance information against which fares could be checked (Hyde).

There has been no comprehensive study of British road maps.

References

Andrews, J. H. (1969) *George Taylor and Andrew Skinner: Maps of the roads of Ireland*. Shannon: Irish University Press. [Facsimile of the 1778 road book].

Chubb, T. (1927) *The printed maps in the atlases of Great Britain and Ireland 1579–1870*. London: Homeland Association. Reprinted, Folkestone: Dawson, 1974.

Fordham, Sir H. G. (1924) *The road-books and itineraries of Great Britain, 1570 to 1850: a catalogue with an introduction and a bibliography*. Cambridge: University Press. [For several other works on British roads by Fordham see Smith (1988), pp. 122–31].

Harley, J. B. (1970) *John Ogilby: Britannia. London 1675* [facsimile edition]. Amsterdam: Theatrum Orbis Terrarum.

Harvey, P. D. A. (1991) *Medieval maps*. London: British Library.

Hindle, B. P. (1988) *Maps for local history*. London: Batsford, pp. 98–106.

Hyde, R. (1979) Maps that made cabmen honest, *The Map Collector* **9**, 14–17.

Kingsley, D. (1982) Printed maps of Sussex 1575–1900, *Sussex Record Society* **72**, 358–76.

MacEachran, A. M. and G. B. Johnson (1987) The evolution, application and implications of strip format travel maps. *Cartographic Journal* **24** (2), 147–58.

Nicholson, T. R. (1983) *Wheels on the road: road maps of Britain 1879–1940*. Norwich: Geo Books.

Shirley, R. W. (1988) *Printed maps of the British Isles 1650–1750*. London: The Map Collector Publications and British Library. pp. 10–12.

Smith, D. (1985) *Victorian maps of the British Isles*. London: Batsford. pp. 84–91.

Smith, D. (1988) *Maps and plans for the local historian and collector*. London: Batsford, pp. 113–23.

Wallis, H. M. and A. H. Robinson (1987) *Cartographical Innovations: an International Handbook of Mapping Terms to 1900*. Map Collector Publications in association with International Cartographic Association, pp. 21–3, 57–8, 61–7.

16 Fire Insurance Plans   Gwyn Rowley

Fire Insurance Plans were first produced in Britain in the early eighteenth century. They developed from the specific requirements of fire insurance underwriters whose pressing needs demanded both an understanding of the physical characteristics of a structure to be insured and the spatial concentration of policy holders, so as to limit a company's exposure, liabilities and losses in case of a conflagration.

London's Guildhall Library holds the earliest surviving fire plans in the form of a pocket book compiled by Thomas Stibbs, Surveyor to the London Assurance Office, dated 1746–7. Premises of individual traders are represented, with the name of the insurer and a description of the building's construction materials. This book, marked 'vol 13', is the only survivor of the series which probably commenced in 1733–4. Guildhall Library also holds the Sun Fire Office Survey Book, 1794–1807, a volume of 88 fire plans carried out by William Pilkington, Surveyor of Buildings to the Sun Fire Assurance Company. Pilkington annotated each plan with its particular fire risk.

J. T. Loveday, Surveyor of Risks to the Phoenix Fire Office, began his 'London waterside Surveys' on the City bank of the Thames between London Bridge and Blackfriars Bridge and sold these manuscript plans to the Phoenix. He then surveyed on his own behalf the wharves and granaries between London Bridge and Tower Dock on the north bank, and between London Bridge and the Globe Granary, Rotherhithe, on the south bank, a task that occupied him for two and a half years. His *London Waterside Surveys* was published in 1857. Loveday established the practice of colouring to indicate materials: pink for brick, light brown for brick-and-timber, yellow for timber and blue for glass.

The London Wharf and warehouse Committee plan books, 54 volumes prepared for the Committee between 1863 and 1903 by A. B. Crockett and Charles Freemen adopted a colouring system similar to Lovedays. These plans, now in the Guildhall Library, are mostly of docks and Thames-side wharves but include a few of their proprietors' inland warehouse properties.

The requirements for fire insurance led, in nineteenth century North America, to the emergence of fire insurance plans as quite specialized cartographic productions (Hayward, 1977; Library of Congress, 1981).

From about 1885 one company, the Charles E. Goad Company, dominated production of these plans in Britain (Rowley, 1984A and B, and 1988). The Goad FIPs were first produced for urban centres within the British Isles in 1886 and within ten years the central parts of all the major towns and cities were covered. The areas of particular interest included the Central Business Districts of the larger urban areas, major commercial regions and industrial districts – particularly warehousing and transport termini – railways, ports and canals.

These large scale plans depict, by means of colour and symbol, impressive information on the use to which buildings were put (in some cases supplying the company's name), internal and external building constructions, building height, street widths and names, property numbers and property lines and of course various fire-related information on the location of water supplies and building materials. Goad also produced plans showing the extent and effects of specific conflagrations; the Guildhall Library has examples which include the outcome of one fire at West India Dock in 1895, and another in Jewin Street in 1897.

Once the Goad FIPs were completed for a centre they would be placed in a large atlas. Individual sheets generally measure 25 inches (63.7cms) by 21 inches (54cms). The key plan within each volume is usually at 300 feet to 1 inch (1:3600) while the general scale for the individual FIPs is 40 feet to 1 inch (1:480). Fifty three centres were covered in 126 volumes. The most extensive coverages are those of Birmingham, Leeds, London, Glasgow, Liverpool and Manchester. Following the issue of an initial volume, new surveys would be undertaken, the plans updated and a new edition published every five years or so. Copies of these various editions provide a quite remarkable fount of spatial information upon our evolving urban areas.

Yet fire insurance plans remain largely unknown and unused, although the British Library, the Guildhall Library, Manchester City Library and a number of local libraries have interesting collections of the Goad plans. Such plans, it is suggested, are the single most important cartographic source for considering the development of the major British towns and cities and industrial districts in the period of quite remarkable change between *c*.1885 and *c*.1970.

References.

Hayward, R.J. (1977) *Fire Insurance Plans in the National Collection.* Ottawa, Public Archives.

Library of Congress (1981) *Fire Insurance Maps in the Library of Congress.* Washington DC, Library of Congress.

Rowley, G. (1984A) *British Fire Insurance Plans.* Old Hatfield: C. E. Goad.

Rowley, G. (1984B) An introduction to British fire insurance plans, *The Map Collector* **29**, 14–19.

Rowley, G. (1988) The patterns of fire: British fire insurance plans, *The Geographical Magazine* **60**, 38–41.

17 Navigable waterways and railway maps

David Smith

Plans of canals and railways accompanied construction schemes as they came into being and during their subsequent operation. Their antecedents are the plans of river improvements and waggonways that preceded canals and railways. From 1793, private canal or waterworks' Bills submitted to Parliament involving new works or compulsory acquisition of land had to be accompanied by a plan of the proposed works. Railway Bills were included from 1803, with elaborate new procedures introduced in 1836. Plans were required not only for full routes but also for branches, extensions, doublings and even the smallest alterations. Many plans submitted to Parliament underwent a process of progressive amendment. Canals were surveyed again in the event of takeover by competing railway companies anxious to utilise the same route.

Large-scale transport maps tend to delineate only the line of route and the land either side, extending to a distance of about 1/4 mile and portraying the full range of landscape features in detail. Each land plot to be acquired was numbered to correspond with its description in a Book of Reference. Additional features found on or accompanying strip maps include larger-scale insets of towns or important estates, distance tables, schedules of estimated costs, tidal ranges, population details, competitive mileages by rival routes, notes of potential freight, and plans and drawings of associated infrastructure such as bridges, stations, tunnels, viaducts and aqueducts. Longitudinal sections showing the level of the ground in relation to the height or depth of the works were frequently included with plans from 1795, being required for railways from 1836 at specified scales. Also from 1836, small-scale maps showing the general direction of railway lines were required but many have failed to survive.

Scales of deposited plans vary widely, often being much larger than those legally required. Standing Orders progressively increased required scales over the years, notably for railway plans which from 1836 had a minimum scale requirement of 4 inches to the mile with built up areas to be much enlarged, particularly to delineate the impact of terminus construction.

Early deposited plans are manuscript drawings, either plain or coloured, on paper or parchment. From 1795, it was required that they should be engraved and printed. However, once the appropriate large-scale Ordnance Survey sheets became available it was sufficient to superimpose proposals onto the Ordnance landscape. Since plans presented to Parliament were subject to the scrutiny of opponents and formed the basis of legislation, they generally represent relatively accurate records, although some railway mapping, particularly during periods of 'mania', was rushed through by incompetent, inexperienced surveyors.

In addition to the detailed large-scale plans submitted to Parliament, promoters required route feasibility surveys, and construction and maintenance demanded comprehensive engineering plans, often simply superimposed onto existing Ordnance and Tithe Survey maps. Later, maps were prepared to facilitate efficient working.

The most reliable network maps, recording route ownership, co-ownership, through-running facilities and other railway information, are those produced and regularly revised on a semi-official basis by employees of the Railway Clearing House, notably Zachary Macaulay and, especially, John Airey, and later by the House itself. Small-scale maps of lines or networks illustrated a scheme's prospectus, publicity, propaganda, timetables, guides and handbooks. Network and regional maps accompanied contemporary accounts and histories and were issued commercially in sheets, atlases, topographies and as wall maps, and, to satisfy popular interest, in periodicals such as the *Gentleman's Magazine*. Unfortunately, however, most promotional maps superimposed communication details on a landscape copied from existing small-scale maps by careless engraving or lithography because accuracy was unimportant. General network maps frequently confused projected with constructed schemes and portrayed those never built. The most reliable are those published by George Bradshaw and the engineers themselves and those prepared for official purposes.

Select bibliography

Some archives produce listings of their transport maps and the Railway and Canal Historical Society maintains an index of document locations.

Brunel University Library (1986) *Railway Maps and the Railway Clearing House. The David Garnett Collection in Brunel University Library.* Uxbridge: Brunel University Library. Contains articles by David Garnett and others, and a full bibliography of articles on railway maps by David Garnett.

Fowkes, E. H. (1963) *Railway History and the Local Historian.* York: East Yorkshire Local History Society.

Hadfield, C. (1955–56) Sources for the history of British canals, *Journal of Transport History* **2**, 80–89. The *Journal* has published other articles which refer to sources for waterway and railway maps and ancillary records, see: Bond, M. (1959–60) **4**, 37–52; Dyos, H. J. (1955–56) **2**, 11–21 and (1957–58) **3**, 23–30; Johnson, L. C. (1953–54) **1**, 82–96; Simmons, J. (1953–54) **1**, 155–69; Wardel, D. B. (1955–56) **2**, 73–9. See also: Cobb, H. S. (1969) in *Archives* **9**, 73–9, and Robbins, M. (1953) in *Railway Magazine* **99**, 228–9, 276. Innumerable works cover transport plans incidentally in the study of transport history, particularly those on canals by Charles Hadfield.

Harley, J. B. (1977) *Maps for the Local Historian. A Guide to the British Sources.* London: Standing Conference for Local History, 40–2, 45–50.

Hindle, P. (1988) *Maps for Local History.* London: Batsford. pp.107–18.

Moir, D. G. (1983) with a Committee of the Royal Scottish Geographical Society. *The Early Maps of Scotland to 1850.* Edinburgh: Royal Scottish Geographical Society, vol. 2, 57–122.

Skempton, A. W. (1977) *Early Printed Reports and Maps (1665–1850) in the Library of the Institution of Civil Engineers.* London: Institution of Civil Engineers.

Skempton, A. W. (1987) *British Civil Engineering, 1640–1840: A Bibliography of Contemporary Printed Reports, Plans and Books.* London and New York: Mansell Publishing Ltd.

Smith, D. (1985) *Victorian Maps of the British Isles.* London: Batsford. pp. 82–3, 91–103.

Smith, D. (1988) *Maps and Plans for the Local Historian and Collector.* London: Batsford. pp. 35, 112–3, 123–34.

Smith, D. (1993) *Canal and Railway Plans, Short Guides to Records No.42.* (Pamphlet, 6pp.) London: Historical Association.

Torrens, H. S. (1974) Early maps of the Somersetshire canal, *Cartographic Journal* **11**, 45–7. For further discussion see: Eyles, J. M., 47–8 and Torrens, H. S. (1975) **12**, 49.

18 Metal mining maps   Roger Burt

The most commonly used sources for locating abandoned mine sites are the old series 6 inch to the mile Ordnance Survey maps and other local and regional surveys that provide details of a wide range of industries and other features. In this sense, mining historians share a common resource. The 'general' maps have been discussed at length elsewhere, however, and attention here will be confined to sources particular to mining.

At the detailed local level, mining historians are fortunate in having access to a very large number of surviving plans and carefully drawn surveys of mining districts. These date primarily from the last half of the nineteenth century but earlier documents, going back to the fifteenth century, can be found. The various sources are too numerous to list in detail, but enquiry at any major archival collection in, or relating to, the mining districts, is likely to reveal a number of useful documents. It is possible here only to give an impression of the range of material available.

The main collection of detailed mine plans was compiled originally, from the mid nineteenth century, by the Mining Records Office at the Museum of Practical Geology. This passed to the Home Office after 1883 and continued to receive material, under the auspices of the Health and Safety Inspectorate, until the present day. Under the terms of the 1872 Metalliferous Mines Act, the collection received the abandonment plans (usually to a scale of 25 inches to the mile) of all mines employing more than twelve persons underground. Periodic lists of the plans deposited were published by the Inspectors of Mines, appended to the annual *Mining and Mineral Statistics of the United Kingdom of Great Britain and Ireland*, appearing in the British Parliamentary Papers (1). With the regional run down of the industry in the late nineteenth and early twentieth centuries, these lists grew quickly in length, and soon enumerated many thousands of workings. In recent years, the collection, previously held centrally, has been distributed to the appropriate county record offices, where now they are generally available for inspection, either in original or photographic form.

As well as abandonment plans, local archives often have other plans made by the mining companies themselves or by the landowners who leased out their mineral rights. Some of the largest and most important collections of landowner plans are still privately held and not normally open for public inspection. The archives of the Earl of Falmouth, at Tregothnan House, the Dukes of Devonshire, at Chatsworth and the Duchy of Cornwall, at 10 Buckingham Gate, are good examples. To a lesser extent, national collections of company documents in the Guildhall Library, City of London, and the Public Record Office, BT 31 collection, can sometimes reveal useful plans and sections of workings, below and above ground. This is something of a mixed bag but certainly worth checking both for domestic and overseas mines. Finally, Crown Estate and other estate records in the Public Record Office and the National Library of Wales are worth checking for occasional maps and plans.

To complement detailed mine plans, and to facilitate the equally important function of relating them to other features and fixing their location, reference can be made to a wide range of maps and surveys of the mining districts. These were often produced during the mid and late nineteenth century to facilitate share broking activities. In the south west, the work of Robert Symons is particularly well known and a number of his surveys can be found in the Cornwall Record Office at Truro. His son, Brenton, also produced mining maps of areas of Wales. (2) Tithe maps and apportionments; maps accompanying Canal and Railway Bills; published Maps and Memoirs of the Geological Survey, dating from the 1840s; and a range of county histories and local history and natural history society journals can also prove very useful.

It is clear that the great bulk of available material relates to the nineteenth and twentieth centuries, but useful earlier documents are available for some areas. A map of the important Somerset Mendips lead mining district, sometimes dated 1470, but probably mid or late 16th century (3), is probably the oldest, followed by a mid 16th century map of the Cornish trade routes, showing some mines, found in the Cecil Papers at Hatfield House. (4) Very few others appeared before the now well-known sketch of the silver mines of Central Wales, published in 1670.(5) Arguably, most mining was still too small, dispersed and lacking in visual impact to warrant much notice by early map makers.

By the early eighteenth century, however, the scale of mining was growing fast and mining maps were increasing in number. William Waller produced surveys of the Cardiganshire mines in the years around 1700 and that district was again surveyed at the mid-century by Lewis Morris.(6) The Cornwall Record Office has various maps relating to tin bounds and particular mining districts, such as Poldice bal, dating from the last years of the seventeenth century. Some of the regional histories that began to be published around that time also included useful surveys of mine sites.(7) By the early nineteenth century, books on mining and the mining districts commonly contained well-drawn and informative maps and sections.(8) There is currently no detailed guide to, or account of, the development of mining cartography, though some help can be derived from work on the history of surveying.(9)

References

1 See, for example, the *Mining and Mineral Statistics of the United Kingdom*, pt.4 1887, in Parliamentary Papers 1888 [C5464] CVII, 369.

2 Brooke, J. (1991) 'The Jeremiah of Mappists', *Journal of the Cornwall Association of Local Historians*, April 1991.

3 J. H. Savory, 'Mendip Mappe', *Proceedings of the Wells Natural History and Archaeology Society* (1913) reproduces and discusses this map.

4 Hunt, R. (1887) *British Mining*, p.134.

5 Pettus, John. (1670) *Fodinae Regales or the History, Laws and Places of the Chief Mines and Mineral Works in England, Wales and the English Part in Ireland*, (reprinted, the Institute of Mining and Metallurgy, 1981).

6 Bick, D. E. (1976) *Old Metal Mines of Mid-Wales Pt 3, Cardiganshire – North of Goginan*, (Newent, 1976); S. J. S. Hughes, *The Cwmystwyth Mines* (British Mining No. 17, 1981)' S. J. S. Hughes, *The Darren Mines* (British Mining No. 40, 1990); Bick, D. and Davies, P. (1993) *Lewis Morris and the Cardiganshire Mines* (National Library of Wales).

7 Borlase, W. (1758) *The Natural History of Cornwall* (Oxford); Pryce, W. (1778) *Mineralogia Cornubensis*.

8 Sopwith, T. (1833) *An Account of the Mining Districts of Alston Moor, Weardale and Teesdale*.

9 Brough, B. H. and Dean, H. (1926) *A treatise on Mine Surveying* and O'Donohue, T. A. (1946) *Field and Colliery Surveying*.

19 Maps in Parliamentary Papers   Susan Gole

Many hundreds of maps of the UK were published in about 900 volumes of the British Parliamentary Papers from the beginning of the 19th century, and maps of Ireland in about 200 volumes. The maps are currently being catalogued for the first time. 'Parliamentary Papers' is a generic term used for four series of publications: Bills and Papers of the House of Lords, Bills of the House of Commons, House of Commons Papers, and Command Papers. Many of the maps were drawn specifically for the purpose, though some were subsequently commercially published. So far only one map has been found with a Bill, and one with an Act. Most occur in the reports of Committees, reports of Commissions, and Accounts and Papers.

The maps themselves cover a wide range, both geographically and thematically. Some, such as three maps of England and Wales, Scotland, and Ireland, were repeated annually from 1865 to 1914 to show the sites of wrecks around the coast. Others depict new electoral boundaries, sites of public works, such as orphanages, workhouses, mines with detailed plans of the workings, railways, canals etc. Each spate of new building in London occasioned a set of plans being placed before the House, many of them on a very large scale.

Though no set is complete, the following libraries hold sets of the Papers: British Library, House of Commons, House of Lords, Bodleian, Cambridge University, National Library of Scotland, Trinity College Dublin, London School of Economics, and the Ford Collection at Southampton University. There is also a set on microfiche (1801–1921) produced by Chadwyck-Healey in 1991 (Cockton 1991).

Several subject indexes have been published but none gives details of the maps (Cockton 1988 and Temperley 1966, for example).

References

Cockton, Peter (1991) *Guide to the Chadwyck-Healey Microfiche Edition.* Cambridge.
Cockton, Peter (1988) *The subject catalogue of the House of Commons Parliamentary Papers, 1801–1900.* Cambridge.
Temperley, Harold and Lillian M. Penson (1966) *A Century of Diplomatic Blue Books 1814–1914.* London, Cassell.

20 Maritime surveys

Christopher Terrell and Helen Wallis

The importance of maritime charts for the history of discovery and exploration, or for studies in the history of navigation itself, is self-evident. What may be less apparent is their use in other areas of historical enquiry.

Sea charts have been defined as maps made for the use of seamen on board ships at sea. As such they might appear to be of limited use to the general historian. However, the seamen was as much interested in the land encountered during a voyage as in the sea; and the ports he intended to berth in were as important as the navigational dangers to be avoided on the way. This helps to explain the apparent paradox that, when looking for historical information on a chart, it is more often the land areas, rather than the sea, that prove rewarding.

Secondly, the charting of coasts was also a landsman's concern. It was considered essential for the defence of the realm.

The earliest printed sea atlas of the British Isles was Lucas Jansz Waghenaer's *Spieghel der Zeevaerdt*, the first atlas of the coasts of western Europe, published at Leiden, 1584–5. The coasts are shown as seen from the sea in a series of bird's eye views. The *Spieghel* was translated into English by Anthony Ashley, clerk to the Privy Council, and published in London with the title *The Mariners Mirrour* in 1588, a few weeks after the Armada. The Dutch and English editions of the atlas, now very rare, became available in facsimile in the 1960s in the 'Theatrum Orbis Terrarum' Series, published at Amsterdam. The *Spieghel* was reproduced in the First Series vol. IV (1964), *The Mariners Mirrour* in Third Series vol. II (1966), both with excellent introductions by R. A. Skelton.

The commissioning of charts for defensive purposes in the 16th century led to large scale mapping of ports and anchorages. In 1539 Henry VIII recruited experts to view all the places along the sea coast. The resulting manuscript charts were based on pilots' and engineers' surveys, on local knowledge and sometimes also on town views. The long view of the south-west coast of England, 1539 (BL Cotton ms. Aug.I.35, 36, 38, 39), is an outstanding example (Barber, p.34). Under Elizabeth I William Cecil Lord Burghley, the Lord High Treasurer, built up a large collection of maps and charts. Some were incorporated from *c*.1570 to 1595 in the 'Burghley-Saxton' atlas, which comprises proofs of Christopher Saxton's county maps, some annotated with coastal and other information, together with additional manuscript maps and charts mainly of strategic areas (BL Royal ms. 18.D.111). Other charts are preserved at Hatfield House, Lord Burghley's country home. These are recorded and some are reproduced in R. A. Skelton and John Summerson, 1971.

Another large collection of manuscript Tudor charts was preserved by Sir Robert Cotton, the Elizabethan antiquary, and is now in the British Library.

With the Restoration of the monarchy in 1660 there was a new impulse to improve the charting of the coasts. Among the mathematical practitioners who set up businesses in London John Seller (fl.1669–1691), chart and compass maker, and map seller, King's Hydrographer from 1671, carried on an unrivalled practice. His *English Pilot* (London, 1671) includes charts of the British Isles, but many were worked up from old Dutch plates, as Samuel Pepys complained. The Admiralty and Trinity House responded to the need in 1681 by commissioning Greenvile Collins, a naval officer, 'to make a survey of the sea coast of the Kingdom'. Collins completed 120 plans of harbours and stretches of coast, but of these only 48 were engraved and published. *Great Britain's Coasting Pilot*, London 1693, with reissues to 1792, met with strong criticism from Pepys and others, but the charts provide good local detail of towns and estuaries.

In the same period, about 1680 to 1690, John Adair was surveying the east coast of Scotland, with support from the Scottish Parliament. The resulting publication was a small sea atlas, *Description of the Sea Coasts and Islands of Scotland* (Edinburgh, 1703). Many of Adair's charts were never engraved. His manuscript surveys are preserved mainly in the Bodleian Library, the Admiralty Library and the National Library of Scotland. Another survey, a joint enterprise of the Navy Board and Trinity House, was undertaken by Edmund Dummer and Thomas Wiltshaw, who in 1698 surveyed eighteen harbours along the south coast investigating possible sites for new dockyards. Nine copies of their report and charts are preserved, three in the National Maritime Museum, three in the British Library and one in the Royal Geographical Society (Robinson, pp.45–6).

In the eighteenth century private individuals undertook charting as amateur hydrographers in response to local needs, to deal with such matters as the silting up of ports. The survey of the Liverpool Harbour, by Samuel Fearon, a shipbuilder, and John Eyes, a land surveyor, 1736–7, published in 1738, is one of the most competent and notable for the first use of the Greenwich prime meridian. The most eminent of the private surveyors who became hydrographers was Lewis Morris, customs officer and antiquary, who survyed the Welsh coast from 1737, producing in manuscript 'Cambria's Coasting Pilot', 2 vols, 1737–42, and *Plans of Harbours, Bars, Bays and Roads in St George's Channel* (London, 1748). A new edition by his son William Morris was published in 1803.

Official surveys of the 18th century showed marked technical progress. Murdoch Mackenzie Senior (1712–97) achieved in his charting of the Orkneys, 1742–49, the most accurate and detailed survey yet attempted in the British Isles. For the first time the survey was based on a triangulation framework and offshore detail was much more accurate. The charts were published in *Orcades* (London, 1750). Mackenzie then surveyed over the next twenty years the west coast of Britain and the whole of the Irish coast. This survey was published in *A Maritime Survey of Ireland and the West of Great Britain* (London, 1776). He was succeeded by his nephew Murdoch Mackenzie Junior, who further advanced the techniques of marine survey.

The military engineer also contributed to the increasingly accurate charting of coastal areas in the eighteenth century, following proposals of the Chief Engineer in 1716 that engineers should be employed in making surveys of the coasts where they had responsibilities. One of the most outstanding was John Desmaretz who surveyed harbours and defensive works in southern England from 1724 to 1755.

The Hydrographic Office was founded in 1795, four years after the Ordnance Survey. Progress in charting was slow, and by 1829 only 44 Admiralty charts of home waters had been published. Francis Beaufort, appointed Hydrographer in 1829, accelerated the process. At his retirement *c.*1855 a total of 255 charts had been completed in what was described as the 'Grand Survey of the British Isles'. Called 'The Father of British Hydrography', Beaufort introduced the Admiralty Chart as we know it today.

Richard Gough's chapter on Charts in his *British Topography*, London, 1780, is probably the earliest survey of the charts of the British Isles. Charts are mainly preserved in the major libraries and maritime offices: the British Library, the Bodleian, Cambridge University Library (which has now acquired the Hanson Collection, previously at the Cruising Association), National Library of Scotland, and Trinity College Dublin, the Hydrographic Office of the Ministry of Defence at Taunton, and the

National Maritime Museum. These holdings are well documented in the appendixes of A. H. W. Robinson, *Marine Cartography in Britain* (1962) which is still the best overall study.

Bibliography

Barber, P. (1992) 'England I. England II' in David Buisseret (ed.) *Monarchs Ministers and Maps*, pp.26–98. Chicago and London: University of Chicago Press.

Campbell, T. (1987) Portolan charts from the late 13th century to 1500, in J. B. Harley and D. Woodward (eds), *The History of Cartography in Prehistoric, Ancient and Medieval Europe and the Mediterranean*, pp.371–483. Chicago and London: University of Chicago Press.

Day, A. (1967) *The Admiralty Hydrographic Service, 1795–1919*. London: HMSO.

Duffy, M. and others (1992) *The New Maritime History of Devon*, vol 1. Exeter: Conway Maritime Press.

Howse, D, and M. Sanderson (1973) *The Sea Chart*. Newton Abbott: David & Charles.

Ritchie, G. S. (1967) *The Admiralty Chart*. London: Hollis & Carter.

Robinson, A. H. W. (1962) *Marine Cartography in Britain*. Leicester University Press.

Skelton, R. A. and Summerson, John (1971) *A Description of Maps and Architectural Drawings in the Collection made by William Cecil, first baron Burghley, now at Hatfield House*. Oxford: The Roxburghe Club.

Smith, David (1988) *Maps and Plans for the Local Historian and Collector*. London: Batsford.

21 Agriculture and land use maps Elizabeth Baigent

Land use is depicted on many maps, but, particularly where it was not the main purpose of the map, such information may be stylised and apparent variation may reflect changing conventions and interpretations rather than real land use change. Often surveys took place long before a map was published so the date of maps may be misleading, especially in areas such as town fringes undergoing enclosure where land use change was rapid. Nonetheless, maps are often the only or the most comprehensive source of information on land use.

Large scale printed county maps date from the sixteenth to the nineteenth centuries. Many, particularly those from the mid-eighteenth centuries onwards, identify such features as woodland, common grazing land, arable land, parks, built areas. quarries, pits and mills. Although much information is reliable, some was incorporated from earlier surveys and field boundaries are usually schematic. Agricultural land use is generally better covered than industrial. Small scale land-use maps of counties were first published in England in the 1790s when the Board of Agriculture began making enquiries into the state of agriculture in the counties. The first true land-utilization map, dated 1800, was by Thomas Milne, an estate and county surveyor, and is entitled 'Milne's Plan of the Cities of London and Westminster'. Only one example of the complete 6 sheet map is known (British Library, K.Top.VI.95).

Drawings for the first edition of the Ordnance Survey's 1 inch to 1 mile maps cover England and Wales south of the Mersey and Humber estuaries at scales of 2, 3 and 5 inches to 1 mile. They date from the 1780s to the 1840s and give much information about land use, although field boundaries may be sketchy. The originals are in the British Library. but microfiche reproductions are widely accessible.

Printed nineteenth-century Ordnance Survey maps give information about land use. The 1 inch to 1 mile maps are difficult to date which complicates their use for the study of land change. 6 inch to 1 mile maps, particularly those published before 1881, show considerable detail of land use.

Between 1855 and 1918 the Ordnance Survey recorded land-use as part of the cadastral mapping and revision at 1:2,500 (6 inches to 1 mile). Until 1884 the maps for each parish were accompanied by a Parish Area

Book (or Book of Reference) which gave the acreage and, before 1880, land use of each land parcel, identified by number on the map. The Area Books cover much of south-east England, Cornwall, north and south Wales and lowland Scotland.

Many eighteenth- and nineteenth-century maps of the environs of towns show the nurseries, hay fields, pleasure gardens, brick kilns and lime pits characteristic of the urban fringe.

Large scale road maps often depict land use to help travellers find their way. Strip maps cover roadside areas alone. (See also above Essays 8, 9, 14 and 16.)

Bibliography

Coppock, J. T. (1968) Maps as sources for the study of land use in the past, *Imago Mundi* **22**, 37–49.

Harley, J. B. (1972) *Maps for the local historian: a guide to the British sources.* London: Bedford Square Press of the National Council of Social Service. Reprinted 1977.

Harley, J. B. (1979) The Ordnance Survey and land-use mapping, parish books of reference and the county series 1:2500 maps 1855–1918. Exeter: University of Exeter, *Historical Geography Research Series* **2**, 59pp.

Hodson, Y. (1989) *Ordnance Surveyors' drawings, 1789-c.1840: The original two manuscript maps of the first Ordnance Survey of England and Wales.* Reading: Research Publications, 154pp.

Laxton, P. (1976) The geodetic and topographical evaluation of English county maps 1740–1840, *Cartographic Journal* **13** (1), 37–54.

Rodger, E. M. (1972) *The large scale county maps of the British Isles 1596–1850: A union list.* Oxford: Bodleian Library. (2nd edition).

Wallis, H. (1981) The history of land use mapping, *Cartographic Journal* **18**, 45–8.

22 Maps of Ireland

J. H. Andrews and Paul Ferguson

There is an extensive literature on Irish map history. It was reviewed by Andrews in 1962, and a bibliography of secondary works was compiled by Ferguson in 1983. Andrews' contribution over the intervening period was reviewed by Whelan in 1992.

Irish cartography begins no earlier than the sixteenth century with the advent of separate maps of Ireland. Before that, the mapping of Europe's outermost Atlantic fringe belongs to the history of other nations and other cultures, with the British Isles taking an inconspicuous place successively in Claudius Ptolemy's Alexandrian world map of the second century AD (Orpen, 1894), in the diagrammatic mappae mundi characteristic of early-medieval Christendom, and in the sea charts produced by Italian and Iberian navigators in the fourteenth century and after (Michael Andrews, 1923). These sources provided the information on Ireland which appeared on early printed maps of the British Isles (Shirley, 1991), but only from c.1540 did Ireland assume a definite cartographic identity in the many English military and political maps that were the surveyors' and engineers' contribution to the forward policy pursued by Tudor governments (Andrews, 1970; Edwards and O'Dowd, 1985). In this connection the maps of Robert Lyth (1567–71), the two John Brownes (uncle and nephew, 1583–90), Francis Jobson (1587–98) and Richard Bartlett (1601–2) (Hayes-McCoy, 1964) are particularly notable. Much of their work remained shut away in government offices or in private archives such as those in the collection of George Carew, Lord President of Munster (O'Sullivan, 1983). Some of these maps were used without acknowledgement in the compilations of foreign cartographers such as Gerard Mercator (1564, 1595) and Abraham Ortelius (1573), and later in the maps of the Englishman John Speed (1611), whose version of Ireland found general acceptance for most of the seventeenth century (Andrews, 1972).

War and the threat of war continued to inspire distinctive maps in Ireland as in other countries, but by Speed's time military campaigns were becoming a less important cartographic influence than the confiscation of landed property. The emphasis shifted to the measurement and plotting of numerous small territorial divisions at large scales. William Petty is pre-eminent among the organisers of these plantation surveys, for the magnitude of his 'admeasurement down', since known as the 'Down Survey' (1655–9); and also his original concept of working up the results into an atlas of all the Irish provinces and counties, the *Hiberniae delineatio* of 1685 (Goblet, 1930). The manuscript maps for the Down Survey and the atlas, with related papers, came to the British Library in 1992 by purchase from the family of Lord Lansdowne, the descendants of Sir William Petty.

Though published in London, Petty's famous atlas may be accepted as characteristically Irish in its evocation of the utilitarian character of plantation cartography (Andrews, 1969). Its outline appeared in most of the general maps of Ireland published by British and foreign cartographers between *c.*1690 and the advent of the Ordnance Survey. Such longevity does little credit to Petty's successors. Once the supply of new plantation surveys dried up in 1703, few Irishmen were willing to carry out cartographic research for its own sake, a major exception being Daniel Beaufort, whose ecclesiastical maps of Ireland (1792) was rightly admired as a masterpiece of careful scholarship (Ellison, 1987).

Petty's real bequest to eighteenth-century Ireland was the country's flourishing class of land-surveyors (Andrews, 1985). Some of them made maps of complete counties, including several that were engraved in Dublin, but their main interest was in the manuscript mapping of farms and estates (Eden, 1975–9). This remained an Irish preoccupation even after the visit to Dublin in 1754–60 of the celebrated Anglo-French cartographer John Rocque (?1704–62), who through his pupils (especially Bernard Scalé) exercised more influence in Ireland on estate surveying than on the kind of printed map that Rocque himself had specialised in (Andrews, 1967). Certainly no cartographer of Irish extraction ever equalled the magnificent plan of Dublin which Rocque published in 1756 (Andrews, 1977). Also notable was the military survey of southern Ireland by Charles Vallancey R.E., 1776–85 (British Library, K.Top.L1. 31–2) (Andrews, 1966). Vallancey's work was used by Aaron Arrowsmith, the London publisher, in his large map of Ireland (1811).

Another generation of innovators, several of them Scotsmen or with Scottish connections, appeared in Ireland after the union of 1801 and were especially active in the mapping of roads, canals and harbours, exploiting new cartographic techniques and achieving new standards of accuracy. Prominent in this group were William Bald, Richard Griffith, William Duncan and William Edgeworth. Most of them spent some time practising as independent civil engineers under central or local government control, particularly in surveys for the Irish Bogs Commission of 1809–14 and in preparing several county maps that were by-products of the bogs survey. Printed maps of counties received limited funding from Grand Juries, the county authorities responsible for road improvements, under an Act of 1774 which led to the mapping of 25 counties at a scale of between one or two inches to the Irish mile, some being surveyed more than once. These maps varied greatly in content and accuracy but those based on theodolite triangulation were of a high standard. The highpoint of this genre was achieved in Bald's 25 sheet map of County Mayo completed in 1830.

Some engineers, such as William Armstrong in County Armagh, tried to apply these standards of precision to the traditional subject-matter of Irish estate surveying, but their efforts were overtaken by the arrival of the Ordnance Survey, a large and efficient government map-making agency directed by officers of the Corps of Royal Engineers (Andrews, 1975b). The newcomers began by publishing maps of the whole of Ireland at the scale of six inches to one mile (1833–46), and then by widening their range in the later nineteenth century to embrace almost every other kind of map (Andrews, 1993). During the second quarter of the century, Dublin, and the Ordnance Survey in particular, was at the cutting edge of cartographic innovation, for example, in engraving by William Dalgleish, in geological mapping by Richard Griffith (Davies, 1983) and in Henry Harness' and Thomas Larcom's representations of thematic information, as presented in the *Atlas to accompany the Second Report of the Railway Commissioners, Ireland* (Dublin: HMSO, 1838) (Robinson, 1955, 1982). But this golden age was short-lived and it ended when the Survey's attention was refocussed on Great Britain in the 1850s. Private large scale cartography in Ireland was stifled by Ordnance Survey competition and land surveyors largely became copyists thereafter. On the other hand, commercial publishers mostly outside Ireland found it profitable to reduce and restyle the Survey's small scale work for a growing tourist and recreation market.

References

Andrews, John H. (1962) 'Ireland in maps: a bibliographical postscript', *Irish Geography* 4 (4), 234–43.

Andrews, John H. (1966) 'Charles Vallancey and the map of Ireland', *Geographical Journal* **132**, 48–61.

Andrews, John H. (1967) 'The French school of Dublin land surveyors', *Irish Geography* 5 (4), 275–93.

Andrews, John H. (1969) Introduction to Sir William Petty's *Hibernia delineatio quod hactenus licuit perfectissima studio Guilielmi Petty.* Facsimile reproduction of the 1685 edition, together with a reproduction of William Petty and Francis Lamb's *Geographical description of ye Kingdom of Ireland* (c.1689). Shannon: Irish University Press.

Andrews, John H. (1970) 'Geography and government in Elizabethan Ireland', in N. Stephens and R. Glasscock (eds.) *Irish geographical studies in honour of E. Estyn Evans*, pp.178–91. Belfast: Department of Geography, Queen's University.

Andrews, John H. (1972) 'An Elizabethan surveyor and his cartographic progeny'. *Imago Mundi* **26**, 45.

Andrews, John H. (1974) *History in the Ordnance map, an introduction for Irish readers.* Dublin: Ordnance Survey. 2nd edition, with new preface and bibliography, Newtown, Montgomery: David Archer, 1993.

Andrews, John H. (1975a) 'Two maps of eighteenth-century Dublin and its surroundings, by John Rocque'. Introduction of facsimiles of *An exact survey of the city and suburbs of Dublin, 1756* and *An actual survey of the county of Dublin, 1760.* Folkestone, Kent: Margary.

Andrews, John H. (1975b) *A paper landscape: the Ordnance Survey in nineteenth-century Ireland.* Oxford: Clarendon Press.

Andrews, John H. (1985) *Plantation acres: a historical study of the Irish land surveyor and his maps.* Belfast: Ulster Historical Foundation.

Andrews, Michael C. (1923) 'The map of Ireland, AD 1300–1700', *Belfast Natural History Society Proceedings*, 1922–3, 9–33.

Davies, Gordon L. Herries (1983) *Sheets of many colours – the mapping of Ireland's rocks, 1750–1890.* No.4 in Historical Studies of Irish Science and Technology. Dublin: Royal Dublin Society.

Eden, P. (ed.) (1975–9) *Dictionary of land surveyors and local cartographers of Great Britain and Ireland, 1550–1850.* Folkestone, Dawson.

Edwards, R. D. and M. O'Dowd (1985) 'Maps and drawings', in Edwards, R. D. and M. O'Dowd (eds.) *Sources for early modern Irish history, 1534–1641*, pp.106–28. Cambridge: Cambridge University Press.

Ellison, Cyril C. (1987) *The hopeful traveller: the life and times of Daniel Augustus Beaufort LL.D., 1739–1821.* Kilkenny: Boethius Press.

Ferguson, Paul J. (1983) *Irish map history: a select bibliography, 1850–1983, on the history of cartography in Ireland.* Dublin: University College, Department of Geography.

Goblet, Yann M. (1930) *La transformation de la géographie politique de l'Irlande au XVIIe siècle dans les cartes et essais anthro-*

pogéographiques de Sir William Petty. 2 vols. Paris: Berger-Levrault.

Hayes-McCoy, Gerard A. (1964) *Ulster and other Irish maps, c.1600*. Dublin: Stationery Office for the Irish Manuscripts Commission.

Orpen, Goddard H. (1894) 'Ptolemy's map of Ireland', *Journal of the Royal Society of Antiquaries of Ireland* **24**, 115–28 and **25** (1895), 179–80.

O'Sullivan, William (1983) 'George Carew's Irish maps', *Long Room*, 15–25.

Robinson, Arthur H. (1955) 'The 1837 maps of Henry Harness', *Geographical Journal* **121**, 440–50.

Robinson, Arthur H. (1982) *Early thematic mapping in the history of cartography*. Chicago and London: University of Chicago Press.

Shirley, Rodney W. (1991) *Early printed maps of the British Isles, 1477–1650*. 3rd revised edition. East Grinstead: Antique Atlas Publications.

Whelan, Kevin (1992) 'Beyond a paper landscape – John Andrews and Irish historical geography', in F. H. A. Aalen and K. Whelan (eds.) *Dublin city and county: from prehistory to present*, pp.379–424. Dublin: Geography Publications.

23 Maps of Scotland　　　　　　　Jeffrey Stone

Students of the history of Scottish maps are fortunate in that they have been very well served for many years by the carto-bibliographic work of eminent Secretaries and members of the Royal Scottish Geographical Society. *The Early Maps of Scotland*, first published in 1934 to commemorate the jubilee of the Society, was rapidly revised and re-issued in 1936. More recently, many years of assiduous data collection by D. G. Moir, in circumstances of increasing interest in the subject, resulted in the publication of the third edition in two volumes. Part 1 of the first volume comprises a history of Scottish maps in twelve chapters, followed by biographical notes on Scottish cartographers and engravers, and this part of the work has been overtaken by new research. However, the rest of the two-volume work, whilst no longer recording every known map, is still close to the ultimately definitive record of Scotland's rich cartographic heritage and fortunately is widely available. Furthermore, an annotated bibliography of the literature of Scottish maps and mapmaking prior to the Ordnance Survey is available in a comprehensive second edition (Moore).

Only about a hundred maps of the whole of Scotland were published before 1750. They include maps by well known names such as Abraham Ortelius, Gerard Mercator, Willem Blaeu and John Speed, as well as by cartographers with closer Scottish connections such as John Leslie, Robert Gordon, John Adair, and Herman Moll. Particular mention must be made of the large collection of sixteenth- and seventeenth-century manuscript maps of Scotland by Timothy Pont, Robert and James Gordon, and John Adair, in the National Library of Scotland. Between 1750 and 1850 the trickle of maps of the whole of Scotland became a flood, with more than 300 different maps recorded.

Topographical maps of Scottish counties constitute by far the largest single category of maps, commencing with the detailed coverage provided by Joan Blaeu in 1654, but including maps for most counties by Herman Moll, Thomas Kitchin, Andrew and Mostyn Armstrong, Thomas Brown, John Lothian, William Blackwood, Adam Black, William Johnston and, most notably, John Thomson (1832). In addition, a great many individual county surveys were made.

Railway plans are exceeded in number only by county maps. Early plans of projected railways which never materialised date from 1817. There are more than 400 recorded plans dating from the next three decades which can be studied in conjunction with a rich literature on nineteenth-century Scottish railways.

Town plans are also a prolific field, with over 400 recorded items prior to 1850. They include several early maps, such as James Gordon's Edinburgh (1647) and Aberdeen (1661). There are also notable later plans of such smaller towns as James Tait's Lochmaben (1786). However, the outstanding item in this category is the town atlas of Scotland by John Wood (1828), which includes 48 of his 50 detailed town plans.

Marine charts of Scotland are a fourth field of notable achievement with some 230 charts dated prior to 1850. The east coast at first received attention, with charts by the Dutch hydrographer Lucas Jansz Waghenaer being particularly influential from 1583. The Northern Isles were also the subject of early surveys. The more difficult west coast was tackled by Murdoch Mackenzie from 1751.

Smaller categories of Scottish maps, each of which contain over 100 items recorded prior to 1850, include historical maps, road maps and canal plans. Geological maps have proved to be a rich subject of recent study, as they are contemporaneous with Scotland's nineteenth-century excellence in this field discipline. Military mapping is associated with road maps in origin, in particular with the eighteenth-century road and bridge building in Scotland by General George Wade, 1724–43. Following the 1745 uprising, the military survey of 1747–55 made Scotland one of the best-mapped countries. The survey of the Highlands, 1747 to 1752, was undertaken by William Roy (1726–90), with Paul Sandby as draughtsman. The survey of southern Scotland proceeded from 1752 to 1755. The manuscript fair copy of the survey, together with the field sheets, is preserved in the British Library (K.Top.XLVIII.25., Maps C.9.b.) and depicts all of mainland Scotland at a scale of about 2 inches to a mile (c.1:36,000). Photographic reproductions are available in various libraries in Scotland.

Another prolific episode in the mapping of Scotland was consequent upon the improving movement in the eighteenth and nineteenth centuries, and gave rise to a great many detailed and accurate surveys before and after the reformulation of the rural landscape. These documents, many of them in manuscript, remain dispersed. Some are still in estate offices of both highland and lowland Scotland, others have found their way into the accessible public map collections of Scotland.

Bibliography

Adams, I. H. (1966, 1970, 1974); Adams I. H. and L. Timperley (1988) *Descriptive List of Plans [in the] Scottish Record Office*, 4 vols, Edinburgh: Vols 1–3 published by HMSO, vol 4 by Scottish Record Office.

Moir, D. G. (1973, 1983), with a Committee of the Royal Scottish Geographical Society. *The early maps of Scotland to 1850*, 2 vols, Edinburgh: Royal Scottish Geographical Society.

Moore, J. N. (1991) The historical cartography of Scotland. *O'Dell Memorial Monographs* **24**. Aberdeen: University of Aberdeen.

O'Donoghue, Y. (1977) *William Roy, 1726–1790, Pioneer of the Ordnance Survey*. London: British Museum Publications for the British Library.

Stone, J. C. (1987) The study of the early maps of Scotland – the way ahead, in M. Wood (ed.), *Cartography: the way ahead*, 77–86. Norwich: Geo Books.

Stone, J. C. (1989) *The Pont manuscript maps of Scotland. Sixteenth century origins of a Blaeu atlas.* Tring: Map Collector Publications.

Wilkes, M. (1991) *The Scot and his maps.* Motherwell: Scottish Library Association.

24 Maps of Wales   Robert Davies

There is no comprehensive history of the mapping of Wales. It mirrors that of England in many aspects but with some significant differences. North (1935) discusses the development of the outline of Wales up to 1600, and North (1937) describes the work of Humphrey Lhuyd, who made the first map to show Wales on its own. These studies were expanded by Evans (1964) and Gruffydd (1968).

Wales was included in the first modern topographic survey of England and Wales begun by Christopher Saxton about 1573. The survey survives as two major cartographic works, the county atlas of 1579 and the wall map of 1583. The recent discovery of a 'proof state' of a map of Wales of about 1580 is discussed in Owen (1987). Wales's own Elizabethan historian and topographer, George Owen of Henllys, is the subject of a study by Charles (1973). The surveys of Saxton and Owen became the basis for a long series of county maps that would dominate the cartography of the region during the seventeenth and early eighteenth centuries.

The eighteenth century was a period of extraordinary activity of county surveys. Walters (1968) describes this development as it relates to Wales. The new surveys of South Wales by Bowen *c*.1720 and John Evans of North Wales, 1795, are examples of regional mapping, while Yates's map of Glamorgan, 1799, William Williams's map of Denbigh and Flint, 1720, Singer's Cardiganshire, 1803 are the only Welsh examples of this genre of large scale county maps. The printed maps of some Welsh counties have been listed. The most comprehensive carto-bibliography is for Monmouthshire (Michael, 1985); and Lewis has prepared incomplete lists for Merioneth (1951), Cardiganshire (1955), Breconshire (1972) and Radnorshire (1977); North (1965) discusses the maps of Glamorgan and Perkins (1970) lists some maps of Dyfed. Jones (1977) lists the maps of Radnorshire and Jones (1987) the maps of Montgomeryshire. These maps are the stepping stone between the surveys of Saxton and Owen at the end of the sixteenth century and the maps published by the Ordnance Survey in the nineteenth century. Oliver (1992) details the history of the small scale survey of Wales in his carto-bibliography which accompanies the best facsimile reproduction of the earliest state of the one inch to the mile maps. The large scale surveying of the Ordnance Survey in Wales at 6 inches and 25 inches to the mile was supplemented by town plans at a scale of 1:500. Some towns were mapped at their own expence at a scale of 1:528. Moore (1973) details the town plans of Glamorganshire.

Bassett (1967) records the advance of geological mapping in Wales and Evans (1969) deals with the marine charts and maritime surveys. Lewis Morris, *Plans of harbours, bays ... in St George's Channel*, 1748, was a particular landmark in the history of Welsh maritime surveys. Robinson (1968) and Robinson (1979) list Morris's maritime surveys, while Bick and Davies (1994) include details of Morris's work for the mining industry.

The publication of topographic, nautical and thematic maps was paralleled with the steady development of large scale manuscript estate maps during the period *c*.1575 to *c*.1825. Davies (1982) describes the collections of estate plans housed at the National Library of Wales and Thomas (1992) lists the estate maps of Glamorganshire. The golden age of estate surveying in Wales was 1750–1850, slightly later than England. The importance of Welsh estate surveys was the subject of Thomas (1966); Thomas (1985) discusses the activities of the land surveyor in Wales 1750–1850, and Evans (1977) has recalled the ascendancy of the estate surveyor in Carmarthenshire.

Chapman (1992) has listed the enclosure maps of Wales and gives a useful bibliography of the literature relating to the enclosure of lands in Wales, while Davies (1993) provides a detailed study of the tithe maps of Wales. These maps herald the demise of the private estate surveyor since any further mapping could be copied from the tithe maps. The manuscript surveys of the private practitioners were finally replaced by the large scale maps of the Ordnance Survey after about 1875. The maps included with auctioneers' sale particulars of many of the large estates as they were disbanded after 1875 are also useful sources for the late nineteenth century. Goad fire insurance plans are available for Cardiff, Swansea and Newport.

The maps sought by historians may be found in many different places and institutions. It is always best to start with the obvious local sources at the local library, record office or museum, and thence to proceed to regional and national collections. The strengths of these local collections are detailed in the individual entries in Part II below.

The National Library of Wales has the most comprehensive map collection in Wales and is open to all ticket holders. There are no published catalogues of its map collection. Enclosure maps (Chapman 1992) and plans of public undertakings and communications are usually found in local record offices. These also have estate maps not found at the National Library of Wales. Some record offices have published guides to their collections, such as Veysey (1984, 1991) for Clwyd and Morgan (1988, 1990) for Powys, but most maps can only be found by consulting catalogues and lists on site, or the annual reports of the county archivists.

Select Bibliography

Bassett, D. A. (1967) *A source-book of geological, geomorphological and soil maps for Wales and the Welsh Borders.* Cardiff: National Museum of Wales.

Bick, D. and P. W. Davies (1994) *Lewis Morris and the Cardiganshire mines.* Aberystwyth: National Library of Wales.

Chapman, J. (1992) *A guide to parliamentary enclosures in Wales.* Cardiff: University of Wales Press.

Charles, B. G. (1973) *George Owen of Henllys: a Welsh Elizabethan.* Aberystwyth: National Library of Wales.

Davies, R. (1982) *Estate maps of Wales 1600–1836 [An exhibition catalogue].* Aberystwyth: National Library of Wales.

Davies, R. (1993) *An atlas of the tithe maps of Wales.* Aberystwyth: National Library of Wales.

Evans, M. C. S. (1977) The pioneers of estate mapping in Carmarthenshire. *Carmarthen Antiquary* **13**, 52–64.

Evans, O. C. (1964) *Maps of Wales and Welsh cartographers.* London: Map Collectors Circle, No.13.

Evans, O. C. (1969) *Marine plans and charts of Wales.* London: Map Collectors Circle, No.54.

Gruffyd, R. G. (1968) Humphrey Llwyd of Denbigh: some documents and a catalogue, *Transactions of the Denbighshire Historical Society* **17**, 54–107.

Jones, J. E. (1987) Montgomeryshire on old maps, *Montgomery Collections* **75**, 9–28.

Jones, I. E. (1977) The mapping of Radnorshire before the Ordnance Survey, *Transactions of the Radnorshire Society* **47**, 13–24.

Lewis, M. G. (1951) The printed maps of Merioneth, 1578–1900, in the National Library of Wales, *Journal of the Merioneth Historical and Record Society* **1**, 162–79.

Lewis, M. G. (1955) The printed maps of Cardiganshire, 1578–1900, in the National Library of Wales. *Journal of the Cardiganshire Antiquarian Society* **2**, 244–76.

Lewis, M. G. (1972) The printed maps of Breconshire, 1578–1900, in the National Library of Wales. *Brycheiniog* **16**, 139–74.

Lewis, M. G. (1977) *The printed maps of Radnorshire.* Aberystwyth: National Library of Wales.

Michael, D. P. M. (1985) *The mapping of Monmouthshire.* Bristol: Regional Publications.

Moore, P. (1973) Glamorgan town plans, *Glamorgan historian* **9**, 157–72.

Morgan, R. (1989) Powys Archives 1984–1989, *Brycheiniog* **23**, 13–20.

Morgan, R. (1992) Powys Archives 1990–91, *Brycheiniog* **24**, 7–9.

North, F. J. (1935) The map of Wales before 1600 AD, *Archaeologia Cambrensis* **90**, 1–69.

North, F. J. (1937) Humphrey Lhuyd's Maps of England and Wales, *Archaeologia Cambrensis* **92**, 11–63.

North, F. J. (1965) Glamorgan in maps – the maps of Glamorgan, *Glamorgan Historian* **2**, 13–29.

Oliver, R. R. (1992) Cartobibliography: Wales. *The Old Series Ordnance Survey maps of England and Wales.* vol. **6**. Lympe Castle: Harry Margary.

Owen, D. H. (1987) Saxton's proof map of Wales. *The Map Collector* **38**, 24–5.

Perkins, A. (1970) Some maps of Wales, and in particular of the counties of Pembrokeshire, Cardiganshire and Carmarthenshire, *Carmarthen Antiquary* **6**, 59–82.

Robinson, A. H. W. (1968) Lewis Morris, an early Welsh hydrographer, *Transactions of the Anglesey Antiquarian Society* [vol. for 1968], 38–48.

Robinson, A. H. W. (1979) Lewis Morris, chartmaker extraordinary, *The Map Collector* **8**, 32–6.

Thomas, C. (1966) Estate surveys as sources in historical geography, *National Library of Wales Journal* **14**, 451–68.

Thomas, C. (1985) Land surveyors in Wales 1750–1850: the Matthews Family. *Bulletin of the Board of Celtic Studies* **32**, 216–32.

Thomas, H. (1992) *A catalogue of Glamorgan estate maps.* [Cardiff]: Glamorgan Archives Publications.

Veysey, A. G. (1984) Guide to the parish records of Clwyd. [Hawarden]: Clwyd Record Office.

Veysey, A. G. (1991) *A handlist of the Denbighshire Quarter Sessions records.* Hawarden: Clwyd Record Office. vol.1, 1–68. 'Enclosure awards and deposited plans of public undertakings'.

Walters, G. (1968) Themes in the large scale mapping of Wales in the eighteenth century, *Cartographic Journal* **5**, 135–46.

Williams, D. H. (1990) *Atlas of Cistercian lands in Wales.* Cardiff: University of Wales Press.

25 Place names and gazetteers   Francis Herbert

Nicholas Carlisle in the Preface to his *Topographical Dictionary* (1808), listed the categories of persons who would surely find his work useful, concluding with 'Students, Authors, and generally ... all Persons of Research, who may require authentic Information respecting the local, statistical, and other facts and circumstances relating to the Kingdom of England'. The terms 'topographical dictionary', 'gazetteer', 'index', or 'alphabetical table' have been applied since at least 1677–80 to an alphabetical arrangement of toponyms (Adams, 1680); the distinction between them is generally that the latter are simpler listings of names with references to a map grid or geographical co-ordinates, whilst the former may be expected to indicate geographical location with additional geographical, statistical, and historical matter.

From Fullarton (1840–2) onwards it was common to include a 'General Introductory Article' or 'Summary' (Wilson, 1866–69) or 'General Survey' (Groome, 1882–85), thus providing an up-to-date geographical overview of a country through one or more essays. Statistical data in gazetteers increased as more Acts of Parliament relating to the population were passed, notably the inclusion of more reliable census figures (decennially from 1801, except for Ireland); many works from the 1830s give comparative figures, within main text or in separate tables, of latest and earlier results. During the nineteenth century etymologies were more often catered for, by including a 'Glossary; or explanation of some of the Welsh [etc.] words which most frequently occur in composition with the names of places (Carlisle, 1811).

Indexes were often a conscious and inherent contextual adjunct to a map – whether that of a country, a county, or a city. A seventeenth-century 'alphabetical table' was often a separately-printed letterpress work to accompany its copperplate engraved map. In the first quarter of the nineteenth century county maps by the Greenwood brothers provided a series of separate indexes (up to 340 pages for Surrey, 1823); towards the century's end toponymic or street indexes were usually bound into covers of town or county maps, especially those issued for cyclists. Conversely, many county maps were published as adjuncts to gazetteers; but this does not imply a direct relationship as regards information content. Alternatively, the Ordnance Survey's town maps were either alluded to as sources of data (Lewis, 1837) or were referred to directly by citing the sheet number (Sharp, 1852; Groome, 1882–85). Emphasising the Victorian progress of industrialisation, some gazetteers included maps of railways (red overprint on 'Scotland' in Wilson (1854–57)), of canals ('Inland-Navigation Map' [*sic*] of c.1865 for England and Wales in Hamilton (1863–68)), or of maritime safety ('The lighthouses and inland navigation of the British Isles' in Bartholomew (1887)). Gazetteers, then, are also cartographic source material and should not be ignored.

References

Adams, J. (1680) *Index Villatis; Or, an Alphabetical Table of all of the Cities, Market-Towns, Parishes, Villages, and Private Seats, in England and Wales.* London: Adams. A map (with 'Alphabeticall Table') was published in 1677.

Bartholomew, J. (1887) *Gazetteer of the British Isles: statistical and topographical: with appendices and special maps and charts.* Edinburgh: Black.

Brabner, J. H. F. (1894–5) *The comprehensive gazetteer of England and Wales.* London; Edinburgh; Dublin: Mackenzie. 6 vols.

Carlisle, N. (1808) *A topographical dictionary of England; exhibiting the names of the several cities, towns, parishes, tythings, townships, and hamlets, . . .* London: Longman, Hurst, Rees and Orme. 2 vols. (No maps).

Carlisle, N. (1810) *A topographical dictionary of Ireland; exhibiting the names of the several cities, towns, parishes, and villages, . . .* London: Miller. (No maps).

Carlisle, N. (1811) *A topographical dictionary of the Dominion of Wales; exhibiting the names of the several cities, towns, parishes, townships, and hamlets, . . .* London: Carlisle. (No maps).

Carlisle, N. (1813) *A topographical dictionary of Scotland, and of the islands in the British seas; exhibiting the names of the several cities, royal burghs, parishes, villages, and islands, . . .* London: Nicol; Edinburgh: Bell and Bradfute. 2 vols. (No maps).

Fullarton, A. (1840–42) *The topographical, statistical, and historical gazetteer of Scotland.* Glasgow; Edinburgh; Aberdeen; Dundee; Dumfries; London: Fullarton. 2 vols.

Gorton, J. and (for Irish and Welsh articles) Wright, G. N. (1831–33) *A topographical dictionary of Great Britain and Ireland.* London: Chapman and Hall. 3 vols. 'With fifty-four quarto maps, drawn and engraved by Sidney Hall'.

Groome, F. H. (1882–85) *Ordnance Gazetteer of Scotland: a survey*

of Scottish topography – statistical, biographical, and historical.
Edinburgh; London; Glasgow; Aberdeen: Jack. 6 vols.

Hamilton, N. E. S. A. (1863–68) *The national gazetteer: a topographical dictionary of the British islands.* London: Virtue. 3 vols. '... illustrated with a complete county atlas, and numerous maps'

Index Nauticus: British Isles. (1820) London: Hydrographic Department, Admiralty. No charts; 'When a name appears on more than one chart, only the largest scale chart is quoted.'

Lewis, S. (1831) *A topographical dictionary of England, comprising the several counties, cities, boroughs, corporate and market towns, parishes, chapelries, and townships, and the islands of Guernsey, Jersey and Man, with historical and statistical descriptions* ... London: Lewis. 4 vols.

Lewis, S. (1833) *A topographical dictionary of Wales, comprising the several counties, cities, boroughs, corporate and market towns, parishes, chapelries, and townships, with historical and statistical descriptions* ... London: Lewis. 2 vols.

Lewis, S. (1837) *A topographical dictionary of Ireland, comprising the several counties, cities, boroughs, corporate, market, and post-towns, parishes and villages, with historical and statistical descriptions* ... London: Lewis (and reprint Port Washington, N.Y.; London: Kennikot Press, 1970).

Lewis, S. (1846) *A topographical dictionary of Scotland, comprising the several counties, islands, cities, burgs and market towns, parishes, and principal villages, with historical and statistical descriptions* ... London: Lewis. 2 vols.

Parliamentary gazetteer of England and Wales, The (1840–43) London; Edinburgh; Glasgow: Fullarton. 4 vols. 'Illustrated by a series of maps forming a complete county-atlas of England, and by four large maps of Wales'.

Parliamentary gazetteer of Ireland, The (1844–46) Dublin; London; Edinburgh: Fullarton. 3 vols.

Sharp, J. A. (1852). *A new gazetteer; or, topographical dictionary of the British islands and narrow seas* ... London: Longman, Brown, Green and Longmans. 2 vols. (No maps).

Wilson, J. M. (1854–57) *The imperial gazetteer of Scotland; or dictionary of Scottish topography ... forming a complete body of Scottish geography, physical, statistical, and historical.* Edinburgh; London; Dublin: Fullarton. 2 vols. 'Illustrated with a complete county atlas, various chorographical maps, plans of forts, harbours, ...'

Wilson, J. M. (1866–69) *The imperial gazetteer of England and Wales; embracing recent changes in counties, dioceses, parishes, and boroughs*

... Edinburgh; Glasgow; London; Dublin; New York: Fullarton. 6 vols. Issued with *Index to atlas* [or *Imperial map*] *of England and Wales* (1869) as separate items, but maps and charts included in gazetteer also.

Carlisle, in all four references given here, listed the topographical works which he had consulted. Apart from that of 1811, he also commented on earlier works, noting their originality or plagiarism.

This survey excludes re-issues and new editions. A reference work still of value is John P. Anderson (1881) *The book of British topography: a classified catalogue of the topographical works in the Library of the British Museum* [now British Library] *relating to Great Britain and Ireland.* London: Satchell, reprinted with introduction by Jack Simmons, Wakefield: EP Publishing, 1976.

Table of geographical regions covered in the gazetteers.

	England	Wales	Scotland	Ireland	Berwick upon Tweed	Isle of Man	Scilly Isles	Channel Islands
Adams (1680)	X	X						
Carlisle (1808)	X			X				
Carlisle (1810)				X				
Carlisle (1811)		X						
Carlisle (1813)			X		X	X	X	X
Lewis (1831)	X				X	X	X	X
Gorton (1831–33)	X	X	X	X	X	X	X	X
Lewis (1833)		X						
Lewis (1837)				X				
Fullarton (1840–42)			X					
Parliamentary (1840–43)	X	X			X	X	X	X
Parliamentary (1844–46)				X				
Lewis (1846)			X	X				
Sharp (1852)	X	X	X	X	X	X	X	X
Wilson (1854–57)			X					
Hamilton (1863–8)	X	X	X	X	X	X	X	X
Wilson (1866–69)	X	X			X		X	X
Groome (1882–85)			X					
Bartholomew (1887)	X	X	X	X	X	X	X	X
Brabner (1894–95)	X	X			X	X	X	X
Index Nauticus (1920)	X	X	X	X	X	X	X	

26 Map collecting

Peter Barber and Tony Campbell

The major collections of early maps in the British Isles reflect royal, which largely means governmental, activity. Sadly, much of the cartographic collection built up by the Tudor and Stuart monarchs was destroyed in the Whitehall fire of 1698 (Wallis, 1981). Significant fragments from the collections of Henry VIII are, however, to be found in the British Library's Cotton Collection, in the Public Record Office and in Hatfield House (Barber). Moreover, numerous items from the collections of Charles II and James II are included in the Dartmouth Papers in the National Maritime Museum and amidst George III's Topographical Collection in the British Library, which also includes atlases and single maps owned by William III, Queen Anne and William, Duke of Cumberland. George III's Topographical Collection, held since 1928 in the British Museum, now British Library, is the largest surviving collection of its kind, with 51 of the 124 numerical 'volumes' devoted to the British Isles. Combined with the old Royal Library, which came to the Museum in 1757, the royal collections represent the largest single gathering of British maps and atlases in the country. George III's Topographical Collection should be considered alongside his Maritime Collection (also in the British Library) and his Military Map Collection (in the Royal Library, Windsor).

In the absence of any clear distinction between state and private documents, some important collections of national importance passed into private hands. The most notable of these was amassed by William Cecil, Lord Burghley, Elizabeth's chief minister. A large part of this survives at Hatfield House (Skelton & Summerson). Maps that were once owned by Burghley can also be found in the Public Record Office and in the collection of the antiquary Sir Robert Cotton (1571–1631). The Cotton Collection came to the British Museum at its foundation in 1753 and is particularly rich in Tudor and earlier maps and charts. In addition to the Public Record Office and the British Library, Belvoir Castle, the seat of the Dukes of Rutland, contains a significant collection of mid-Tudor military mapping acquired by the Manners family (Colvin).

Important private collections of British cartography were put together by Samuel Pepys (1633–1703) (preserved at Magdalen College, Cambridge – see Tyacke), by Richard Gough (1735–1809), antiquary (given to the Bodleian Library, Oxford – see Walters) and by John Innys (1695–1778), stationer, in his *General System of Cosmography* (vols LXVII-XCIX) which, since about 1750 has been housed at Holkham Hall, Norfolk, the seat of the Earls of Leicester (Wallis, 1993).

The Duke of Buccleuch also has a significant collection of eighteenth-century military maps at Boughton House, Northants., inherited in the female line from the second Duke of Montagu and his father-in-law, the first Duke of Marlborough, who were both Masters General of the Ordnance. The reverse process, the dispersal of collections through auction, is documented for the period since 1790 (Harley & Walters).

The Public Record Office brings together the greatest number of maps, accumulated along with official documents. Some of these official papers are retained by the originating departments. One such is the Hydrographic Office at Taunton, whose extensive holdings include handwritten and printed surveys of the British coasts going back to the mid 18th century. Those are complemented by the hydrographic (and general) material at the National Maritime Museum. Much of this belonged to a private collection amassed by A. G. H. Macpherson and acquired by Sir James Caird.

[For notes on the various special collections see the appropriate subject section: for local collections see under the relevent geographical heading].

References

Barber, P. M. (1984) The Manuscript Legacy. *The Map Collector* **28**, 18–24.

Barber, P. M. (1992) England I: Pageantry, Defense and Government: Maps at Court to 1550, and England II: Monarchs, Ministers and Maps, 1550–1625, in D. Buisseret (ed.) *Monarchs, Ministers and Maps. The Emergence of Cartography as a Tool of Government in Early Modern Europe*, pp. 26–98. Chicago: University of Chicago Press.

Colvin, H. M. et al. (1982) *The History of the King's Works. Volume IV 1485–1660 (Part II)*. London: HMSO.

Harley, J. B. and G. Walters (1978) English map collecting 1790–1840: a pilot study of the evidence in Sotheby sale catalogues, *Imago Mundi* **30**, 31–55.

[Public Record Office] (1967) *Maps and plans in the Public Record Office. vol. I, British Isles, c.1410–1860*. London: HMSO.

Skelton, R. A. (1972) *Maps: a historical survey of their study and collecting.*

Chicago and London: University of Chicago Press.

Skelton, R. A. and J. Summerson (1971) *A description of maps and architectural drawings in the collection made by William Cecil, first Baron Burghley, now at Hatfield House.* Oxford: Roxburghe Club.

Tyacke, S. (1989) *Catalogue of the Pepys Library at Magdalen College, Cambridge. Vol 4, Music, maps and calligraphy.* Cambridge: Brewer.

Wallis, H. M. (1973) The map collections of the British Museum Library, in Wallis, H. M. and S. Tyacke (eds.) *My head is a map*, pp.3–20. London: Francis Edwards and Carta Press.

Wallis, H. M. (1981) The royal map collections of England, *Centro de Estudos de Cartografía Antiga: Separatas 141.* Coimbra.

Wallis, H. M. (1984) A Banquet of Maps, *The Map Collector* **28**, 2–10.

Wallis, H. M. (1993) Discovery at Holkham Hall, *Colonial Williamsburg* **15** (3), 49–53.

Walters, G. (1978) Richard Gough's map collecting for the British Topography 1780, *The Map Collector* **2**, 26–9.

PART II

THE REPOSITORIES

Sources of information for Part II

Work on the *Guide* began in the late 1970s and 1980s when some 300 questionnaires were sent out from the Map Library of the British Library to Record Offices, Universities, Cathedral and Public Libraries, and to the commercial and private institutions, museums and societies thought to be holding old maps. The project was then delayed by administrative changes within the British Library, but was revived in 1992. A further 200 questionnaires were distributed, yielding a total of some 450 positive returns. The questions asked were these:

1 Name and address of collection; telephone and fax numbers.

2 Title and/or name of Officer-in-charge.

3 Please provide a short description of your map collection, pointing out groups of special interest to historians; stating for example, whether there are manuscript as well as printed maps, what dates are covered, and whether the provenance of the maps is of historical importance.

3a Please state whether the collection includes maps of areas outside the British Isles. *This question was later deleted as it led to confusion in other sections.*

4 Please list published catalogues (both past and present) of the collection, noting sections relevant to maps, and any other unpublished handlists etc. available for readers.

4a Please list any publications (both past and present) on particular maps or on the map collection as a whole, and any reproductions of maps.

5 Types of map in your collection for period c.1150–1900. Please indicate with a tick which categoris of map are to be found in your collection. (The 17 types are listed in the Key to Part II entries, p. 104).

6 Please add any further comments on the type of map you have in your collection.

7 Are there any other notable local collections which might include maps? If so, please provide the name of the person to write to and the address.

8 If your collection is not usually open to readers, please state conditions of entry, e.g., 'by appointment only'.

The quality of the entries was, as might be expected, extremely variable.

Archivists and librarians were not always conversant with the historical importance of their map holdings; indeed in many repositories the maps had not been listed. Elsewhere, officers sent printouts of their entire stock of maps, leaving us to select from brief entries, sometimes lacking names or dates, or indications as to which were manuscript or printed, which originals, and which copies.

The information supplied was rearranged, and printouts returned to each repository for checking, and for any specific problems to be clarified. Volunteers visited many of the repositories to amplify the returns. At this stage it became apparent that many telephone numbers had recently changed, and that several offices and libraries were about to remove to new addresses, or to be temporarily rehoused whilst their original premises underwent building works. Where we were forewarned, such removals have been signalled.

We cannot claim to have contacted every repository, and of those we did contact, some declined to be included, some could not supply sufficient information to justify an entry, and others did not respond. It is always worth asking County Archivists if they know of other holders who will respond to specific enquiries, or who may have placed copies of maps in the local Record Office.

A note on stray manuscript maps

Manuscript maps have come to rest outside the area to which they refer for a number of reasons. The principal collections lay with the monarch and government departments, consequently maps of every part of the kingdom can be found within the Public Record Offices, the Ordnance Survey Offices, the Royal Collection at Windsor, the British Library and the National Libraries of Wales, Scotland and Ireland. Many landowners held distant estates which had come to them through conquest, inherit- ance, marriage, purchase or bequest. This might be expected with the great landed families, but it applied to a lesser extent also to minor families, and bequests of land or property were an important source of wealth for the ancient colleges and hospitals, livery companies and parishes. National and diocesan archives hold estate maps of properties from a wide area. Maps of roads, rivers, canals and railways normally extend over more than one county. There have always been collectors of antiquarian or specialist maps; the donations of Richard Gough, now in Oxford's Bodleian Library, and of the Eyles Collection of geological maps at the University of Bristol are examples. There are several collections of maps and papers of engineers and surveyors who worked in different parts of the country.

When the printouts for the *Guide* were sent for checking, each repository was asked to identify any stray maps, but it soon became clear that maps in many deposited private estate collections had not been listed in a way which enabled a response to be given easily. It may be taken for granted that many repositories hold maps covering adjacent counties. The list which follows is therefore selective, and the geographical regions only loosely defined.

Stray maps of Central England have come to rest in repositories numbered 9, 14 ...., and similarly for the other regions listed.

Central England, 9, 14, 23, 24, 29, 30, 32, 34, 35, 37, 39, 69, 94, 108, 116, 163, 185, 197, 235, 260.
East Anglia, 9, 14, 15, 22, 84B, 94, 116, 122, 163, 190, 197.
Northern England, 23, 29, 30, 34, 35, 36, 37, 116, 121, 122, 175, 177, 188, 189, 191, 196, 204, 206.
Southern and southeastern England, 23, 24, 27, 36, 37, 175, 189.
Southwestern England, 24, 30, 35, 37, 60, 84B, 94, 122, 175, 187, 188, 190, 191, 192, 197, 200, 244.
Wales, 22F, 24, 59A, 110, 116, 118, 122, 170, 187, 188, 190, 194, 201, 206.
Scotland, 7, 20, 118, 170.
Ireland, 9, 69, 84B, 99, 102, 108, 137, 244.

Maps in the colleges of the Universities of Oxford and Cambridge

Elizabeth Baigent and Sarah Bendall

Many of the colleges of the Universities of Oxford and Cambridge were founded in the middle ages or early modern period and were endowed with substantial land holdings. Many of these estates were close to the Universities, notably in Oxfordshire, Berkshire, Cambridgeshire and East Anglia, but others were situated throughout Britain. Their remoteness meant that College Fellows often had no personal knowledge of the estates and needed detailed information about them, a need which increased as the estates were developed more intensively, for example through agricultural improvements such as enclosure, mineral exploitation and urban development. Colleges therefore commissioned maps of their land holdings and later acquired printed maps, especially Ordnance Survey maps, which covered their estates.

The estate maps of the Colleges are undoubtedly their most important cartographic holdings. In addition, some of the wealthier Colleges have sizeable holdings of printed maps and atlases but this material is duplicated in other libraries to which readers will have easier access.

The Oxford Brookes University, formerly Oxford Polytechnic, and the Anglia Polytechnic University, which amalgamated polytechnics in Cambridge and Chelmsford, are completely separate institutions of recent foundation with no significant map holdings.

ABBREVIATIONS

CARN	County Archive Research Network
CRO	County Record Office
BL	British Library
NLS	National Library of Scotland
NLW	National Library of Wales
NMS	National Museums of Scotland
NRA	National Register of Archives
OS	Ordnance Survey
RO	Record Office

Beds.	Bedfordshire
Berks.	Berkshire
Bucks.	Buckinghamshire
Cambs.	Cambridgeshire
Cards.	Cardiganshire
Derbys.	Derbyshire
Glam.	Glamorgan
Glos.	Gloucestershire
Hants.	Hampshire
Herefs.	Herefordshire
Herts.	Hertfordshire
Hunts.	Huntingdonshire
Lancs.	Lancashire
Leics.	Leicestershire
Lincs.	Lincolnshire
Merion.	Merionethshire
Middx.	Middlesex
Mon.	Monmouthshire
Mont.	Montgomery
Norfk.	Norfolk
Northants.	Northamptonshire
Northum.	Northumberland
Notts.	Nottinghamshire
Oxon.	Oxfordshire
Pembs.	Pembrokeshire
Ruts.	Rutland
Shrops.	Shropshire
Som.	Somerset
Staffs.	Staffordshire

Suff.	Suffolk
Warwicks.	Warwickshire
Westmd.	Westmorland
Wilts.	Wiltshire
Worcs.	Worcestershire
Yorks.	Yorkshire

Old standards of length, and map scales

In medieval and later centuries the definition of standards was extremely vague and uncertain. Thus the standard for long measure, fixed by Henry I in 1101, commanded that the ancient 'ulna' or 'arm', equivalent to the yard, should correspond to the length of his own arm. The kingdoms of England, Scotland and Ireland, as well as the Isle of Man and Channel Islands employed various measures of length. The legal standards, usually in the form of a wooden or iron rod, by which the towns and cities of the kingdoms regulated commerce and thus cadastral surveys, differed locally and could differ again from those in customary usage.

The statute mile of 1760 yards was introduced as legal standard in 1593, but was used only in London and its environs. John Ogilby, in his road atlas *Britannia* (1675), wrote that 'Vulgar Computations' were widely accepted and normally gave lengths greater than the statute mile. His practice was to record (1) the direct horizontal distance (as the crow flies); (2) the vulgar computation; and (3) the actual 'dimensuration in statute miles', measured by the perambulator. The *Britannia* is a major source for understanding the history of English land measurement.

At the Act of Union in 1707, English weights and measures were introduced into Scotland but did not entirely displace the old Scottish measures. Prior to the Weights and Measures Act of 1824 which introduced Imperial Measure, Scottish measure was often by the ell, equal to 37.2 English inches, 30 ells corresponding to 31 English yards. Similarly, 48 Scottish acres were equal to 61 English acres. The Irish inch and the Welsh inch both corresponded to the English inch, but the Irish mile contained 6720 English feet against the 5280 feet of the English and Welsh miles.

From the late 18th century, Parliament sought to define a standard yard, which could be accurately made in the form of a brass bar and be preserved in the Exchequer, with copies sent to various cities within the three Kingdoms, so that local standards, surveyors' chains, rods and rules, could be manufactured according to the legal measure. Standards, in the form of brass marker pins and engraved strips of brass, were often embedded in the wall, or the ground, adjacent to the Town Hall or other governmental building, where some have survived to the present day.

Ogilby used a scale of one inch to one mile in his *Britannia* and was thus responsible for the increasing acceptance of this scale for regional maps. When in 1759 the Royal Society of Arts offered a premium for the best county survey 'upon the scale of one Inch to a Mile', this scale came into general favour. The Ordnance Survey, established in 1791, introduced it for the small scale national survey of the country, starting with the 1801 map of Kent.

References

Connor, R. D. (1987) 'The mile and the league', Chapter 5, in his *The weights and measures of England*, pp. 68–78, with references.

Harley, J. B. (1972) *Maps for the Local Historian*, p.69.

Harley, J. B. (1970) Introduction, in the reprint of John Ogilby, *Britannia*, London 1675, pp. v–xxiii.

Seebohm, F. (1914) 'Part II, the old British Mile', in his *Customary Acres ... a series of unfinished essays*, pp. 79–93.

Seymour, W. A. (ed.) (1980) *A history of the Ordnance Survey*, p.11.

Old English standards of length:

1 foot = 12 inches
1 yard = 3 feet

Old English standards of area:

1 acre = 4840 square yards
1 rood = 1210 square yards

Imperial to metric

1 inch = 2.54 centimetres
1 yard = 0.9144 metre
1 acre = 0.4047 hectare

Printed map scales

Representative fraction

1 : 500	approx. 10 feet to 1 mile
1 : 528	10 feet to 1 mile
1 : 1056	60 inches to 1 mile
1 : 2500	approx. 25 inches to 1 mile
1 : 10,560	6 inches to 1 mile
1 : 25,000	approx. $2\frac{1}{2}$ inches to 1 mile
1 : 63,360	1 inch to 1 mile
1 : 126,720	1 inch to 2 miles

Manuscript map scales

Representative fraction	1 inch on the map represents:
1 : 192	16 feet
1 : 240	20 feet
1 : 360	30 feet
1 : 480	40 feet
1 : 594	3 rods, poles or perches, or $\frac{3}{4}$ chain
1 : 792	4 rods etc., or 1 chain
1 : 1584	8 rods etc., or 2 chains
1 : 2376	12 rods etc., or 3 chains
1 : 3168	16 rods etc., or 4 chains
1 : 3960	20 rods etc., or 5 chains
1 : 4752	24 rods etc., or 6 chains
1 : 6336	32 rods etc., or 8 chains
1 : 7920	40 rods etc., or 10 chains
1 : 9504	48 rods etc., or 12 chains
1 : 11,880	60 rods etc., or 15 chains
1 : 12,672	64 rods etc., or 16 chains

KEY TO ARRANGEMENT OF ENTRIES

'GUIDE'   ADDRESS

No   TELEPHONE (See Note 1)   FAX

ACCESS

'Open', 'By Appointment' or otherwise restricted. See Note 2.

INDEX

Published and unpublished catalogues etc.; lists and indexes available only on site. Some map collections are unlisted and students must rely on guidance from the archivist. Some document collections which include maps have copies of their lists at the National Register of Archives. See Note 3.

SUMMARY

Groups of maps held; principal and important examples; special collections; date ranges; mention of manuscript or otherwise rare maps from outside the area where there are uncommon. Where published catalogues are available, the summary has been kept short.

DETAIL

Codified from Question 5: Types of maps held. See Note 4.

PUBLICATIONS OF MAPS HELD

Published articles and books which reproduce maps or plans from the collection.

FACSIMILES OR REPRODUCTIONS ON SALE

Copies of popular maps and plans offered for sale by the library or Record Office concerned. See Note 5.

Notes to key

1 Telephone and fax numbers are given with the new UK area dialling codes operative from 16 April 1995, with the former prefix 0 replaced by 01.

2 'Open' repositories give access during permitted hours to all members of the public, without notice being required. It was decided not to give opening hours as these are subject to change. 'By appointment' and 'By written appointment' are conditions imposed where search-room space or staff time are limited, or the scholar's bona fides must be checked.

A 'Reader's Ticket' may be required before entry is allowed to certain national and university libraries. CARN reader's tickets are required at those Record Offices participating in the County Archive Research Network; they are obtainable free of charge on production of identification, and are valid for a period. 'Library of last resort': Some private collections will, upon written application with full details, exceptionally grant access to scholars for the purpose of examining documents not available anywhere else.

Even where the holding institution is a public body or a library, documents may be in a distant store and not immediately available. Enquirers are strongly recommended to write in the first instance.

3 NRA (National Register of Archives) listings can be seen at the Royal Commission for Historical Manuscripts, Quality House, Quality Court, Chancery Lane, London WC2A 1HP, but for copyright reasons may not be copied there.

4 Detail key:

1   General and regional maps of the British Isles
2   General and regional maps of Wales
3   General and regional maps of Scotland
4   General and regional maps of Ireland
5   Thematic maps, e.g., showing the distribution of coal mines, particular crops, or the extent of industrialization, etc.
6   County maps,   (a) atlas and small scale maps
                           (b) large scale, i.e. 1" or more to a mile
7   Town plans and views
8   Maritime surveys
9   Military maps

10   Ordnance Survey   (a) 1" to 1 mile
                       (b) 6" to 1 mile
                       (c) 25" to 1 mile

Local maps and plans:—
11   Estate
12   Enclosure
13   Railway
14   Canal
15   Road
16   Insurance plans
17   Parish maps.   (a) Tithe
                    (b) Parochial assessment
                    (c) Others

5 Reproduction maps: Many libraries and record offices sell local sheets
from the Godfrey Edition of old Ordnance Survey maps, a reprint series
whose coverage is being actively extended.

ENGLAND

1   Public Record Office

Address Ruskin Avenue, Kew, Richmond, Surrey TW9 4DU
and Chancery Lane, London WC2A 1LR

Telephone (both Offices) (0181) 876 3444   *Fax*   (0181) 878 8905
ext. 2497

Access By Reader's ticket, obtainable at either Office, upon
proof of identity.

Index *Published catalogue: Maps and plans in the Public Record
Office*, vol I, *British Isles, c.1410–1860* (HMSO, 1967).
Card catalogues, arranged topographically and by date.
The Kew catalogue includes material at Kew and Chancery Lane, that at Chancery Lane describes only material
held there.
Card indexes to names of draughtsmen, surveyors, cartographers etc., and to maps commonly cited by their
military references, and Admiralty charts. At Kew only.
Summary calendar, ordered geographically, of unextracted maps (which remain with other documents in
their class, awaiting a full catalogue description). At
Kew only.
Class lists to those classes consisting only of maps.
Available at Kew and Chancery Lane.
British Transport Historical Records registers describe
the core collection of these maps. At Kew only.

A Records Information leaflet, 'Maps in the Public
Record Office', is available free of charge and should be
consulted for the whereabouts and availability of the
records. Other leaflets describe certain classes which
contain maps.

Summary The Public Record Office is the national repository for
records accrued by government departments and courts
of law within England and Wales. Documents are pre-

sently kept at Chancery Lane and at Kew, where they are readily available; others are in outlying stores where notice is required for their production. There is no map collection as such. Several million maps and plans are known to exist among the records, covering all parts of the globe and ranging over many centuries in date, of which less than a quarter of a million have been identified and described in detail. The remainder are listed with brief descriptions, or remain undiscovered in the records of which they form a part.

The following classes consist entirely or largely of maps and plans, or contain correspondence and papers which are known to include maps (the class code precedes the heading; dates refer to the commencement of the class, not necessarily the date of its earliest maps.)

ADM, *Admiralty and Secretariat Papers*, charts, plans of harbours, defences etc., from 1660.

Greenwich Hospital Surveys, maps of Hospital estates in Cumberland and Northumberland, from 1547.

AN, *British Transport Commission*, track detail, from north-eastern railways, from 1883.

BD, *Welsh Office*, local authority planning maps from 1854.

C, *Close Rolls*, enclosure awards and maps, small plans relating to trust deeds, from 1204.

COAL, *National Coal Board and Power*, land use, geology and deposits, coal and metalliferous mining, 19th century.

CP, *Court of Common Pleas*, Recovery Rolls, enclosure awards and maps, 1582–1837.

CRES and LRRO, *Crown Estate Commission* and its predecessors, Royal Parks and estates, and individual Crown properties, enclosures, leases (many with plans), coal and minerals prospecting licenses, from 16th century. *Land Revenue Records Office*, forests, parks and estates in England, Wales, Isle of Man and Alderney, and lands reclaimed under various Harbour Acts etc., from 1560.

DL, *Duchy of Lancaster*, boundaries of manors, extents and valuations, Henry VIII to Victoria.

DSIR, *Geological Survey Board*, specimen sheets from 1853.

DURH, *Palatinate of Durham*, enclosure awards, 1632–1834.

E, *Exchequer*, (a class rich in topographical information of all kinds). Exmoor Forest enclosure, 1817–18, Special Commissions of Enquiry relating to concealed lands (ie, those of dubious title), debts, encroachments, tithes, woods, marshlands, seabanks, mills, boundaries and ports, Elizabeth I to Victoria.

F, *Forestry Commission*, land in the following forests: Dean, New, Parkhurst, Delamere, Chopwell, Hazelborough, Salcey, Alice Holt, Bere, Woolmer, Bentley, Dymock, Hainault, Whittlewood and Wychwood, from 1608.

HLG, *Housing and Local Government*, maps submitted by local authorities, and those deposited under Acts of Parliament, from 1800.

IR, *Inland Revenue*, tithe maps and associated documents, from 1805.

MAF, *Agriculture, Fisheries and Food*, enclosure awards etc., in England and Wales under the Acts of 1845–1899, deregulation of metropolitan commons from 1867, exchange of glebe lands from 1841, Fisheries Department, salmon and freshwater fisheries, fish weirs and other structures, sea fisheries and shellfish areas, harbours, from 1852, lowland area flood sheets from 1894.

MEPO, *Metropolitan Police Office* maps defining administrative districts, some locating public houses, from 1894.

MH, *Ministry of Health* Poor Law Union plans from 1861.

MT, *Transport Departments* Ramsgate Harbour deeds etc. from 1613. Railway papers including plans of lines, junctions, bridges, etc. from 1840, light railway plans from 1896 in England, Scotland and Northern Ireland. Plans relating to the Channel Tunnel works of 1866–70.

OS, *Ordnance Survey Dept.* miscellaneous manuscript and engraved maps from 1777 for Channel Islands,

Isle of Man, and parts of England. OS military maps, mostly England and Hants., from 1861. Parish Boundary Sketch Maps and Boundary record maps including Scotland, 1843–92.

PC, *Privy Council* registers relating to changes in ecclesiastical and political boundaries from 1540, but maps only from 19th century.

RAIL, *British Transport Historical Records*, a vast group including rail, inland waterways and canals, towns, ports and local areas.

RG, *General Register Office*, registrars' districts for England and Wales from 1861, but some series incomplete.

SP, *State Paper Office* domestic and Irish, maps mostly from 16th and 17th centuries, some later.

T, *Treasury*, municipal and Parliamentary Boundaries Commission, 1831–6, and various maps and plans of public buildings, harbours and roads in England, Ireland and Scotland, from 1668.

TITH, *Tithe Redemption Commission*, boundary awards, 1839–60, with maps attached, delimiting parishes and townships in England and Wales.

WO, *War Office*, Ordnance Office, military properties in the British Isles from 17th century.

WORK, *Works Dept.* Epping Forest Commission maps made between 1860 and 1880. Ancient Monuments, which include stone circles and other extensive field monuments and sites. Royal Parks and pleasure gardens, from 1701. Miscellaneous plans of roads, railways, the River Thames, 18th century maps of London. Government property, naval and army establishments, from the 18th century.

Detail   All categories.

2

British Library, Map Library and Department of Manuscripts

Address
Great Russell Street, London WC1B 3DG
NB The library departments of the British Museum were transferred to the newly founded British Library in 1973.
The British Library will be moving to St Pancras within the next few years.

Map Library

Telephone
(0171) 323 7700   *Fax*   (0171) 323 7780

Department of Manuscripts

Telephone
map enquiries (0171) 323 7701
admission (0171) 323 7513/4   *Fax*   (0171) 323 7513

Humanities and Social Sciences (General Library)

Telephone
(0171) 323 7676   *Fax*   (0171) 323 7736

Access
Map Library: By British Library Reader's pass or by providing signed proof of identity.
Department of Manuscripts: By Manuscripts Reader's pass (supplementary to the normal British Library Reader's pass), for which a letter of recommendation is required.
Humanities & Social Sciences: By British Library Reader's pass.

2A

Map Library

Index
'The map collections of the British Library'. This 20-page leaflet, sent free on request, should be consulted first. It includes opening hours, reading lists etc.
The ... catalogue of printed maps, charts and plans ... Photolithographic edition to 1964 (1967), and *Ten-year*

supplement, 1965–1974 (1978).

'Cartographic Materials File, 1975–', accessible via BLAISE-LINE.

Catalogue of manuscript maps, charts and plans and of the topographic drawings in the British Museum, 3 vols (1844, 1861; reprinted, 1962). [The three published catalogues listed above are currently being converted: once merged with the post-1974 file, they will be issued on a single CD-ROM].

Summary

The British Library contains the major collection of British Isles mapping. The greatest number of maps and atlases are held in the Map Library, the national map library of the U.K., but most of the highly important collection of manuscript maps are preserved in the Department of Manuscripts and much of the early atlas collection is kept in the General Library. Parliamentary papers and official reports, many containing maps, are held in Official Publications & Social Science Service. Although material must generally be seen in the department concerned, the overlap between the catalogues and their forthcoming amalgamation makes it more sensible to consider the BL as a whole. Those approaching the BL for the first time are recommended to visit the Map Library for general directions to the collections.

As the premier legal deposit library in the U.K., the Map Library holds a comprehensive collection of British production for the period since 1911, and sizeable holdings prior to that date. Among the large historical collections of British mapping held in or across the various departments, the following can be specifically mentioned:

Ordnance Survey: the most complete collection of OS mapping (the OS store at Southampton having been bombed in 1940). This comprises the Ordnance Surveyors' Drawings (1789–*c*.1840) – the originals for the first edition one inch survey – and continues with all editions of each of the various scales for Britain and all of Ireland.

Town plans: all the very large-scale OS town plans from the Victorian period are held, as well as a number that were locally published. There is also a large holding of the detailed Goad fire insurance plans (1886–1970).

George III's collections: 51 of the notional 124 'volumes' of George III's Topographical Collection contain material relating to the British Isles – maps, charts, drawings, architectural plans and views, both printed and manuscript. Further British material is contained in the Maritime Collection.

Tudor mapping: the maps and plans formerly in the possession of Sir Robert Cotton (1571–1631), one of the earliest surviving collections of manuscript maps, form one of the most significant gatherings of Tudor cartography.

Crace collection: the notable collection of London maps and plans assembled by Frederick Crace, Commissioner for Sewers, was acquired in 1880. (The Map Library holds fiches of the views and the few plans housed in the British Museum's Department of Prints and Drawings).

Admiralty charts: a comprehensive collection, from 1800.

Roy's Scotland: William Roy's great military Survey of Scotland (1747–55) is held in various versions, field sheets, fair copy, etc.

Estate maps: nearly a thousand estate maps and atlases, mostly in the Department of Manuscripts, dating from the 1570s onwards.

Manuscript cartographic documents: some thousands of hand-drawn maps and documents relating to British cartography from the Middle Ages onwards are contained in the foundation collections of the British Museum (1753) and those added later (Additional MSS etc). Among these can be mentioned the Anglo-Saxon world map (c.1000), the maps of Britain and the itinerary maps of Matthew Paris (13th century), Laurence Nowsell's map of England, Wales and Ireland (1564), and several manuscript county surveys by John Norden.

Printed county maps: a very large collection of county atlases (from the proofs of Christopher Saxton's maps onwards) and large-scale county maps.

Sale catalogues: of estates, 19th and 20th century, arranged by county.

Cartographic history: documents, in the Department of

Manuscripts, relating to surveying practice, operations and personnel, map acquisition, and map publishing. Of particular significance are papers relating to Elizabethan and Jacobean surveys, those concerning the Egmont estates in County Cork, and the John Warburton archive (Lansdowne Mss 886–901).

History of cartography: a large collection of monographs and pamphlets, including catalogues of BL exhibitions.

Detail   All categories

Publications of Y. Hodson, *Ordnance Surveyors' Drawings, 1789–1840*,
maps held   (Reading: Research Publications, 1989).

H. M. Wallis, 'The map collections of the British Museum Library', in H. M. Wallis and S. Tyacke, *My head is a map* (1973), pp. 3–20.

H. M. Wallis, 'A Banquet of Maps', *The Map Collector* **28** (Sept. 1984), 2–10.

2B Department of Manuscripts

Index   *Catalogue of the Manuscript Maps, Charts and Plans and of the Topographical Drawings in the British Museum*, (vol I, General maps, England, Beds.,- Lincs.; vol II, England, Middlesex – Yorks., Wales, Scotland, Ireland, France; vol III, remainder of the world) 1844 and 1861, reprinted 1962. The catalogue lists items now to be found either in the Department of Manuscripts or in the Map Library.

Maps acquired since publication of the foregoing are described in the volumes of the *Catalogue of Additions* ... and indexed therein under the place, as well as under the heading 'Maps and Plans'.

Summary   The collection contains entirely manuscript maps ranging from, for example, the Matthew Paris map of England (13th century) to military maps of the mid-nineteenth century. There are three large collections of maps which are especially notable: (1) Cotton Ms Augustus I and II containing maps probably from the state papers, 15th to early 17th century; (2) Add mss 17641–17676, the Bauza collection of maps relating to

South and central America, 17th to early 18th century; (3) Add mss 57636–57722, the Royal United Services Institution collection: military maps, 18th and 19th century, including the collection of Field-Marshal Lord Amherst.

Detail	1, 2, 3, 4, 7, 9, 11, 12, 13, 14, 15
Publications of maps held	Owing to the large number of unique manuscript maps in the collection, there have been many writings on individual maps or collections and it is not possible to indicate them here. Many of the maps have been widely reproduced.
Facsimiles and reproductions on sale	The individual Christopher Saxton county maps (1570s), Boazio's 'Ireland', (1599), John Speed's 'Scotland' (1610). (Available from the British Library Publications Sales Unit, Boston Spa, Wetherby, West Yorkshire LS23 7BQ). Selected maps are reproduced as postcards. A full photo/repro service for all the material held.

AVON

3   Bristol Record Office

Address   'B' Bond Warehouse, Smeaton Road, Bristol BS1 6XN

Telephone   (01179) 225692

Access   Open.

Index
E. Ralph (ed.) *Guide to the Bristol Archives Office* (1971).
I. M. Kirby (ed.) *Diocese of Bristol: a catalogue of the records of the Bishop and Archdeacons and of the Dean and Chapter* (1970).
A Catalogue of historic maps in Avon (Avon County Council, c.1984).
Map and Plan schedule, and catalogues of collections which include maps and plans, available on site.

Summary
Maps and plans of the City Council, manuscript and printed, from 1497. Maps and plans of the Diocese of Bristol, manuscript and printed, from the 18th century. Maps and plans in deposited collections, e.g. those of landed estates, surveyors, charities etc., manuscript and printed.
OS, 1:2500 series for Bristol area, c.1880-1948; 1:500 town plans of the City, c.1880. Ashmead, 1 inch to 50 feet town plans of the City, 1855, corrected to 1874.

Detail
5, 7, 10b,c, 11, 12, 13, 15, 16, 17a,c

Publications of maps held
T. Chubb, *A descriptive catalogue of the printed maps of Gloucestershire, 1577–1911* (Bristol and Gloucestershire Archaeological Society, 1912).
J. S. Pritchard, 'Old plans and views of Bristol', *Transactions of the Bristol and Gloucestershire Archaeological Society* **48** (1926), 325–353.
M. D. Lobel and E. M. Carus-Wilson, *Bristol*, in M. D. Lobel and W. H. Johns (eds), *The Atlas of historical towns*. vol. 2 (1975).
R. Hall Warren, 'Braun's map of Bristol, commonly called Hoefnagle's', *Clifton Antiquarian Club Proceedings* **5** (1900-1903), 62–74.
A Gloucestershire and Bristol Atlas (Bristol and Gloucestershire Archaeological Society, 1961).

Facsimiles and reproductions on sale
Donne's 'Bristol' (1773); Lavar's 'View of the environs of Bristol' (1887);
Bristol parish boundaries, c.1900 (xerox); Ancient parishes of Bristol
(xerox); South Gloucester, North Somerset parishes, 1830; plan of
Bristol, 1479 (as a postcard).

4   Bath City Record Office

Address   Guildhall, Bath BA1 5AW

Telephone   (01225) 461111 ext. 2420/1   *Fax*   (01225) 448646

Access   Open.

Index   None.

Summary
Maps of Bath by Jones, 1572, Gilmore, 1694, Thorpe, 1742, Cotterell's
survey of Bath, 1852. The collection consists mainly of 19th century
printed maps, which include a few railway, canal and road maps.

Detail
7, 10a,b,c, 13, 14, 15, 17a

5   Bath Central Library

Address   19 The Podium Centre, Northgate Street, Bath BA1
              5AN

Telephone   (01225) 428144   *Fax*   (01225) 331839

Access   Open.

Index
Unpublished catalogue, compiled by R. M. Wright, *A descriptive list of
the published plans of the City of Bath and its environs, 1588–1816* (1925).

Summary
City plans, numerous from c.1770 onwards. Published county maps of
Somerset including those by Christopher Saxton, J. Jansson, Blaeu,
Robert Morden, G. F. Cruchley, and of Gloucestershire and Wiltshire.
Charlcombe and Northstoke tithe maps, 1839, and two maps of the
Charlcombe estate, 1863 and 1864. Manuscript survey of an estate in
the parish of Langridge, 1755, by John Hinde. Local 1st edition OS;
later OS material includes geological maps, 1 inch to 1 mile soil survey,

agricultural land classification, land utilization. The Library holds an example of John Rennie's 'Plan of the proposed navigable canal between the River Kennet at Newbury ... and the River Avon at Bath ...' (1793) and the copy of 1810 showing the canal completed. There is also a manuscript 'Plan of the Somerset Coal canal with the Rail Roads and Lines and Lockage ... joining the Kennett and Avon canal at the Dundas Aqueduct' which is undated but may be early 19th century.

Detail
6b, 7, 10a,b,c, 13, 14, 15

6   Bristol Reference Library, Central Library

Address   College Green, Bristol BS1 5TL

Telephone   (01179) 299147   *Fax*   (01179) 226775

Access   Open. Prior notice is required to produce original maps and researchers are advised to enquire in advance if facsimiles are not suitable.

Index
Card catalogue of maps, arranged by theme and cartographer, on site. Departmental Local Studies leaflet refers to map collection.

Summary
A variety of maps particularly relating to the City of Bristol, manuscript and printed, the earliest being J. Millard's 'Famous city of Bristol and its suburbs' (1673). Various maps by Benjamin Donne from 1769, William Champion's 'Plan of Bristol Channel from the Key to the Hot Wells' (1767), George C. Ashmead's 'Bristol' (1828 and 1855).
A wide range of Bristol town plans are contained in the city guide books which date from the early 19th century.

Detail
1, 2, 3, 4, 5, 6a,b, 7, 10c, 11, 12, 13, 14, 15, 17a

Publications of maps held
A Gloucestershire and Bristol Atlas. (Bristol and Gloucestershire Archaeological Society, 1961).
M. D. Lobel, *An atlas of historic towns,* vol 2. (1975).
J. E. Pritchard, 'Old plans and views of Bristol', *Bristol and Gloucestershire Archaeological Society Transactions* **48** (1926), 325–353.

Facsimiles and reproductions on sale
Twenty-eight various prints of maps.

7   University of Bristol Library

Address   Tyndall Avenue, Bristol BS8 1TJ

Telephone   (01179) 288014   *Fax*   (01179) 255334

Access   Open.

Index
Indexes on site.

Summary
Early atlases, c.1570–1800. Road books, for various parts of England, mainly 18th century. The Eyles Collection of early geological books, periodicals and maps, bequeathed to the University Library in 1986, holds geological maps, mainly 1800–1850, including those of William Smith. These are printed maps annotated with manuscript geological information.

Another listed collection of early geological maps is held in the Department of Geology. Non-members of the University should apply in the first instance to the Special Collections (Cartography) Librarian.

Detail
1, 2, 3, 4, 5, 6a, 7, 10a, 11, 13, 15

8   The Society of Merchant Venturers

Address   8 The Promenade, Bristol BS8 3NH

Telephone   (01179) 733104

Access   By written appointment.

Index
E. Ralph, *Guide to the archives of the Society of Merchant Venturers of Bristol* (Bristol, c.1988).

Summary
During its long history the Society has acquired land and property, some held in trust for various charities, other properties in the city of Bristol held in its own right. In the late 17th century it acquired the two manors

of Clifton, and later, estates outside Bristol. The estate records include maps and plans referring to these properties, notably:

Manor of Clifton: survey and plan of Clifton, by De Wilstar, 1746; maps and plans of the manor, roads, 18th and 19th centuries.

Manor of Monkton Stogursey, Somerset: survey 1860; survey and plan of the manor of Monkton and Priory of Stogursey, by De Wilstar, 1744; maps of Stogursey, 1841, 1904.

Manor of Beere in Cannington, Somerset: survey and plan of Beere, by De Wilstar, 1744.

Manor of Locking, Somerset: maps of Locking, 1816, 1883 and 1905; maps of the fields bordering the manor of Locking, 1904, survey and plan of the manor, by De Wilstar, 1745.

Detail
11

BEDFORDSHIRE

9   Bedfordshire County Record Office

Address   6 County Hall, Cauldwell Street, Bedford MK42 9AP

Telephone   (01234) 228833   *Fax*   (01234) 228619

Access   Open.

Index

A Catalogue of maps in the Bedfordshire County Muniments (Bedfordshire County Council, 1930).

Catalogue of the Enclosure Awards, Supplementary Catalogue of Maps, and Lists of Awards upon Tithe, in the Bedfordshire County Muniments (Bedfordshire CC, 1939).

Guide to the Russell Estate Collections for Bedfordshire and Devon to 1910 (Bedfordshire CC, 1966).

Card index, arranged in sections: Printed County Maps, by date and by cartographer; Index of Maps arranged by parish; Awards; Out County Maps, on site.

Summary

(1) Printed County Maps include those of Christopher Saxton, John Speed, Michael Drayton etc., some reproductions but many originals. (2) Maps attached to deeds, enclosure awards etc. Woburn Estates: five atlases, 1840-1900, of the Duke of Bedford's estates in Beds., Bucks., Cambs., Norfolk, Northants., and Hunts. (3) Maps from other counties, including properties of the Duke of Tavistock in Buckinghamshire; an estimated 750 rolls of plans once the property of Sir Albert Richardson, former President of the Royal Institution of British Architects, some of which pre-date 1900; and the Russell Collection which has a good collection of printed Irish County Maps by John Rocque: Armagh (1760), Cork (1759), Dublin, City and Suburbs (1756), City, Harbour and Bay (1757), Dublin County (1760), and by John Ridge, Down (1755).

Detail

4, 6a,b, 7, 10a,b,c, 11, 12, 13, 15, 17a

Publications of maps held
B. Chambers, *Printed maps of Bedfordshire, 1576-1900*, Bedfordshire *Historical Records Society* **62** (1983).
B. Chambers. 'T. Jefferys "The County of Bedford Surveyed ... 1765" ', *Bedfordshire Historical Records Society* (1983).
F. G. Emmison, *Some types of Common Field Parish* (Standing Conference for Local History, 1965), deals with a number of Bedfordshire Enclosure Maps.
G. H. Fowler, 'Bedfordshire in 1086, an analysis and synthesis of Domesday Book', *Quarto Memoirs* vol 1, *Bedfordshire Historical Records Society* (1922).
G. H. Fowler, 'Four pre-enclosure village maps', *Quarto Memoirs* vol 2, *Bedfordshire Historical Records Society (1928–36)*.

Facsimiles and reproductions on sale
Maps of Bedfordshire: by A. Bryant (1825) (in four sections); by John Speed (1610); of Bedford Town, by M. Reynolds (1841). Many dyelines of Bedfordshire county and parish maps are available, also some parish maps from the Bedfordshire Historical Records Society.

10   Bedford Estate Archives

Address   Woburn Abbey, Woburn MK43 0TP

Telephone   (01525) 290666   *Fax*   (01525) 290271

Access   By appointment only, on production of two references and with the permission of the Marquess of Tavistock and the Trustees of Bedford Estates. Search fee.

Index
None.

Summary
Woburn Abbey and Park plans, manuscript and printed, 18th to 20th centuries. Woburn Estate plans, mostly printed, 20th century.
Bloomsbury Estate plans, manuscript and printed, a very few from the 17th century, the remainder 18th to 20th centuries.
Miscellaneous plans, e.g. bound volume of Irish estates of the 6th Duke of Bedford, 19th century.

Most of the pre-1913 estate records are held at local County Record Offices, as follows:

Bedfordshire C.R.O., those relating to Beds. and Bucks.

Cambridgeshire C.R.O., Fenland drainage records.

Devon C.R.O., those relating to Devon, Dorset and Cornwall.

Hampshire C.R.O., those relating to Hants.

Greater London R.O., those relating to Covent Garden and other Middlesex estates, excluding Bloomsbury.

Detail
11

BERKSHIRE

11   Berkshire Record Office

Address   Shire Hall, Shinfield, Reading RG2 9XD

Telephone   (01734) 233182   *Fax*   (01734) 233203

Access   Open

Index

F. Hull, *Guide to the Berkshire Record Office* (1952) for enclosure and tithe maps, and estate maps under collection.

P. Walne, (ed.), *A Catalogue of Inclosure Maps in the Berkshire Record Office* (1955), superseded by card index on site.

Index to enclosure maps; Index to tithe maps; Catalogue of estate maps, arranged by parish; Catalogue of printed county maps, arranged by cartographer; index to surveyors of manuscript maps; index to deposited plans, arranged by title and number of scheme, and by parish.

Summary

Printed and manuscript maps of Berkshire, 17th to 19th centuries. The collections are fully described and comprehensively indexed. Printed county maps, by well-known publishers and dating from early 17th century, originals and reproductions. Some 300 manuscript maps, and photocopies of maps held elsewhere. Family estate papers. Deposited Plans, largely 19th century, dealing with various schemes including railways, canals, bridges, waterworks, gasworks, tramways.

Detail

6a,b, 10a,b,c, 11, 12, 13, 14, 15, 17a,c

12   Royal County of Berkshire, Department of Libraries &c.

Address   Reference Library, Berkshire Local History Collection, Abbey Square, Reading RG1 3BQ

Telephone   (01734) 509247   *Fax*   (01734) 589039

Access   Open.

Index

Map Section in *Local Collection Catalogue of Books and Maps relating to Berkshire* (Reading Libraries, 1958), with *Supplement; Books added 1956–66* (1967) includes an index of cartographers.

Card indexes of local maps, and of Estate Catalogues, on site.

Summary

The Map Section refers entirely to printed maps, with sections on (1) county maps, 1574–1898 arranged chronologically; (2) other maps of local interest, including the River Thames, Windsor Forest, roads, canals, railways, arranged chronologically, 1607-1895; (3) maps of towns in Berkshire (Abingdon, Maidenhead, Newbury, Reading, Wallingford, Windsor), 1610-1895.

The card index to local maps includes OS at 1 inch, $2\frac{1}{2}$, 6 and 25 inches to the mile, 19th and 20th century, arranged by parish, with a few outside the county, and county and Reading maps arranged by cartographer, which overlaps with the published catalogue.

Estate catalogues date from the 19th century; there are also volumes of Insurance Plans of Reading, from 1895.

Detail

6a,b, 7, 10a,b,c, 11, 13, 14, 15, 16

Facsimiles and reproductions on sale

Various maps, mostly of the county, available.

13   The Royal Collection

Address   Royal Library, Windsor Castle, SL4 1NJ

Telephone   (01753) 868286   *Fax*   (01753) 845910

Access   By written application for prior appointment.

Index

The Military Maps (1) are listed by place and by date.

For Hollar's maps (2) see Richard Pennington, *A descriptive catalogue of the etched work of Wenceslaus Hollar 1607–1677* (Cambridge University Press, 1982), pp.104–116.

A typed handlist for the Topographical Collection (4).
County atlases (5) are included in the general Library card catalogue, to be computerised.
The loose maps (6) are being listed; the Geological and OS maps (7 & 8) are unlisted.

Summary
(1) The principal group of maps within the Royal Collection is King George III's Military Map Collection (also known as The Cumberland Collection), dating from the 16th to 19th centuries and mainly in manuscript. Only a very few refer to the British Isles, including (a) a small number relating to the Civil War, with a manuscript map by Sir Bernard de Gomme of the Battle of Edgehill (1842); (b) maps relating to the Irish War (1689–1691) and the Jacobite Risings of 1715 and 1745; (c) domestic military mapping in south coast areas during the early part of the Seven Years War (1750s); (d) plans of encampments in southern Britain from the 1760s to the 1780s by Captain Daniel Paterson; (e) mapping exercises by officers from the Royal Military College, High Wycombe (early 1800s).
(2) A collection of 76 general and county maps of the British Isles (including later states) by Wenceslaus Hollar.
(3) The most notable early survey is John Norden's 'Description of the Honor of Windesor' (1607).
(4) A Topographical Collection, mainly printed views relating principally to Great Britain, contains about 200 cartographical items, including 20 maps of London and 17 of Berkshire (16th to 19th centuries).
(5) The Library holds some county atlases, e.g. Christopher Saxton (1579), John Speed (1675), John Norden (1723).
(6) A collection of loose maps (17th to 19th centuries) principally of Europe, of which only two folders relate to the British Isles.
(7) Sets of early, hand-coloured, geological mapping (Old Series, 1 inch) of England and Wales, together with coverage of the coalfields, and sections.
(8) OS 6 inch maps; incomplete; not currently available for study.

Detail
1, 3, 4, 5, 6a,b, 7, 9, 10a,b, 11, 13

Publications of maps held
The Military Maps are available on colour microfiche: *The Cumberland Collection from the Royal Library* (Ormonde Publishing, 1987), obtainable from Mindata Ltd., Bathwick Hill, Bath BA2 6LA.

R. Pennington, *A descriptive catalogue of the etched work of Wenceslaus Hollar 1607-1677* (1982), pp.104-116.

Norden's map of Windsor Castle is reproduced in various publications, including Robin Mackworth-Young, *The history and treasures of Windsor Castle* (1982), p.33.

A Royal Miscellany from the Royal Library, Windsor Castle. Catalogue of an exhibition held in The Queen's Gallery, Buckingham Palace, 1990; items 77, 222–226.

Yolande Hodson, 'Prince William: Royal map collection', *The Map Collector* **44** (1988), 2–13.

Facsimiles and reproductions for sale
John Norden's map of Windsor castle is reproduced as a Royal Collection postcard.

14   The Aerary

Address   Dean's Cloister, St George's Chapel, Windsor Castle SL4 1NJ

Telephone   (01753) 857942 or if no reply, 865538

Access   By appointment.

Index
J. N. Dalton, *Manuscripts of St George's Chapel, Windsor Castle* (Windsor, 1957), with addenda to other College properties.

Summary
Maps of lands owned by the College of St George, including Tithe Apportionment, some manuscript, dating from early 17th to mid 19th centuries. These lands are located in the counties of Berks., Bucks., Cambs., Devon, Essex, Hants., Herefs., London and Middlesex, Norfolk, Oxon., Somerset, Surrey, Warwicks., and Worcs. Railway and canal maps, early 19th centuries

Detail
7, 11, 12, 13, 14, 17a

15 University of Reading, The Library

Address   Whiteknights, Reading RG6 2AE

Telephone   (01734) 318770   *Fax* (01734) 312335

Access   By appointment.

Index
Checklist to 'Illustrations of Northamptonshire'.
N. E. Butcher, *The history and development of geological cartography; catalogue of the exhibition of geological maps in the University Library* (Reading, 1967).

Summary
The University houses the following Collections.
In the Geography Department Map Collection:
(1) Partial collection of Old Series 1 inch to the mile OS maps; set of OS 6 inches to the mile, 1st edition for Berkshire; John Rocque's 'Berkshire' (1761); many facsimiles of large-scale county maps.
In the Rural History Centre:
(2) Various estate maps and surveys dating from the 18th century, relating to Berkshire, Kent, Lincoln, Nottingham and Wiltshire.
(3) The Farm Records Collection, including farm and estate maps, manuscript and printed, chiefly 19th century. (Presently housed in the University Library).
(4) The Ransomes Collection, which contains a volume of maps and plans of the firm's Orwell Works, Ipswich, with surrounding properties, 19th century.
(5) Open Spaces Society Collection, with 47 maps, 1765–1899, mostly English counties, including some overprinted OS maps.
In the University Library:
(6) 'Illustrations of Northamptonshire', comprising nearly 1000 prints, drawings and watercolours of Northants. interest, including maps of the county, plans and views of estates, etc. (Overstone Library).
(7) The isotype Collection of Otto and Marie Neurath, containing maps and town plans from the 16th to 19th centuries, a considerable number brought together as an aid in designing a pictorial system of communication. (Housed in the Department of Typography and Graphic Communication).
(8) Various atlases and sheet maps from the 17th to 19th centuries, including a 1st edition (pre-railways) set of OS sheets at 1 inch to the mile (Stenton Library), Rocque's 'Berkshire (1761), geological maps by

William Smith and George Bellas Greenough, and many antiquarian books containing maps.

Detail
1, 2, 3, 4, 5, 6a, b, 7, 9, 10a, b, 11, 13

16   Eton College

Address	Provost and Fellows Library and Eton College Records, Penzance, Eton College, Windsor SL4 6DB
Telephone	(01753) 858991 ext. 117
Access	By written appointment.

Index
Eton College Records, vol 51, compiled in 1964, is a typescript calendar by H. N. Blakiston comprising 421 pieces, indexed by names of engravers, surveyors, map-makers etc.

Summary
Manuscript maps in the Archives relating to the College holdings. Printed maps – a small collection of atlases and loose maps.

Detail
1, 6a,b, 10a,b,c, 11, 13, 17a.

Publications of maps held
E. M. Elvey, *A Handlist of Buckinghamshire Estate Maps* (Buckingham Record Society, 1963) refers to maps in the collection.

BUCKINGHAMSHIRE

17   Buckinghamshire Record Office

Address   County Offices, Aylesbury HP20 1UA

Telephone   (01296) 382587   *Fax*   (01296) 383166

Access   Open. CARN reader's ticket required.

Index
Buckinghamshire Record Office, Occasional Publications No.4: A Catalogue of Maps (1961), a duplicated booklet with index.

E. M. Elvey, *A Handlist of Buckinghamshire Estate Maps* (Buckinghamshire Record Society, 1963) includes many in the RO collection.

General map index on site.

Buckingham Archaeological Society maps (on temporary deposit) have been inserted into the general map index.

Summary
A general mixed collection of manuscript and printed maps with examples of the major types occurring in Record Offices. It includes a full set (around 100) of enclosure maps but relatively few tithe maps. The major part of the collection dates from post-1700 and there are no maps earlier than 1600 with the exception of the Boarstall cartulary map, c.1450. There are photographic copies of maps held elsewhere.

The Buckinghamshire Archaeological Society's map collection has been deposited in the Record Office pending repairs to the County Museum where it is normally held.

Detail
6a,b, 7, 9, 10a,b,c, 11, 12, 13, 14, 15, 17a,b,c

Publications of maps held
C. Birch and J. Nuttall, *Maps of Buckinghamshire* (Buckingham, 1978).

P. D. A. Harvey, 'Boarstall, Buckingham', in R. A. Skelton and P. D. A. Harvey (eds.), *Local maps and plans from medieval England* (1986), pp. 211–219.

Buckinghamshire Estate Maps (Buckingham Record Society, 1964).

R. A. Croft and D. C. Mynard, *The changing landscape of Milton Keynes,*

Bucks. Archaeological Society Monograph Series No.5 (1993), obtainable from Oxbow Books, Oxford. Includes large-scale facsimiles and tracings of some Record Office maps.

Facsimiles and reproductions on sale
A reproduction of the enclosure map of Weston Turville, Bucks., 1788, forms part of an archive teaching unit (No.1) on Parliamentary Enclosure, published by the Record Office.

18 Buckinghamshire Archaeological Society

Address	c/o The County Museum, Church Street, Aylesbury HP20 2QP
Telephone	(01296) 696012
Access	By appointment. The map collection is on temporary deposit at the Buckinghamshire Record Office whilst repairs are being carried out at the Museum.

Index
E. M. Elvey, *A Handlist of Buckinghamshire Estate Maps* (Buckingham Record Society, 1963) includes Bucks. Archaeological Society maps together with others in public and private custody.
Typed list of other maps is available.

Summary
Manuscript maps of Buckinghamshire estates, early 17th century to 1861. Ashendon, 8 maps, 1624–1837; Wotten Underwood and Woodham, 3 maps, 1649–1745; Shenley, 3 maps, 1693–1771; Great Linford, 2 maps, 1641 and 1678; Wendover, 1620, companion to map of the manors of Ellesborough, Chequers and Mordaunts in Buckinghamshire Record Office. Printed map, A. Bryant, *County of Buckingham from an actual survey*, 1824, at 1 inch to 1 mile.

Detail
6a,b, 11

Publications of maps held
Buckinghamshire Estate Maps (Buckingham Record Society, 1964).

CAMBRIDGESHIRE

19   Cambridgeshire Record Office

Address   Shire Hall, Cambridge CB3 0AP

Telephone   (01223) 317281   *Fax*   (01223) 317201

Access   Open. CARN reader's ticket required.

Index
Index to maps and unpublished lists of tithe enclosure records on site.
A. S. Bendall, *Maps, land and society: a history with a cartobibliography of Cambridgeshire estate maps, c.1600–1836* (1992).

Summary
The following are of special interest: Bedford Level Corporation land drainage maps, of fens in Cambs., Hunts., Lincs., Norfolk and Suffolk, mainly manuscript, 182 in number, dating between 1604 and 1928. Maps of the North Level, approximately 300 in number, from the Drainage Board, *c.*1754 to 20th century.
Draft enclosure maps, showing old and new boundaries, of 25 parishes in Cambridgeshire (excluding the Isle of Ely), 1801–46. Parochial assessment of University and College property under the Cambridge Award Act of 1856.

Detail
6a, 7, 10a,b,c, 11, 12, 13, 14, 15, 17a,b

Publications of maps held
D. Souden, *Wimpole Hall* (The National Trust, 1991), reproduces detail from Benjamin Hare's Wimpole estate map (1638).
Royal Commission on Historical Monuments, *West Cambridgeshire* (1968) reproduces detail from Benjamin Hare's Wimpole estate map (1638), Orwell, enclosure map (1837), and Kingston Wood Farm estate map (1720).
M. Spufford, *Contrasting communities* (1974), includes detail from the map of Chippenham Lordship, 1712.
E. Lynam, 'Maps of the Fenland', in *Victoria County History of Huntingdonshire*, vol.3 (1936) refers to the Bedford level Corporation maps.

H. G. Fordham, *Cambridgeshire maps, a descriptive catalogue* (1908) refers to printed county and land drainage maps.

Facsimiles and reproductions on sale
Cambridgeshire, by William Kip (1607), by John Blaeu (1648). Huntingdonshire, by John Blaeu (1645), by John Speed (1662), by Thomas Jefferys (1768). Town of Huntingdon by Thomas Jefferys (1768). Cambridgeshire with Hunts., Northants., Beds. and Rutland, by Christopher Saxton (1576). John Ogilby's Roads (1675): from Oxford to Cambridge, from Cambridge to Coventry, from Huntingdon to Ipswich, from London to King's Lynn. John Bodger's 'Chart of the Beautiful Fishery of Whittlesea Mere' (1786).

20 County Record Office

Address	Grammar School Walk, Huntingdon PE18 6LF
Telephone	(01480) 425842 *Fax* (01480) 459563
Access	Open. CARN reader's ticket required.

Index
G. H. Findlay, *Guide to the Huntingdonshire Record Office* (Huntingdon, 1958), pp.24–7, lists briefly the maps then held.
P. G. M. Dickinson, *Maps in the County Record Office, Huntingdon* (St Ives, 1968).
Maps received since 1968 are listed with other records in the accessions lists in *Annual Reports of the Northants. and Hunts. Archives Committee* (1968–74) and *Cambridgeshire County Council Annual Reports of the County Archivist* for 1974 onwards.

Summary
Maps in the Office relate chiefly to ancient Huntingdonshire. For a few classes they include also the Soke of Peterborough, until 1965 in Northamptonshire.
(1) Official maps, including a virtually complete series of enclosure maps for Hunts. and for the Soke of Peterborough, 1768-1903, either as originals or as photographic copies (for several parishes however no map was made or survives); diocesan and parish copies of tithe maps 1837–1936; deposited plans of public utility schemes (especially railways) 1836–

20th century; and town plans of Godmanchester for the Local Board of Health, 1853.

(2) Estate maps, c.1590–20th century. The most important collection is that of the Montagu family of Kimbolton Castle, Earls and Dukes of Manchester, which includes records of the Bernard and Sparrow families of Brampton. A series of maps of Kimbolton including those by Stirrup (1673) and Cosmo Wallace (1763–4) are notable amongst these. Other estate collections with notable maps are those of Montagu of Hinchingbrooke, Earls of Sandwich, including a survey of their Hunts. estates (1757), Thornhill of Diddington, including Boxworth, Cambs., by Hayward (1650) and Fellowes of Ramsey, notable for farming plans (19th century). There are a few estate plans for areas outside Huntingdonshire.

(3) Military maps: a small number of miscellaneous manuscript and printed plans, 17th-20th centuries, including those of the King's army during the Scottish campaign of 1639.

(4) Printed county maps of Hunts. and maps of the fens, 17th-20th centuries.

(5) OS maps of all scales including photostats of drawings for the one-inch Old Edition and complete First Edition 1:2500 county series for Hunts.

Detail
1, 2, 3, 4, 5, 6a,b, 7, 8, 9, 10a,b,c 11, 12, 13, 14, 15, 17a,c

Publications of maps held
Hausted's map of Glatton (1613) reproduced in the *Victoria County History of Huntingdonshire*, iii (1936), 176.

Most enclosure and principal estate maps were published as 16 x 20 inches photographs for subscribers by Huntingdonshire County Council in 1937–40.

Facsimiles and reproductions on sale
Huntingdonshire, with Cambs., Northants., Beds., and Rutland, by Christopher Saxton (1576). Huntingdonshire, by Joannes Blaeu (1645), by John Speed (1662), by Emanuel Bowen (1749), by Thomas Jefferys (1768). John Ogilby's 'Road from Huntingdon to Ipswich' (1675). Jefferys' 'Town of Huntingdon' (1768). Jonas Moore's 'Great Levell of the Fenns' (1720). John Bodger's 'Chart of the Beautiful Fishery of Whittlesea Mere' (1786).

21   Cambridgeshire Libraries, Cambridge-shire Collection

Address   Central Library, 7 Lion Yard, Cambridge CB2 3QD

Telephone   (01223) 65252   *Fax*   (01223) 62786

Access   Open.

Index

Duplicated 'Guide to the catalogues and indexes'.

Catalogue of Cambridge maps, 1800–1920, unpublished list with annotations.

The indexes to Cambridge and to Cambridgeshire are arranged by name, by subject, and chronologically, with an index to plans of Cambridge buildings by name and by village. They refer to sheet maps and to maps in books etc.

Summary

The Cambridge Collection contains virtually a complete file of engraved maps of Cambridge and Cambridgeshire from the 16th century, and in addition, OS maps at all scales, from 1886.

Detail

6a,b, 7, 10a,b,c,

Publications of maps held

J. W. Clark, *Old plans of Cambridge, 1574–1798* (1921).

H. G. Fordham, 'Cambridgeshire maps, an annotated list, 1579–1800', *Cambridgeshire Archaeological Society Proceedings*, **11** (1903-4), 101-73 and **12** (1906-8), 152-231.

E. Lynam, 'Maps of the Fenland', in *Victoria County History of Huntingdonshire*, iii (1936) refers to the Bedford Level Corporation maps.

Wisbech Society, 'Old maps of Wisbech and the Fenland, an exhibition.' (1954), and 'Old Fenland Maps, an Exhibition Catalogue' (1976).

Facsimiles and reproductions on sale

Richard Lyne's 'Cambridge' (1574).

22   Cambridge University Library

Address   West Road, Cambridge CB3 9DR

Telephone   (01223) 333000   *Fax*   (01223) 333160

Access   By reader's ticket; non-members of the University apply in writing.

22A   Map Library

Index
Card catalogue and indexes, arranged by place and by name, on site.

Summary
A copyright (legal deposit) library. Comprehensive coverage of British printed maps and atlases, 1579 onwards, including town plans, county maps, maritime charts, and thematic (e.g. geological) maps.
Detailed specialisations: Approximately 1000 manuscript maps including plans, estate and parish maps. Large sections on (1) Cambridgeshire, (2) particulars of sale for properties throughout Great Britain, (3) topographic postcards.
Complete coverage of OS maps at all scales (apart from OS First Edition 1:2500, and town plan series, which is incomplete).

Detail
1, 2, 3, 4, 5, 6a,b, 7, 8, 9, 10a,b,c, 11, 12, 13, 14, 15, 16, 17c.

22B   Rare Books Department

Index
The Hanson Collection is itemised in the main Library Catalogue and a shelf list is held in the department.

Summary
The Hanson Collection of the Cruising Association, acquired in 1990, comprises some 700 items dating from 1490 to the 19th century. The collection, brought together by Herbert James Hanson from 1914 to 1956, includes many general and maritime atlases of British interest, together with books and pamphlets.

Department of Manuscripts and University Archives

22C University of Cambridge Archives

Index

H. E. Peek and C. P. Hall, *The archives of the University of Cambridge, an historical introduction* (Cambridge, 1962), Appendix B, gives 'Muniments of Title relating to University Property', with covering dates but does not itemise.

D. M. Owen, *Cambridge University Archives, a classified list* (Cambridge, 1988) identifies plans of holdings.

Handlists on site.

Summary

Maps and plans of Cambridge from the late 18th century.

Maps and plans of University Estates, within Cambridge and in the counties of Cambs., Cheshire, Hants., Hunts., Lincs. and Norfolk, 18th to 20th centuries.

Plans from Commissioners of Sewers, records, including River Ouse (1618–20).

Detail

5, 7, 10a,b, 11, 12, 17b,c,

Publications of maps held

J. R. Ravensdale, *Liable to floods* (1974), reproduced the River Ouse map (1618–20) on the dust jacket.

D. N. Stroud, *Capability Brown* (1975), reproduced Brown's scheme for laying out the Backs.

22D Ely Dean and Chapter Archives

Index

Provisional handlist on site.

Summary

Most estate maps and documents are in the Church Commissioners' records (Ely Chapter estates). Estates maps for Ely Chapter properties, located in Cambridgeshire, Suffolk, and London (St Andrew's, Holborn).

There is one 17th century example, the rest dating from the late 18th and 19th centuries.

Detail
11, 17a, c

22E   Ely Diocesan Records

Index
D. M. Owen, *Ely Records* (1970), lists maps.

Summary
Tithe apportionment maps for Cambridgeshire, and maps associated with Orders in Council (parish boundaries) and consecration deeds. Small maps of various properties in Cambridgeshire and London (Serjeant's Inn), dating from 1787 to 1878, together with miscellaneous estate books. Most estate maps and documents are in the Church Commissioners' records (Ely Bishopric Estates.)

Detail
11, 17a, c

22F   Queens' College Archives

Index
Handlist on site.

Summary
Maps of Queens' College estates, in Beds., Cambs., Carmarthens., Essex, London, Northants., and Suffolk, dating from 17th to 19th centuries. Two atlases of College estates maps, dating from early 19th century.

Detail
11

23   Clare College, College Archives

Address   Cambridge CB2 1TL   Located at: Memorial Courts,
                  Queens Road

Telephone   (01223) 333228   *Fax*   (01223) 333219

Access   By appointment.

Index
Catalogue on site.

Summary
Manuscript and annotated OS maps for the College estates, dating from 1634 to the present. The estates were located in the counties of Cambs., Hunts., Beds., Berks., Bucks., Derbys., Dorset, Essex, Glos., Hants., Herts., Kent, Lancs., Leics., Lincs., Middx, Norfolk, Northumb., Som., Staffs., Suffolk, Surrey, Sussex, Sutherland, Warwicks., Wilts., Worcs. and Yorks.

Detail
10b,c, 11, 12, 14, 17a,c

24   Christ's College, The Archives

Address   St Andrew's Street, Cambridge CB2 3BU

Telephone   (01223) 334900   *Fax*   (01223) 334967

Access   By written appointment.

Index
In course of preparation (1994).

Summary
Maps and plans of the College buildings and of the College estates. These were located in the counties of Cambs., Devon, Essex, Herefs., Herts., Hunts., Kent, Leics., Lincs., Mons., Norfolk, Notts., Pembs. and Suffolk.

Detail
11

25   Corpus Christi College, College Archives

Address   Cambridge CB2 1RH   Located at: Trumpington Street

Telephone   (01223) 338066   *Fax*   (01223) 338061

Access   By written appointment.

Index
Catalogue on site.

Summary
Maps of College estates in Cambridgeshire, Northamptonshire and Suffolk from 1654.

Detail
11

26   Downing College, College Muniments

Address   Cambridge CB2 1DQ   Located at: Regent Street

Telephone   (01223) 334800   *Fax*   (01223) 467934

Access   By written appointment.

Index
Catalogue on site.

Summary
Town plans of Cambridge, 18th and 19th centuries. Plans and maps of the College and its grounds; plans and maps of the College estates in Cambridgeshire. The holdings include a volume of manuscript plans, drawn in colour on parchment, showing farms in the parishes of Croydon, Tadlow, East Hatley, Guilden Morden and Gamlingay, Cambridgeshire, all part of the estates of Sir George Downing, founder of the College. The surveys, by Joseph Cole, date to *c*.1750.

Detail
7, 11

27 Emmanuel College, College Archives

Address   Cambridge CB2 3AR   Located at: St Andrew's Street

Telephone   (01223) 334292   *Fax*   (01223) 334426

Access   By written appointment.

Index
Card indexes on site.

Summary
Maps of the College's estates in the City of Cambridge, Cambs., Essex, Kent, Leics., Lincs., City of London, Norfolk, Surrey and Warwicks., dating from 1656.

Detail
10b, c, 11

28 Gonville and Caius College, College Archives

Address   Cambridge CB2 1TA   Located at: Trinity Street

Telephone   (01223) 312211   *Fax*   (01223) 332456

Access   By written appointment.

Index
Handlist on site. The estate maps are also listed in the *Registrum Magnum*, the general catalogue of the College Muniments.

Summary
Maps and printed maps with memoranda relating to the ancient possessions of the College. They date from the 18th and 19th centuries. The estates are mainly in Cambridgeshire with some outlying properties in Hertfordshire, Dorset and Devon.

Detail
10a,b, 11, 12, 17a,c

Publications of maps held
J. Venn (comp.), *Biographical History of Gonville and Caius College 1349–1897* (1897 etc), vol. IV, has an Appendix giving general information on the estates.

29   Jesus College, College Archives

Address   Cambridge CB5 8BL   Located at: Jesus Lane

Telephone   (01223) 339439   *Fax*   (01223) 3324910

Access   By written appointment.

Index
Catalogue on site.

Summary
Maps of College estates in the counties of Beds., Cambs., Essex, Herts., Hunts., Leics., Suffolk, Surrey and Yorks., dating from the early 18th century.

Detail
5, 7, 10a,b,c, 11, 12, 13, 15, 17a,b,c

30   King's College, Muniment Room

Address   Cambridge CB2 1ST   Located at: King's Parade

Telephone   (01223) 350411   *Fax*   (01223) 314019

Access   By written appointment.

Index
King's College catalogue No.4 includes maps, arranged alphabetically, with other listings by date and place.

Summary
Mainly manuscript maps and plans of the College estates, ranging in date from 1612 to 1898. The estates were located in the counties of Beds., Berks., Bucks., Cambs., Cornwall, Devon, Dorset, Essex, Glos., Hants., Kent, Lancs., Lincs., London, Middx, Norfolk, Suffolk, Sussex, Warwicks., Wilts. and Yorks.

Detail
11

31 Magdalene College, The Pepys Library

Address Magdalene Street, Cambridge CB3 0AG

Telephone (01223) 332100   *Fax* (01223) 63637

Access By written appointment.

Index
S. J. Tyacke, 'Maps', in *Catalogue of the Pepys Library at Magdalene College Cambridge. Vol 4: Music, maps and calligraphy*, ed. J. Stevens (Woodbridge: D. S. Brewer, 1989), pp.i–xxiii, 1–67.

Summary
The collection amassed by Samuel Pepys (1633–1703) contains many atlases, maps and charts, of which an important part relates to the British Isles and surrounding seas, and especially to London. Pepys, with his long association with the Admiralty and Trinity House, was acquiring contemporary mapping from the 1660s, in one of the most flourishing periods of English mapmaking. His major sources of provenance were the London map-sellers John Seller for sea atlases and charts, Richard Mount for navigational books and sea atlases, and John Burston in the 1660s, and later John Thornton, for manuscript charts. Items relating specifically to the British Isles number 135 to 198 in Tyacke's catalogue.

Detail
1, 6, 7, 8

32 Pembroke College, College Archives

Address Cambridge CB2 1RF   Located at: Trumpington Street

Telephone (01223) 338100   *Fax* (01223) 338163

Access By written appointment.

Index
On site.

Summary
Maps of College estates, located in the counties of Cambs., Derbys., Essex, Norfolk, Rutland and Suffolk.

Detail
11

33   Peterhouse College, College Archives

Address   Cambridge CB2 1RD   Located at: Trumpington Street

Telephone   (01223) 338200   *Fax*   (01223) 337578

Access   By written appointment.

Index
Card index on site.

Summary
Maps and plans are associated with documents relating to the College itself and to its estates in Cambridgeshire and Rutland.

Detail
11

34   St Catharine's College, College Archives

Address   Cambridge CB2 1RL

Telephone   (01223) 338343   *Fax*   (01223) 338340

Access   Accredited scholars only, by written appointment.

Index
Maps are listed in the well-indexed *Catalogue of Documents* (1930), on site.

Summary
There are maps, plans, deeds and other documents relating to the College itself and to its estates in Cambs., Warwicks. and Yorks., dating from the 17th century.

Detail
11

35 St John's College, College Archives

Address   Cambridge CB2 1TD   Located at: St John's Street

Telephone   (01223) 338631   *Fax*   (01223) 338600

Access   By written appointment.

Index
Handlists, arranged by estate, on site.

Summary
Mostly manuscript maps from *c.*1600 to 1900. Some are the results of surveys for the College by Watford, Freeman and Hutson. Some interesting 17th century maps with representations of houses. The areas covered include the College itself, and lands in Berks., Cambs., Derbys., Devon, Essex, Kent, Lancs., Lincs., Middx, Norfolk, Notts., Rutland, Salop, Suffolk, Surrey, Wilts., Yorks. Many late 19th century plans showing development areas in Cambridge. OS maps, mostly at 25 inches to the mile, some coloured.

Detail
5, 10b,c, 11, 12, 17a,c

36 Sidney Sussex College, Muniment Room

Address   Cambridge CB2 3HU   Located at: Sidney Street

Telephone   (01223) 338824   *Fax*   (01223) 338884

Access   By written appointment.

Index
Catalogue on site (in progress, 1994).

Summary
Maps of College estates in the counties of Cambs., Kent, Lincs. and Yorks.

Detail
7, 11, 12, 17a,b

37 Trinity College

Address   Cambridge CB2 1TQ   Located at: Trinity Street

Telephone   (01223) 338488   *Fax*   (01223) 338564

Access   By written appointment.

Index
Lists and calendars available in the Library.

37A College Archives

Summary
Maps and plans of the College and its estates in Beds., Bucks., Cambs., Durham, Essex, Herts., Isle of Wight, Leics., Lincs., Middx, Northants., Notts., Staffs., Surrey, Suffolk, Warwicks., Westmor. and Yorks..

Detail
11

37B Trinity College Library

Summary
John Norden's 'The generall perambulation & delineatio of Cornwall', 1607, manuscript.

Detail
6

Publications of maps held
W. L. D. Ravenhill, 'John Norden's Manuscript Map of Cornwall and its Nine Hundreds', text and reproduction (University of Exeter, 1972).

38 Cambridge Antiquarian Society

Address   Museum of Archaeology and Anthropology, Downing Street, Cambridge CB2 3DZ

Access   By written appointment.

Index
Card index on site.

Summary
About 180 maps, including some photographic copies. A small number cover adjacent counties but most relate to the town and county of Cambridge and were bequeathed by H. P. W. Gatty of St John's College. They date from the 18th and 19th centuries and include maps from printed books.

Detail
6a,b, 7, 12, 17a

39 Wisbech and Fenland Museum

Address   Museum Square, Wisbech PE13 1ES

Telephone   (01945) 583817

Access   By appointment.

Index
Handlist to local collections on site.

Summary
The map collection falls into two categories:
(1) Local material, covering estates and farms in the area, parish maps, and, most importantly, drainage of the fens. These cover lands in Cambridgeshire and the adjoining counties of Norfolk and Lincolnshire.
(2) Early printed maps and atlases, from the collection of Alexander, Baron Peckover of Wisbech, in 1928.

Detail
1, 6a,b, 7, 8, 9, 10a,b,c, 11, 12, 13, 14, 15, 16, 17a,b,c,

Publications of maps held
Old maps of Wisbech and the Fenland, Wisbech Society Exhibition, 1954.
Old Fenland Maps, Wisbech Society Exhibition, 1976.
Old Fenland Maps, Wisbech and Fenland Museum Exhibition, 1993.

Facsimiles and reproductions on sale
Reproductions, 'Town plan of Wisbech' (1830). 'Wisbech Hundred Maps of 1597, copied by Thomas Watts' (1657).

CHESHIRE

40   Cheshire Record Office and Chester Diocesan Record Office

Address   Duke Street, Chester CH1 1RL

Telephone   (01244) 602559   *Fax*   (01244) 603812

Access   Open. Appointment advisable.

Index

C. M. Williams (ed.), *Cheshire Record Office Guide*, Cheshire County Council (1991).
Card index of maps on site.

Summary

Estate maps: mainly from *c*.1750 to 1850, with some earlier examples from late 16th century. Some out-county maps are held, including one of Woodplumpton, Lancs. (1759). Photocopy of Survey of Manor of Bidston (1665).

Tithe maps: for all townships in pre-1974 Cheshire (except for 25 not subject to tithe) and for some in 'new' areas in Cheshire, that is, the Warrington/Widnes area.

Enclosure maps and plans, 1767–1898, in Cheshire Quarter Sessions records.

Deposited plans of railways, canals and other public undertakings from 1792, in Cheshire Quarter Sessions records.

OS maps: good coverage of 1st edition (*c*.1874) and 2nd edition (*c*.1898) at 6 and 25 inches to the mile, and some urban plans at 10 feet to the mile, including Nantwich (1851).

Detail

5, 6a,b, 7, 10a,b,c, 11, 12, 13, 14, 15, 17a

41   Chester City Record Office

Address   Town Hall, Chester CH1 2HJ

Telephone   (01244) 324324 ext. 2110   *Fax*   (01244) 324338

Access   Open.

Index

Unpublished lists of most of the Chester printed maps and the Quarter Sessions plans on site.

Handlist of the Grosvenor family Cheshire Estates (accessible on application for permission from the Estate Office via the City Record Office.)

Summary

Maps relating to Chester: printed maps, c.1580–1938, including some 1 inch, 6, 25 and 50 inches OS sheets. Quarter Sessions deposited plans: canals (1772–1793), railways (1824–1913), roads, bridges and tramways (1824–1902). Plans of the River Dee Admiralty Enquiry, 1850, showing the River Dee from c.1600 to 1849. Chester Archaeological Society manuscripts: 24 printed maps of the county, c.1648–1849.

Estate maps and plans, enclosure and tithe maps, etc, from the Grosvenor family which are preserved at the Eaton Estate Office, Eaton Hall, Eccleston, Cheshire, and with permission can be made available for research at the City Record Office.

Detail

6a, 7, 8, 10a,b,c, 13, 14, 15

Facsimiles and reproductions for sale

Contact and dyeline copies of: 'Chester' by G Braun, from *Civitates Orbis Terrarum* (1572–1618); 'Chester' by A. de Lavaux (1745); plan of the intended canal from Chester to Middlewich, by R. Murray (1772); by J. Wood (1833).

42   Cheshire County Council, Warrington Library

Address   Museum Street, Warrington WA1 1JB

Telephone   (01925) 31873   *Fax*   (01925) 411395

Access   Open.

Index

Handlist to maps and plans to 1908 in *Catalogue of the Reference Library, 1898–1908.*
Maps in the Reference Library are contained in the card catalogue on site.
Maps in the Local Collection are entered in the sheaf catalogue to that collection, on site.
Some loose small-scale maps are indexed as part of the broadside catalogue card index on site.

Summary
Maps and atlases occur within the Reference Library Collection and the Local Studies Collection. Printed and manuscript maps, mostly 18th century or later. Library stock acquired since 1760, date of the foundation of Warrington Circulating Library, now part of Warrington Library, founded in 1848. Cover is strongest for Lancashire, Cheshire and particularly the Warrington area.

Detail
1, 6a,b, 7, 10a,b,c, 11, 12, 13, 14, 15

CLEVELAND

43   Cleveland County Archives

Address   Exchange House, 6 Marton Road, Middlesbrough TS1 1DB

Telephone   (01642) 248321

Access   Open.

Index
No index to maps.

Summary
The maps all relate to the area of the post-1974 county of Cleveland and the vast majority are for the period from 1850. The collection contains:
(1) Maps produced by local authorities from the mid-19th century onwards relating to roads, housing schemes etc.
(2) OS maps.
(3) Maps in deposited collections, the largest being the Owners of the Middlesbrough Estate, relating to urban develoment of Middlesbrough and Saltburn from the mid 19th century onwards.
(4) Tithe maps.

Detail
10b,c, 11, 12, 13, 17a

44   Cleveland County Libraries, Central Reference Library

Address   Victoria Square, Middlesbrough TS1 2AY

Telephone   (01642) 263358/9   *Fax*   (01642) 230690

Access   Open.

Index
Maps are incorporated in the Library catalogue which is in process of being computerised, but the main map collection is not yet entered on the new system.

Summary
Cleveland County equates with part of the old south-east of County
Durham (Hartlepool, Stockton, Billingham and adjacent areas) and the
north-east of the old North Riding of Yorkshire (Thornaby, Yarm,
Nunthorp, Eston, Redcar, Saltburn and the coast south to Staithes and
Guisborough, with adjacent areas).
The collection includes both current and historical maps, the latter mainly
of local interest. The area covered varies with the scale and type of maps,
the core being the present County Cleveland, extending into County
Durham and Yorkshire, with some maps of north-east England where
relevant. Maps of all scales, subject coverage and date are collected in
order to build as complete a visual picture of the area as possible. Of
the pre-1900 maps, a few are manuscript, but the majority are printed,
either originals or reproductions of various types. The earliest representation of the area is a photocopy of the Burghley map of County
Durham, and then the maps of Christopher Saxton.

Detail
4, 5, 6a,b, 7, 10a,b,c, 13, 15, 17c.

Publications of maps held
The River Tees, two centuries of change (Cleveland County Libraries in
   conjunction with the Cleveland and Teesside Local History Society,
   1976). An album of plans with descriptive notes illustrating the development of the River Tees estuary into a major port during the past 200
   years.
Middlesbrough's history in maps (Cleveland and Teesside Local History
   Society, 1980). An album of maps and plans from the 17th to the 20th
   centuries, with text.
The history of Stockton and Thornaby in maps (Cleveland and Teesside
   Local History Society, 1982). An album of reproductions of old maps
   and plans, with text.

CORNWALL

45   Cornwall County Record Office

Address   County Hall, Truro TR1 3AY

Telephone   (01872) 73698 / 74282 ext. 3127   *Fax*   (01872) 70340

Access   By appointment. CARN reader's ticket required.

Index

Indexes in progress in 1994: (1) All estate plans pre-1840; present total of 1200 entries according to farm/tenement, arranged by parish. (2) Plans of abandoned metalliferous mines, arranged by mine name, parish and a basic grid plot on OS 2nd edition (1906) six-inch plans. (3) Comprehensive index of all plans, arranged by location and parish.

Summary

Maps and plans are grouped under the following heads: estate, metalliferous mining, utilities and printed county maps.

Principal and important items are (1) The estate maps of Joel Gascoyne for the period 1693–1698 including the 'Lanhydrock' atlas, available in microform, b/w negatives and colour slides; plans of abandoned mines, including detailed underground and surface workings for the period c.1750 onwards; district mining plans for the nineteenth century; tithe map coverage for over 90% of the county; OS 1:500 of nine major towns. Some maps covering Devon.

Detail

5, 6a,b, 7, 8, 9, 10a,b,c, 11, 12, 13, 14, 15, 17a

Publications of maps held

W. L. D. Ravenhill, 'Joel Gascoyne – a cartographer with style', *Geographical Magazine*, **44** (1972), 335–341.

W. L. D. Ravenhill, 'Joel Gascoyne, a pioneer of large-scale county mapping', *Imago Mundi*, **26** (1972), 60–70.

W. L. D. Ravenhill and O. J. Padel, 'A Map of the County of Cornwall Newly Surveyed by Joel Gascoyne', text and reproduction, *Devon and Cornwall Record Society*, New Series, **34** (1991).

W. L. D. Ravenhill, 'John Norden's Manuscript Map of Cornwall and its Nine Hundreds', text and reproduction (University of Exeter, 1972).

Facsimiles and reproductions on sale
OS First Edition 1:2500 (c.1880); District Mining Plans (leaflet available).
W. L. D. Ravenhill and O. J. Padel, 'A Map of the County of Cornwall Newly surveyed by Joel Gascoyne', *Devon and Cornwall Record Society*, New Series, **34** (1991).

46   The Royal Institution of Cornwall, The Courtney Library

Address	Royal Cornwall Museum, River Street, Truro TR1 2SJ
Telephone	(01872) 72205
Access	Open, but written enquiry recommended in the first place. By appointment for microfilms.

Index
Card catalogue on site.

Summary
The maps relate to Cornwall only. Generally maps arising from estate business of local families, mostly manuscript, from late 17th century onwards. Notable are the maps, 1690–8, by George Withiell, philomath of Penryn and Holsworthy.
Several hundred maps of mining areas.
Large scale OS maps, 1880 and 1906–8 editions, on microfilm.

Detail
1, 5, 6a, 10a,b,c, 11, 13, 15, 17a

Publications of maps held
J. B. Harley and E. Stuart, 'George Withiell, A West-Country Surveyor of the late-seventeenth century', *Devon and Cornwall Notes and Queries*, **35** (1982), 95–114.

Facsimiles and reproductions on sale
Photocopies of many small maps available for consultation and purchase.

CUMBRIA

47A   Cumbria Record Office, Carlisle

Address   Cumbria Record Office, The Castle, Carlisle CA3 8UR

Telephone   (01228) 812416/812391

Access   Open, but some material is outhoused and notice is required for production. CARN reader's ticket required.

Index

Unpublished handlists to:

Maps of Cumberland, Westmorland (some) and Carlisle.

Enclosure maps. Deposited plans of public utilities: railways, roads, harbours, docks amd tramways.

Railway station and line plans, railway bridge plans.

School plans. Minerals plans (some unlisted). Tithe maps.

Index to Carlisle City building byelaws plans c.1850–1934.

Building byelaws plans for the following urban and rural areas: Cleator Moor, Maryport, Millom, Penrith, Whitehaven, Wigton, Workington and North Westmorland R.D.C.

Summary

Public maps, e.g. enclosure and tithe; estate maps from c.1700. Maps of Whitehaven and Maryport, both of which were 'planted towns'; Whitehaven, founded in the 1680s, is said to be the first planted town since Winchelsea. Mineral plans, especially coal iron and lead mining.

Detail

1, 2, 3, 4, 5, 6a,b, 7, 8, 9, 10a,b,c, 11, 12, 13, 14, 15, 16, 17a,b,c

47B   Cumbria Record Office, Kendal

Address   Cumbria Record Office, County Offices, Kendal LA9 4RQ

Telephone   (01539) 814330/814329

Access   Open. CARN reader's ticket required.

Index
Typescript *Catalogue of pre-Ordnance Survey estate maps 1667–1861.*
Handlists of tithe and enclosure maps, deposited plans, highway diversions and deposits containing maps, on site.
Index on site, arranged by subject, including maps.

Summary
Manuscript and printed maps 1667–c.1930, mainly relating to the historic county of Westmorland, with some major deposited collections having maps relating to Cumberland, Lancashire and Yorkshire.

Detail
1, 4, 5, 6a,b, 7, 8, 10a,b,c, 11, 12, 13, 14, 15, 17a,c

47C Cumbria Record Office, Barrow

Address	Cumbria Record Office, 140 Duke Street, Barrow-in-Furness LA14 1XW
Telephone	(01229) 831269
Access	Open. CARN reader's ticket required.

Index
Handlist on site for most of the relevant collections.
List of records and plans from Duke of Buccleugh's Furness Estate, copy at NRA.
Information sheet, listing the more important maps and summarising others, is available.

Summary
Printed and manuscript maps covering the County Borough of Barrow-in-Furness, including Borough Surveyors maps, 1867–1950; Building Inspectors plans, 1870–20th century.
Dalton-in-Furness UDC: Surveyors plans; Building Inspectors plans, 1874–20th century.
Duke of Buccleugh's Furness estate: maps and plans, including perambulations of manors in Furness, enfranchisements and mineral royalties, 1850–1940s. Also iron mining plans: boreholes and shafts, 1850–1940s.
Furness Railway: miscellaneous lineside and property plans, 19th-20th centuries.
Thomas Butler & Son, solicitor, Broughton-in-Furness: local estate plans, 19th century; sales particulars with maps, 1830s-1950s.

Hart Jackson, solicitor, Ulverston: estate plans including Crosby Gyll Park (1634); other areas, 1746–20th century.

Originals or reproductions of most enclosure maps and of all tithe maps issued in Furness and South West Cumberland, 19th century.

County maps: reproductions of W. Yates's Lancashire (1786); originals of C. Greenwood's Lancashire (1818); T. Hodgson's Westmorland (1828). M. Mackenzie's chart of coast between Heversham and St Bees (1775).

OS maps: Furness area of North Lancashire: almost complete coverage at 6 and 25 inches to 1 mile. For various towns, plans at 126 inches to the mile (1:500), editions of the late 1840s-1913 and 1930s. Ulverston town centre at 60 inches to 1 mile, 1852. South West Cumberland: many sheets from 6 and 25 inches to the mile, editions of 1860s-1900, with further sheets from the incomplete surveys of the 1920s.

Reproductions of H. Merryweather's map of Dalton-in-Furness (1825); J. Wood's map of Ulverston (1832).

Detail
5, 6, 7, 8, 10b,c, 11, 12, 13, 15, 17a

48   Cumbria County Library, Barrow Library, Furness Collection

Address   Ramsden Square, Barrow-in-Furness LA14 1LL

Telephone   (01229) 820650   *Fax*   (01229) 870234

Access   Open.

Index
No index to maps.

Summary
The collection consists of OS maps at 1 inch, $2\frac{1}{2}$, 6, 25, and 50 inches to the mile, and some 1:500 scale plans of Barrow. OS coverage extends to the Furness area generally, although not complete for all editions. Other maps comprised in the Furness Collection have been deposited with the Barrow Record Office, but remain the property of the Library Service.

Detail
7, 10a,b,c

DERBYSHIRE

49   Derbyshire Record Office

Address   Ernest Bailey Building, New Street, Matlock DE4 3AG.

Telephone   (01629) 580000 ext. 7347

Access   Open. Users are required to register. Appointment advised, especially for use of microfilmed material.

Index

J. C. Cox, *Records of the County of Derby* (1899) lists highway diversions and deposited plans to that date.

H. Nichols, *Local maps of Derbyshire to 1770: an inventory and introduction* (Matlock, Derbyshire Library Service, 1980).

Derbyshire Record Office, *Tithe maps in Derbyshire Record Office* (1991), and *Enclosure maps in Derbyshire Record Office* (1992).

C. C. Handford, 'Some maps of the County of Derby, 1577–1850', *Derbyshire Archaeological Society*, 1971.

Handlists on site, and at NRA.

Summary

The map collection consists of the County Council's own holdings, and maps and plans occurring among deposits in the Office. The Council holds an almost complete set of county maps from 16th to 20th century and extensive collections of OS 1:2500, 6 inch, $2\frac{1}{2}$ inch and 1 inch in various editions; county, district, parish, ward and highway maps, printed or drawn for local government purposes; almost complete sets of plans of public undertakings deposited under Act of Parliament from 1792; enclosure maps private and statutory, 17th century onwards; tithe rent charge apportionment plans mid-19th century; private estate and business maps and plans, late 16th century onwards, including mining plans, sale catalogue plans, and accompanying surveys.

Detail

5, 6a,b, 7, 10a,b,c, 11, 12, 13, 14, 15, 17a,b,c

Publications of maps held

P. P. Burdett, 'Map of Derbyshire, 1791', *Derbyshire Archaeological Society*, 1975.

50A Derbyshire County Library, Matlock

Address Local Studies Department, County Offices, Smedley Street, Matlock DE4 3AG

Telephone (01629) 580000 *Fax* (01629) 580350

Access Open.

Index
Card index on site.

Summary
Printed maps relating to Derbyshire, 1577 to date. OS sheets of Derbyshire, various dates, various scales. Mid-nineteenth century Geological Survey maps. Plan of Ashover lead-mine (1803). Cross-sections of railway tunnel between Dronfield, Bradway Tunnel and Sheffield. A few 18th century canal maps.

Detail
5, 6a,b, 7, 10a,b,c, 13, 14

Facsimiles and reproductions for sale
John Speed's 'Derby' (1610).

50B Derbyshire County Library, Derby

Address Derbyshire Local Studies Department, 25b Irongate, Derby DE1 3GL

Telephone (01332) 255393

Access Open.

Index
Maps and plans are listed in section 3 of *Manuscripts and archives: a list of the major items in Derbyshire County Library* (1975).
Notes on maps in the major Local Studies Departments of Derbyshire Libraries generally are in *Derbyshire Local Studies Collections* (1976).

Summary
Maps of Derbyshire, 1577 to date; maps of Derby, 1610 to date. These include general small-scale maps, maps for specific purposes, e.g. proposed railways and canals, licensed houses, parliamentary and ward boundaries, and larger-scale maps for specific purposes, e.g. street improvements in Derby, and lead veins. Geological Survey maps: 1 inch

(*c*.1852–55 and 1890). Approximately 150 tithe maps for Derbyshire parishes.

OS maps include 1 inch (1880–90), 6 inch (1880–90), 25 inch (1st edition, c.1879, 2nd edition, c.1900) but none give complete coverage of Derbyshire. For Derby only: 50 inch (1899), 1:500 (1883).

Detail
5, 6a, 7, 10a,b,c, 11, 12, 13, 14, 15, 17a

Facsimiles and reproductions on sale
John Speed's 'Derby' (1610) and 'Derbyshire' (1610); Moule's 'Derbyshire' (1837).

50C   Derbyshire County Library, Chesterfield

Address   Chesterfield Central Library, New Beetwell Street, Chesterfield S40 1QN

Telephone   (01246) 209292

Access   Open.

Index
M. Jobling (comp.), *Ordnance Survey plans of Derbyshire, c.1875-1940, a Union List* (*c*.1988, a listing now out of date).
Looseleaf catalogue on site.

Summary
A basic collection of general Derbyshire maps covering early and modern editions, dating from Christopher Saxton's map of 1577 onwards. Mainly printed maps with some facsimiles and photocopies of originals. Some specialisation in the local area. Total map stock is approximately 2900, of which 2000 are OS sheets, including those dating after 1900. Additional microfilm provision: OS, 1st and 2nd edition at 6 inches to 1 mile, 1st, 2nd and 3rd editions at 25 inches to 1 mile, full county coverage.

Detail
6a,b, 7, 10a,b,c, 11, 12, 13, 15, 17a

Facsimiles and reproductions on sale
Burdett's 'Derbyshire'(1791).

DEVON

51   Devon Record Office

Address   Castle Street, Exeter EX4 3PU

Telephone   (01392) 384253   *Fax*   (01392) 384208

Access   Advise by letter. Some documents in distant store. Proof of identity required. Search Room charges with exemptions.

Index
'Brief Guide: Part I (Official and Ecclesiastical)', pp. 33–40 lists deposited plans and pp.52–73 lists tithe maps and enclosure awards.
Card index on site. Handlists on site and at NRA.

Summary
Manuscript maps include: (1) in Exeter City Archives, large volume of maps of properties owned by Exeter City Chamber, 1744–1758 with some later additions. J. Coldridge's large-scale map of the City of Exeter (1818–19); maps and plans relating to railways, turnpikes, canals, etc., in Devon, deposited with the Exeter Clerk of the Peace, chiefly 19th century. (2) Estate maps, maps showing location of mines, canals, turnpike roads, etc., covering dates 17th to 19th centuries.
Printed maps include copies of 17th and 18th century maps of Exeter. 28 large scale (1:500) OS maps covering the City of Exeter, chiefly 1876. John Wood's map of Exeter (1840).
Maps of abandoned mines, on microfiche.

Detail
5, 6a,b, 7, 10b,c, 11, 12, 13, 14, 15, 17a

Publications of maps held
H. S. A. Fox, in R. A. Skelton and P. D. A. Harvey (eds), *Local maps and plans from Medieval England* (Oxford, 1986), pp.163–170 and 329–336, illustrates and discusses two maps from the Exeter City Archives.

52   North Devon Record Office

Address   Tuly Street, Barnstaple EX32 7EJ

Telephone   (01271) 388607   *Fax*   (01271) 388599

Access   Open. Proof of identity required. Admission charges with exemptions.

Index
Card index and handlists on site.

Summary
The office holds the records of the old borough of Barnstaple, important deposits from local landowners, and parish records from the ancient parishes within the borough and in North Devon. The Pitts Tuckers collection of 18th and 19th century maps is of particular interest; it derives from the Barnstaple solicitors Pitts Tucker, established c.1860, who handled estates in Devon and Cornwall. Some Admiralty charts are held.

Detail
7, 8, 10a,b,c, 11, 12, 13, 14, 15, 17a,c

53   West Devon Record Office

Address   Unit 3, Clare Place, Coxside, Plymouth PL4 0JW

Telephone   (01752) 385909

Access   Proof of identity required. Search Room charges with exemptions.

Index
Maps are included in *A Guide to the Archives Department of Plymouth City Libraries, Part 1. Official Records* (Plymouth Corporation, 1962).
Leaflet No.12 *Maps at West Devon Record Office.*
Card index, hand lists and indexes to deposited collections, on site.

Summary
The Office holds the records of the Plymouth Corporation dating from 1486, deposits from local landowners and solicitors, and parish records from many of the ancient parishes within the city and surrounding district. There is an extensive collection of over 3000 printed and manuscript maps, dating from the 17th century to the present. Good holdings of OS maps include Plymouth at 1:500 (1860s survey) and a

series of mid-19th century building plans of St Aubyn properties in Devonport. Devon tithe maps on microfiche.

Detail
1, 6b, 7, 10a,b,c, 11, 12, 13, 17a,c

Publications of maps held
E. Stuart, *Lost landscapes of Plymouth: maps, charts and plans to 1800* (Stroud, Sutton, 1991).

54 North Devon Local Studies Centre

Address   Tuly Street, Barnstaple EX32 7EJ

Telephone   (01271) 388607   *Fax* (01271) 388599

Access   Open.

Index
No index to maps.

Summary
Mainly well-known standard printed sheet maps of the county of Devon (a few of adjoining counties), 16th to 19th centuries. Maps of Great Britain covering the same period, contained in atlases or books, such as W. R. Shepherd, *Shepherd's Historical Atlas* (London, 1956), R. F. Treharne and H. Fullard, *Muir's Historical Atlas* (London, 1969). Early large scale OS maps of North Devon on microfiche.

Detail
6a,b, 7, 10a,b,c

Facsimiles and reproductions for sale
A limited selection.

55 Torquay Local Studies Library

Address   Torquay Central Library, Lymington Road, Torquay TQ1 3DT

Telephone   (01803) 217673   *Fax* (01803) 217680

Access   Open.

Index
Handlist on site and available.

Summary
Small number of historic maps and town plans of Torquay. Early OS maps for Torbay area.

Detail
6a, 7, 10a,b,c

56 Plymouth Central Library, Local Studies Library

Address   Drake Circus, Plymouth PL4 8AL

Telephone   (01752) 385909   *Fax*   (01752) 385905

Access   Open.

Index
No index to maps.

Summary
Printed maps only, 17th to 19th centuries, of Devon and Cornwall, and of Plymouth, Devonport and Stonehouse. Small collection of facsimiles of atlases and maps of England, Wales and Ireland, mostly 17th century. Copies of Camden's *Britannia*, 3 vols, 1789, and Cary's *County Atlas*, 1801–8.
A few 19th century Hydrographic Office charts of Plymouth Harbour and other parts of S.W. England.
Some OS maps on microfilm.

Detail
1, 5, 6a,b, 7, 8, 10a,b,c, 16

Facsimiles and reproductions for sale
Civil War defences etc. (1643). Devonshire by Benjamin Donn (1765). Plan of Plymouth, Stonehouse, Dock etc. by S. Elliott (1820). Borough of Plymouth by J. Cooke (1820). 'Cooke's Strangers Guide, or pocket plan of the three Towns' (1827). 'The Three Towns' (1830). Plan of Plymouth, Stonehouse and Devonport by R. Brown (1840). Plymouth, Devonport and Stonehouse, by J. Tallis (1860), by W. Wood (1865), by W. H. Maddock (1881). 'The environs of Plymouth. Shewing the new forts' by W. Wood (1868).

57   West Country Studies Library

Address   Castle Street, Exeter EX4 3PQ

Telephone   (01392) 384216   *Fax*   (01392) 384208

Access   Open, appointment advisable.

Index
Computerised and card indexes on site.

Summary
The bulk of the pre-1900 map collection is housed in the West Country Studies Library with a few items in the Reference Library. The maps, nearly all printed, relate almost exclusively to Devon and the West Country with over 600 sheets prior to 1900, of which half are OS maps. There are some 150 maps of Devon or the West Country in general, dating from *c.*1600 onwards, some 50 county maps of Cornwall and Somerset, and about 100 town plans, mainly of Exeter and Plymouth. The 1:500 town plans and the 25 inch OS maps are on microfilm.

Detail
1, 5, 6a,b, 7, 8, 10a,b,c, 11, 13, 14, 15, 16

Facsimiles and reproductions for sale
Georg Braun, 'Civitas Exoniae (vulgo Excester)' (1618), engraved by Remigius Hogenberg; Sutton Nicholls, 'A true plan of the City of Excester' (1725); C. Tozer, 'Plan of the City and suburbs of Exeter' (1792); J. Britton, 'Exeter, 1803', from *The beauties of England and Wales*; R. Brown, 'The City of Exeter' (1835); J. Tallis, 'Exeter' (c.1852).

58   Exeter Cathedral Archives

Address   Diocesan House, Palace Gate, Exeter EX1 1HX

Telephone   (01392) 495954, pm only.

Access   By appointment.

Index
Typescript handlist and index on site.

Summary
Manuscript maps: a small group of manorial maps of estates of the Dean and Chapter of Exeter, all made between c.1770 and c.1870, usually accompanying valuations; one enclosure award and map of Bampton,

Oxfordshire (1821). Maps of parts of Exeter, late 16th century. Railway, road maps and plans, 19th century, some accompanying deeds.
Printed maps: a few county maps of Devon and city plans of Exeter, casually acquired.

Detail
6a, 7, 11, 12, 13, 15

59A   Exeter University

Address   University Library, Stocker Road, Exeter EX4 4DT

Telephone   (01392) 263869

Access   Non members of the University, by personal application to the Librarian or Deputy Librarian.

Index
Maps are listed in the main card catalogue on site and in a handlist.

Summary
The Constable and Townsend collections contain some 113 loose maps, largely of English and Welsh counties, including a number from the 16th and 17th centuries and extending to the 19th century. There are also some plans of Exeter and one or two Devon county maps. No manuscript maps.

Detail
1, 2, 6a, 7

59B   Geography Department, Map Library

Address   Amory Building, Rennes Drive, Exeter EX4 4RJ

Telephone   (01392) 263248   *Fax*   (01392) 263342

Access   By personal application to the Map Curator.

Index
Card index on site.

Summary
The collection contains 19th-century maps of Cornwall, Devon, and Dorset; a number of atlases and early editions of OS maps. Benjamin Donn's 'Devon' (1765) and the reprint; Christopher and John Green-

wood's 'Devon', surveyed in 1825–6, published in 1827, Camden's 'Britannia' (1722). Numerous facsimiles of early maps.

Detail
1, 2, 3, 4, 6a,b, 10a,b,c

60   The North Devon Athenaeum

Address   North Devon Library and Record Office, Tuly Street, Barnstaple EX32 7EJ

Telephone   (01271) 42174   *Fax*   (01271) 388599

Access   Open.

Index
Library index on site.

Summary
'A Map of Devon, with the City of Exeter' by Benjamin Donn, dated 1765 (1st? edition); facsimile edition of Benjamin Donn's 'Map of Devon', published by DCRS 1965; O.S. County of Devon 6 inch maps dated 1880–90; John Ogilby, 'Map of Devon and Cornwall' (1675); facsimile edition, 9 sheets, published by Devon Books 1984; Barnstaple Borough Parliamentary Boundary (Reforms Act 1832), del. C. Ingrey, London; OS. (Old Series) 1 inch to 1 mile Devon and Cornwall (1809) (1st Edition) by William Mudge, sheets 21 to 27; 'New Map of England' published by G. and J. Carey, London, half-inch to 1 mile, Part I sheets 1, 2, 8 and 9 published 1 July 1820, Part II sheets 3, 11, 12, 16 and 17 published 2 July 1821.

Detail
6a,b, 7, 10a,b

DORSET

61   Dorset Record Office

Address   Bridport Road, Dorchester DT1 1RP

Telephone   (01305) 250550   *Fax*   (01305) 224839

Access   Open.

Index
Parish index and subject index, including maps, on site.

Summary
Some printed but mainly manuscript maps, with photocopies of a few in other collections, spanning 17th to 20th centuries but mainly 18th and 19th centuries. Almost entirely of Dorset, but some of other counties where an estate archive covers land outside Dorset. Plans deposited with Quarter Sessions records in connection with proposed boundaries, docks, harbours, electricity, water and gas undertakings, and tramways. Plans in connection with Justices' certificates altering roads.

Detail
6a,b, 7, 10a,b,c, 11, 12, 13, 14, 15, 17a,c

Publications of maps held
The Archives of Dorset: Catalogue of an exhibition to mark the first 30 years of the Dorset Record Office (1986), includes a section on 'Dorset maps'.
Town and County: Catalogue of an exhibition of maps showing the County of Dorset and its Towns.

Facsimiles and reproductions on sale
Part of John Ogilby's map of roads between London and Weymouth (1675). County of Dorset by Langley (1817).

62 Dorset Natural History and Archaeological Society

Address   Dorset County Museum, Dorchester DT1 1XA

Access   By appointment.

Index
No index to maps.

Summary
Printed maps, dating from the end of the 18th century, covering the county of Dorset only.

Detail
6a,b, 7, 9, 10a,b,c, 11

COUNTY DURHAM

63   Durham County Record Office

Address   County Hall, Durham DH1 5UL

Telephone   (0191) 3833253   *Fax*   (0191) 3860958

Access   By appointment.

Index
S. C. Newton, *The Londonderry Papers, catalogue of the documents deposited in the Durham County Record Office by the 9th Marquess of Londonderry* (Durham, 1967).
Handlists, indexes and catalogues on site. Lists of major collections at NRA.

Summary
Maps and plans are contained in the records of County Council and Local Authorities, businesses (including National Coal Board), solicitors, and estate agents, and within family and estate papers, parish records and miscellaneous deposits. There is a collection of OS plans at scales of 1:10560 and 1:2500 for County Durham only.

Detail
1, 5, 6a,b, 7, 10a,b,c, 11, 12, 13, 15, 17a,c

64   The Dean and Chapter Library

Address   The College, Durham DH1 3EH

Telephone   (0191) 386 2489

Access   By appointment.

Index
Lists on site.

Summary
Printed maps and atlases in the Printed Books Collection: J. Jansson, sets of maps and town plans (*Novus Atlas*, 1646–50); Mercator, *Atlas Minor*, 1607/10; Ortelius, *Theatrum orbis terrarum*, 1570; Nomenclator

Ptolemaicus 1584; Jansson, *Illustriorum principumque urbium ... tabulae*, 1657 (8 vols.)

Detail
1, 6a,b, 7, 13

65 Durham University

Access   Open to non-members of the university who must provide proof of identity. Advance notice recommended.

65A Durham University Library, Archives and Special Collections

Address   Palace Green Section, Durham DH1 3RN

Telephone   (0191) 374 3001   *Fax*   (0191) 374 7481 (University Office)

Index
R. M. Turner, *Maps of Durham, 1576–1872, in the University Library, Durham, including some other maps of local interest* (Durham, 1954).
A. I. Doyle, *Maps of Durham, 1607–1872, in the University Library, Durham, a supplementary catalogue* (Durham, 1960).
Unpublished sheaf catalogue of maps, printed and manuscript, of Co. Durham and places and areas within it, of all dates.
Loose printed maps are also entered in the general catalogues of the Library.

Summary
The collection of loose maps is largely of printed maps of County Durham and areas within and adjacent to it, 16th to 20th century, with a few manuscript maps, mostly 18th century estate plans from County Durham and, among the Earl Grey papers, 19th century estate plans from Northumberland. Maps of other areas and of the British Isles as a whole are almost entirely in 17th to 19th century printed atlases among the early printed book collections.

Detail
1, 2, 3, 4, 5, 6,a,b, 7, 8, 10a,b,c, 11, 13, 14, 15

Publications of maps held
G. Manley, 'Some notes on maps of the county of Durham in the

University Library', *Durham University Journal* **27** (1931), 127–33.
G. Manley, 'The Plancius map of England, Wales and Ireland, 1592',
Geographical Journal **84** (1934), 252–3.

65B Durham University Library, Archives and Special Collections

Address   Section at 5 The College, Durham DH1 3EQ

Telephone   (0191) 374 3610   *Fax*   (0191) 374 7481 (University
                     Office)

Index
Durham Bishopric Halmote Court Records: Handlist of documents relating
to Enclosure Awards, 1957; handlist of subsidiary manorial Documents,
1959; unpublished list of additional maps and plans.
Durham Diocesan Records: List of Tithe Apportionments and Plans for
County Durham, 1971.
List of the Baker Baker Papers, vol. 6, 1971, Deeds ... Books ... Maps
    and Plans.
List of the Shipperdson papers, 2 vols, 1972–3.
List of Shafto (Beamish) papers, 1976.
Unpublished lists and indexes of plans in the Durham Dean and Chapter
Muniments, the Church Commission Durham Bishopric and Dean and
Chapter estates deposit, the Durham Diocesan records, the Gibby Papers,
the Howard of Naworth papers, and of OS plans, chiefly of Durham
and Northumberland.

Summary
The material falls into two groups: (1) The records of the Dean and
Chapter and of the Bishopric of Durham, and (2) family collections.
Both groups include manuscript and printed maps.
Inclosure Plans occur in several collections; Tithe Plans for the parishes
in the historic County Durham.
The many OS plans at 6 and 25 inches to the mile in the Bishopric
Halmote Court Records bear manuscript notes and colourings.
Maps in the family collections reflect the interests and occupations of
the family members; they are mainly estate plans but also include plans
arising from the commercial concerns of the family.
In the muniments of the Dean and Chapter there are four medieval maps
of areas in the county of Durham: Tursdale beck, c.1430–1442, two of

Durham, 1439–c.1442 and 1440–c.1445, and Witton Gilbert, mid-15th century.
Most maps relate to County Durham, Cumberland, Northumberland and Westmorland. Most are manuscript and date from the 18th and 19th centuries, although there are some important 17th century plans, mostly of Cumberland. The few Derbyshire maps include a 1686/7 map of Taddington in the Booth and Lazenby Papers.

Detail
1, 5, 6a,b, 7, 8, 10a,b,c, 11, 12, 13, 14, 15, 17a,c

Publications of maps held
M. G. Snape, and M. G. Snape and B. K. Roberts, in R. A. Skelton and P. D. A. Harvey (eds.), *Local maps and plans from medieval England* (1986), pp. 171–94, 203–210 and 229–36, reproduce and discuss the four medieval maps from the Durham Dean and Chapter muniments.
M. Bonney, *Lordship and the urban community: Durham and its overlords, 1250–1540* (Cambridge, 1990), pp.248–9, reproduces and discusses a 16th century plan from the Durham Dean and Chapter Muniments.
M. W. Beresford, 'East Layton ... in 1608. Another early cartographic representation of a Deserted Village site', *Medieval Archaeology* **11** (1967), 257–60, concerns plans and a survey in the Baker Baker Papers, 72/249.
T. H. B. Graham (ed.), *The Barony of Gilsland, Lord William Howard's survey taken in 1603*, Cumberland and Westmorland Antiquarian and Archaeological Society, Extra Series **16** (1934), concerns the field book accompanying an early 17th century set of estate plans.

65C Department of Geography

Address Science Laboratories, South Road, Durham DH1 3LE

Telephone (0191) 374 2000   *Fax* (0191) 374 2456

Access By appointment.

Index
Handlist of atlases and maps.

Summary
The Department holds some 40 atlases and county maps covering the entire British Isles, and about 35 relating to northeast England.
The first group includes 'A navigation chart for British waters' by A. Jacobsen, 1670; chart of the Channel, 1750; A. Zatta's 'England and

Wales', and 'Ireland', 1778; N. Sanson's 'Principality of Wales' of 1658, 'Scotland beyond the Tay' and 'Scotland below the Tay', both of 1665; G. and D. Robert's 'Ireland', 1750, and 'Scotland', 1757; and county maps by J. Speed, C. Saxton, H. Overton, R. Morden, J. Cary, etc. Among the northeastern maps are charts and coastal maps, including 'Wells to Tynemouth' by J. A. Colum, 1632; 'North Sea coast' by J. van Keulen, 1683; 'Holy Island' by Greenvile Collins, 1695; county maps of Durham, by J. Jansson, 1647, by J. Speed, 1620, and others of 18th and 19th century date, and of Northumberland, by H. Hondius, 1630, J. Blaeu, 1650, by P. Lea, 1689, by A. and M. Armstrong, 1787; road maps, London to Berwick, 1720 and 1765, Bishoprick of Durham, anon., 1560, and by R. Morden, 1695, and Durham wards by C. Greenwood, 1819.

Detail
1, 2, 3, 4, 6a,b, 7, 8, 15

ESSEX

66A   Essex Record Office

Address   Essex Record Office, County Hall, Victoria Road South, Chelmsford CM1 1LX

Telephone   (01245) 430067   *Fax*   (01245) 352710

Access   By appointment. CARN reader's ticket required.

Index

F. G. Emmison (ed.), *Catalogue of maps in the Essex Record Office, 1566–1860* (revised edition, 1947), with *Supplements*, (1952, 1964, 1968).

F. G. Emmison (ed.), *County Maps of Essex, 1576–1852: A handlist* (1955), copies augmented with additions available on site.

Card index on site.

Summary

In addition to usual Record Office holdings, as a low-lying maritime county, there are maps prepared for Commissioners of Sewers. The value of many of the maps lies in their close association with related documents, which illuminate agricultural practices etc. in the county over more than three centuries.

Detail

1, 5, 6a,b, 7, 8, 9, 10a,b,c, 11, 12, 13, 14, 15, 16, 17a,b,c

Publications of maps held

A. C. Edwards and K. C. Newton, *The Walkers of West Hanningfield: mapmakers extraordinary* (London, 1984).

F. G. Emmison and R. A. Skelton, ' "The Description of Essex" by John Norden, 1594', *Geographical Journal* **123** (1957), 37–41.

A. Stuart Mason, *Essex on the map* (Essex RO, 1990).

Facsimiles and reproductions on sale

Reproductions of maps of Essex: by John Norden (1594), by Johannes Blaeu (1645), by John Ogilby and William Morgan (1678).

66B   Essex Record Office

Address   Essex Record Office, Southend Branch, Central Library, Victoria Avenue, Southend-on-Sea SS2 6EX

Telephone   (01702) 612621 ext. 215   *Fax*   (01702) 469241

Access   By appointment. CARN reader's ticket required.

Index
F. G. Emmison (ed.), *Catalogue of maps in the Essex Record Office 1566–1860* (revised edition, 1968) includes maps now transferred to this Branch Office.
F. G. Emmison (ed.), *County Maps of Essex, 1576–1852: A handlist* (1955).

Summary
Southend Branch Office holds those maps relating to the area of the Rochford Hundred, with the exception of the largest in size, which have been retained at the Office in Chelmsford.

Detail
6a,b, 10a,b,c, 11, 17a

Publications of maps held
A. C. Edwards and K. C. Newton, *The Walkers of West Hanningfield, mapmakers extraordinary* (London, 1984).
F. G. Emmison, 'The Art of the mapmaker', in his *Catalogue of maps in the Essex Record Office* (1947), pp.vii–xv.
A. Stuart Mason, *Essex on the map* (Essex RO, 1990).

Facsimiles and reproductions for sale
Essex, by John Norden (1594), by Johannes Blaeu (1645), by John Ogilby and William Morgan (1678), by John Oliver (1696).

66C   Essex Record Office

Address   Essex Record Office, Colchester and North East Essex Branch, Stanwell House, Stanwell Street, Colchester CO2 7DL

Telephone   (01206) 572099

Access   By appointment. CARN reader's ticket required.

Index

F. G. Emmison (ed.), Catalogue of maps in the Essex Record Office 1566–1860, with *Supplements* (1952, 1964, 1968).

F. G. Emmison (ed.), *County Maps of Essex, 1576–1852: A handlist* (1955).

Summary

Estate and tithe maps mostly of Colchester and North East Essex.
Town plans of Colchester.

Detail

5, 6a,b, 7, 10b,c, 11, 17a

Publications of maps held

A. C. Edwards and K. C. Newton, *The Walkers of West Hanningfield, mapmakers extraordinary* (London, 1984).

A. Stuart Mason, *Essex on the map* (Essex RO, 1990).

Facsimiles and reproductions on sale

Essex, by John Norden (1594), by Johannes Blaeu (1645), by John Ogilby and William Morgan (1678).

GLOUCESTERSHIRE

67   Gloucestershire Record Office

Address   Clarence Row, Alvin Street, Gloucester GL1 3DW

Telephone   (01452) 425295   *Fax* (01452) 426378

Access   Open. CARN reader's ticket required. Admission fee.

Index
Handlists on site and with National Register of Archives.

Summary
Printed and manuscript maps relating to Gloucestershire. Maps occur amongst the deposited papers of local families or solicitors, as well as amongst the official records of County Council, Quarter Sessions and Diocese. Estate maps date from 1595 but are for the most part late 18th or early 19th century. Quarter Sessions records include Enclosure Award plans and plans of public schemes such as canals and railways. Diocesan records include a good series of Tithe maps. Large scale OS maps of all editions.

Detail
6a,b, 7, 10a,b,c, 11, 12, 13, 14, 15, 17a,b,c

Publications of maps held
T. Chubb, *A Descriptive Catalogue of the Printed Maps of Gloucester, 1577–1911* (Bristol and Gloucestershire Archaeological Society, 1912).
R. Austen, Additions to, and Notes on, the 'Descriptive Catalogue ...' by Thomas Chubb, *Transactions of the Bristol and Gloucestershire Archaeological Society* **39** (1916), 233–64.
A Gloucestershire and Bristol Atlas (Bristol and Gloucestershire Archaeological Society, 1961), contains reproductions of early maps, and a diagram showing county boundary changes *c*.1800–1960.

Facsimiles and reproductions on sale
Gloucestershire by Johannes Blaeu (1648).

68 Gloucester County Library, The Gloucester Collection

Address Brunswick Road, Gloucester GL1 1HT

Telephone (01452) 426979 *Fax* (01452) 521468

Access Open.

Index

Catalogue of the Gloucestershire Collection (1928), arranged topographically by subject and place.
Printed and card indexes to date, on site.

Summary

The material relates only to Gloucestershire and forms part of the Library's extensive Local History Department. The collection includes published and unpublished maps, of various dates, relating to the county or parts of it, and is comprehensive and of great historical interest.

Detail
6a,b, 7, 10a,b,c, 15

HAMPSHIRE

69   Hampshire Record Office

Address   Sussex Street, Winchester SO23 8TH

Telephone   (01962) 846154   *Fax*   (01962) 878681

Access   Open. CARN reader's ticket required.

Index

'Transport in Hampshire and the Isle of Wight – a Guide to the Records' (Hampshire Archivist's Group, 1973), lists Deposited Plans and other plans of communications.

Handlists of Tithe and Enclosure Awards and Deposited Plans on site.

Card Index arranged alphabetically by place.

Summary

Printed maps in the collection include incomplete series of OS at 6 and 25 inches to 1 mile, 1st, 2nd and 3rd editions, for Hampshire and the Isle of Wight, and small scale (up to 1 inch to the mile) county maps from the 17th to 20th centuries. Manuscript maps include tithe (c.1840), enclosure (mainly late 18th-19th centuries) and a number of estate maps, a few dating from the 17th, but mostly from the 18th centuries. Many of these form part of large collections of documents deposited by great landed families, Bolton, Chute, Heathcote, Jervise, Kingsmill, Normanton and Wickham, among others (lists for these at NRA). There are also plans deposited with the Clerk of the Peace from the late 18th century onwards. There are a few manuscript maps relating to Isle of Wight, Berks., Bucks., Devon, Dorset, Essex, Herefs., Lincs., Middx., Northants., Oxon., Som., Surrey, Sussex, Wilts., and some Irish estate maps among the Heathcote and Normanton archives.

Detail

5, 6a,b, 7, 10a,b,c, 11, 12, 13, 14, 15, 17a,c

Facsimiles and reproductions on sale

14 reproduction maps accompanying *Maps of Portsmouth before 1801* (Portsmouth Record Series vol. 4) and a portfolio, are sold individually or as a set.

'Hampshire' by John Norden (1595).

Postcards of extracts of estate maps, Compton (1735), Eastgate, Winchester (1748) and Hyde, Winchester (1753).

70   Portsmouth City Records Office

Address   3 Museum Road, Portsmouth PO1 2LE

Telephone   (01705) 829765   *Fax*   (01705) 874079

Access   Open. CARN reader's ticket required.

Index
Unpublished catalogues of map collections on site.

Summary
Manuscript and printed maps of Portsmouth and South East Hampshire, from 1719.
Charts and Reviews of the Fleet, from 1750; geological maps, from 1884; plans of Portsmouth fortifications, barracks and Dockyard, from 1747, some as photocopies.
OS maps, at 1 inch to 1 mile, 1810–11, 1895; at 6 inches to 1 mile, from 1857; at 1:2500, from 1860; at 1:500 (Portsmouth only), 1862–1884, 1867–1904.
Photocopies of many maps held elsewhere.

Detail
6a,b, 7, 8, 9, 10a,b,c, 11, 12, 13, 14, 15, 17a,c

Publications of maps held
D. Hodson (comp.), *Portsmouth Record Series No.4: Maps of Portsmouth before 1801* (1978). Lists maps held at Portsmouth RO and elsewhere in UK, Ireland and France, with introduction and appendices.

Facsimiles and reproductions on sale
'Early Portsmouth Maps', a portfolio of 14 maps of Portsmouth and Gosport, c.1584–1775, in association with the above Record Series volume. (Portsmouth RO does not hold the originals).
Alan Godfrey Editions of OS maps of parts of Portsmouth, 1896 (Hants sheets 83.07, 83.09, 83.11), with historical commentary and extracts from street directories. (Other editions are in preparation).

71 Southampton City Archives

Address   Civic Centre, Southampton SO9 4XR

Telephone   (01703)   832251 / 223855   ext. 2251   *Fax*   (01703)
832424

Access   Open.

Index
Sections 3 and 8–10 (maps and plans) in *Southampton Records; 1. Guide to the Records of the Corporation and Absorbed Authorities in the Civic Record Office* (Southampton Corporation, 1964).
Transport in Hampshire and the Isle of Wight. A Guide to the Records, (Hampshire Archivists Group, 1973). (NB These publications also describe records housed elsewhere in the county.)
Typewritten handlists on site.

Summary
OS maps of Southampton and immediate neighbourhood. John Norden's 'Hampshire' (1595). Town maps, including Thomas Milne's 1 inch map of 1791. Town plans;(1) manuscript plan on 33 sheets of Town for Improvement Commissioners (1846) at 60 inches to the mile; (2) OS plans, 1868–70, 10 feet to the mile; (3) manuscript map of Portswood (1658); (4) many 19th and 20th century plans for local authority purposes (water, drains, planning, improvements, roads, etc.), from 1800 onwards. Plans on leases of council properties, mostly from about 1820. Sale plans, 19th and 20th centuries.

Detail
6a,b, 7, 10a,b,c, 11, 13, 14, 15, 16, 17a

Publications of maps held
E. Welch (ed.), *Southampton Maps from Elizabethan Times* (Southampton Corporation, 1964). A portfolio of 24 maps, with separate introduction.

Facsimiles and reproductions on sale
Facsimile maps of different dates, showing the historical development of Southampton, with descriptive leaflets: Manor of Portswood (1658), Southampton in 1771, 1800, 1802, 1842 and Southampton District in 1698 and 1791. Photocopies of Southampton (1611, 1907).
'Plan of Southampton, 1846'. A set of three sheets from detailed plan of town made by the OS in 1846.
Dyeline maps: Trade maps of Southampton (1477/8, 1620); Continental

origins of Southampton Huguenots; OS map of Southampton (1866) scale 6 inches to 1 mile; Southampton (1875).

72A   Southampton University

Address   The Hartley Library, Cope Collection, Highfield, Southampton SO9 5NH

Telephone   (01703) 593335   *Fax*   (01703) 593939

Access   Open. Readers must provide evidence of identification.

Index
Detailed card index to the entire collection on site.

Summary
The Cope Collection, based on the bequest of the Rev. Sir William Cope, holds a range of printed maps of Hampshire dating from the 17th century. Facsimiles of earlier maps are also available.
OS coverage is limited although the collection does include some books of reference to Hampshire parishes in the 1860s and 1870s.

Detail
1, 6a, 10a

72B   Department of Geography

Address   Department of Geography, Southampton SO9 5NH (Entered from Salisbury Road or University Road)

Telephone   (01703) 592228   *Fax*   (01703) 593729

Access   Open.

Index
Unpublished handlist for a University exhibition which included a number of maps held by the Department: M. J. Clark, *A catalogue of maps and plans of Hampshire and Southampton – an exhibition for the University Arts Festival* (Southampton University, Department of Geography, nd).

Summary
Primarily a university and departmental working collection of recent

maps in support of teaching and research. Several categories of pre-1900 material, as follows:
(1) Late 19th century OS maps at various scales. (2) A selection of county maps, mainly of Hampshire. (3) Various plans of Southampton docks proposals, local canals proposed, etc. Also 'A plan of the intended navigable canal from Basingstoke ... to the River Thames', by Benjamin Davies (1769); ditto, 'from Andover to Redbridge', by J Lodge (1772); ditto 'from Basingstoke to the River Wey', by W Faden (c.1777). (4) One manuscript map of Southampton and the River Itchen, undated but probably late 16th or early 17th century.

Detail
6a,b, 7, 8, 10a,b,c, 14

Publications of maps held
E. Welch (ed.), *Southampton maps from Elizabethan times* (Southampton Corporation, 1964) contains a representation of the Elizabethan manuscript map (see 4 above), which formed part of the collection of the Hartley Institute, forerunner of the University. Notes accompanying the map discuss its date and value to historians.

73 Winchester College

Address	Winchester SO23 9NA
Telephone	(01962) 864242 (Bursar's Office)
Access	The College Archives and The Fellows' Library are separately administered. Both are accessed by written appointment.

Index
To the College archives as a whole, J. H. Harvey, 'Winchester College Muniments', *Archives* **5** No.28 (1962). College estates papers list is held at NRA.
To the books in the Fellows' Library, W. F. Oakeshott, *Winchester College Library before 1750* (Bibliographical Society, 1954); J. M. G. Blakiston, *Winchester College Library in the 18th and early 19th centuries* (Bibliographical Society, 1962); P. Yeats-Edwards, *Short title Catalogue of the Printed Books in the Strong Room of the Fellows' Library* (1973).

Summary
The holdings of the Archives include maps relating to the College estates, nearly all from 18th and 19th centuries.

Those of the Fellows' Library include the collection bequeathed by E. G. Box, which includes road-books with maps from the 16th century to the early 19th century.

Detail
1, 6a, 7, 8, 9, 10a, 11, 12, 17a

Publications of maps held
For maps from the Fellows' Library:

W. F. Oakeshott, 'Some Classical and Medieval ideas in Renaissance Cosmography'. Reprinted from *Fritz Saxl 1890–1948, a volume of memorial essays*, edited by D. J. Gordon (London, 1959), pp.245–260 and Plate 12.

W. F. Oakeshott, 'Medieval geography in Winchester College Library', *School Library Review* **2** No.2 (1938), 43–80 (Library Association, School Libraries Section).

HEREFORDSHIRE AND WORCESTERSHIRE

74A   Hereford and Worcester Record Office

Address   County Hall, Spetchley Road, Worcester WR5 2NP

Telephone   (01905) 763763 ext. 6350   *Fax*   (01905) 763000

Access   Open, but booking required for maps which are on film. CARN reader's ticket required.

Index
Indexes on site, arranged chronologically, by place and by cartographer etc.
Handlists: plans deposited with the Quarter Sessions; tithe and enclosure plans; plans deposited with the former Worcestershire County Council.

Summary
The main holdings of maps comprise:
(1) Maps held on deposit with the Quarter Sessions Court and those held by the former Worcestershire County Council by statutory deposit, such as enclosure plans and awards and plans of public undertakings such as canals and railways.
(2) Microfilms of Worcestershire tithe plans held at the Public Record Office.
(3) Microfilms of OS maps, 1st edition, 25 inches to 1 mile, for Worcestershire (1882–90).
(4) OS maps at 6 and 25 inches to 1 mile of Worcestershire, from the 1880s to the present day.

Detail
5, 6a,b, 10a,b,c, 12, 13, 14, 15, 17a,c

Publications of maps held
B. S. Smith, 'The Dougharty family of Worcester, estate surveyors and mapmakers, 1700–1760', *Worcestershire Historical Society, New Series* **5** (1967).

74B Hereford and Worcester Record Office

Address   St Helen's Church, Fish Street, Worcester WR1 2HN

Telephone   (01905) 763763 ext. 5922

Access   Open. CARN reader's ticket required.

Index
Indexes on site, arranged chronologically, by place and by cartographer etc.
Handlists: plans deposited with the Quarter Sessions; tithe and enclosure plans; plans deposited with the former Worcestershire County Council.

Summary
The main holdings of maps comprise:
(1) Copies of tithe maps for the majority of parishes in the Diocese of Worcester.
(2) Large numbers of privately-deposited estate and other maps.
(3) 19th century canal, property and other plans amongst the Worcester Corporation's archives.
Of particular interest are some 67 maps of Worcester, dating from 1577 to the 19th century, collected by Alderman Palfrey of Stourbridge. They include maps by Christopher Saxton, John Speed and John Ogilby.

Detail
5, 6a,b, 10a,b,c, 11, 12, 13, 14, 15, 16, 17a,c,

Publications of maps held
B. S. Smith, 'The Dougharty family of Worcester, estate surveyors and
  mapmakers, 1700–1760', *Worcestershire Historical Society, New Series*
  5 (1967), 138–80.

74C Hereford Record Office

Address   The Old Barracks, Harold Street, Hereford HR1 2QX

Telephone   (01432) 265441

Access   Open, but booking required for maps which are on film.
               CARN reader's ticket required.

Index
Handlist to maps on site.

Summary

The holdings comprise:

(1) Manuscript maps held by the former County Council by statutory deposit, that is, enclosure awards, plans of public undertakings, such as turnpikes, canals, railways etc.

(2) The Records of the Diocese of Hereford which include Diocesan copies of tithe maps for the majority of parishes.

(3) Large numbers of privately deposited estate maps.

In all these cases, archive provenance is of primary importance in evaluating the evidence contained in the plans.

One collection of special interest is a fine series of 74 printed maps from the County collection by George Marshall of Breinton. These maps range in date from Christopher Saxton's maps of 1577 to modern OS maps.

Detail

5, 6a,b, 7, 10a,b,c, 11, 12, 13, 14, 15, 17a,b,c

75   Hereford Cathedral Library

Address   The Cathedral, Hereford HR1 2NG

Telephone   (01432) 359880   *Fax*   (01432) 355929

Access   By appointment.

Index

Card index of loose printed maps, catalogued within the estates to which they appertain, separate list of maps held, on site.

Summary

Printed maps:

(1) Maps in printed volumes: British Isles in Ptolemy, *De Geographia* (Ulm, 1486) and Strabo, *Rerum Geographicarum,* (1571).

County maps in William Camden's *Britannia*, by Christopher Saxton in the edition of 1610, and by Robert Morden in the editions of 1695, and 1653.

(2) Separate maps of the county of Hereford: about 30 maps, c.1607–1850, mounted in albums or framed, including those of Christopher Saxton from Camden's *Britannia* (1607, 1637 and 1665), John Speed (1610), Blaeu (1645), Jan Jansson (1646), Richard Blome (1673), Robert Morden (*c.*1695), Herman Moll (*c.*1724) and (1753), Emanuel Bowen (*c.*1749), Greenwood (1834). John Ogilby's 'Road from Hereford to Leicester' and 'Road from Bristol to Chester' (*c.*1698).

(3) Plans of the city of Hereford, by Taylor (1757) and Cole (1806).
Manuscript maps:
Estate maps and surveys of properties of the Dean and Chapter, Dignitaries, Prebendaries, the vicars Choral of Herefordshire, late 18th to early 19th centuries. Estate maps for Hospital Charities, St Ethelbert's Hospital (Herefs.), St Katharine's, Ledbury (Herefs./Glos. border) and other charities endowed with estates in Radnorshire, 18th to 19th centuries.

Detail
1, 6a, 7, 11, 17a,c

The Hereford Mappa Mundi

Now in the care of Trustees, this famous map was made in Lincoln by Richard of Haldingham, *c.*1285, with the Welsh castles added *c.*1289. The British Isles are rendered in some detail.

HERTFORDSHIRE

76   Hertfordshire Record Office

Address   County Hall, Hertford SG13 8DE

Telephone   (01992) 555105   *Fax*   (01992) 555644

Access   Open. CARN reader's ticket or Hertford Record Office day ticket required.

Index
A Catalogue of Manuscript Maps in the Hertfordshire Record Office (Hertford, 1969), covering manuscript enclosure, tithe, and estate maps to 1850 and continued in typescript on site.

Summary
The Office holds a large collection of printed and manuscript maps dating from the 16th to the 19th centuries, as well as photocopies or photographs of a few local maps held in other collections or in private hands. The printed maps include a good series of county maps from Christopher Saxton's map of 1577 and including the larger-scale surveys produced by A. Dury and J. Andrews in 1766 and Andrew Bryant in 1822. A fairly good series of mid to late 19th century OS maps of the county at 1, 6, and 25 inch scales; deposited plans relating to canal, railway, gas, electricity, waterworks and sewerage projects; and miscellaneous plans from sale particulars. The manuscript maps include enclosure and tithe maps, the latter covering as a whole probably in excess of 85% of the total area of the county, and road diversion maps from the Quarter Sessions records, but in the main consist of estate maps, those from the archives relating to the Ashridge, Gorhambury and Panshanger estates being particularly notable for both quantity and quality.

Detail
3, 5, 6a,b, 7, 9, 10a,b,c, 11, 12, 13, 14, 15, 17a,b,c

Publications of maps held
H. G. Fordham, 'Hertfordshire maps: a descriptive catalogue of maps of the county, 1579–1900', *Transactions of the Hertfordshire Natural History Society*, (1901–3–5 and 1907).

D. Hodson, *The printed maps of Hertfordshire, 1577–1900* (Folkestone: Dawson, 1974).

V. G. Scott and T. Rook, *County maps and histories of Hertfordshire* (London: Quiller Press, 1989).

HUMBERSIDE

77   South Humberside Area Archive Office

Address   Town Hall Square, Grimsby DN31 1HX

Telephone   (01472) 353481

Access   Open.

Index
Maps dating before 1880 are summarised in *Guide to the South Humberside Area Archive Office* (1993).
Lists of all maps dating before 1947, on site.

Summary
All maps relate to the ancient county of Lincolnshire. There is no map collection as such; maps, both printed and manuscript, have been deposited with the archives of the various public bodies for which this Office is the offical repository, as well as by private owners. The earliest map held is of Humberston manor (1707).
Among the Parliamentary enclosure awards, deposited by parish councils, are maps for Barnoldby le Beck (1770), Great Grimsby (1840) and Scawby (1771).
Large-scale printed maps of 19th century Grimsby.
Goad Fire Insurance plans for Grimsby.
The Sheffield Papers, listed at NRA, transferred from the Scunthorpe Borough Museum to this Office, include many estate surveys dating from the 18th and 19th centuries.

Detail
10c, 11, 12, 16

Facsimiles and reproductions for sale
Dyeline copies of the 1840 enclosure map of Great Grimsby (town centre only).

78   Hull City Record Office

Address   79 Lowgate, Hull HU1 2AA

Telephone   (01482) 595102 / 595110   *Fax*   (01482) 595062

Access   Open.

Index

No index to maps.
Lists of individual archive groups, which include maps, on site and at
   NRA.

Summary

Published maps, including OS, for Hull and district, from the 18th
century.
Manuscript maps forming part of archival collections, mostly Hull and
adjacent areas.
Marine charts, mostly relating to the River Humber, and including both
published and private (notably Humber Conservancy) charts.

Detail

7, 8, 10a,b,c, 11, 12, 13, 15

79   University of Hull, Brynmor Jones Library

Address   Cottingham Road, Hull HU6 7RX

Telephone   (01482) 465265   *Fax*   (01482) 466205

Access   By appointment; apply in writing to the University
           Archivist.

Index

B. Dyson, *Yorkshire maps and plans in the archives of the University of
   Hull* (Hull: University of Hull Centre for Regional and Local History,
   1990).
Items in the Archives are listed in detailed calendars.
Local (Yorkshire) items are entered on computer database.
Card catalogue of items held in the Map Room, on site.

Summary

The Library's holdings are located in two places.
The Division of Archives and Special Collections in the Main Library

building contains about 2000 maps for this period, most relating to Yorkshire and South Humberside. There are manuscript maps and plans of local landed estates, as well as antiquarian and printed maps. The earliest map dates from 1604. Holdings of enclosure plans are particularly interesting, and are frequently complemented by matching pre-enclosure plans.

The separately located University Map Room also holds about 460 antiquarian and printed maps, including facsimiles of maps from the mid-13th century onwards for all parts of the British Isles.

Detail
1, 2, 3, 4, 5, 6a,b, 7, 10b, 11, 12, 15, 16

Facsimiles and reproductions on sale
'Bishop-ricke of Durham, Cumberland, Westmoreland, York-shire and parte of Linconshire' by Wenceslaus Hollar (1640s).
'East Riding of Yorkshire' (1753) and 'North Riding of Yorkshire' (1785) by Emanuel Bowen.
'Famous map of the County of York' by Thomas Dix (1820).
'East Riding of Yorkshire' by Christopher Greenwood (c.1831).
'Railway and telegraph map of Yorkshire' by G. F. Crutchley (c.1865).

KENT

80A   Kent Archives

Address   Centre for Kentish Studies, County Hall, Maidstone
                 ME14 1XQ

Telephone   (01622) 694363

Access   Open but appointment recommended. CARN reader's
                 ticket. Fee payable by overseas researchers.

Index
F. Hull, *Catalogue of Estate Maps, 1590–1840* (Maidstone: Kent County
   Council, 1973). Other maps are referred to in F. Hull, *Guide to the
   Kent County Archives Office* (Maidstone: Kent County Council, 1958),
   the *First Supplement* (1971), and E. Melling (ed.) *Second Supplement,
   material added 1969–80* (1983).
Typescript catalogue of maps, and index of printed plans on site.

Summary
Principally a collection of estate maps from *c.*1590 but supplemented by
official plans, e.g. the Rochester Diocesan set of tithe maps; some
parochial copies for Canterbury Diocese; sewers maps from *c.*1640
especially Romney Marsh area; deposited plans of public utilities; and a
few waste-land enclosure maps. Printed plans of Kent and of the Channel
coast from *c.*1590.
OS maps from Mudge onwards, but incomplete.
Photocopies of some early estate maps still in private ownership within
the county.

Detail
5, 6a,b, 7, 10a,b,c, 11, 12, 13, 14, 15, 17a,b

Publications of maps held
F. Hull, *Catalogue of Estate Maps, 1590–1840* (1973).
F. Hull, *Kentish maps and mapmakers* (1973).

Facsimiles and reproductions for sale
Symonson's 'Kent'(1719) engraved by Samuel Parker.

195

80B Thanet Branch Archive Office

Address   Ramsgate Library, Guildford Lawn, Ramsgate, CT11 9AY

Telephone   (01843) 593532   *Fax* (01843) 852692

Access   Open.

Index
Unpublished handlists, catalogues and card index on site.
Published catalogues for the former Kent Archives Office only.

Summary
The Archive collection includes printed County series of Ramsgate area; manuscript maps, plans and drawings of plots and estates in Thanet area and Ramsgate Harbour.
The Local Studies Library collection has printed large scale maps of Ramsgate and the surrounding area.

Detail
6b, 7, 10b,c, 11, 13

80C Rochester upon Medway Studies Centre

Address   Civic Centre, Strood, Rochester ME2 4AW

Telephone   (01634) 732714   *Fax* (01634) 732756

Access   Local Studies Library open; Archives by appointment.

Index
Card index to maps in Local Studies collection, which includes street index to OS 25 inch to 1 mile county series. Catalogue and card index to maps and plans in Archives.
F. Hull, *Guide to the Kent County Archives* (1958) partly relates to collections held at this office.

Summary
Local Studies:
Chatham fortifications: large scale plans, various dates from about 1886 onwards, showing interior details.
Tithe maps for Rochester and Chatham.
OS maps, 1st and 2nd editions onwards, at 25 inches to the mile. Also 1:500 Town centre maps, late 19th century onwards.
Estate maps, 17th and 18th centuries.

Maps and plans of the River Medway, various dates.

Archives:
(1) Local Authority archives, especially City of Rochester and Borough of Chatham, mainly 19th century, and local (Kent).
(2) Some parish tithe and enclosure maps, mainly 18th to 20th centuries, and local (Kent).
(3) Many maps in family estate collections, e.g. Darnley of Cobham Hall, and Best of Boxley and Chatham, including the south-east of England and Kent, mainly 18th to 20th centuries.

Detail
6a, 7, 8, 9, 10b,c, 11, 12, 13, 14, 15, 16, 17a,b,c

81   Heritage Room, Kent Arts and Libraries

Address	Folkestone Library, 2 Grace Hill, Folkestone CT20 1HD
Telephone	(01303) 850123 *Fax* (01303) 242907
Access	Open, but a few days notice is needed to produce some maps and plans which are in a distant store.

Index
Kent Maps and Plans (Library Association, 1992) includes Library Collections throughout Kent, and some Archives Offices, though not South East Kent in detail.
Card catalogue for Archives, on site.
Card Catalogue for Local Studies, in preparation.

Summary
The Heritage Service based at Folkestone Library covers the Local Studies Collection, the South East Kent Archives Office and Folkestone Museum. The collections are rich in material on the whole of the Shepway District Area, including Folkestone, Hythe, Capel, Romney Marsh and Elham Valley.

The Archives Office holds maps within the records of the Folkestone Town Council, such as Borough Engineers Plans, lighting and sewers; private company papers, and sales particulars. Other maps include the Royal Military Canal, Shorncliffe Camp and various railway plans.

The Local Studies Collection holds Hills' 'Cheriton' (manuscript, 1713), various printed maps of the area, plus early maps and plans for the Radnor Estate and the South Eastern Railway and Harbour.

OS maps: Folkestone, at 10 feet to the mile and at 50 inches to the mile (1873), at 25 inches to the mile (1887); for Shepway, at 6 inches to the mile (1877 and 1898), and at 25 inches to the mile (1898).

Detail
6a, 10a,b,c, 17a

82 Canterbury Cathedral Archives

Address   The Precincts, Canterbury CT1 2EH

Telephone   (01227) 463510   *Fax*   (01227) 762897

Access   By appointment. CARN reader's ticket required. Fee payable by overseas researchers.

Index
Unpublished catalogues of tithe maps, of estate maps, and of some city plans.

Summary
A collection of about 150 Cathedral estate maps and plans of the City, 18th and 19th centuries; a few printed maps; 2 maps of Canterbury, 16th and early 17th centuries; books of maps and plans of the city, 18th and early 19th centuries; sketch map of Cliff marshes, c.1385; maps of Kent. 'Les glorieuses conquêtes du Roy de France' (1694). Some 19th century railway maps; tithe maps for Canterbury diocese parishes.

Detail
7, 9, 10b,c, 11, 13, 14, 17a

Publications of maps held
F. Hull, 'Cliffe, Kent, late 14th century', in R. A. Skelton and P. D. A. Harvey (eds), *Local maps and plans from medieval England* (Oxford, 1986), pp.99–105 illustrates the map of Cliff.

Facsimiles and reproductions on sale
Kent, by Cary (1787), by Seller (1710), by Speed (1611).
Plan of Wye (1746). Thanet by Hall (1792).

83   Maidstone Museum and Art Gallery

Address   St Faith's Street, Maidstone ME14 1LH

Telephone   (01622) 794497   *Fax*   (01622) 602193

Access   By appointment.

Index
Card index to estate maps on site.

Summary
Estate maps throughout Kent; some parish maps; town plans; OS maps. Mostly printed, with a few manuscript maps on a very small scale, e.g. local parishes. Dates from 1626 but mostly from the 1840s. OS maps, 1868 onwards.

Detail
6a, 10b,c, 11

84   Institution of Royal Engineers

Address   Brompton Barracks, Chatham ME4 4UG.

84A   Royal Engineers Library

Telephone   (01634) 844555 ext. 2416

Access   By appointment.

Index
No index to maps.

Summary
The collection consists of documents, photographs, maps and plans relating to the history of military engineering worldwide.
OS and Geological Survey of Great Britain and Ireland.
17th and 18th century maps and plans of military installations and European cities.
There is a section dealing with military survey as the Royal Engineers not only produced maps for the armed forces but were involved in many international boundary surveys in the 18th and 19th century.

Detail
1, 7, 8, 9, 10a,b,c

84B   Royal Engineers Museum

Telephone   (01634) 406397   *Fax*   (01634) 822371

Access   By appointment.

Index
Card index on site.

Summary
The maps are miscellaneous and do not form part of any official or working collection. They have been deposited by various army departments and individuals.
Plans and surveys of Medway, Chatham Dockyard, forts and landward defences, late 17th to mid-19th century.
Miscellaneous 19th century barracks plans.
Military maps, e.g. maps for Colonel Twiss's report on the defence of Ireland, 1803.
Plans of Dover Castle, Gravesend blockhouse, Newhaven fort, Portsmouth forts, Plymouth, Pendennis Castle, Yarmouth etc., mainly 18th century.

Detail
1, 4, 6b, 7, 8, 9, 10a,b, 11

Facsimiles and reproductions for sale
'Plan of Chatham Lines shewing their state in the Year 1786'.

85   Rochester Bridge Trust

Address   The Bridge Chamber, 5 The Esplanade, Rochester ME1 1QE

Telephone   (01634) 843457 / 846706   *Fax*   (01634) 840125

Access   By appointment.

Index
Maps are summarised in *Rochester Bridge Trust and the New College of Cobham, Kent: Guide to the classification and indexing of records* (1954).

Summary

The Trust's collection of some 120 maps includes plans and drawings of River Medway bridges, estate map book (1717), and individual estate maps of Rochester, 1687 onwards, Delce and Nashenden, 1596 onwards, Dartford, 1596 onwards, Faversham, 1596 onwards, Frindsbury, 1767 onwards, Gillingham, 1882, Isle of Grain, early 17th century onwards, Halstow, 1717 and 19th century, Langdon, 1596 onwards, Strood, 1695 onwards, London, Leadenhall Street, 1687 onwards, Tilbury (Essex), 1735 onwards.

In the New College holding there are 12 surveys and maps of Chalke, Shorne and West Thurrock (Essex), 1598–1885.

Detail

11

LANCASHIRE

86   Lancashire Record Office

Address   Bow Lane, Preston PR1 2RE

Telephone   (01772) 263039   *Fax*   (01772) 263050

Access   Open. CARN reader's ticket required.

Index

R. Sharp France, *Guide to the Lancashire Record Office* (Preston, 1985) and J. D. Martin, *Supplement, 1977–1989* (Preston, 1992).
Typescript handlist of county maps, on site.

Summary

The core collection consists of OS maps from 1845, enclosure maps, and for those areas not enclosed before 1836, a fine collection of sealed tithe maps and awards. In addition there are Parliamentary deposited plans for all road, rail, canal and utility undertakings, dating from 1792 to the late 19th century.

The local authority collections contain boundary maps, and occasionally, as in the case of Preston, sewerage plans, *c.*1850 and 1890, while the Preston Medical Officer of Health reports *c.*1890 include maps showing the incidence of infectious diseases.

The Office has notable collections of estate records including those of Lord Derby's and Lord Sefton's estates, both of which contain a number of maps. Also of particular note are the plans of the coal workings in the Burnley coalfield which survive among the Kay-Shuttleworth estate papers. The estate maps date from the 16th century and include a colourful map of Burtonwood, *c.*1580 and one of Penwortham, *c.*1590. Among the 17th century holdings are a series of plans showing the roads from Lancaster to Warrington. These are dated 1684 and are thought to have been drawn by Dr Kuerden during his research for a history of Lancashire, which was never published.

Detail

5, 6a,b, 7, 10b,c, 11, 12, 13, 14, 15, 17a

87   Lancashire District Libraries, Local History Collections

Address   Market Square, Lancaster LA1 1HY

Telephone   (01524) 63266

Access   Open.

Index

Drawn-out map index for 25 and 50 inch plans, and sheaf catalogue on site.

Summary

Lancaster Library is an official Manorial repository. Its holdings include printed and manuscript maps. The main sources of maps are (1) Lancaster Borough and City Administration; (2) Family and estate documents; (3) Lancaster Port Commissioners, there are a few plans of the Port of Lancaster and Glasson Dock; (4) others acquired by purchase.

Detail

1, 5, 6a,b, 7, 8, 10a,b,c, 11, 12, 13, 14, 15, 17a,b,c

Facsimiles and reproductions on sale

Lancashire, by Christopher Saxton (1577), by Robert Morden (1695), by Yates (1786), by Greenwood (1818). Yorkshire by Christopher Saxton (1577). Harrison and Sale's guide to the East Lancashire Railway map (1849). Leeds to Liverpool Canal map (1770).

LEICESTERSHIRE

88   Leicestershire Record Office

Address   Long Street, Wigston Magna, Leicester LE18 2AH

Telephone   (01162) 571080   *Fax*   (01162) 571120

Access   Open.

Index

Reports 1 to 7 of the former Leicestershire County Record Office.

B. L. Gimson and P. Russell, *Leicester maps, a brief survey* (Leicester, 1947). The Leicestershire Record Office holds examples of most of the maps illustrated and described in this publication.

Lists and schedules on site, some duplicated at NRA.

Summary

Chief groups are tithe and enclosure maps, estates maps, deposited maps and plans of railways, canals etc., and printed county and OS maps at all scales. The areas covered are the former counties of Leicester, Rutland and the City of Leicester. The date range is mainly within 17th to 20th centuries.

Detail

1, 5, 6a,b, 7, 10a,b,c, 11, 12, 13, 14, 15, 16, 17a,c

Publications of maps held

B. L. Gimson and P. Russell, *Leicester maps, a brief survey* (Leicester, 1947).

P. K. Baum, *Antique Maps of Leicestershire* (Leicester, 1972).

Facsimiles and reproductions on sale

J. Blaeu, 'Leicestershire' (1645) and 'Rutland' (1663). Plan of Leicester by J. Fowler (1828), plan of Hinckley by J. Robinson (1782), plan of Oakham (1787), Leicester by J. and T. Spence (1879).

LINCOLNSHIRE

89   Lincolnshire Archives

Address   St Rumbold Street, Lincoln LN2 5AB

Telephone   (01522) 525158   *Fax*   (01522) 530047

Access   Open, advance notice preferred. CARN reader's ticket required.

Index
Card indexes on site:
(1) General, arranged alphabetically by parish.
(2) Separate indexes to enclosure and tithe awards.
Archivists' Reports vols 1–26 (1948–77) have been indexed up to 1968 and give separate entries for maps and plans.

Summary
There is no map collection as such but maps are found in many archive collections, including those of the Diocese of Lincoln and the former county councils of Lindsey, Kesteven and Holland. They include enclosure and tithe maps, deposited plans of public undertakings such as railways and canals, estate plans in various private deposits, etc. There are a few early maps but most date from the 18th and 19th centuries.

Detail
1, 2, 3, 4, 6a, 7, 8, 9, 10a,b,c, 11, 12, 13, 14, 15, 17a,b

Publications of maps held
Ray Carroll (ed.), *The Printed Maps of Lincolnshire, 1576–1900: a cartobibliography* (Lincolnshire Record Society, forthcoming).

90   Lincolnshire Library Service, Lincolnshire Collection

Address   Reference Library, Free School Lane, Lincoln LN2 1EZ
             NB The Lincolnshire Collection will be rehoused during 1994–6 while a new library is built.

Telephone   (01522) 549160   *Fax*   (01522) 535882

Access   Open.

Index
Sheaf catalogue, Vol 1. to the City of Lincoln, Vols 2 and 3 to the parishes, arranged alphabetically.
Card index to railway plans. Other typewritten lists on site.

Summary
The maps are mostly printed and from the 19th century onwards, but include some earlier ones of the county (from 1756) and of the city (from 1610) and castle. There is a small collection of railway plans, 1840s to 1880s. Modern reconstructions by R. C. Russell of Lincoln enclosure maps between 1740 and 1822, illustrating the changes from strip to field farming.

Detail
1, 6a,b, 7, 10a,b,c, 11, 12, 13, 14, 15

Publications of maps held
Ray Carroll (ed.), *The Printed Maps of Lincolnshire, 1576–1900: a cartobibliography* (Lincolnshire Record Society, forthcoming).

91   Lincolnshire City and County Museum

Address   Broadgate, Lincoln LN2 1HQ

Telephone   (01522) 530401

Access   By appointment.

Index
Handlist to maps of Lincolnshire in the county's museums and elsewhere, on site.

Summary
County maps of Lincolnshire, road maps by John Ogilby and others; town plans of principal Lincolnshire towns, and a few estate or area maps. A copy of A. Armstrong's original 1 inch to the mile map of Lincolnshire (1766/9), with list of subscribers. Copies of 1st edition 1 inch OS map of Lincolnshire.

Detail
6 7, 8, 10a, 11, 15ba

92   Spalding Gentlemen's Society

Address   Broad Street, Spalding PE11 1TB

Telephone   (01775) 724658

Access   By appointment.

Index
None.

Summary
Seventy six maps, mainly printed maps and plans relating to Lincolnshire, with particular reference to Spalding and its environs. The earliest authoritative local map is an excellent detailed map of Spalding, 1732. There are two John Ogilby maps of 1675, and several surveys of Lincolnshire, including those by A. Armstrong (1776), by Bryant (1818), and by C. and J. Greenwood (surveyed in 1827–8, published in 1831). There is also a map of London in 1560 (engraving by Vertue of 1743).

Detail
6b, 8, 10a,b,c, 11, 12, 15, 17a

GREATER LONDON

93 Bank of England, Archive and Records Management Section

Address Threadneedle Street, London EC2R 8AH

Telephone (0171) 601 4889 / 5096 *Fax* (0171) 601 5808

Access By appointment.

Index
Typewritten catalogue of maps and plans on site.

Summary
The main map collection is listed under two headings:
'Premises, site and surroundings, 1677–1934' contains site plans, street plans of wards and plans of Sir John Houblon's house and garden (including some modern copies). An engraved plan of Broad Street and Cornhill Wards, 1755, by Benjamin Cole.
'Premises, building and rebuilding, 1731–1945' shows plans of the Bank and alterations during its period on the present site. They include work by John Tracy, 1731, and Richard Grimes, ?c.1731; Thomas Malton, 1790; R. Morris, c.1790, Sir John Soane (Rotunda, alterations in Lothbury, 1795–1812), Walter Payne (1824–34), William Hayward, Surveyor to the City, 1847.

Detail
7, 10, 17c

94 St Bartholomew's Hospital, Archives Department

Address West Smithfield, London EC1A 7BE

Telephone (0171) 601 8152 Fax (0171) 601 7899

Access By appointment.

Index
Typescript catalogues of planbooks and maps, 16th to 20th centuries, on site.
Database catalogue in course of preparation will supersede existing typescripts.

Summary
Maps of the Hospital site in London and of the Hospital's estate property in London, Middx., Cambs., Essex, Hants., Herefs., Herts., Kent, Lincs., Northants., Oxon., Somerset, Surrey and Warwicks. The earliest are by Ralph Tresswell, 1587, of Hospital properties in Downham, Hatfield Broadoak, Little Burstead and Little Wakering (Essex), and Bishop's Stortford (Herts.). Other estate maps are dated between 1588 and 1957. Plans of the Hospital site date from the early 17th century onwards.

Detail
11

Publications of maps held
Reproductions of early 17th century plans of the Hospital site, from a planbook attributed to Martin Llewellyn, were published by the London Topographical Society in 1950–5.

95   Bishopsgate Institution

Address   230 Bishopsgate, London EC2M 4QH

Telephone   (0171) 247 8895   *Fax*   (0171) 638 2249

Access   Open.

Index
Card catalogue, arranged chronologically and by author etc., on site.
Card catalogue of deeds; List of documents relating to the Tillard Estate, both of which contain some plans.

Summary
A collection of over 1000 maps, covering the London area only, c.1650 to the present, with emphasis on the City. All major London area maps are represented, by originals or reproductions, Most substantial holdings after 1850. A few manuscript maps, of St Helen's (Bishopsgate) parish (1816), of a field at Hoxton, (?late 18th century); of properties in and near Devonshire Square (1767), and north of Camomile St (1787), of St Botolph parish, c.1860.

There are deeds from the late 15th century which, from about 1800 onwards, often have maps or plans attached. The Tillard Estate, Spitalfields (1716–1914) has some plans, mostly from the later 19th century.

Detail
7, 10a,b,c, 11, 15, 17b

96 British Museum, Department of Prints and Drawings

Address   Great Russell Street, London WC1B 3DG

Telephone   (0171) 636 1555   *Fax*   (0171) 323 8999

Access   Reader's ticket normally required. Visitors may be admitted with a letter of introduction for a single visit. In some cases identification by means of a valid passport may be required.

Index
Antony Griffiths and Reginald Williams, *The Department of Prints and Drawings in the British Museum: User's Guide* (London, British Museum, 1987), describes the scope of the collection, and its many indexes, catalogues and other lists.

Summary
The Department has never collected maps, and many that were once in its holdings were transferred to the Map Room of the British Museum, now the British Library, and to the Department of Manuscripts, as appropriate. There are however some important atlases and maps, collected partly by accident and partly as examples of engraving. The bound volumes include Ptolemy's *Cosmographia*, 1462 (i.e. 1477), Berlinghieri's *Geographia*, Florence, 1482, Ptolemy's *Cosmographia*, Rome, 1508, Saxton's *Atlas of England and Wales*, c.1579, Richard Blome, *England exactly described or a guide to travellers in a complete set of the counties of England*, London, 1715.
Of the sheet maps, a large number are bound in various extra-illustrated volumes as follows: Edward Hyde, first Earl of Clarendon (1609–74), *The History of the Rebellion and Civil War in England*, 1702–4, extra-illustrated and bound in 8 fol. vols, 1796 with manuscript index. Bulstrode Whitelocke (1605–75), *Memorials of the English Affairs, from the beginning of the Reign of King Charles the First, to King Charles the Second his happy Restauration*, 1st edition, 1682., extra-illustrated with 579 prints

and bound in two folio vols. in 1796, with manuscript index (Companion to Clarendon's *History*). Thomas Pennant (1726–98), *Some Account of London*, 1793 (1st edition was 1790: this is 3rd edition), extra-illustrated and bound in 14 folio vols by John Charles Crowle, with manuscript index. Vol.XIII is especially important and includes 16 large scale maps of London from the 16th to 18th centuries. Thomas Pennant, *Some account of London, Westminster and Southwark*, printed for the illustrator (n.d., c.1942). Extra-illustrated with 1607 illustrations by Hermann Marx between 1938 and 1942.

The maps in the Crace Collection, assembled by Frederick Crace (1779–1859) mainly between 1829 and 1859, were transferred to the Map Room in 1933, and the views were retained in the Department of Prints and Drawings. (See *A Catalogue of maps, plans and views of London, Westminster and Southwark, collected and arranged by Frederick Crace*, edited by his son John Gregory Crace, 1878.) There are, however, some other maps in the Crace Supplement, which comprises the rest of the Department's collection of London typography arranged in the same order as the Crace collection. The entire Crace collection is available on microfilm.

Examples of most of Wenceslaus Hollar's maps are held, including the unique impression of the West Central district of London.

The Schreiber collection of fans, presented by Lady Charlotte Schreiber (1812–95) includes a map of Westminster (unmounted) and a map of Warwickshire (mounted). The collections of trade cards include those of map and chart sellers. There are many sets of geographical playing cards bequeathed by Lady Charlotte Schreiber. They include the only complete set of the most famous English geographical cards, signed W. B. of 1590.

Detail
1, 2, 3, 4, 7

97   Brunel University Library

Address   Kingston Lane, Uxbridge UB8 3PH

Telephone   (01895) 274000   *Fax*   (01895) 232806

Access   Open.

Index
The Airey and Railway Clearing House maps are listed in *Railway maps and the Railway Clearing House* (Brunel University Library, 1986).

Summary
The Transport History Collection includes the Garnett map collection, mainly 19th century maps relating to railway history but also many OS and Bartholomew maps. The collection is particularly strong in Airey and Railway Clearing House maps and junction diagrams.

Detail
1, 2, 3, 4, 10a, 13

98   Church Commissioners

Address   1 Millbank, London SW1P 3JZ

Telephone   (0171) 222 7010   *Fax*   (0171) 233 0171

Access   Restricted; strictly a library of last resort. Recommended approach is through County Record Office in the area of interest.

Index
No index to maps.

Summary
A collection which has accumulated over the years in connection with the work of the Church Commissioners, and their predecessors the Governors of Queen Anne's Bounty and the Ecclesiastical Commissioners. A great number are still referred to in connection with present day matters.
There are four groups of material: (1) cuttings from maps on which the Commissioners' land agents marked the properties which passed to the Commissioners from 1840 onwards; (2) maps which Bishopric and Chapter Estate managers passed to the Commissioners with their estates. These date from the 17th century forwards. These maps have in the main been passed to CROs but some of the estates lie outside the proper area of the Bishopric. (3) an incomplete set of OS maps from 1860 marked with ecclesiastical parish boundaries; (4) copies of sealed maps relating to Orders in Council dealing with changes in parish boundaries, the originals now at PRO, in the Privy Council register, class PC 2.

Detail
11, 17c

99 The Clothworkers' Company

Address   Clothworkers' Hall, Dunster Court, Mincing Lane, London EC3R 7AH

Telephone   (0171) 623 7041   *Fax*   (0171) 283 1289

Access   By written appointment, after supplying details of study and a written reference.

Index
No index to maps.

Summary
All maps are manuscript and connected strictly with the Company's properties in London, Essex, Kent and Ulster at dates between the Company's incorporation in 1528 and the present.

Detail
11

Publications of maps held
J. Schofield, *The London Survey of Ralph Treswell* (London Topographical Society, Pub. 135, 1987).

100 Duchy of Cornwall

Address   10 Buckingham Gate, London SW1E 6LA

Telephone   (0171) 834 7346

Access   By written appointment.

Index
The catalogue is being revised, along with the collection.

Summary
The collections relating to the Duchy's extensive holdings are at present undergoing major revision. At the time of going to press, no date could be given for completion of this work.

Detail
1, 10a, 11, 17a

101 Geological Society Library

Address   Burlington House, Piccadilly, London W1V 0JU

Telephone   (0171) 734 5673   *Fax*   (0171) 439 8975

Access   The Archives Collection is open to bona fide researchers by appointment with the Hon. Archivist. (The General Library Map Collection is restricted to members only).

Index

Catalogue of books and maps in the Library of the Geological Society of London (1846, with Supplements, 1856, 1860, 1863). (This catalogue includes some material now in the Archives).

Handlist of manuscript maps in the Archives.

List of maps in the Greenough Collection.

Sheppard's list of 19th century geological maps of the British Isles, unpublished, all on site.

Summary

Manuscript maps and field mapping by 19th century geologists, among these, Roderick Impey Murchison (1792–1871), George Bellas Greenough (1778–1855), Charles Moore of Bath (1815–81) and William Smith (1769–1839). Original manuscript maps include L. A. Necker's geological map of Scotland (1808) and John Farey's geological sections through England (1807–12).

The Greenough Collection comprises printed maps from Britain and worldwide, mostly with geological annotations.

Detail
5

102 Inner Temple Library

Address   The Honourable Society of the Inner Temple, London EC4Y 7DA

Telephone   (0171) 797 8217   *Fax*   (0171) 797 8224

Access   By written appointment with letter of recommendation. (Library of last resort).

Index

Typed handlist of maps and plans on site.

Catalogue of the Library of Inner Temple (1833) is a class catalogue with atlases and maps included under 'Geography, topography, voyages and travels'.

Summary
Small collection of printed atlases, charts and maps, of 18th and 19th century date. Specialist material related to maps, plans and drawings of the Temple and Inner Temple (1863) as well as documents of interest to lawyers such as Irish Railway Commission material – plans and sections of lines, 1837–8.

Detail
1, 6a, 7, 10a, 11, 13

103   The Leathersellers' Company

Address   15 St Helen's Place, London EC3A 6DQ

Telephone   (0171) 588 4615

Access   By written appointment.

Index
No index to maps.

Summary
The Company possesses title deeds to properties from 1600 onwards but these are unlisted and have to be sought amongst the general collection of deeds and other documents. There is a bound volume of 'Plans of the Estates belonging to the ... Leathersellers ... and to Various Trusts under their Management situate in the City and the counties of Kent, Hertford and Middlesex' surveyed by Andrew Wilson, 1871, and another 'Sketch Plan of the Leathersellers' Buildings and Adjacent Property' also by Wilson, 1877. A manuscript copy, 'Plan of the Lewisham Award, 1819', shows place names, proprietors and acreages. 'Plan of Sydenham Common, 1813', by Lance, coloured manuscript. A Sale Plan of estates at Upper Sydenham, 1865.

Detail
11

104 University of London Library, Map Collection

Address	Senate House, Malet Street, London WC1E 7HV
Telephone	(0171) 636 8000 *Fax* (0171) 436 1494
Access	Open to members of the University validated by their school or institute and to others on application. External users may be charged a fee.

Index
Card catalogue arranged by area and date.

Summary
A general collection of world coverage with emphasis on modern maps, but including much material of historical interest, e.g.:
(1) A good selection of London maps, 1572–1900; facsimiles and historical maps from the 13th century to 1900.
(2) All facsimile reproductions of the London Topographical Society.
(3) OS 6 inches to 1 mile, 1st edition, for Ireland and Scotland.
(4) OS 1 inch to 1 mile, 1st edition, for England and Wales.
(5) A good selection of world and regional atlases, originals and facsimiles, Ptolemy to 1900.
(6) A selection of canal, turnpike and railway maps in the Goldsmith's Library (Economic and Social History).
(7) Wyatt Collection of early maps of Buckinghamshire.

Detail
1, 2, 3, 6a, 7, 10a,b, 13, 14

105 Institute of Historical Research Library

Address	Senate House, Malet Street, London WC1E 7HU
Telephone	(0171) 636 0272 *Fax* (0171) 436 2183
Access	Open to members of the Institute, otherwise by appointment.

Index
Classified catalogue of maps and plans on site.

Summary
Collection of printed maps and atlases, some reproductions, principally

dating from the 18th and 19th centuries. Some coverage of British Isles and counties, but strongest in maps of London.

Detail
1, 2, 3, 4, 5, 6a, 7, 9, 10a, 13, 15

106   University of London, King's College

Address   Map Room, Chesham Building, Strand, London WC2R 2LS

Telephone   (0171) 873 2599 (Map Room Office)   *Fax*   (0171) 872 0207
(071) 873 2139 (Library Office)

Access   Open to members of the University, otherwise by appointment.

Index
Unpublished handlists to Atlases and to Antiquarian Maps, also other indexes, on site.

Summary
A collection from the late Professor Wooldridge, of folded geological maps, dating from *c.*1820–1880, extending widely over Britain and elsewhere and including early Geological Survey maps.
A collection of bound atlases dating from *c.*1740 to 1820, believed to have come from the London Institution early this century, including three atlases of sea charts, printed and from various sources, and ten other miscellaneous European atlases.

Detail
5, 8, 10a,b,c

107   University College London, Library

Address   Gower Street, London WC1E 6BT

Telephone   (0171) 387 7050   *Fax*   (0171) 380 7373

Access   Open to members of the University, otherwise on application.

Index
Atlases acquired since 1982 (and some obtained earlier) appear on the

LIBERTAS on-line catalogue. Other atlases are indexed under that heading in the main author catalogue. Card index to maps in the London History Library, arranged alphabetically by author/publisher, also by date and by area covered.

Summary
The London History Library holds about 500 printed maps and atlases of London from the 18th century onwards, including reproductions of some earlier maps. The reproductions are largely those of the London Topographical Society, some local societies and libraries, the Guildhall Library, the London County Council and the Ordnance Survey.
A few maps are held which are not listed in J. Howgego, *Printed maps of London c.1553–1850* (1978) or in R. Hyde, *Printed maps of London, 1851–1900* (1975).

Detail
6a,b, 7, 10a,b,c, 11, 17c

108   The Mercers' Company

Address   Mercers' Hall, Ironmonger Lane, London EC2 8HE

Telephone   (0171) 726 4991

Access   By appointment.

Index
Card indexes on site, to estate archives under name of donors.

Summary
Maps and plans of the Company's properties, principally in the City of London and environs, Kent and Bucks. Other counties represented include Beds., Essex, Glos., Herts., Lincs., Northumb., Shrops., Surrey, and Northern Ireland. The maps date from the 17th century onward.

Detail
11

Publications of maps held
Jean Imray, *The Mercers' Hall* (London Topographical Society, 1991).
I. G. Doolittle, *The Mercers' Company, 1597–1959* (1994).

109   Middle Temple Library

Address   The Worshipful Society of the Middle Temple, Middle Temple Lane, London EC4Y 9BT

Telephone   (0171) 353 4303   *Fax*   (0171) 538 6674

Access   By appointment, following written application to the Librarian.

Index
No index to maps.

Summary
The Society holds some early atlases in its rare books collection and atlases and maps in its later reference collection. The early atlases include various editions of Ortelius: *Theatrum orbis terrarum* (French edition), Antwerp, 1587, (Latin edition), Antwerp 1603, *Thesaurus Geographicus*, Antwerp, 1587; also Camden's *Britannia*, 1695, with other copies and editions; the Mercator-Hondius world atlas, 1636; Herman Moll's *Atlas Royal*, 1708–19.
Later works include 'Maps and Sections of the Railways of Great Britain', George Bradshaw, 1839; 'A New Parliamentary and County Atlas of Great Britain and Ireland', by W. Hughes, A. H. Keane, London, J. S. Virtue, 1885; Stanford's 'Map of Parliamentary Boroughs within the County of London', 1900.
OS 5th edition, one inch to the mile series.

Detail
1, 5, 6a,b, 10a, 13

110   Morden College

Address   19 St German's Place, Blackheath, London SE3 0PW

Telephone   (0181) 858 3365   *Fax*   (0181) 293 4887

Access   By written application to the Clerk to the Trustees.

Index
In process (1994) of being added to the archive database.

Summary
The collection consists mainly of architects' and surveyors' manuscript plans of the Morden College estates at Greenwich Marshes (Manor of Old Court), Maidenstone Hill, Chatham and Rochester (Kent). These

are on vellum, drawn by James Roffen (1732), John Holmes, (1732/39), and Michael Searles senior and junior (1771). A book of manuscript maps on vellum, by Timothy Skinner (*c*.1745), of the Coggeshall area of Essex, where the College has fee-farm property. There is a book of plans dealing with separate properties in the area which was drawn up about the end of the 18th century. The collection also includes numerous surveyors' plans of individual properties and related local areas drawn up in the 18th and 19th centuries, also a map of the mining district of Cardiganshire, in particular Brynglas lead mine.

Detail
5, 10a,b, 11, 13

111   National Maritime Museum

Address	Library, Manuscripts Section and Maritime Information Centre, Romney Road, Greenwich, London SE10 9NF
Telephone	(0181) 312 6672 *Fax* (0181) 312 6632
Access	Printed atlases held in the Library are available on demand. Manuscripts and charts are available by appointment. Access to certain items is restricted but microfilm or facsimile may be available.

Index
National Maritime Museum, Catalogue of the Library, Vol 3, 2 parts (1971) includes only charts and maps in atlases. The NMM Library Catalogue may be consulted via On-Line Public Access (OPAC) terminals in Library.
Handlist of manuscript Sea Charts and Pilot Books executed before 1700 (1973).

Summary
Topographical atlases are in the Caird Library, charts and sea atlases with the Curator of Hydrography, manuscript atlases are in the Manuscripts Section.
The Museum holds a large collection of printed and manuscript charts which aims to provide historical coverage of hydrographic practice and endeavour from the 16th century to the present day. Up to the 18th century the content is international but after 1830 it consists mostly of

British Admiralty charts. A complete set of current British Admiralty charts is also available for reference.

Collections of special interest to historic studies in the British Isles include the Dartmouth collection of manuscript plans of ports and fortifications in the British Isles and Channel Islands (c.1665).

Detail
1, 2, 3, 4, 5, 6a, 7, 8

Publications of maps held
D. Howse and M. Sanderson, *The Sea Chart* (Newton Abbot: David & Charles, 1973).

112 National Army Museum, Department of Archives, Photographs, Film and Sound

Address Royal Hospital Road, London SW3 4HT

Telephone (0171) 730 0717 *Fax* (0171) 823 6573

Access Readers ticket, to be obtained in advance of visit.

Index
Comprehensive card index and calendars of large collections of maps and plans, on site.

Summary
The maps in the Archive Collection are for the most part contained in the papers of officers of the British and Indian Armies. They include both printed and manuscript maps and plans, none earlier than c.1700, and the majority dating from the 19th and 20th centuries. Most are either battle plans, or maps which otherwise illustrate some facet of a military campaign. Maps of the British Isles are not particularly numerous, comprising annotated Ordnance Survey and other maps for use on manoeuvres; plans and maps of camps and fortifications; and road surveys, all later than 1800.

Detail
1, 3, 4, 9, 10a

113 Natural History Museum Library

Address   Cromwell Road, London SW7 5BD

Telephone   (0171) 938 9191   *Fax*   (0171) 938 9290

Access   Readers ticket required, or by appointment.

Index
Card index on site.

Summary
A specialist library but with certain holdings of historical interest. The catalogue indicates about 500 maps published between 1700 and 1900, e.g., the 'Downland Survey' (1840–41). The geological section is strong on maps published between 1800 and 1900, Notable are: 'Mineralogical Map of the Western Counties of England' (1797), Berger's geological map of N. E. Ireland (1816), William Smith's geological maps, and his atlas 'Delineation of the Strata of England and Wales' (1815). A few manuscript maps are held, usually relating to collection of specimens. It is worth noting that the long runs of scientific periodicals also contain important early maps and historical information.

Detail
1, 2, 3, 4, 5, 6a,b, 10a,b,

Publications of maps held
A. G. Davies, 'Notes on Griffith's geological maps of Ireland', *Journal of the Society for the Bibliography of Natural History* **2** (1950), 209–11.
A. G. Davies, 'William Smith's Geological Atlas and the later history of the plates', *Journal of the Society for the Bibliography of Natural History* **2** (1952), 388–95.
J. M. Eyles, 'William Smith (1769–1839): a bibliography of published writings, maps and geological sections, printed and lithographed', *Journal of the Society for the Bibliography of Natural History* **5** (1968), 87–109.

114 The Records of the House of Lords and the House of Commons

Address   Record Office, House of Lords, London SW1A 0PW

Telephone   (0171) 219 3074   *Fax*   (0171) 219 2570

Access   By appointment.

Index
M. F. Bond, *Guide to the Records of Parliament* (HMSO, 1971), pp.71–90 and 229.
Manuscript registers of Deposited Plans (arranged by Parliamentary Session) 1794 to date, on site.
Database of Private Bill Records 1794–1827, on site.

Summary
The collection consists almost entirely of plans of canals, docks and harbours, railways and tramroads, turnpike roads, bridges and other public works. Standing Orders required copies of canal plans to be deposited with each House of Parliament from 1794 onwards, and by 1814 they covered all the other works mentioned. The early plans are often in manuscript and vary from 2 inches to 24 inches to the mile. In 1836 it was specified that railway plans should be at least 4 inches to the mile with enlarged plans ($\frac{1}{2}$ inch to 100 feet) for built-up areas. Most of the plans after the 1830s are printed. Later plans were often drawn on OS sheets and most are prefaced by a small-scale OS map giving an outline of the plan. The deposits continue to the present day.

Detail
10a,b, 13, 14, 15

Publications of maps held
M. F. Bond, 'Materials for Transport History amongst the Records of Parliament', *Journal of Transport History* **4** (1959–60), 37–52.
H. S. Cobb, 'Parliamentary records relating to internal navigation', *Archives* **9** (1969), 73–9.
C. Hadfield, 'Sources for the history of British canals', *Journal of Transport History* **2** (1955–6), 80–9.

115   Royal Geographical Society, Map Room

Address   1 Kensington Gore, London SW7 2AR

Telephone   (0171) 589 5466   *Fax*   (0171) 584 4447

Access   Open.

Index
The sole published catalogue of manuscript and printed cartographic materials is *Catalogue of [the] Map Room of the Royal Geographical*

Society. March, 1881 (1882), London: Murray, listing 'all the maps in the Society's collection on 31st March 1881'; the large numbers of sheets of the OS, of the Hydrographic Office, The Admiralty, and of the Great Trigonometrical Survey of India were omitted as their own institutional catalogues were held and suitably annotated. Notices or articles in the Society's *Proceedings* (New Series), 1879–92 and *Geographical Journal* (from 1893) are normally the only way of tracing pre-1900 material accessioned after publication of the 1881/82 *Catalogue* (search *via* annual or decennial indexes). The current card catalogue has two main retrieval facilities: author (alphabetical, then title, order); and geographical (hierarchical 'general' to 'special' system – extraterrestrial, world, oceans, continents, and countries – arranged within each category alphabetically then chronologically, with subject headings added when pertinent). Index (or 'key') diagrams for many multi-sheet map series are on site only.

Summary
Manuscript material derives chiefly from mid-19th century to mid-20th centuries and reflects RGS's policies of collecting scientific geographical information from its members or sponsored parties on exploratory travels abroad. At the same time efforts were made towards collecting older items to show the historical progress of geographical discovery: thus a MS copy of the *mappa mundi* of Richard of Haldingham (or de Bello) in Hereford cathedral was commissioned in 1830. A county atlas of the British Isles of c.1605 has maps engraved by P. van der Keere and MS texts and coats-of-arms on versi. Another county atlas, *The Theatre of the Empire of Great Britain* (1611/12), has many proof states of John Speed's maps. There are some 'special' collections – whether by theme or donor – which may be split between the Map Room and Library. Most relevant here are those of M. C. Andrews in 1934 (for British Isles and constituent parts); Sir H. G. Fordham (British and French road books and itineraries, and publications of John Cary firm); G. B. Greenough in 1855 (including 18th and 19th century county, canal, and railway maps – usually with MS annotations and/or colouring concerning geology and natural resources); and Lord Rennell of Rodd (including MS maps of James Rennell of 1750s). See Freeman, M. J. and J. Longbotham *The Fordham Collection: a catalogue* (1981), Norwich: Geo Abstracts. [Institute of British Geographers: Historical Geography Research Series; No.5]; and Cook, A. S. (1978) 'James Rennell's manuscript maps in the RGS collection', *Geographical Journal* **144**, 157–159.

Detail
1, 2, 3, 4, 5, 6a,b, 7, 8, 9, 10a,b, 13, 14, 15

Publications of maps held
English county maps in the collection of the Royal Geographical Society,
with introduction and notes by Edward Heawood (1932) London:
RGS, reproduces some early engraved maps.

116   Royal Society of Arts, Library and Archives

Address   6–8 John Adam Street, London WC2N 6EZ

Telephone   (0171) 930 5115   *Fax*   (0171) 839 5805

Access   By appointment.

Index
No index to maps.

Summary
Atlas of Richard Horwood's 'Plan of the Cities of London and Westminster' (1803), tinted to distinguish parishes. Atlas of some 25 plans of proposed canals, printed, with hand colouring, including a large profile and plan of the Thames-Severn Navigation, mostly from Acts of Parliament, 1790–6. 28 survey sketches of roads in Surrey and Hampshire, undated.

12 maps of agricultural improvements in various parts of England, early 1800s, accompanied by written descriptions. Those schemes which the Society rewarded were published in its *Transactions*, usually without the map.

Sundry other 18th and 19th century maps and plans, including manuscript 'Plan of a cut and dam ... north of Rye Harbour,' (1796), and chart of the approaches to King's Lynn (1812); printed Robert Sayer's 'Road Map of the British Isles' (1772), 'Lights on the coast of Ireland' (1834). Six sheets of Richard Horwood's 'County of Berkshire' (1752).

The counties represented are Berks., Brecknock, Cambs., Cards., Cheshire, Derby, Devon, Essex, Hants., Herts., Hunts., Lancs., Lincs., Middx., Monmouth, Norfolk, Northants., Notts., Oxon., Rutland, Shrops., Staffs., Suffolk, Surrey, Sussex, Warwicks., Wilts., Yorks.

Detail
1, 2, 5, 6, 8, 14, 15

117   Royal College of Physicians of London

Address   11 St Andrew's Place, London NW1 4LE

Telephone   (0171) 935 1174   *Fax* (0171) 487 5218

Access   Open to Fellows, Members and Licentiates, otherwise by appointment.

Index
Card indexes on site, to archives, and to printed works, both by name only.

Summary
Printed atlases and coastal maps of the 16th and 17th centuries, bequeathed to the College in 1680 with the library of Henry Pierrepoint (1606–80), 1st Marquis of Dorchester. Two manuscript maps of estates at Burmarsh, Kent (1733), owned by the College, and High Ongar, Essex (1728), formerly owned by the College, both unsigned. A few plans of sites and buildings, printed and manuscript, 18th and 19th centuries.

Detail
7, 8, 11

Publications of maps held
Maps and atlases: Catalogue of an exhibition (London: Royal College of Physicians, 1972).

118   Science Museum Library and Archives

Address   South Kensington, London SW7 5NH

Telephone   (0171) 938 8234   *Fax* (0171) 938 8213

Access   Open.

Index
Within the General Catalogue at 912(410) (Maps: Great Britain), on cards for material accessioned before 1983, thereafter on computer. The index is to printed maps, arranged by country, then region, then town, and within these groups, by theme.
Maps found amongst the archives are identified as the archive collections are being entered on the Library database.

Summary
Printed thematic maps, relating to transport and industry. These include

prospectuses for proposed railways and canals; road, waterway, railway, steamboat and coach route maps; levels and lengths for railways and canals; land use, mining and electricity supply maps; agricultural and port developments; reproductions of early atlases and maps by Christopher Saxton and others. The road maps date from c.1750, the industrial maps from the 19th century.

The following archive collections contain manuscript and annotated printed maps:

Berry, waterworks in London, and New River, c.1740 onwards.

Gibb, Docks, waterworks, railways and lighthouses in England and Scotland.

G.W.R., 19 ground plans of railway stations, mostly scaled at 40 feet to 1 inch, 1880s.

Hawksley, engineers. Waterworks constructed by Hawksley, May & Hawksley, and their successors, at Nottingham, c.1847; Oxford, 1883; Whitehaven, 1849; Norwich, 1850; New River, 19th century; Merthyr Tydfil, 19th century; Wexford, 1877.

Industrial Monuments Survey.

Neumann, plans of railway bridges and viaducts.

Simmons, 300 annotated OS maps dating from the early 19th century showing locations of water and windmills throughout England and Wales.

Taylor & Sons, engineers. Deposited plans from Parliamentary Plans for water and sewage works in southern England and Wales.

Detail
1, 5, 6a,b, 7, 13, 14, 15

119   Sir John Soane's Museum

Address   13 Lincolns Inn Fields, London WC2A 3BP

Telephone   (0171) 405 2107   *Fax*   (0171) 831 3957

Access   By appointment.

Index
Forthcoming concise catalogue (1994).

Summary
Three sets within the architectural drawings collection are:
Drawer 57: Set 1. 16 maps of England and overseas. Set 2: 18 Maps and

Plans, London and Westminster, improvements. Set 3: Plans of Cities etc., England and Europe, 1766–1826.

Detail
1, 7, 11

120 The Society of Antiquaries of London

Address   Burlington House, Piccadilly, London W1V 0HS

Telephone   (0171) 734 0193   *Fax*   (0171) 287 6967

Access   By appointment.

Index
Unpublished catalogue of manuscripts, and card indexes to printed books, prints and drawings, contain references to maps. A new catalogue of the Society's holdings is being prepared.
M. W. Barley, *A Guide to British Topographical Collections* (Council for British Archaeology, 1974), gives further information on the Society's holdings.

Summary
The atlases include Ortelius's *Theatrum orbis terrarum* (Antwerp, 1595); Braun and Hogenburg's *Civitates orbis terrarum*, 6 vols, (1592–1618); John Speed's *Theatre* (1676), (2 copies, one with *A Prospect of the most famous Parts of the World*).
The Harley Collection comprises 8 folio volumes of prints and drawings, including maps and plans of London and the Home Counties, collected by Edward Harley, Earl of Oxford (1689–1741). Vol.4 for example, includes 'Middlesex' by John Norden, printed and sold by John Garrett (a proof); 'The River Thames' by Francis Mathew, engraved by Thomas Jenner (1660); 'The Newest and Exactest Mappe of the Famous Citties of London and Westminster' by Thomas Porter (c.1655), edition of c.1670, printed and sold by Robert Walton; Wenceslaus Hollar's 'A Map or Groundplot of the Citty of London', sold by John Overton, 1666; John Leake's survey of the City of London in 1666, engraved by George Vertue, 1773. John Ogilby and William Morgan's plan of London in 20 sheets (1678); 'A Plan, Section and Elevation of the Fleet Market by 1737' published by George Dance.
Examples in vol.7 which includes Norfolk, are 'The Groundplot of Kings Lyn' (1692?), manuscript, and 'Chart of the Jurisdiction of the Admiralty King's Lyn in the Mayoralty of Henry Bell 1693', surveyed by C. Merit.

The Coleraine Collection of British Topography, late 17th and early 18th century, bequeathed by Henry Hare, third Baron Coleraine (1693–1749), covers the British Isles in seven volumes. It includes maps, town plans and archaeological plans. In vol.6, 'A Survey of the Conduits &c to Whitehall, St James &c.' 1718, manuscript; 'A Survey & Ground Plot of the Royal Palace of Whitehall, 1680, Surveyed by Jno. Fisher. G. Vertue, 1747'.

The collection of Edward James Willson of Lincoln (1787–1854), architect and antiquary, was compiled around 1808–53, with some earlier material, mostly 18th century. It includes maps and plans of the County and City of Lincoln, fen drainage plans, estates in Old Bolingbrooke, etc.

In the Society's own collections there are archaeological maps and plans, many of them engraved by George Vertue FSA, the Society's engraver; for example, 'An accurate Survey of some Stupendous Remains of Roman Antiquity on the Wolds in Yorkshire, Survey'd and drawn by John Haynes of York, 1744, Geo. Vertue sculp.'

Detail
1, 6a,b, 7, 10a,b,c,

Publications of maps held
The unique example of the 2nd edition of Thomas Porter's plan of London, c.1670, was reproduced by the London Topographical Society, Publication No.5, 1898.

121   The Society of Jesus, Archives of the British Province

Address   114 Mount Street, London W1Y 6AH

Telephone   (0171) 493 7811

Access   By written appointment.

Index
No index to maps.

Summary
A collection of plans of estates, Roman Catholic parishes, and church properties, in Yorkshire, Lancashire, Oxfordshire and Surrey, 19th century. These occur in bound volumes of lettters and papers and are often only rough sketches.

There is also a group of about 40 printed town and county maps, almost entirely 18th and 19th century.

Detail
7, 11, 17c

122   Corporation of London Records Office

Address   Guildhall, London EC2P 2EJ

Telephone   (0171) 332 1251   *Fax*   (0171) 332 1119

Access   Open.

Index
Card index and schedules on site.

Summary
All maps of official provenance, reflecting the Corporation's activities as
a local authority and as a major landowner and leaseholder both in the
City and outside. Attention is drawn to the following:
Bridge House Estates, with property in Deptford, Lewisham, Southwark
and Stratford. Manuscript maps from the 15th century onwards.
Royal Contract Estates held by the City in the 17th century and nearly
all sold by the end of the century. The lands were in all parts of England
and Wales. A few 17th century plans including Exeter Castle (Devon)
ground and farms in Dorset and Croyland (Lincs.).
Conduit Mead Estate, part of the above, retained. Covers Oxford St –
Bond St area in London. Maps from 1694 onwards.
Finsbury Estate, leased by the Corporation from medieval times to 1867.
Plans from 1641 onwards.
Brandsburton Estate (Yorks. East Riding), property of Emanuel Hos-
pital. Plans from c.1700 onwards.
Open Spaces owned and maintained by the Corporation, often outside
the City boundary. The most important are Epping Forest, Burnham
Beeches (Bucks.), Kent and Surrey Commons, Highgate Wood, Queen's
Park Kilburn, West Ham Park. Plans, 19th century.
NB – the majority of leases of Corporation property including the Bridge
House, Conduit Mead and Finsbury Estates have ground plots attached
from 1675 onwards.

Detail
5, 7, 10b,c, 11, 13, 14, 15, 16, 17c

Publications of maps held
J. H. Harvey, 'Four 15th century London Plans', *London Topographical*

Record, **20** (1952), 1–8 (plans of Deptford, Southwark Bar, St George's Bar, Carter Lane).

P. E. Jones 'Four 15th century London Plans', *London Topographical Record,* **23** (1972), 35–59 (plans as above).

B. R. Masters, 'The Public Markets of the City of London Surveyed by William Leybourne in 1677', *London Topographical Society Publication* No.117 (1974).

J. R. Sewell, 'Plans of the Artillery Ground and Fields in Finsbury', *London Topographical Society Publication* No. 120 (1977), reproduces plans of 1641 and 1705.

R. Hyde, 'A survey of the City of London rediscovered', *Journal of the Society of Archivists* **4** No.2, (1970), 141–2, large scale ward maps by Samuel Angell and Michael Meredith, not reproduced.

123   Guildhall Library, Print Room

Address   Aldermanbury, London EC2P 2EJ

Telephone   (0171) 260 1862/3   *Fax*   (0171) 260 1119

Access   Open.

Index

Card indexes on site, to collections in the Print Room, and in the Manuscript Room, arranged by place and by the various institutions and companies.

J. Howgego, *Printed maps of London, c.1553–1850* (1975)

R. Hyde, *Printed maps of Victorian London, 1851–1900* (1975).

I. Scouloudi, *Panoramic views of London, 1600–1666* (London: Guildhall Library, 1953).

Summary

The majority of the holdings relate to the City of London, with a small amount of material covering other parts of the British Isles. Various London institutions and Livery Companies have deposited their archives in the Guildhall Library. These archives include maps and plans of properties within the City and outside it. Some of these maps and plans are held in the Print Room, others in the Manuscripts Room. (Records of the Corporation of London should be sought in the City Record Office.) The principal deposited map collections are:

Armourers' and Braziers' Company, plans of the Hall and tenements, 1679–1881, some by Joseph Fitcombe. Plan of Globe Yard Estate by Charles J. Shoppee (1858), plans and elevations of Britannia Place

Almshouses, Bishopsgate Street, showing proposed rebuilding, c.1880.
Bakers' Company, plans and elevations of almshouses in Mare Street, Hackney (1895) by C. Herbert Shoppee.
Barber Surgeons' Company, litho plans and elevations of new buildings in Monkwell Street (1862) by C. J. Shoppee, etc.
Bowyers' Company, plan of the lordship of Isley Walton, Leicester, (1854) by C. F. Cheffins.
Brewers' Company, Wyotts Manor, South Mimms (1594) by Ralph Treswell. Maps and plans of properties in Hertfordshire, the City and north-west London, 17th to 19th centuries.
Broderers' Company, Part of Stifford Manor, Essex, by Bernard Scale (1780) and resurveys to 1843.
Butchers' Company, Plans of properties in Lambeth and City, 19th century.
Clothworkers' Company, their bargehouse and garden in Lambeth, (1654), almshouses (c.1790) and other estates in Islington (1848), and in Southwark and Deptford, 19th century.
Coopers' Company, estates at Ratcliffe, Middlesex, early 19th century, by George Smith.
Cutlers' Company, Aldersgate Street estate (1837).
Drapers' Company, almshouses at Southwark, rebuilt 1820, and at Crutched Friars, by J. W. Archer (1851).
Fishmongers' Company, survey and terrier of lands at Bray, Berkshire, belonging to Jesus Hospital (1672) by Robert Chelsham. Many plans of properties and lands in the City, Southwark and Kent, 18th and 19th centuries.
Goldsmiths' Company, property in Foster Lane (1830).
Haberdashers' Company, plans of the Manor of Knighton, Staffordshire, and a farm at Woodsease, Shropshire (1783) by Jno. Dugleby.
Innholders' Company, plans of premises behind their Hall in Upper Thames Street (c.1880).
Ironmongers' Company, plans of property north of Old Street, Finsbury, by 'Edw. G.'(1592) and later resurveys. Plans of lands and properties in the City, Hackney, Stepney, Poplar and the Isle of Dogs, in East and West Ham, Barking, and Bradwell-on-Sea, Essex, and at Woolwich, Kent, 18th and 19th centuries. Surveys of the Manor of Lizard in Coleraine, County Londonderry, 18th and 19th centuries.
Joiners' Company, Plans of streets adjacent to their Hall in Upper Thames Street and other properties (1839).
Merchant Taylors' Company, plan of the Hall and adjacent properties (1845).
Vintners' Company, Survey of farms at Boxley (1741) by Alexander Bittle,

and at Wavering Street, Kent. Volumes of plans of properties in the City (1808) by Jesse Gibson, and resurveys, (1808 and 1856).

Wax Chandlers' Company, plan of property around Upper Thames Street (1882).

The D'Oyley Collection, maps and plans relating to Epping Forest and its environs, surveyed by William D'Oyley and his son William junr. The earliest dated map is 1820, the latest is 1880.

Detail

1, 2, 3, 4, 5, 6a,b, 7, 8, 9, 10a,b,c, 11, 14, 15, 16, 17a,b,c

Publications of maps held

R. Hyde, 'Notes on a collection of London insurance surveys, 1794–1807', *Journal of the Society of Archivists* **4** (1971), 327–9.

R. Hyde, 'Seven manuscript Thames charts by Greenvile Collins', *Journal of the Society of Archivists* **5** (1974), 38–40.

Facsimiles and reproductions for sale

Wenceslaus Hollar, 'London after the Great Fire' (1666).

J. Oliver, 'London, Westminster and Southwark' (c.1680).

J. Fairburn, 'London and Westminster' (1797).

Banks' 'Balloon View of London' (1851).

Ogilby and Morgan, 'Survey of the City of London' (1676) (Guildhall Library with Harry Margary).

William Morgan, 'London Actually Survey'd' (1682) (Guildhall Library with Harry Margary).

124   Westminster City Archives

Address   NB In 1994 both branches of Westminster Archives will transfer into a new building, 10 St Anne's Street, SW1.

124A   Victoria Library, Archives Department

Address   160 Buckingham Palace Road, London SW1W 9UD

Telephone   (0171) 798 2180   *Fax*   (0171) 798 2181

Access   Open.

Index

Card index on site to maps and plans in the collection, and to reproductions issued by the London Topographical Society etc., arranged alphabetically by place. There is also a catalogue referring to printed maps of London in books kept in the Archives Department.

Summary
The maps collection at Victoria Library consists of originals and reproductions, providing a comprehensive series of maps of south Westminster (the former City of Westminster) and of London as a whole, mostly printed and dating from the late 17th century. The Grosvenor Estate collection includes about 10,000 maps and plans, dating from the mid-18th century.

Detail
7, 10c, 11, 12, 13, 14, 15, 16, 17c

Publications of maps held
Set of six maps of the parish of Westminster (1755), from John Strype's edition of John Stowe's *A Survey of the Cities of London and Westminster ...*, (1754).

124B Marylebone Library, Archives Department

Address   Marylebone Road, London NW1 5PS

Telephone   (0171) 798 1030   *Fax*   (0171) 798 1019

Access   Open.

Index
Card index on site which lists the maps chronologically under these headings: London, Marylebone, Paddington, Westminster insurance plans, OS, and other London boroughs.
A. Cox-Johnson, *Handlist to the Ashridge Collection on the history and topography of St Marylebone* (St Marylebone Libraries Committee, 1959), includes a sizeable group of maps.

Summary
There are almost 1500 maps in the collection. The former boroughs of Paddington and St Marylebone became part of the City of Westminster in 1965 and the collection specialises in these areas. It also includes a large number of general maps of London and some plans of the Grand Junction Canal and the Great Central Railway.
The collection includes a number of manuscript maps and there are photostat copies of maps of the private estates in both Marylebone and

Paddington from the 18th to 20th centuries. The printed maps include a survey of St Marylebone to a scale of 26 inches to 1 mile by Peter Potter giving individual house numbers (three editions, 1821–*c*.1832) and a number of surveys of both parishes to a scale of 20 inches to 1 mile by George Lucas (1846–62), which also give house numbers. There is an almost complete set of OS maps of the area from the first 60 inches to 1 mile edition of the 1860s to the current 1:1250 series and good coverage of its commercial zones by the Goad insurance plans, 1889–1968.

The Ashbridge Collection, a private collection of material relating to St Marylebone bequeathed in 1945 by Arthur Ashbridge, District Surveyor to the former borough, includes printed maps of London of *c*.1680–1850.

Detail
6, 7, 10c, 11, 13, 14, 15, 16, 17c

Publications of maps held
'Plan of the Parish of St Marylebone in the County of Middlesex' by Peter Potter (*c*.1832), reprinted by Westminster City Libraries and the St Marylebone Society, 1979.

125   Greater London Record Office

Address   40 Northampton Road, London EC1R 0HB

Telephone   (0171) 332 3820 (Catalogue Room)   *Fax*   (0171) 833 9136
(0171) 332 3821 (Maps and prints)

Access   Open.

Index
Manuscript maps:
London mss indexes
Official bodies' maps and plans are identified in GLRO General Index.
Middlesex mss indexes
Middlesex Sessions deposited plans have a card index arranged by site.
London deposited records
Indexed in GLRO place names index.
Middlesex deposited records
Index arranged by place, accessions listed up to 1979, thereafter in GLRO index.

Printed maps:
No published catalogue but a series of information leaflets on the Collection and aspects of it are available.
Card catalogue on site.

Summary
The GLRO collections relate mainly to the former counties of London and Middlesex, with some material from outside this area. The origins of the maps have led to their being classed under 'London' or 'Middlesex' heads with both groups having printed and manuscript maps. The London and Middlesex Collections were formerly housed separately, which accounts for the present structure of the maps and plans collections and their indexes.

London, manuscript maps from official sources:
(1) Commissioners of Sewers, 1703–1852, printed and manuscript volumes and rolls (indexed within maps index). Also Metropolitan Commissioners of Sewers. Notebooks on sewers associated with the first OS, 1848–52. The Metropolitan Board of Works collections include contract drawings and deposited plans for sewers and other subjects including Thames floods.
(2) Office of Works papers on parks include plans of Battersea, Kennington and Victoria Parks, from 1841. Plans of bridge approaches etc, at Chelsea, Battersea.
(3) London County Council, from 1889: Deposited plans under Bills promoted by the LCC; large number of miscellaneous plans associated with the wide spectrum of LCC activity.
Many other official records, referenced in the general index where plans are noted. LCC street numbering plans, from 1865; road improvement plans.
(4) Goad insurance maps, analysed by date of sheet, for LCC and City areas, from 1887.

Middlesex, manuscript maps from official sources:
(1) Middlesex Sessions Records: deposited plans (with card index by subject, listed chronologically). The Middlesex County Council took over in 1889. Justices' administration of asylums and bridges, plans of county property from 1718.
(2) Enclosure plans and awards for the county of Middlesex.

London, deposited records:
(1) Tithe maps for the Diocese of London (north of the river Thames), and some parish copies for the area south of the river Thames (Diocese of Winchester).

(2) Church and ecclesiastical property in Orders of Council, deeds etc., for Surrey parishes of the Diocese of Winchester.
(3) St Thomas's Hospital estates deeds; maps and plans listed divided between estates in London and those in the country, located in Berks., Cambs., Essex and Derby (including coal mines area) dating from 1628.
(4) Bedford estates (Covent Garden and Surrey estates), including plans of Howland Wet Dock.
(5) Foundling Hospital Bloomsbury estates.
(6) Sons of the Clergy estates, north London (Holloway) and country, with area maps and property plans.
(7) Charterhouse estates, London and country, maps and plans listed within the main series.
(8) Maryon-Wilson estate, Charlton etc. (LCC area).
(9) Northampton estates at Clerkenwell and Canonbury, listed within the main series.
(10) In the Manorial series: map of the manor of Paris Garden, 1627, including site of theatre.

Middlesex, deposited records, Separate index, arranged by place, to 1979.
(1) Tithe maps and parish copies for the Diocese of London and Middlesex.
(2) Northwick estate.
(3) Jersey estates, Osterley and west Middlesex.
(4) Important maps relating to the development of suburban Middlesex.
(5) The collections of solicitors, surveyors, and estate agents are rich in plans.
(6) Newdigate estates at Harefield etc., from 1680s, with surveyors' field books etc.
(7) Thames Water. A large collection of maps and plans relating to the Metropolitan Water Board and its predecessor companies, some of whose premises and property lay wholly or in part south of the Thames, many of 19th century and some of earlier dates.

Printed maps
There are some 15,000 maps. The area covered is that part of London and its environs included within the pre-1965 counties of London and Middlesex. The Collection also includes small unsystematic holdings of Essex, Kent and Surrey maps. The period covered is from c.1553 to date, but strongest on 18th and 19th centuries. The types of maps are almost exclusively printed, with a few manuscript estate maps. Extensive holdings of OS plans (very extensive holdings of large-scale OS plans) but no series complete. A group of experimental MS plans at 5 and 10 feet to

1 mile, compiled by surveyors of the Metropolitan Commission of Sewers foreshadow OS large plans. The main series are:

(1) Ordnance Survey. London and environs, 1 inch to 1 mile, c.1800–1959; London 1 inch to 5 feet to 1 mile, various dates c.1810–1930s; Middlesex, 6 and 25 inches to 1 mile, 1860s-1938; Essex, Kent and Surrey (areas adjacent to London), 6 and 25 inches to 1 mile, 1860s.

(2) London General. Maps of whole or part of London (as defined at the time of publication) including pre- and near-Fire maps, 18th century versions of schemes for re-building City, and other maps of 19th and 20th century date.

(3) Boroughs. Maps covering areas within a single Metropolitan Borough (and therefore within the boundaries of the former County of London) arranged by Metropolitan Borough regardless of date.

(4) Outer Boroughs. Maps covering areas within a single London Borough (outside the area of the former County of London but within the boundaries of Greater London) arranged by London Borough regardless of date.

(5) Environs. London (as defined at the time of publication) and environs, 1611–1939, at small scale.

(6) Counties. Maps of counties, or parts of them, adjacent to London, from late 17th century, i.e. Beds., Bucks., Essex, Hants., Herts., Hunts., Middlesex, Surrey, Sussex.

(7) Geological. A few, for the London area only.

(8) Rivers, canals and docks. A small series, London area only.

(9) Water supply. Mainly of water companies' areas, late 19th century.

(10) Thematic. On specific subjects, late 19th century, i.e. boundaries, education, services, transport, land use and planning, traffic, Royal Commission on London, various.

(11) Proposals. Proposed schemes and designs (not necessarily executed).

Detail
5, 6a,b, 7, 10a,b,c, 11, 12, 13, 14, 15, 16, 17a,b,c

Facsimiles and reproductions on sale
Facsimiles of the following maps are available (publication numbers in brackets):
London, by Georg Braun and Frans Hogenberg (1572), (100 b&w, 171 col.), by Jacobus de la Feuille (c.1690), (101), by John Rocque (1769), (102); UK Newspaper/Surrey (1832) (103). Environs, by John Rocque (1769), (106). Middlesex, by John Norden (1593), (170 col.), by John Ogilby (1672), (104), by John Warburton (1749), (105).

126 Museum of London

Address   London Wall, London EC2Y 5HN

Telephone   (0171) 600 3699   *Fax*   (0171) 600 1058

Access   By appointment.

Index
Card index on site.

Summary
A collection of printed maps, both originals and reproductions, covering London and its environs and dating from the 16th century onwards. Some of the maps are exhibited in the Museum galleries. Most, if not all, the material in this collection is also available at the Guildhall Library.

Detail
1, 5, 6a, 7, 17c

Facsimiles and reproductions on sale
'Moorfields in 1559' (London Museum, 1963).
'London in maps', (P Glanville, *The Connoisseur*, 1972).
'Londinium Feracissimi Angliae Regni Metropolis' of Braun and Hogenburg (1575), (coloured facsimile entitled 'Tudor London').
'A New plan of the City of London, Westminster and Southwark', (facsimile entitled 'London in 1720,).
'District Railway map of London' (5th edition, 1892), (Coloured facsimile).

127 Museum in Docklands, Library and Archive

Address   Unit C14, Poplar Business Park, 10 Prestons Road, London E14 9RL

Telephone   (0171) 515 1162   *Fax*   (0171) 538 3869

Access   Strictly by appointment only.

Index
Computerised list of maps available on site.

Summary
A specialised collection, being principally confined to maps of the

enclosed Port of London, and to the tidal portion of the River Thames between Teddington and the estuary. One group of maps belongs to the Port of London Authority and is on loan to the Museum of London, of which the Docklands Library and Archive is a branch. The period 1799–1805 is particularly well covered, as this is when the earliest enclosed docks were built. Only the east side of London, from London Bridge down to Blackwall, is strongly represented. Another important group is the Thames Conservancy charts of the River Thames, being large scale plans which show the layout of the buildings fronting the river from Central London down to Greenwich, and dating from c.1840 to 1890.

All these maps were working tools and have suffered as a result of much handling and storage in poor conditions before passing into the Museum's hands. Consequently many are in poor condition.

Maps of particular significance are: Manuscript plan of Hermitage Dock (c.1600), probably by Richard Poulter; manuscript map on vellum of the parish of Stepney, including the Isle of Dogs, by Joel Gascoyne (1703); The Thames from London Bridge to Woolwich, chart by David Steel (1802); The William Vaughan book of maps of the West India and London Dock (1799).

Detail
5

Publications of maps held
W. Ravenhill, 'Joel Gascoyne's Stepney', *Guildhall Studies in London History* **2** (1977), 200–212.

128 London Borough of Barnet, Hendon Library

Address	The Burroughs, Hendon, London NW4 4BQ Located at: Archives and Local Studies Centre, Hendon Catholic Social Centre, Chapel Walk, Egerton Gdns, NW4
Telephone	(0181) 202 5625 ext. 55 *Fax* (0181) 202 8520
Access	By appointment.

Index
Indexes to the Archives and the Local History Collection, arranged by subject, place and persons. Separate index available by district, on site. Printed listing of all OS maps in the collection.

Summary

The London Borough of Barnet covers the areas of the former Hendon B.C. (Hendon U.D.C. 1895–1932); Finchley B.C. (Finchley U.D.C. 1895–1933); Barnet U.D.C., East Barnet, and Friern Barnet Urban Councils. OS maps for the whole area of the borough, at 25 inches to 1 mile for 1864, 1896, and later, and for part of the borough, at 6 inches to 1 mile for 1873, 1897 and later. Tithe maps (copies) are available for Edgware, Finchley, Friern Barnet, Hendon, Monken Hadley and South Mimms. There are enclosure maps for Chipping and East Barnet in 1817 and Finchley in 1814.

The collection also includes a number of estate maps from the 18th to 20th centuries, a large number of plans of roads and buildings, mainly 19th century and later, maps produced by local authorities, geological, land use, and other special maps and county maps of Middlesex from the 17th century. A small collection of sale catalogues, which include plans, dates from the later 19th century.

Detail

6a, 7, 10a,b,c, 11, 12, 13, 15, 17a

Publications of maps held

Local Maps and Views, 1600–1850 (1972) includes reproductions of Middlesex (1610) and Middlesex and Hertfordshire (1724) from the collection, plus others of maps held elsewhere.

Facsimiles and reproductions on sale

Alan Godfrey Edition of old OS maps, local sheets only.
'A Map of ye County of Middlesex' by Richard Blome (1672).

129 London Borough of Barking and Dagenham, Valence Library, Local Studies Collections

Address   Becontree Avenue, Dagenham RM8 3HT

Telephone   (0181) 592 6537 Valence Library
(0181) 592 4500 ext. 4293 Valence House Museum

Access   Prior telephone advised.

Index

Index to maps in Valence Reference Library.
Handlist: Barking and Dagenham, a select list (1969, updated 1976).

Essex and Dagenham: a catalogue of books, pamphlets and maps (2nd edition, 1961).

Summary
Printed maps, and a few manuscript maps, of Essex, especially Barking and Dagenham area. Photocopies of maps of these areas from other collections. Land sale catalogues with maps (originals and photocopies), from late 19th century. There are three published charts: The Thames Estuary by A. H. Jaillot (1693), Essex and Suffolk coasts by Greenvile Collins (1686), Essex and Kent coasts by J. van Keulen (1686), and one manuscript chart, 'The Thames from Galleon's Reach to Erith Reach' by Jonas Moore. Three manuscript plans of interest are: land at Marks Gate, surveyed by Nicholas Howard (1764); plan of a Dagenham estate by James Turnbull; and 'Copyhold lands ... of the manor of Cockermouth, ... called Long Hide Farm' (Dagenham) (c.1793). The collection includes 'Dagenham maps 1948' by C. J. Hart, a two-volume compilation of maps of Dagenham, largely copies, from the 16th to the 20th centuries, with comments.

Detail
6a,10a,b,c, 11, 12, 13, 14, 15, 17a

130 London Borough of Bexley, Libraries and Museums Department, Local Studies Section

Address   Hall Place, Bourne Road, Bexley DA5 1PQ

Telephone   (01322) 526574 ext. 217/8   *Fax*   (01322) 522921

Access   Open.

Index
Card index on site.

Summary
Maps of the whole of Kent. Most of the historically important county maps from Christopher Saxton (1575) onwards, as originals or facsimiles. Maps covering the London Borough of Bexley, mostly from mid-18th century to date. Many printed OS, tithe, enclosure, etc., with a few estate plans, of the Danson estate in Bexley, from the 18th century, and others.

Detail
6a, 7, 10a,b,c, 11, 12, 13, 15, 17a

131   London Borough of Brent Library Service

Address   Grange Museum of Local History, Neasden Lane, London NW10 1QB

Telephone   (0181) 452 8311

Access   Open.

Index
Card catalogue, arranged by names of surveyors, institutions etc., by place, and by subject, on site.

Summary
The London Borough of Brent incorporates the former boroughs of Willesden and Wembley. Wembley was originally part of Harrow parish, with the ancient parish of Kingsbury.
The earliest large-scale maps are enclosure and tithe maps, early 19th century. The main series of OS maps are: 1 inch to 1 mile, 1st edition, 1822 and subsequent; 6 inches to 1 mile, 1875 and 1891 (Willesden only); 25 inches to 1 mile, 1st edition, 1865 and 2nd edition, 1896, for most of the borough; 60 inches to 1 mile, 1891–3, (Willesden only). The collection also includes a number of estate maps, maps produced by the local authority, geological and other special maps. Old county maps of Middlesex and London, dating from the late 16th century, manuscript and printed originals and reproductions. Particularly noteworthy are the maps of the estates of All Souls College, Oxford, in Willesden (1589), of which photocopies are held.
Many old building plans, dating from the 1800s onwards, have been deposited. There are also two volumes of sales catalogues in the Wood Collection, which include a number of plans from about 1871–80.

Detail
6a,b, 7, 10a,b,c, 11, 12, 13, 17a,c

132   London Borough of Bromley, Central Library, Local Studies Section

Address   High Street, Bromley BR1 1EX

Telephone   (0181) 460 9955 ext. 261   *Fax*   (0181) 313 9975

Access   Appointment recommended.

Index
Card index including maps, on site.

Summary
The Local History Collection and the Archives both contain maps. Major historical maps of Kent, 16th to 19th centuries including facsimiles and reproductions.
OS, 6 inches to 1 mile, some 1st edition, 2nd edition complete for Kent.
Maps for the area of the London Borough of Bromley: OS, 6 and 25 inches to 1 mile 1st editions incomplete, 2nd edition 6 inches to 1 mile complete, 1 inch, various dates. Three OS reference books to Bromley, Hayes and Lewisham, 1864, with a map. Street maps of London, early 19th century.
The archives section has a few estate maps, 18th and 19th centuries, manuscript, photographic copies and tracings, of properties in Bromley, Lewisham and Sydenham.

Detail
5, 6b, 7, 10a,b,c, 11, 12, 13, 14, 15, 17a

133   London Borough of Camden Archives

Address   NB Both branches of Camden Archives will be brought together at Holborn Library in the near future.

133A   Holborn Library, Local Studies and Archives

Address   32–38 Theobalds Road, London WC1X 8PA

Telephone   (0171) 413 6342

Access   By appointment.

Index
Card catalogue for Local History Collection including maps, arranged by district, date and subject, on site.

Summary
Holborn Library holds material relating to the former Borough of Holborn, and some archives for Camden as a whole. There are many reproductions, and photocopies of originals in other collections. Originals include 18th century printed maps of local parishes and various other

17th to 19th century printed and manuscript maps, some showing properties and occupiers.

OS maps: two sheets covering Holborn northwards to Camden Town, at 12 inches to 1 mile, surveyed 1848–51. Several sheets covering most of Holborn and parts of St Pancras, at 6, 25 and 60 inches to 1 mile, 1862/73 and revised editions, 1893/5, etc.

Detail
6a,b, 7, 10a,b,c, 11, 13, 14, 15, 17c

Facsimiles and reproductions on sale
'Hampstead' (1814) by Newton; 'St Andrew Holborn' (1755); 'St Giles in the Fields' (1755).

133B Swiss Cottage Library, Local Studies and Archives

Address   88 Avenue Road, London NW3 3HA

Telephone   (0171) 413 6522

Access   Open

Index
Card index, sub-divided into districts, then arranged chronologically, on site.

Summary
Swiss Cottage Library holds material relating to the former Boroughs of Hampstead and St Pancras, and Camden as a whole (some Camden material is kept at Holborn Library). Later prints and photographs form a large part of the collection. There are detailed manuscript maps of St Pancras parish, with field books, by John Thompson, 1804. The Library holds the Ambrose Heal Collection, largely of local interest and including a number of printed maps. There are Goad's Insurance maps from *c.*1891.

Of special interest are 'Map of the Manor of Belsize (1679), 'Trigonometric survey of Hampstead' (1680), a copy of the 'Manor of Hampstead Map' by James Ellis (1762), scale about 1:2000, with accompanying field book, 'Map of Hampstead' (1814) by J. Newton, scale about 1:9000, and a copy of the tithe map of Hampstead with list of owners and occupiers (1839).

OS 'skeleton series' surveyed 1848–51, at 12 inches to 1 mile for Euston and Camden Town, and at 60 inches to 1 mile for Hampstead Heat and

Highgate. At least one edition for all Camden of the 6 and 25 inches to 1 mile series, and for most of Camden for the 60 inches to 1 mile series.

Detail
6a,b, 7, 10a,b,c, 11, 13, 14, 15, 16, 17a

Facsimiles and reproductions on sale
'Hampstead' (1814) by Newton.

134   London Borough of Ealing, Central Library, Local History Library

Address	103 Ealing Broadway Centre, Ealing W5 5JY
Telephone	(0181) 567 3656 ext. 37
Access	Open.

Index
Card dictionary catalogue, with maps indexed under name, place, owner of property, surveyor, cartographer, etc.

Summary
As a result of a fire the vast majority of maps, including OS sheets pre-1960s, are photocopies.
Maps are local to the old Borough of Ealing or the old County of Middlesex; places covered include Acton, Bedford Park, Brentford, Castlebar, Dormers Wells, Drayton Green, Ealing, Ealing Green, Greenford, Hanwell, Middlesex, New Brentford, Northholt, Old Brentford, Perivale, Pitshanger, South Ealing, Southall, Twyford, West Ealing. The library has a good collection of OS sheets. Some interesting maps are: 'Great Greenford' by R. Binfield (1776); 'New Brentford' by W. T. Warren (1838), 'Historical map of the Parish of Ealing' by William Nichols (1822); 'Ealing Tithe Map' by William Tress (1839); Northholt enclosure map by James Trumper (1835); an unsigned manuscript map of an estate in Hanwell (1790).

Detail
6a, 7, 10b,c, 11, 12, 17a

Facsimiles and reproductions on sale
'Parish of Ealing', 1777 and 1822/8. Cary's 'Survey of Middlesex' (1786), Ealing and environs.
Alan Godfrey Edition of old OS maps for the area.

135 London Borough of Enfield, Libraries and Museums

Address   Local History Unit, Town Hall, Green Lanes, Palmers Green, London N13 4XD.

Telephone   (0181) 982 7453

Access   By appointment.

Index
Typescript list of OS maps. Rest of the collection unlisted.

Summary
The collection covers the former boroughs of Enfield, Edmonton and Southgate. At the core is a collection of over 1000 large scale maps (6, 25 and 50 inches to 1 mile, 5 feet to 1 mile) from 1866/7 to the present day. The collection includes enclosure maps for Enfield and Edmonton and a plan of the Forty Hall Estate, Enfield. Also included is a collection of printed maps of Middlesex (unlisted).

Detail
6a, 10,b,c, 11, 12, 14, 15

136 London Borough of Greenwich, Local History Library

Address   'Woodlands', 90 Mycenae Road, Blackheath, London SE3 7SE

Telephone   (0181) 858 4631

Access   By appointment.

Index
Handlist to the Martin Collection on site.

Summary
Maps in the collection fall into three groups:
(1) A Kent collection of county maps plus maps and plans of individual towns and villages in the county. There are many original prints and some manuscript maps, dating from the mid-17th century. Areas covered include royal properties at Greenwich and Woolwich dockyards, Blackheath, Charlton, Erith, Plumstead, Staplehurst and Lee.
(2) Maps relating to the London Borough of Greenwich, including

reproductions and copies, arranged in date order. The earliest is a tracing of work undertaken at Greenwich palace from 1430. Administration and development of the district, housing developments, railways, roads, sanitation etc. are all covered. Many OS maps at various scales from mid-19th century.

(3) The Martin Collection, local material donated by Alan Roger Martin, contains several hundred plans, ground sites, and maps, of domestic and commercial properties, wharves, stables, estates, gravel pits, railways etc, from the 17th century onwards.

Detail
5, 6a,b, 7, 8, 10a,b,c, 11, 12, 13, 15, 17a,c

137   London Borough of Hackney Archives

Address   Rose Lipman Library, De Beauvoir Road, London N1 5SQ

Telephone   (0171) 241 2886

Access   By appointment.

Index
Catalogue of maps in the Dawson Library, A. T. Brown, *John Dawson; his life and Library*, 3 vols, typescript (Thesis submitted for FLA, 1973).

Summary
Printed maps of London, 18th century onward. Printed maps and surveys of Hackney parish, 18th century and later.
A small number of manuscript maps, mainly of Hackney parish 18th century and later.
The earliest detailed maps of the area date from 1745 when Peter Chassereau made a map of Shoreditch. John Rocque's survey (1745) provides the earliest map of Hackney and Stoke Newington and better maps were made from the survey by W. H. Ashpital, revised by John Edmeston (1831), and a survey by C. Miller of Stoke Newington (1846). There are tithe maps of Hackney (1843) and Stoke Newington (1848), and estate maps and sale plans of smaller areas.
OS coverage begins with the 'Skeleton' plan series of 1848 (with later revisions) showing roads only, 25 and 60 inches to 1 mile sheets for Hackney and Stoke Newington. Thereafter there is coverage at 25 inches (1870) at 60 inches (1894–6) with a few gaps, and at 6, 25 and 60 inches for all Hackney.

The John Dawson Library, a deposited collection which includes 4 volumes of printed maps which he collected during his lifetime. Dawson (1692–1765) was an officer of HM Customs and Excise, resident in Shoreditch. British items in his collection include H. Moll's Irish maps.

Detail
6a,b, 7, 10c, 11, 13, 17a,b,c

138 London Borough of Hammersmith and Fulham

138A Archives and Local History Centre, The Lilla Huset

Address   191 Talgarth Road, London W6 8BJ

Telephone   (0181) 741 5159   *Fax*   (0181) 741 4882

Access   By appointment.

Index
General indexes on site. These include references to maps and plans in deposited collections which have been listed. Some index references to maps and plans amongst inherited records.
Card indexes to Metropolitan Borough of Hammersmith Engineer's Department plans of council projects, and 28,000 Drainage Application plans (1860s to 1970s), indexed by address.
Local history card indexes include references to surveyors/publishers of printed maps in the collections.

Summary
Maps and plans which are archives. Many deposits come from firms of solicitors, local businesses, bridge companies, churches and some private persons. There are a few maps and plans dating from the 17th and 18th centuries but the majority relate to development of the area in the 19th century, including Maclure's Parish of Fulham (1853) and Roberts' Parish of Hammersmith (1853).
OS maps dating between 1865 and 1900 at 1:1056 and, of Hammersmith, at 25 inches to the mile from 1863 onwards.
Also other printed county and local maps, from the 18th century onwards.

Detail
6a, 7, 10b,c, 11, 15, 17a,b,c

Facsimiles and reproductions on sale
Fulham and Hammersmith Local History Society has published the following maps with descriptive notes: Ogilby's 'Western roads out of London' (1675, part); Rocque (1746), Salter (1830), Parish of Fulham by Maclure (1853), Parish of Hammersmith by Roberts (1853).

138B   Hammersmith Area Reference Library

Address   Shepherds Bush Road, London W6 7AT

Telephone   (0181) 576 5053   *Fax*   (0181) 576 5053

Access   Open.

Index
No index to maps.

Summary
Port of London, Select Committee maps, c.1800.
Most London Topographical Society maps of 15th century London onwards (published from 1885). (Includes Salway 1811 reprint for Kensington Turnpike Trust).
Some London and Middlesex Archaeology reprints.
John Speed, 'England' (1953 reprint).
Wyld's 'London and Southwark'(1825, original).
Camden's 'Britannia', county plates in bound volumes.
Rocque's 'London, Westminster and Southwark' (1745).
Reprint of the OS 1 inch 1st edition, with railways.

Detail
6, 7, 10a

138C   Fulham Reference Library

Address   598 Fulham Road, London SW6 5NX

Telephone   (0181) 576 5252   *Fax*   (0171) 736 3741

Access   By appointment for maps.

Index
Card index on site identifies maps.

Summary

Reprint of the 1st edition OS of Great Britain, loose in sheets, with the railway lines added. The set is almost complete.
Reproductions of the London Topographical Society and the Fulham and Hammersmith Historical Society.

Detail
10a

139   Haringey Archives Service, Bruce Castle Museum

Address   Lordship Lane, London N17 8NU

Telephone   (0181) 808 8772

Access   By appointment.

Index
Card index on site.
Typescript 'A Catalogue of Maps relating to Tottenham from 1619 to 1936' compiled by C. H. Rock (1938), on site.
Archives Handlist No.1, Deposited Parish Records, on site.

Summary

There are two collections here: Local History, and Archives. Together they hold about 600 maps, covering the whole of the Borough of Haringey (the former Boroughs of Tottenham, Hornsey and Wood Green), the surrounding districts, and the old County of Middlesex. The archives cover the parishes of All Hallows, Tottenham, and St Mary's, Hornsey. Most of the historic maps (i.e. John Speed and Rocque) and later commercial maps are represented. There is good coverage of OS maps on all scales from 1863 as well as the usual parochial maps in manuscript. Where originals are not held, copies are generally available, as for example Thomas Milne's Land Use Survey of London and Environs in 1800. As a typical local collection, there is a large number of detailed area plans, inherited for the most part from previous local authorities. There are also three volumes of Estate Auction Prospectuses, 1851–1913, with plans, relating to Tottenham, Edmonton and Wood Green.
Most noteworthy items are: (1) A 19th century copy of 'A Survey of the Manors of Tottenham' (1619) by Thomas Clay for the Earl of Dorset, Lord of the Manor. (2) Survey of Tottenham (1817), scale about 25

251

inches to 1 mile. (3) Tottenham Tithe Map (1844), scale 25 inches to 1 mile. (4) Map of Tottenham Marshes published by I. N. Walter (1822), scale 32 inches to 1 mile, (coloured lithograph, 5ft x 2ft). (5) Photographic copy of the Hornsey Enclosure Award of 1816 (original at Greater London Record Office). (6) Almost complete coverage of the modern borough on OS sheets at all scales, from the 25 inches to 1 mile edition of 1864. (7) Map of the parish of Tottenham engraved by Bowler and Triquet for William Robinson's *History of Tottenham*, (1818), from a survey by Wyburn, 1798. (8) 'A Plan of an Estate . . . near Stamford Hill . . . belonging to William Earl of Radnor' (1767). Tinted copy of original with Hackney Libraries. (9) 'Plan of the turnpike roads from the Stone's End, St Leonard's Shoreditch, to the further part of the Northern Road . . . Enfield' surveyed by James Chilcott and engraved by Gale and Butley, 1810.

Detail
5, 6a,b, 10a,b,c, 11, 12, 15, 17a

140 Harrow Local History Collection

Address   The Reference Library, PO Box 4, Civic Centre, Station Road, Harrow HA1 2UU

Telephone   (0181) 424 1056   *Fax*   (0181) 424 1971

Access   Open

Index
Handlist to the main collection. Card index arranged by name of publisher, surveyor, engraver etc. on site

Summary
The map section of the Local History Collection consists in the main of printed maps and plans of Harrow and district from the early 19th century to date, including an extensive though not comprehensive collection for the area of OS maps and plans on the 1 inch, up to 25 inches to 1 mile scales, from the first edition of each scale (ie from 1822) onwards. There are only a few manuscript maps, the most important of which is the Harrow Enclosure map of 1817 which accompanies the parish copy of the Award, but photographic copies are held of the most important large-scale maps of the area held by the Greater London and Public Record Offices. There is also a collection of about 1000 printed county maps of Middlesex and of the environs of London, ranging in date from

the early 17th to the early 20th centuries, and a small number of 19th and early 20th century street plans and atlases of London.

Detail
6a,b, 10a,b,c, 11, 12, 13, 15, 17a,b,c

Publications of maps held
A. Dark, *The Harrow Enclosure 1796–1817: a guide to the primary sources.* Harrow Schools Local Resource Bank No.2. (LB of Harrow, 1976).

A. Dark, *From rural Middlesex to London Borough: the growth and development of Harrow illustrated with maps* (LB of Harrow, 1981).

Facsimiles and reproductions on sale
'Mapp of ye County of Middlesex with its Hundreds' by Richard Blome (1672).

141 London Borough of Hillingdon, Local Heritage Service

Address   Central Library, 22 High Street, Uxbridge UB8 1HD

Telephone   (01895) 250702   *Fax*   (01895) 239794

Access   Open.

Index
Unpublished catalogue on site.

Summary
Some 1000 items forming part of the Local Collection and covering in some detail the town of Uxbridge, the former urban districts of Ruislip, with Northwood, Hayes and Harlington, and of Yiewsley, with West Drayton. OS cover at 25 inches to 1 mile of the Uxbridge Union parishes (i.e. approximately the area of the present LB of Hillingdon). There are also some maps of Middlesex and Buckinghamshire. The collection includes some manuscript maps of Ruislip farms, c.1770, and the grounds of Swakeleys Manor House by S. Driver (1774). Marginal to the Local collection is the 'Uxbridge Panorama' – two long strips of cloth with views down the entire length of Uxbridge High Street, drawn in pen and ink c.1800. It identifies the occupiers of every building.

Detail
6a,b, 7, 10a,b,c, 11, 12, 13, 14, 15, 17a

142   London Borough of Hounslow

142A   Chiswick Library, Local Studies Collection

Address   Duke's Avenue, London W4 2AB

Telephone   (0181) 994 5295 / 1008   *Fax*   (0181) 995 0016

Access   Open.

Index
An Introduction to the material in the public libraries illustrating the history and development of Brentford and Chiswick (1957); Section A: Maps, lists the principal maps from 18th century to 1957.

Summary
Chiswick Library houses material relating to the old Brentford and Chiswick Borough and the parishes of Chiswick and Old and New Brentford. Maps range in date from the 17th century onward.

Detail
1, 6a,b, 7, 10a,b,c, 11, 13, 14, 15, 16, 17a,b

Facsimiles and reproductions on sale
Map of the County of Middlesex, 17th century.
The Alan Godfrey Edition of old OS maps, c.1894–7, for the area of Brentford and Chiswick.

142B   Hounslow Library, Local Studies Collection

Address   24 Treaty Centre, High Street, Hounslow TW3 1ES

Telephone   (0181) 570 0622   *Fax*   (0181) 569 4330

Access   Open.

Index
No index to maps.

Summary
Hounslow Library houses maps relating to the old Heston and Isleworth Borough, and the parishes of Heston and Isleworth, as well as material

relating to the parishes of Feltham, Hanworth and Bedfont. Dates range from 17th century onward.

Detail
1, 6a,b, 7, 10a,b,c, 11, 12, 13, 14, 15, 16, 17a,b

Facsimiles and reproductions on sale
'Map of the Manor of Isleworth/Syon' by Moses Glove (1635).
Map of the County of Middlesex, 17th century.
The Alan Godfrey Edition of old OS maps, *c*.1894–7, for the area of Isleworth and Norwood Green.

143 London Borough of Islington

143A Central Library, Local History Collection

Address	2 Fieldway Crescent, London N5 1PF
Telephone	(0171) 609 3081
Access	By appointment.

Index
Handlist 'Index to maps in the Collection of the Islington Central Reference Library'.

Summary
The collection includes copies of relevant portions of maps by John Rocque, Richard Horwood, Ralph Agas and others. Islington local maps include those of 1735, 1793, 1801, 1828, 1841, 1853 and 1877, besides OS maps. An Islington map of especial interest, with numbered key in book form to plots of land, showing ownership and occupation, is the Survey (1806) of the parish of St Mary, Islington, by R. Dent, scale approximately 200 feet to 1 inch. Copy of the Tithe Redemption Land Commission Map of 1848 with numbered key. Maps of Finchley Cemetery, 1854 and 1891. Copies of relevant portions of maps by John Rocque, Richard Horwood, Ralph Agas and others.
OS sheets, 5 feet to 1 mile, for 1869–71 and 1892–96.

Detail
6a, 7, 11, 14, 15, 17a,c

Facsimiles and reproductions on sale
Full-size reproductions: 'Clerkenwell' by R. Wilkinson (1805); 'Plan of the Parish of St Mary, Islington' by J. Dower (c.1853); 'Parish of Clerkenwell' (1865) by James Wyld, reproduced from W. J. Pinks, *History of Clerkenwell* (1865).

143B Finsbury Library, Finsbury Local History Collection

Address   245 St John Street, London EC1V 4NB

Telephone   (0171) 278 7343 ext. 25

Access   By appointment.

Index
Index in progress (1994).

Summary
Some estate maps and plans; parish maps, notably T. Horner, 'Plan of the Parish of Clerkenwell' (1808) at a scale of 100 feet to 11 inches.
London maps – the earlier being mainly printed copy maps, but including Bowles' map of London and Westminster (1803), and Cary's 'Map of London and Vicinity' (1825).
Good collection of OS maps of 1894–6, some with manuscript annotations regarding boundary changes, for Metropolitan Borough of Finsbury area.

Detail
7, 10b,c, 11, 17c

Facsimiles and reproductions on sale
'Clerkenwell' by R. Wilkinson (1805); 'Plan of the Parish of St Mary, Islington' by J. Dower (*c.*1853). 'St Mary, Islington' by R. Cheighton, (pub. S. Lewis, 1841) and 'Parish of Clerkenwell' taken from W. J. Pink's *History of Clerkenwell, 1865),* both republished by the London & Middx. Family History Society.
Alan Godfrey Edition of old OS maps, various sheets.

256

144 London Borough of Lambeth, Archives Department

Address   Minet Library, 52 Knatchbull Road, London SE5 9QY

Telephone   (0171) 926 6076

Access   By appointment.

Index

Maps and plans are listed in Section V of W. Minet and C. J. Courtney, *A Catalogue of the Collection of Works relating to the County of Surrey contained in the Minet Public Library* (Aberdeen University Press, 1901), and Section V of its *Supplement to the Catalogue* (London, 1923).

M. Y. Williams, *A Short Guide to the Surrey Collection* (Borough of Lambeth, 1965).

Indexes, arranged by cartographer and other names, and by place, on site.

Summary

The Minet Library houses the Surrey Collection, formed by William Minet and donated by him as as a public library in 1890. The scope of the collection was the whole of the pre-1888 county of Surrey. (Present collecting policy is confined to the geographical area of the London Borough of Lambeth.) There are manuscript and printed maps from the 17th century onwards.

OS maps at 60 inches to 1 mile, 1870–76, for the London Borough of Lambeth only. OS maps at 6 inches to 1 mile, 1848, 1870–6, 1894–6 and subsequent revisions, for the whole county. Estate maps for properties throughout the county, dating from the 17th century, occur within the deposited family papers.

Detail

1, 5, 6a,b, 7, 10a,b,c, 11, 12, 13, 14, 15, 16 17a,b,c,

Publications of maps held

Some maps from this collection are reproduced in J. Howgego, *Printed maps of London c.1553–1850* (1978); and R. Hyde, *Printed maps of Victorian London, 1852–1900* (1975).

145   London Borough of Lewisham, Local History Centre

Address   119–201 Lewisham High Street, London SE13 6LG

Telephone   (0181) 852 5050/7087   *Fax*   (0181) 297 0927

Access   Open.

Index
Card catalogue, arranged chronologically, by place and by subject, on site.

Summary
The Centre's holdings principally relate to the Borough of Lewisham, but with some cover of Great London and Kent, including Blackheath, Brockley, Chislehurst, Croydon, Eltham, Greenwich, Mottingham, Orpington, Plumstead, etc. The maps, originals and reproductions, range in date from the late 16th century to the present. They fall essentially into two groups:
(1) A local studies collection, chiefly of printed maps, with copies of manuscript maps held elsewhere. It includes OS, town, parish and local government maps, sale plans, road, railway and canal plans, and copies of tithe and enclosure maps.
(2) Maps and plans among the official and deposited archive collections. These include some estate plans, plans of individual buildings, and a quantity of late 19th to 20th century highway and drainage plans produced by the local Board of Works. The archive collection includes papers of the Baring family with estates at Lee; the Mayow Wynell Adams family of Sydenham; the Hardcastle family at New Cross; and plans of the Evelyn estates at Deptford. Other items of note are 18th century plans of the Red House (Victualling Yard) at Deptford.
1st edition OS sheets for southern England from Kent to Cornwall, and for parts of East Anglia and the East Midlands.

Detail
1, 5, 6a,b, 7, 10a,b,c, 11, 12, 13, 14, 15, 17a,c

Facsimiles and reproductions on sale
The Alan Godfrey Edition of old OS maps for the area.

146 London Borough of Merton.

146A Morden Library, Civic Centre

Address   London Road, Morden SM4 5DX

Telephone   (0181) 545 4039   *Fax*   (0181) 545 4037

Access   Open.

Index
No index to maps.

Summary
This branch of Merton Libraries covers the parishes of Merton and Morden. Maps of Surrey by Emanuel Bowen, Cary and J. Edwards (1811, part only of the county) and some facsimiles. OS sheets at 25, 50 and 60 inches to 1 mile for the locality. Administration maps, agricultural land use classification, and Geological Survey of South London. Photocopy of an estate map showing properties along the River Wandle, 1820.

Detail
5, 6a,b, 10b,c, 11, 13, 14, 17a

Facsimiles and reproductions on sale
'Surrey' by E. Bowen.
The Alan Godfrey Edition of old OS maps for the parishes of Merton and Morden.

146B Mitcham Reference Library

Address   London Road, Mitcham CR4 2YR

Telephone   (0181) 648 4070/6515   *Fax*   (0181) 646 6360

Access   Maps on closed access within the open Reference Library.

Index
No index to maps.

Summary
This branch of Merton Libraries covers the parish of Mitcham. Good range of OS maps of the district at 6 and 25 inches to 1 mile, from c.1850 to the present. 19th century sale plans; estate maps and plans

including Hall Place (1780); Makepeace's Mill Estate, Mitcham (1845); Tooting (1835, 1843 and 1854). Reproductions of maps by Christopher Saxton, John Norden, John Speed, Cary, John Senex and John Rocque.

Detail
10b,c, 11, 13, 14, 17a

Facsimiles and reproductions on sale
The Godfrey Edition of old OS maps, Mitcham parish, 1865.

146C   Wimbledon Reference Library

Address   Wimbledon Hill Road, London SW19 7NB

Telephone   (0181) 946 1136   *Fax*   (0181) 944 6804

Access   Open.

Index
Handlist on site.

Summary
This branch of Merton Libraries covers the parish of Wimbledon. Mainly printed maps; those of local interest include Thomas Milne's 'Land use of London and environs' (1800), proposed railways, 1863, the local parts of John Rocque's 'London and 10 miles around' (1746) at about $5\frac{1}{2}$ inches to 1 mile; and his London, Westminster and Southwark, at about 26 inches to 1 mile (1746). Reform Bill 'New map of the County of Surrey divided into Hundreds'; Early maps of Surrey by E. Bowen (1760), by Cole (1808), by R. Morden (1695), by John Rocque (1762), R. Rowe's 'Dorking' (c.1858), John Speed, 1610. Edwards' 'Wimbledon and Carshalton' (1819) at about 2 inches to 1 mile; Wimbledon Common Improvements (largely new roads) (1864). Copies of those parts relating to Wimbledon parish of the Parliamentary Deposits plans, submitted by railway, canal and water supply companies which undertook works in the district.

Detail
5, 6a,b, 7, 10b,c, 11, 13, 14, 17c

Facsimiles and reproductions on sale
Surrey, by John Speed (1610), by Emanual Bowen (c.1760).
'Survey of London' by John Rocque (1746), parts for Mitcham, Merton and Morden, and Wimbledon.
The Godfrey Edition of old OS maps: the parishes of Merton, Mitcham, Morden and Wimbledon, and Wimbledon Village (all dated 1865).

147 London Borough of Newham, Stratford Reference Library

Address Water Lane, London E15 4NJ

Telephone (0181) 534 4545 ext. 25662

Access Open.

Index

Maps are listed in the *Guide to local material available in the Reference Library*: Section 7, Maps and Surveys.

Summary

John Rocque's 'Survey of London (1741–5): several originals of the Newham section. Photocopy of J. James, 'Map Book of Plaistow' (1742): a manuscript book by the bailiff of the manors from 1742 to 1790, giving successive owners of fields and houses. Some notes on land use. (Original in Essex RO.) Commissioners of Sewers: surveys for West Ham and parts of East Ham in the 1740s and for West Ham in the 1850s. Presentment books for the latter. Copy of P. Le Neve, 'East Ham' (1800), a draft map at 10 inches to 1 mile, giving owners and occupiers and land use. J. Clayton, 'Survey of the Parish of West Ham' (1821) at 40 inches to 1 mile, with manuscript reference book. General Board of Health, 'Map of West Ham (1855). West Ham Board of Health, Plan, 60 inches to 1 mile (1860–65). J. Chapman and P. André, 'Map of the County of Essex' (1772, published 1777).

OS of Essex, East Ham and West Ham at various scales from 1805 to date; complete set at $2\frac{1}{2}$ inches to 1 mile for Essex, 6, 25 and 50 inches for East Ham and West Ham.

Detail

1, 10a,b,c, 11, 13

Publications of maps held

Three maps of West Ham (unidentified extracts, dated 1745, 1886 and 1936) reproduced in D. McDougall (comp.), *Fifty years a Borough, the story of West Ham, 1886–1936* (West Ham, County Borough Council, 1936).

Facsimiles and reproductions on sale

The above maps of West Ham, 1745, 1886 and 1936.

148   London Borough of Southwark, Local Studies Library

Address   211 Borough High Street, London SE1 1JA

Telephone   (0171) 403 3507

Access   Open.

Index
Card catalogue on site, arranged by date with indexes under subject and cartographers.
OS maps listed by OS sheet numbers and by the library's own grid system.

Summary
The London Borough of Southwark covers the former Metropolitan Boroughs of Bermondsey, Camberwell and Southwark, which in turn superseded ten civil parishes in 1900. The maps treat the area from the 16th century onwards. There are substantial groups of municipal and estate plans, both mainly 19th century and largely manuscript. A few estate plans are significantly earlier. There are many original maps of London, c.1770–1830, and facsimiles or earlier ones. The library's 25,000 property deeds have many attached plans, chiefly 18th and 19th century.

Detail
5, 6b, 10b,c, 11, 12, 13, 15, 16, 17b,c

Facsimiles and reproductions on sale
The Alan Godfrey Edition of old OS maps at 25 miles to the inch, for the area.

149   London Borough of Sutton, Sutton Heritage Service: Archives and Local Studies Department

Address   Central Library, St Nicholas Way, Sutton SM1 1EA

Telephone   (0181) 770 4747   *Fax*   (0181) 770 4777

Access   Open, but restricted hours.

Index
Archive and Local Studies Guide has a section on maps and also on the Archive Collections.

Indexes to maps in the Archive Collections, and catalogues to maps in the Local Studies Collections, on site.

Summary
The map collection covers the area of the London Borough of Sutton in detail and the County of Surrey in general.
The Archive Collection holds some manuscript maps and a large collection of sale catalogues. Efforts have been made to acquire copies of manuscript maps held elsewhere; there is a good holding of maps of the River Wandle.
Tithe and enclosure maps, covering the area of London Borough of Sutton.
Early county maps of Surrey, e.g. those by John Norden, John Speed and John Rocque (reproductions, with a few originals)
OS maps at 6 and 25 inches to 1 mile, for the area of the London Borough of Sutton, and at 1 inch to 1 mile for Surrey.

Detail
6a,b, 7, 10a,b,c, 11, 12, 17a

150   London Borough of Tower Hamlets, Local History Library

Address   Bancroft Library, 277 Bancroft Road, London E1 4DQ

Telephone   (0181) 980 4366 ext. 129

Access   Open, but appointment recommended.

Index
Card index on site, arranged alphabetically by place.

Summary
The London Borough of Tower Hamlets is made up of nine parishes: Stepney, Limehouse, Whitechapel, St George's in the East, Spitalfields, Shadwell, Wapping, Bethnal Green and Poplar. The collection includes about 500 pre-1900 maps and plans, mostly later than 1700, manuscript and printed. There are also general maps of London covering the borough, and some copies of manuscript maps in other collections.

Detail
6a,b, 7, 10b, 11, 13, 17c

Publications of maps held
W. Ravenhill, 'Joel Gascoyne's Stepney', *Guildhall Studies in London History*, **2**(4) (1977), 200–212.

151 London Borough of Waltham Forest, Waltham Forest Archives

Address   Vestry Museum, Vestry Road, Walthamstow, London E17 9NH

Telephone   (0181) 509 1917 or (0181) 527 5544 ext. 4391

Access   By appointment.

Index
Card index on site, arranged in sections according to former parishes, chronologically, with index of authors of all sorts.
S. D. Hanson, *A Walthamstow Bibliography* (Walthamstow Antiquarian Society, 1971) contains a short list of the more important maps of Walthamstow.

Summary
The collection relates to Essex, London and its environs, and more particularly, Stratford, Leyton, Leytonstone, Forest Gate, and the parishes of Walthamstow, Chingford, Wanstead, covering the years from 1699. The manuscript maps include: 'Manor of Ruckholt' (1721) by Thomas Archer; Walthamstow etc. levels (1818) by James Walker; survey of Low Leyton Level (1747) by John Noble; the manors of Woodford and Wanstead (1815–6) by John Doyley, with some terriers; drainage maps of Leytonstone (1867) by J. K. Doyley; survey of the manor of High Hall, Walthamstow (1699) by A. Forbes. Printed maps include some early county maps, from the 17th century, and some 1st edition OS sheets.

Detail
5, 6a,b, 7, 10a,b,c, 11, 12, 13, 15, 17a,b,c

Facsimiles and reproductions for sale
The Alan Godfrey Edition of old OS maps, for the Waltham Forest area.

152 London Borough of Wandsworth, Local History Collection

Address   Battersea District Library, Lavender Hill, London SW11 1JB

Telephone   (0181) 871 7467

Access   Open.

Index
No index to maps.

Summary
The collection holds maps and plans relating to the parishes of Battersea, Putney, Streatham, Tooting Graveney and Wandsworth. They are mainly printed or facsimile but do include some manuscripts, e.g. the Manor of Wimbledon (1787), the Springfield Estate (1839), and plans of buildings, mainly municipal. Several volumes of plans of areas in Wandsworth and Battersea with descriptions of individual properties sold by auction in 1835–6. Deposited Plans, including railway schemes.

Detail
10c, 11, 13, 15, 17a

Facsimiles and reproductions on sale
'Wandsworth and district' by John Rocque (1760).
Stanford's 'Library map of London' (1862), sheet 18, Clapham and Balham.
The Alan Godfrey Edition of old OS maps, for the area of the Borough of Wandsworth, dates between 1898–1916.

GREATER MANCHESTER

153   Wigan Archives Service

Address   Town Hall, Leigh WN7 2DY

Telephone   (01942) 672421 ext. 266   *Fax*   (01942) 602007

Access   By appointment.

Index
Wigan Record Office Guide (1976).
Lists and calendars to the relevant collections on site.

Summary
Wigan Record Office preserves records of about fourteen pre-1974 authorities; public records such as Quarter and Petty Sessions, and hospitals; school records, and many private papers and business deposits. OS 6 inches to the mile for most of Wigan and District (1846–9); 25 inches to the mile, 1st, 2nd and 3rd revised editions. Town plans of Wigan at 5 feet to the mile (1848) and 10 feet to the mile (c.1890). Manuscript maps include tithe maps (from 1840), enclosure awards (from 1764–5) and agreements (18th century), and various estate maps.

Detail
1, 5, 7, 10a,b,c, 11, 12, 13, 14, 15, 17a,b,c

Facsimiles and reproductions on sale
Alan Godfrey Edition of old OS maps: 25 inches to the mile 2nd edition (1907–8): Lancashire sheets 93.07, and Wigan area 93.08.

154   Bury Archive Service, Derby Hall Annexe

Address   Edwin Street, (off Crompton Street), Bury BL9 0AS

Telephone   (0161) 797 6697

Access   Open restricted hours, otherwise by appointment.

Index
Handlists on site. Interim guide to collections in preparation.

Summary

The service holds records of local authorities and private bodies in the Bury metropolitan area c.1675 to date. Many of these archive groups include maps and plans, usually in manuscript or as manuscript annotations on OS maps. Among these groups are:

Tithe maps (1838–42); Deposited parliamentary plans of railways and other utilities (1843–1927); Maps and plans of local authority sewer schemes and other projects (1848 onwards); Maps and deed plans for private estates (1750 onwards).

Detail

7, 10b,c, 11, 13, 15, 17a

155   Bolton Archive and Local Studies Service

Address   Central Library, Civic Centre, Le Mans Crescent, Bolton BL1 1SE

Telephone   (01204) 22311 ext. 2179   *Fax*   (01204) 363224

Access   Open.

Index

Guide to Bolton Archive Service (1988), pp.48–50.

Handlists of archive deposits, notably those of Albinson and Jackson (see below) on site.

Microfilm copies of Archive Lists available from Chadwyck Healey (Cambridge).

Summary

Bolton Metropolitan Borough (Greater Manchester since 1974) took in the former areas of Bolton County Borough, Farnworth Municipal Borough and the Urban Districts of Blackrod, Farnworth, Horwich, Kearsley, Little Lever, Turton and Westhoughton, all in Lancashire.

Large scale OS maps, scales ranging from 6 inches to 1 mile to 10 feet to 1 mile, 1845 to date, for Bolton and district as detailed above.

Manuscript maps and plans including estates, industrial premises, roads, railways, canals, and enclosure, 1620–1950, most Bolton and district.

The records of John Albinson of Bolton, land surveyor (1748–1850), and of Joseph Jackson & Sons of Bolton, land agents and surveyors (1777–1950), contain several thousand manuscript maps and plans, among them those of mines and quarries, industrial plants, roads, bridges, railways and canals, waterworks, churches and miscellaneous estate plans.

Detail
6b, 7, 10b,c, 11, 12, 13, 14, 15, 17a,c

156   Salford Archives Centre

Address   658–662 Liverpool Road, Irlam, Manchester M30 5AD

Telephone   (0161) 775 5643

Access   By appointment.

Index
Handlists on site and at NRA.

Summary
The maps held in the Archives Centre have been acquired by the City Archivist. The great majority date from the 19th century onwards. They fall into the following groups:
(1) About 200 OS and other maps of Salford and parts of Lancashire and Cheshire published for the general public.
(2) About 18,000 manuscript maps produced by local authorities from the mid-19th century onwards.
(3) Records of Peel Estates Ltd. and its predecessors, containing several thousand estate, colliery and canal or navigation maps, Lancashire and Cheshire, from the late 18th century onwards.
(4) A small number of other estate, railway and other thematic maps.

Detail
5, 7, 10a,b,c, 11, 13, 14

157   City of Manchester Central Library

Address   St Peter's Square, Manchester M2 5PD

Telephone   (0161) 234 1900   *Fax*   (0161) 234 1963

Access   Open.

Index
Handlists of OS maps covering Manchester and Salford, and local towns and villages, on site.

Summary
The library holds a fairly extensive collection of maps and atlases collected since 1851. There is no map collection as such and material is

divided between subject departments. There is an outstanding collection of local printed and manuscript maps.

Detail
1, 2, 3, 4, 5, 6a,b, 7, 8, 9, 10a,b,c, 11, 12, 13, 14, 15, 16, 17a

Publications of maps held
A. L. Smyth, 'The Ordnance Survey', *Manchester Review* **6** (1953), 513–16.

158   Chetham's Library

Address   Long Millgate, Manchester M3 1SB

Telephone   (0161) 834 7961   *Fax*   (0161) 839 3609

Access   Open.

Index
Bibliotheca Chethamensis ... Catalogus:
Vol I – 1791 : pp.220–22 Tabulae Geographicae.
Vol IV – 1862 : pp.450–52 Chartae Tabulae, &c.

Summary
The Library was founded under the terms of the will of Humphrey Chetham (1580–1653) and has been operating since 1655.

Maps are interspersed throughout the collection which is an historical one and they date from the early 16th century onwards. The collection of William Asheton Tonge (1860–1936) acquired in 1937 is particularly strong in the topography, archaeology and antiquities of Lancashire, Cheshire and Yorkshire.

In addition to atlases and road books there is a collection of separate maps. The earliest is the plan of Manchester and Salford, 1741, published by R. Casson and J. Berry, later editions of this map also being held. Maps by William Green and Charles Laurent (1790s). 'Adshead's maps of the township of Manchester', original survey by R. Thornton, at 80 inches to one mile, 1851. Numerous maps in directories and gazetteers, and plans of individual streets, rivers and buildings.

Item 11399 is 'A Scrap Book of Maps, Plans, Views etc. of Manchester', presented in 1838.

Detail
1, 2, 3, 4, 5, 6a,b, 7, 8, 9, 10b, 11, 12, 13, 14, 15, 17a

Publications of maps held
The Library and, in brief, its maps, are described in
N. Frangopulo, *Rich inheritance* (Manchester, 1969), pp.246–54.
Moelwyn I. Williams, *Directory of Rare Book and Special Collections* (London, 1985), pp.398–401.

159   Stockport Central Library, Library of Social Studies

Address   Wellington Road South, Stockport SK1 3RS

Telephone   (0161) 474 4540/4524   *Fax*   (0161) 474 7750

Access   Open.

Index
Cheshire maps in the Stockport Local History Collection (Stockport Public Libraries, Handlist No.3, 1962) lists only 100 maps from the collection. Handlists on site.

Summary
The Library holds about 2500 maps, both printed and manuscript. The Cheshire county maps begin with Christopher Saxton's map of 1577. OS sheets at 1 inch, 6 and 25 inches to 1 mile, from 1842. Canal and railway maps. An as yet uncatalogued addition to the collection came from the former Stockport Metropolitan Borough and consists of several thousand maps and plans from its various departments.

Detail
6a,b, 10a,b,c, 11, 13, 14, 15, 17a

160   Rochdale Central Library, Local Studies Library

Address   The Esplanade, Rochdale OL16 1AQ

Telephone   (01706) 864915

Access   Open.

Index
Handlist on site.

Summary

A collection of over 600 maps, including estate plans, administrative surveys, railway maps and plans, and tramway plans. Also the Falinge Hamlet Survey (1819), Baines' Town Centre Plan (1824), Butterworth's Town Plan (1829), the first complete survey of the Borough (1831), a town centre survey (1842), and a series of Castleton Township (1844). OS sheets at 6 inches to 1 mile of 1851 and 1892, at 60 inches to 1 mile of 1851, at 25 inches to 1 mile of 1890–1937, and the large-scale 1:500 series printed in 1892, for the Littleborough and Rochdale areas. An extensive collection of manuscript plans made by local surveyor T. L. Whitehead, in the later part of the 19th century, shows various streets and estates in great detail.

Detail
6a,b, 7, 10b,c, 11, 13, 14, 15

161   Salford Local History Library

Address   Peel Park, Salford M5 4WU

Telephone   (0161) 736 2649   *Fax*   (0161) 745 9490

Access   Open.

Index
No index to maps.

Summary
The collection covers the area of the present City of Salford, consisting of Eccles, Irlam, Salford, Swinton, Walkden and Worsley, with a few general Lancashire County maps. It consists mainly of printed maps, chiefly various OS series, from 1845, but also includes copies of 18th century estate plans of the Bridgewater and Trafford estates in the locality.

Detail
6a, 10a,b,c 11, 14

Facsimiles and reproductions for sale
'Manchester and Salford' (1740); Green's 'Salford' (1794).

162   Tameside Local Studies Library, Stalybridge Library

Address   Trinity Street, Stalybridge SK15 2BN

Telephone   (0161) 338 2708 / 3831   *Fax*   (0161) 303 8289

Access   Open.

Index
Guide to the Archive Collection, on site, outlines OS map holdings.
Archive catalogue and library index to Stamford Estate plans (these are also held by NRA).
Card catalogue of OS and county maps.

Summary
OS maps from 1842, covering roughly the area now called Tameside.
Printed county maps for Lancashire and Cheshire, from the 1780s.
Some Stamford Estate plans for the Ashton under Lyne area, c.1800–1950, including plans of railways, waterways, sewerage, bridges and roads, the latter being a private collection of plans pertaining to the former estate of the Earl of Stamford and Warrington.

Detail
6a, 7, 10a,b,c, 11, 13, 14, 15

163   Barclays Records Services, Group Archives

Address   Dallimore Road, Wythenshaw M23 9JA

Telephone   (0161) 902 0421   *Fax*   (0161) 946 0226

Access   By appointment.

Index
Handlist of archives of the former Martin's Bank, includes maps.
The majority of Barclays records are computerised.

Summary
A few maps and plans amongst other property and business documents, including a plan of the houses destroyed and damaged by the fire which began in Exchange Alley, Cornhill in 1748, scale 1 inch to 18 yards, Cruchley's County Map of Glamorgan, three estate plans relating to Heath and Leighton Buzzard, Beds., Map of the course of the North

Staffordshire Railway and of the Trent and Mersey canal; map and sale prospectus for an estate at Scole and Diss, Norfolk (1897); plan of land in the parishes of St Peter and St Mary, Ipswich, at 1 inch to 8 feet.

Detail
2, 10a, 11, 13, 14

164 Salford Mining Museum

Address   Buice Hill Park, Eccles Old Road, Salford M6 8GL

Telephone   (0161) 736 1832

Access   By appointment.

Index
The plan collection is partly catalogued, but uncatalogued material can be made available.

Summary
About 1000 plans, many original, and dating from 1800 onwards, of former mineworkings in the North West, mainly Lancashire and Greater Manchester.
Geological Survey 1st Edition 6 inches to 1 mile, covering the former county of Lancashire. Various strata and geological sections, maps and plans.

Detail
1, 5, 6a,b, 10a,b,c, 11, 13

MERSEYSIDE

165   Merseyside Record Office

Address   4th Floor, Cunard Building, Pier Head, Liverpool L3 1EG

Telephone   (0151) 236 8038   *Fax*   (0151) 236 5827

Access   Open.

Index
No index to maps.

Summary
Some maps in family and estate records, notably 37 plans in the Weld Blundell collection, dating from 1866, mainly relating to the building of Birkdale Park (Southport) and South West Lancashire.

Detail
11

166   Liverpool Record Office and Local History Department

Address   Liverpool Libraries and Information Services, William Brown Street, Liverpool L3 8EW

Telephone   (0151) 225 5417   *Fax*   (0151) 207 1342

Access   Open.

Index
Maps are identified in the Local History Catalogue and Archives lists, on site.
Handlist of Liverpool street maps.
Index to OS maps of Liverpool (25 inches to 1 mile, 1891–1935 editions).

Summary
Coverage of Lancashire and Cheshire, but concentrating on Liverpool. Printed and manuscript maps.
Printed maps: Lancashire from 1610, Cheshire from 1749. Street maps

of Liverpool, from a conjectural map of the 14th century onwards.
Goad Insurance Plans.
Surveys of the Rivers Mersey and Dee and Liverpool Bay, including
Hydrographic Office charts and some earlier printed charts.
OS sheets, at 1, 6, and 25 inches to 1 mile, and 10 feet to 1 mile, from
1845.
There are also maps in relevant archive collections.

Detail
6a,b, 7, 8, 9, 10a,b,c, 11, 12, 13, 14, 15, 16, 17a

167 St Helens Local History and Archives Library

Address   Central Library, Gamble Institute, Victoria Square, St Helens, WA10 1DY

Telephone   (01744) 24061 ext. 2952   *Fax*   (01744) 20836

Access   Open.

Index
Card index and calendars on site.

Summary
Most OS maps of the Borough of St Helens, 1840s to date.
Most local authority building plans submitted to St Helens Improvement
Commissioners, then St Helens Borough Council, from 1850 onwards.

NB. Many of the building plans are in poor condition and those too
fragile to use cannot be made available until they have been conserved.

Detail
5, 7, 10a,b,c, 13, 15

168 University of Liverpool

Address   Sydney Jones Library, Special Collections Department, PO Box 123, Liverpool L69 3DA

Telephone   (0151) 794 2673   *Fax*   (0151) 708 6502

Access   Open to members of the University, otherwise by appointment.

Index

J. Sampson (comp.), *A catalogue of books, printed and in manuscript, bequeathed by T. G. Rylands* (Liverpool, 1900).

Duplicated select list (incomplete) (1977).

Handlist arranged by classification, on site.

Summary

Strong holdings of early atlases scattered in a number of Special Collections, but particularly in the Rylands Collection, bequeathed by Thomas Glazebrook Rylands in 1900. Some charts.

Detail

1, 2, 3, 4, 6a, 8

167   Pilkington Group Archives

Address   c/o Information Management and Storage, Hamlet House, Delftwood Drive, St Helen's, WA9 5JE

Telephone   (01744) 453555

Access   By appointment.

Index

No index to maps.

Summary

Mainly plans of glass works in St Helens and of the estates upon which these works were erected, from the 1770s, with later maps consisting of annotated OS sheets.

Detail

5, 10a,b, 11

WEST MIDLANDS

170 Birmingham Central Library

Address   Chamberlain Square, Birmingham B3 3HQ

170A Archives Division

Telephone   (0121) 235 4217   *Fax*   (0121) 233 4458

Access   Open. CARN reader's ticket required.

Index
Catalogues of various collections which include maps are available on
site and at NRA.
There are no separate handlists.

Summary
The holdings of the Archives Division are largely manuscript:
(1) Maps in family and estate collections: covering Staffs., Warwicks.
and Worcs., 16th to 20th centuries.
(2) Surveyors' collections: railway, canal, road and estate plans relating
to Midland counties, late 17th to 20th centuries.
(3) Birmingham tithe and enclosure plans.
(4) Birmingham town maps, from the 19th century onwards.
(5) Deposited railway and road plans, from the 19th century onwards.
(6) Boulton & Watt Collection: Among the Watt family papers are maps
and plans, probably by John Watt (1687–1737, uncle of James Watt)
surveyor of roads in Scotland (Lanarks., Renfrews., Firth of Forth and
River Clyde, 1720s-30s).
James Watt also worked as a surveyor and engineer on various Scottish
canals during his early years and the collection includes maps of canals,
rivers, lochs and harbours, by him and others such as John Rennie,
printed and manuscript, from the 1770s, including the Caledonian and
Crinan Canals, Port Glasgow, Ayr Harbour, Greenock Harbour and the
River Clyde. James Watt also acquired estates in Wales and the Collection
includes plans of Kinnerton Township, Radnor (1815).

Detail
7, 11, 12, 13, 14, 15, 17a

Publications of maps held
A. F. Fentiman, *John Snape, Land Surveyor 1737–1816. A comprehensive list of his works* (Sutton Coldfield: Fentiman, 1986), lists his works held in Birmingham Library and other libraries and record offices in the Midlands.

170B   Local Studies and History

Telephone   (0121) 235 4549

Access   Open, but advance notice required for pre-1700 material and for access to large quantities of maps.

Index
Handlists on site, but these are no longer correct due to recent restructuring of departments.

Summary
The holdings consist of approximately 48,000 sheet maps and 1600 atlases and books about maps, including modern and non-British material. There are some 18,000 maps of Birmingham, including large scale OS maps, current and historical.
The largest part of the collection relates to antiquarian mapping of England and Wales, and especially of the local area. A few general thematic maps of Britain.
Christopher Saxton's wall map of England and Wales (1583), mounted on cloth and measuring $4\frac{1}{2}$ by 6 feet with heraldic border, one of two surviving examples of the original state.
Numerous pre-1700 atlases donated by W. A. Cadbury (of Cadburys). The George Skett collection (a large private collection donated in 1978), consisting of several thousand OS sheets, including two sets of OS First Series, 1 inch to the mile; also a number of large scale 18th century county surveys.
OS maps, all editions, at 6 inches to the mile for local counties; at 25 inches to the mile for local area.

Detail
1, 6a, 7, 10a,b,c, 11, 12, 13, 14, 16, 17a

171 Dudley Archives and Local History Service

Address   Mount Pleasant Street, Coseley, Dudley WV14 9JR

Telephone   (01902) 880011

Access   Open.

Index
Card catalogue, and draft catalogue (giving details and descriptions) of Dudley Estate plans, on site.

Summary
There are several thousand manuscript and printed plans, dating from the 17th to 20th centuries. The bulk of the holdings relate to the estates of the Earls of Dudley and are part of the family's archive deposited here. There is also a quantity of local authority plans which have been microfilmed.

Detail
5, 6a, 10a,b,c, 11, 12, 13, 14, 15, 17a,b,c

Facsimiles and reproductions on sale
'Plan of the mines of Lord Dudley' by Sheriff (1812).
'Dudley', by Treasure (c.1835) and by Richard (1865, the time of Dudley's incorporation). Town plan of Stourbridge (1837).

172 Sandwell Local Studies Service

Address   Smethwick Library, High Street, Smethwick B66 1AB

Telephone   (0121) 558 2561   *Fax*   (0121) 555 6064

Access   Open.

Index
The map collection is in process of being listed. Readers are advised to consult the archivist in advance of their visit.

Summary
The area covered is that now adminstered by Sandwell Metropolitan Borough Council.
A good holding of large-scale OS maps, chiefly at 25 inches to 1 mile, with some town plans at 1:500. Copies of tithe maps. Maps and plans produced by Borough Councils etc.

For some areas, manuscript maps produced for local Boards of Health (1850s). In some cases these are drawn to large scales and show great detail.

This area was very heavily mined in the 19th century and the collection includes many manuscript plans of mine workings, chiefly of mid to late 19th century date, as well as a large number of mine plans and mine draining plans.

Detail
6a, 7, 10c, 11, 15, 17c

173   Walsall Local History Centre

Address	Essex Street, Walsall WS2 7AS
Telephone	(01922) 721305
Access	Open.

Index
Published *Handlist of accessions to the Archives 1972–1992* (Revised edition) includes a section on maps and plans.
Card catalogue of printed maps on site.

Summary
The Centre holds manuscript and printed maps relating to the Walsall Metropolitan Borough Council area. The earliest manuscript map is the Countess of Mountrath estate map of Walsall (1763).

Detail
1, 5, 6a, 7, 10a,b,c, 11, 12, 13, 14, 15, 17a,b,c

Facsimiles and reproductions on sale
Alan Godfrey Edition of old OS maps, at 25 inches to the mile for the area.

174   Wolverhampton Archives and Local Studies

Address	Central Library, Snow Hill, Wolverhampton WV1 3AX
Telephone	(01902) 312025 *Fax* (01902) 714579
Access	Open.

Index
Unpublished handlists on site.

Summary
County maps relating to Staffordshire.
Manuscript and printed maps, 16th to 20th century, relating to Wolverhampton and district, with the adjoining areas of South Staffordshire. These include official local government plans and plans deposited with the Clerk of the Peace, as well as privately deposited material including local estates, industries, etc.

Detail
1, 5, 6a, 7, 10a,b,c, 11, 12, 13, 14, 15, 17a,c

Publications of maps held
M. Mills (ed.), *Mapping the past: Wolverhampton 1577–1986* (Wolverhampton Public Library, 1993).

Facsimiles and reproductions on sale
'Wolverhampton' by Isaac Taylor (1750).

NORFOLK

175   Norfolk Record Office

Address   Central Library, Bethel Street, Norwich NR2 1NJ

Telephone   (01603) 761349   *Fax* (01603) 761885

Access   Open. CARN reader's ticket required.

Index
J. C. Tingey, *Revised Catalogue of Norwich City Records* (1898).
Guide to the Great Yarmouth Borough Records (1972), including maps
and plans.
Card catalogue, arranged by parish and land surveyor, on site, which
includes Norfolk manuscript maps held elsewhere.

Summary
The Record Office holds estate and parish surveys and other manuscript
maps relating to Norfolk mostly within the period 1580–1900, and
photocopies of maps known to be in private hands. It is particularly rich
in local maps before 1650 by surveyors such as William Haiward, Thomas
Waterman, John Godwin and George Sawer. Maps by Haiward of
Morley (1629) and Gressenhall (1624) have drawings of herdsmen and
their flocks. There is a virtually complete series of enclosure maps for
the county and a tithe apportionment with maps for most of the 700
parishes in Norfolk.
The Norfolk Bishopric and Cathedral properties are particularly well
covered as are the Bickling, Heydon, Stotesham, Earsham, Killington,
Stow Bardolph and Hunstanton estates. Henry Bradfer-Lawrence's extensive collection of West Norfolk maps and copies was accumulated partly
in an effort to locate King John's lost treasure in the Wash. An unusually
early survey comprises three maps of field strips at Shouldham, 1440–
41, in the archives of Sir Ralph L. Hare, Bt. There are considerable
holdings of maps for areas in Cambs., Essex, Lincs., and Suffolk; other
counties represented are Bucks., Cheshire, Cumberland, Devon, Durham,
Herts., Hunts., Kent, Leics., London and Middx., Northants., Surrey
and Yorks.

Detail
11, 12, 13, 14, 15, 17a,c

N.B. On 1 August 1994 fire destroyed a large part of Norwich Central Library. We understand that the vast majority of items in the archives were safely retrieved, though some have suffered water damage. Intending users should seek further details in advance from the Office.

176 Holkham Hall

Address   Wells-next-the-Sea, Norfolk NR23 1AB

Telephone   (01603) 761349   *Fax* (01603) 761885

Access   Admission strictly by appointment with the Librarian. Admission granted for research on original materials not available elsewhere, or not reproduced photographically.

176A The Library

Index
A catalogue is in preparation.

Summary
The Library of the Earls of Leicester (at present administered by Viscount Coke). The Library of Chief Justice Coke (1552–1634) and his heir Thomas Coke (1697–1759), First Earl of Leicester of the first creation, with agricultural and estate records (see next section, 'The Archives') of 'Coke of Norfolk', namely, Thomas William Coke (1752–1842), First Earl of the second creation. Of major importance for British maps is the Innys Collection.
The topographical collection of John Innys, Citizen and Stationer of London (1695–1778) was assembled between about 1714 and 1750. It is entitled 'A General System of Cosmography ... Illustrated by Maps, Plans and Views, Collected from the Most Eminent Authors, Ancient and Modern' There are a total of 113 elephant folio volumes, of which vols.112–113 are indexes. The collection was acquired by Thomas Coke in about 1750. The material from the British Isles totals 34 volumes, numbers 67 to 99. Innys was working as a bookseller and publisher in London from 1710 to 1729, and had access to the products of the map trade, also acquiring important manuscript maps.

Detail

Publications of maps held
On the origins and content of the Innys Collection, see
H. Wallis, 'Discovery at Holkham Hall', *Colonial Williamsburg* (Williamsburg VA, USA) **15** (Spring, 1993), 49–55.
H. Wallis, 'The copperplate maps and the Holkham engravings', *The Map Collector*, **56** (1991), 13–21.

176B The Archives

Address   The Estates Office, Holkham Hall

Index
Handlists on site. Handlists of photographic copies are held in the Map Library of the British Library and in the Bodleian Library.

Summary
The estate plans at Holkham Hall date from 1575 and cover the Norfolk holdings of the Coke family. Those of the late 18th century are notable on account of the agricultural reforms of 'Coke of Norfolk'. Photographic reproductions are held in the Map Library of the British Library and in the Bodleian Library.

NORTHAMPTONSHIRE

177   Northamptonshire Record Office

Address   Wootton Hall Park, Northampton NN4 89BQ

Telephone   (01604) 762129   *Fax*   (01604) 767562

Access   Open.

Index

Card catalogues and indexes on site. Enclosure, tithe and some other types of maps have been listed in summary or detail; lists available on site.

Summary

Manuscript maps of parishes and estates in Northamptonshire and the Soke of Peterborough, from c.1570, and the adjacent counties, with some from other parts of the British Isles; some printed maps of the county, with a few of other counties. OS maps at various scales; plans in sale catalogues of properties; road maps and other maps in books.

Bishop of Peterborough's estates, in London and elsewhere. The Brudenell family archives have a fine collection of estate maps relating to the West Riding of Yorkshire and include some 18th century plans of coal workings. The Finch Hatton maps cover the Earl of Winchelsea's Kent estates in the neighbourhood of Eastwell and Wye.

An important collection of mining plans for ironstone, both underground and open-cast, dating from the beginning of the century. Maps of forests. Maps showing proposed changes in administrative and other areas.

Detail

1, 5, 6a,b, 7, 9, 10a,b,c, 11, 12, 13, 14, 1, 16, 17a,c

178   Northamptonshire Libraries, Northamptonshire Studies Collection

Address   Central Reference Library, Abington Street, Northampton NN1 2BA

Telephone   (01604) 26774/26772   *Fax*   (01604) 230790

Access   Open.

Index

Guides and indexes on site.

Summary

A collection of printed maps, including originals and some copies.
Maps of Northampton, 1610 to date. Maps of Northamptonshire, 1576 to date. Small collection of town and village maps.
OS maps of the county: 1 inch 1st edition (post 1870) reprint. 6 inch 1st edition (1880s), incomplete. 25 inch 1st edition (1886–7), Northampton and surrounding area only. Plans at 2 miles to the inch (1885 edition) for Northampton area.

Detail

6a,b, 7, 10a,b,c, 12, 13, 15, 16

Facsimiles and reproductions for sale

Northampton, by John Speed (1610), by J. Noble and Butlin (1747), by G. Cole and J. Roper (1807), by Wood and Law (1847), by W. W. Law (1891). Northamptonshire, by John Norden, (1591), by William Kip (1610), by Robert Morden (1708), by Hermann Moll (1724), by Thomas Kitchin (1752), by Emanuel Bowen (1760), by A. Bryant (1824–6), by Cole (1838), by Bingley (1842), by Lea (1693), by John Speed (1610), by Jan Jansson (1659), by T. Eyre and J. Ogilby (1791). 'The Road from London to Derby' (1695) by J. Ogilby.

NORTHUMBERLAND

179A Northumberland Record Office

Address Melton Park, North Gosforth, Newcastle-upon-Tyne NE3 5QX

Telephone (0191) 236 2680 *Fax* (0191) 236 2680

Access Open. (Some collections have closure periods.)

Index

Northumberland History: A brief guide to records and aids in Newcastle-upon-Tyne (1962) lists tithe plans, enclosure awards, railway plans.
'The Bell Collection of Plans and Surveys' (handlist to the Bell Collection) lists extensive collection of estate plans relating to Northumberland.
All plans in listed collections are included in the topographical card index.

Summary

Manuscript plans including enclosure awards, tithe awards, Deposited Parliamentary plans, estate maps, coal mining plans. The Office holds the records of the North of England Institute of Mining and Mechanical Engineers of Newcastle upon Tyne, which has maps relating to the northern counties of England.

Detail
1, 5, 6a,b, 7, 8, 9, 10a,b,c, 11, 12, 13, 14, 15, 17,a,c

179B Berwick-upon-Tweed Record Office

Address Council Offices, Wallace Green, Berwick-upon-Tweed TD15 1ED

Telephone (01289) 330044 *Fax* (01289) 330540

Access Open.

Index
No index to maps.

287

Summary

Holdings relate to Berwick-upon-Tweed and North Northumberland, and include:

(1) For Berwick-upon-Tweed, Buck's 'View' (1745); OS at 10 feet to 1 mile, 1852, for Berwick and Tweedmouth; OS at 2 inches to 1 mile, 1852, for Berwick, Tweedmouth and Spittal; tithe maps of Berwick-upon-Tweed, 1840s.

(2) For Berwick-upon-Tweed and North Northumberland, 2nd edition OS maps at 6 inches to 1 mile.

(3) Various estate maps (Ford) and enclosure plans (Holy Island, 1792); Tweedmouth and Spittal, 1799).

Detail

7, 10b,c, 11, 12, 13, 17a

NOTTINGHAMSHIRE

180   Nottinghamshire Archives

Address   County House, Castle Meadow Road, Nottingham NG2 1AG

Telephone   (01159) 581634

Access   Open. CARN reader's ticket required.

Index

H. Nichols, *Local maps of Nottinghamshire to 1800: an inventory* (Notts. C.C.: Leisure Services, 1987) includes all estate maps etc. in the Archives collection.
Card index to all major manuscript and printed maps (other than OS), also arranged by surveyor, on site.

Summary

The collection consists of the following groups:
(1) OS (incomplete) set of all editions pre-1950, at 1 inch, 6 and 25 inches to 1 mile, for Nottinghamshire; some 19th century town plans at 10 feet to 1 mile.
(2) Printed county maps, 16th to 20th century.
(3) Manuscript estate maps, 1619 to 19th century.
(4) Sale plans etc, 19th to 20th century.
(5) Enclosure and tithe maps, 18th to 19th century.
(6) Deposited plans, 19th to 20th century.
Groups 3, 4, 5, and 6 cover Nottinghamshire, with some examples from Derbyshire, Yorkshire, Lincolnshire and a few from other counties.
There are photocopies of major estate maps in private hands, especially William Senior's maps of the Earls of Newcastle's and Devonshire's estates in Nottinghamshire and Derbyshire and many other counties, *c.*1610–1630 (originals at Welbeck Abbey and Chatsworth House), and Christopher Saxton's manuscript plan of Shafton, Yorkshire (1597) (original at Osberton Hall).

Detail

5, 6a,b, 7, 10a,b,c, 11, 12, 13, 14, 15, 16, 17a,b,c

181 British Geological Survey, Library and Records

Address   Keyworth NG12 5GG

Telephone   (01159) 363205   *Fax*   (01159) 363200

Access   Open. Appointment recommended when extensive research is involved.

Index
Lists on computer and as printouts, on site.

Summary
Earth science maps from all parts of the world, 18th century to date. As well as public sheets the collections include many manuscript sheets produced by Survey staff and others.
There are a few estate maps relating to where geological work took place, e.g. sections along railway lines.

Detail
1, 2, 3, 4, 5, 6a, 7, 10b, 11

Publications of maps held
The Library has many indexed articles on the more important geological maps produced before 1900.

Facsimiles and reproductions for sale
Copying and photographic service available.

182 University of Nottingham

Address   University Park, Nottingham NG7 2RD

182A University Library, Department of Manuscripts and Special Collections

Telephone   (01159) 514565   *Fax*   (01159) 514558

Access   By appointment.

Index
Handlists on site and available at NRA, British Library and Copyright Libraries.

Summary

Main collections containing maps and plans are those of Drury-Lowe, Manvers, Middleton, Newcastle, Portland, Denison, Hatfield Chase Corporation, Severn-Trent Water Authority. The bulk are estate maps, and up to *c*.1860 are usually manuscript; later practice was to adapt OS maps. The earliest map is of watermills on the River Allen, Dorset, *c*.1520 (Middleton collection). Fine series of maps for Manvers estates, e.g. Laxton – open field (Manvers Mss). Other maps derive directly out of careers of individuals, e.g. Lord William Bentinck, 1780–1839, who among other interests was a Fenland improver in Norfolk, and the Duke of Newcastle (Portland and Newcastle collections). Also maps and plans in records of drainage and water authorities (Brigg Court of Sewers, Hatfield Chase Corporation, Severn-Trent Water Authority).

Detail
1, 3, 4, 5, 6a, 7, 8, 9, 10a,b,c, 11, 12, 13, 14, 15, 17a

182B Department of Geography

Telephone   (01159) 515456   *Fax*   (01159) 515249

Access   By appointment only for non-members of the University.

Index
Not directly available for consultation.

Summary

The collection is now a reference/archive collection for students and staff of the University, but access is severely limited since there is no longer a full-time librarian and the room once known as the map library is now a multi-purpose teaching/computing room although the bulk of the map collection is still housed there, under lock and key, with access only under the supervision of the Senior Cartographer.
The maps of historical interest are mostly 19th century including 1st edition and early OS.

Detail
1, 2, 3, 4, 5, 6a,b, 7, 8, 9, 10a,b,c

OXFORDSHIRE

183   Oxfordshire Archives

Address   County Hall, New Road, Oxford, OX1 1ND

Telephone   (01865) 815203   *Fax*   (01865) 810187

Access   By appointment.

Index
Indexes and catalogues on site.

Summary
There are manuscript and printed maps from four sources:
(1) maps deposited with Oxfordshire Quarter Sessions under statutory requirememts, e.g. railway, canal and turnpike plans.
(2) maps forming part of evidence produced before Oxfordshire Quarter Sessions, e.g. road diversions.
(3) maps collected by 19th century Clerks of the Peace, e.g. printed county maps.
(4) enclosure maps for most of the county, dating from the late 18th and 19th centuries and tithe maps from the 1830s.
(5) a large number of privately deposited maps, e.g. estate maps from c.1586, printed county maps, turnpike maps. Some of the estate maps form part of large collections of records relating to a particular estate such as that of the Jerseys of Middleton Stoney for the 19th century. The collection includes some material relating to the adjacent counties of Berkshire and Buckinghamshire.
The archives of University College, Oxford, are made available at this office.

Detail
1, 6a,b, 7, 10a,b,c, 11, 12, 13, 14, 15, 17a,c

184 Oxfordshire County Libraries, Centre for Oxfordshire Studies

Address   Central Library, Westgate, Oxford OX1 1DJ

Telephone   (01865) 815749   *Fax*   (01865) 810187

Access   Open.

Index
Sheaf catalogues, arranged by date, personal names, subjects and titles, on site.

Summary
Collection of original, reproduction and photocopies of printed maps of Oxford and Oxfordshire, from 1574 to the present, many taken from atlases. The works of John Speed, Wenceslaus Hollar, Joan Blaeu, Jan Jansson, David Logan, John Ogilby, Robert Morgan, Thomas Gardner, Thomas Kitchen, J. Lodge are represented. Subjects covered include the city of Oxford, its colleges and its fortifications; the county of Oxfordshire in whole and in parts, and with adjacent areas; the Thames, from source to sea; 17th and 18th century roads from Oxford to Banbury, Bristol, Cambridge, Chichester, Derby, Salisbury; two 'hunting maps' of 1834 showing meets of local hunts; plan of the canal from Oxford to Coventry, 1774; railways; and local administration. Many of the maps cover adjacent parts of Berks. and Bucks., the road and river maps extend further afield.

Detail
6a,b, 7, 10a,b,c, 13, 14, 15

Facsimiles and reproductions on sale
Oxford by Agas (1578), Loggan (1675), Faden (1789), Moule (1845); Oxfordshire by Speed, 1605 (1611), by Blaeu (1648), by Greenwood (1834), by Moule (1845); Berkshire, by Speed, 1605 (1611), by Moule (1845); Saxton's 'Oxfordshire, Berkshire, Buckinghamshire' (1574).

185 Bodleian Library

Address   Broad Street, Oxford OX1 3BG.

Access   By reader's ticket; non-members of the University need recommendation.

185A Map Section

Telephone (01865) 277013/277014 *Fax* (01865) 277182

Index

M. Clapinson and T. D. Rogers, *Summary catalogue of post-medieval western manuscripts in the Bodleian Library, Oxford: Acquisitions 1916–75*, vol 2 (Oxford: Bodleian Library, 1991), nos. 48167–48474.

E. M. Rodger, *The large scale county maps of the British Isles 1596–1850: a union list* (Oxford: Bodleian Library, 1972).

'Maplists' series: unpublished lists by topic, in progress. (Copies deposited with other major map libraries).

Card index on site.

Summary

The Bodleian is the library of Oxford University and it is also one of the copyright libraries of the British Isles. Maps and atlases, both originals and facsimiles, have been acquired since the end of the 16th century. Sir Thomas Bodley's agreement with the Stationers' Company in 1610, whereby one copy of every work entered at Stationers' Hall in London was granted by the Company to the Library was continued in later years under the Copyright Acts and brought a large number of cartographical works into the Library. A local topographical collection took form with the arrival of the county maps that were published in the 18th century and was greatly increased when, in 1809, the Bodleian received the library of Richard Gough, the antiquary. This bequest consisted of a large number of books on local topography, together with a large collection of general and county maps.

The Bodleian Map Library now holds:

(1) Printed maps: copyright deposits including most OS issues, a few official deposits, and a large collection of county maps, from the 16th century surveys of Christopher Saxton onwards.

The Todhunter-Allen Collection of atlases and printed maps of Britain, from 1617, formerly held at Lancashire Record Office, is now in the Bodleian Library.

(2) Manuscript maps: a few official deposits (but most of these have been passed to the appropriate Record Offices), and maps from amongst private deposited papers and gifts. These consist largely of estate maps covering all counties of the United Kingdom.

Important items are the Gough Map (*c*.1360), the oldest known road map of Great Britain and probably the oldest British map in the Library; the map of Laxton open fields by Mark Pierce (1635); the map of Oxford by Ralph Agas (1578) and the Hamond map of Cambridge (1592).

Detail
1, 2, 3, 4, 5, 6a,b, 7, 8, 9, 10a,b,c, 11, 12, 13, 14, 15

Publications of maps held
'The Map of Great Britain, circa AD 1360, known as the Gough Map', facsimile with overlays and memoir by E. J. S. Parsons (Oxford, Bodleian Library, reprinted 1970).

Facsimiles and reproductions on sale
The individual Christopher Saxton county maps, 1570s.
The Gough Map, *c*.1360.
Laxton Open Fields map, by Mark Pierce, 1635.

185B   Oxford University Archives

Telephone   (01865) 277152   *Fax*   (01865) 279299

Access   (See above, for reader's ticket); by prior arrangement with the Archivist. Material is usually consulted in Duke Humfrey's reading room in the Bodleian Library.

Index
No index to maps.

Summary
Maps occur among the records of the University's estates. The Archives is responsible only for the administrative records of the University itself. There is no separate list or catalogue of maps; estate records can only be approached via indexes of places. The University's 'ancient estates' of which there may be maps in the Archives include Cookham, Berks (acquired in 1609), Langdon Hills, Essex (1621), the Manor of Bexley, (1622) and Elmley, (1860) both in Kent, Bledington (1756) and Wick Rissington, (1634), both in Glos., Stuchbury, Northants. (1740), Chedzoy, Somerset (1860).

Detail
11

186   The School of Geography

Address   Mansfield Road, Oxford OX1 3TB

Telephone   (01865) 271919   *Fax*   (01865) 271929

Access   By appointment only.

Index
Library catalogue.

Summary
Working collection of maps mainly for undergraduate use, but also 20–25 county atlases dating mainly from the 19th century, with a few earlier examples. OS maps, 1 inch to the mile, all editions. 1st edition Geological Survey maps. Topographical and thematic maps.

Detail
1, 2, 3, 4, 5, 6a,b, 7, 8, 9, 10a,b,c

187   All Souls College, The Codrington Library

Address   Oxford OX1 4AL   Located at: High Street

Telephone   (01865) 279318   *Fax*   (01865) 279299

Access   By written appointment.

Index
Preliminary List of Estate maps (All Souls College): Codrington Library and College archives, List and Inventories No.2 (1987).
Typed handlist also at Bodleian and NRA.

Summary
The collection of Elizabethan and Jacobean maps must be unrivalled. There are 211 estate maps, of which 108 are dated or datable to the period 1579 to 1605. NB Certain maps listed above have been deposited in the Bodleian Library. Detailed descriptions have been made of all the maps. The counties represented include Beds., Berks., Bucks., Kent, Leics., London and Middx., Northants., Oxon., Salop, and Somerset. There are three maps of Wales.

Detail
11, 12, 17a

Reproductions of maps on sale
Filmstrips available from Bodleian Library: All Souls College Archives, Hoveden Survey. Estate maps of the College's lands in survey made for warden Robert Hoveden, 1588–1605.
Roll 231, Estate maps of lands in Beds., Berks., Bucks., Kent, Leics., Middx., Northants., Oxon., Salop and Somerset, with a view of the College (84 frames).
Roll 121B, Close-up of maps of Wheatley, Oxon., showing arable strips and woodlands, 1593–4 (8 frames; The Wheatley maps are included, not in close-up, in Roll 231.)

188 Balliol College

Address   Oxford OX1 3BJ   Located at: Broad Street

188A The Archives

Telephone   (01865) 277777   *Fax* (01865) 277803

Access   By appointment.

Index
Section II H 1/C, in J. H. Jones, *The Archives of Balliol College, Oxford* (Phillimore, 1984), pp. 22–23.
Handlist of the Archives published on microfiche by NIDS (National Inventory of Documentary Sources).
Handlist on site.

Summary
Maps (including two tithe maps) relating to lands owned by the College, the College site, etc. These go with other College records to provide an overall picture of the growth and development of the College and hence provide detailed local information. The estates are located in the counties of Beds., Bucks., Cumbs., Devon, Essex, Glos., Hants., Northumb., Oxon., Radns., Salop, Som., Warwicks. and Worcs.

Detail
5, 10c, 11, 17

188B   The Library

Telephone   (01865) 277777   *Fax*   (01865) 277803

Access   By appointment.

Index
Catalogue in Library.

Summary
Some antique atlases.

Detail
1

189   Brasenose College, The Archives

Address   Oxford OX1 4AJ   Located at: Radcliffe Square

Telephone   (01865) 277830   *Fax*   (01865) 277822

Access   By appointment.

Index
Two unpublished catalogues, 1885–1909 and c.1965.
Card index, 1910 onwards.
Handlist of main estate maps, 1992.

Summary
Maps of College estates, located in the counties of Beds., Berks., Bucks.,
Cheshire, Durham, Essex, Glos., Hants., Herefs., Hunts., Kent, Lancs.,
Leics., Lincs., Middx., Northants., Oxon., Sussex, Warwicks., Wilts.,
Worcs. The maps are mostly manuscript, dating 1750–1975. Seven earlier
maps, c.1500–1738. Provenance generally unrecorded. Other small maps
and plans are to be found among the estate papers and correspondence,
most of which is only roughly listed at present. OS maps from 1st, 2nd
and 3rd editions, endorsed with College information, for use as estate
maps.

Detail
5, 6a, 10b,c, 11, 14

Publications of maps held
Brasenose Quatercentenary Monographs (Blackwell's and Oxford Historical Society, 1909).

190 Christ Church, The Muniment Room

Address   Oxford OX1 1DP   Located at: St Aldate's

Telephone   (01865) 276150   *Fax*   (01865) 276276

Access   By appointment.

Index
A very detailed typescript catalogue is: E. W. Bill, *A Catalogue of Maps, Plans and Drawings, at Christ Church, Oxford* (1953). Copies in Christ Church and in The Library, Lambeth Palace.

Summary
Printed and manuscript maps used in adminstration of Christ Church estates, from 17th century onwards. The estates are located in the counties of Berks., Bucks., Cambs., Cheshire, Devon, Glos., Hants., Herts., Kent, Lancs., London, Middx., Monts., Norfolk, Northants., Oxon., Salop, Som., Warwicks., Wilts., Worcs., Yorks.

Detail
6a, 10b,c, 11

Publications of maps held
D. H. Fletcher, *The emergence of estate maps: Christ Church, Oxford, c.1600 to 1840* (Oxford University Press, forthcoming.)

Reproductions of maps on sale
Filmstrips available from Bodleian Library:
Manuscript estate map of Hillesden, Bucks. Roll 264.6 (8 frames).

191 Corpus Christi College

Address   Oxford OX1 4JF   Located at: Merton Street

191A The Archives

Telephone   (01865) 276717

Access   By appointment.

Index
C. M. Woolgar, *Catalogue of maps and estate plans.* Unpublished manuscript held in the Archives and Bursary.

Summary
Maps of the college estates in Beds., Berks., Bucks., Devon, Glos., Hants., Kent, Lincs., Northants., Oxon., Som., Surrey, Sussex, Wilts. and Yorks. dating from 17th century: printed and manuscript. Some estates were first surveyed in the early 17th century by Matthew Nelson, Thomas Langdon and Henry Wilcock. Some surveys have small scale maps of single tenements, e.g., Langdon on Lincolnshire estate, 1609. There are also annotated OS maps of the College estates.

Detail
11

Publications of maps held
C. M. Woolgar, 'Some draft estate maps of the early seventeenth century', *The Cartographic Journal* **22** (1985), 136–143.
B. Twyne *et al.*, 'Chartarum chirographorum, et aliorum id genus munimentorum, de brevis ... Collegi Corporis Christi in alma universitate Oxon ...' 1627/8, reproduced by the National Register of Archives, see Royal Commission on Historical Manuscripts, *Report of the Secretary to the Commission, 1871–2*, p.14.
J. L. G. Mowat, (ed.), *Sixteen old maps of properties in Oxfordshire (with one in Berkshire) in the possession of some of the colleges in the University of Oxford, illustrating the open field system* (Oxford, 1888) reproduces seven maps by Thomas Langdon, *c*.1605, four of Lower Heyford, Oxon., one of Whitehill, Tackley, Oxon., two of Cowley and Headington, Oxon.
H. Lambert, 'Some account of the Surrey manors held by Merton and Corpus Christi Colleges, Oxford, in the 17th century', *Surrey Archaeological Collections* **41** (1933), 34–49, describes five maps of Egham, Surrey, 1659 and 1829.
F. Turner, *Egham, Surrey : A history* (Egham, 1926), pp.112–13 reproduces part of one of the above maps by Langdon.
J. G. Milne, 'The Berkshire muniments of Corpus Christi College, Oxford', *Berkshire Archaeological Journal* **46** (1942), 38–9 reproduces a map of Streatley and Arborfield, Berks., by Thomas Langdon, 1606.
P. Eden, 'Three Elizabethan surveyors: Peter Kempe, Thomas Clerke and Thomas Langdon' in S. Tyacke (ed.), *English Map making 1500–1650: historical essays* (1983), pp.68–92.
Photographic reproductions of Hampshire 17th-century maps are held at Hampshire Record Office. Photographic reproductions of Oxfordshire (pre-OS) maps held in the Local Studies Section of the Oxford City Library, Westgate, Oxford.

Reproductions of maps on sale
Filmstrips available from Bodleian Library:
Berkshire and Hampshire estates maps of College properties by T. Langdon, 1606. Roll 211F (28 frames).
Estate maps, Glos., Lincs., Oxon., Somerset, Surrey, 17th to 19th centuries. Roll 249.1 (24 frames.)

191B   The Library

Telephone   (01865) 276700   *Fax* (01865) 793121

Access   By written appointment.

Index
Card index on site.

Summary
Printed atlases dating from the early 17th century.

Detail
1

192   Exeter College, The Library

Address   Oxford OX1 3PD   Located at: Turl Street

Telephone   (01865) 279600   *Fax* (01865) 279630

Access   By appointment.

Index
Handlist of maps in college archives (chiefly estate maps).
OS and other published maps in card catalogue.

Summary
Estate maps of college properties in Oxfordshire and Somerset from 16th to 19th centuries. Town plans of Oxford, 1789 etc. Maps of woodlands in Hertfordshire, 19th century.
Some building plans. OS 1 inch, 1805 etc.
Some published maps of Britain, derived from Saxton and from Camden's 'Britannia'.

Detail
1, 5, 6b, 10a, 11, 12, 17a

Publications of maps held
J. L. G. Mowat, (ed.), *Sixteen old maps of properties in Oxfordshire (with one in Berkshire) in the possession of some of the colleges in the University of Oxford, illustrating the open-field system* (Oxford, 1888).

193   Hertford College, The Library

Address   Oxford OX1 3BW   Located at: Catte Street

Telephone   (01865) 279409   *Fax* (01865) 279437

Access   By written appointment with the Archivist or Librarian.

Index
Handlist of earlier printed books is available in the Library.

Summary
Some early printed atlases and 17th- and 18th-century works with maps. Most of these volumes came to Hertford as part of the library of Magdalen Hall, formed *c.*1650 to 1760.
No manuscript maps, since the College has never owned estates.

Detail
1, 6

194   Jesus College

Address   Oxford OX1 3DW   Located at: Turl Street

194A   The Archives

Telephone   (01865) 279700   *Fax* (01865) 279687

Access   By appointment with the Archivist and/or the Estates Bursar.

Index
Handlists on site.

Summary
OS and manuscript estate maps, relating to College property dating from the late 18th and 19th centuries. The College's longstanding link with Wales makes the collection of Welsh maps important. Counties rep-

resented are: Anglesey, Brecon, Bucks., Cards., Carms., Denbigh, Essex, Flint., Glam., Herefs., London, Merion., Mon., Northants., Oxon.

Detail
5, 10b,c, 11

194B The Library

Telephone (01865) 279700 *Fax* (01865) 279687

Access By appointment.

Index
No index to maps.

Summary
A few early printed maps of Oxford, one of Cardiff and one of London, and some pre-1900 atlases are in the Fellows' Library.

Detail
1, 7

195 Keble College, The Library

Address Oxford OX1 3PG Located at: Parks Road

Telephone (01865) 272727 *Fax* (01865) 272705

Access By appointment.

Index

Summary
The Library holds the original (19th-century) plans of the College.

Detail
7

196 Lincoln College

Address   Oxford OX1 3DR   Located at: Turl Street

196A The Archives

Telephone   (01865) 279831   *Fax   (01865) 279802*

Access   By appointment.

Index
No index to maps.

Summary
The College Archive has six maps of College estates in Bucks. and Yorks., dating from the 18th and 19th century.

Detail
1, 11

196B The Library

Telephone   (01865) 279831   *Fax*   (01865) 279802

Access   By written appointment.

Index
No index to maps.

Summary
Published atlases, 18th and 19th centuries, and maps of Oxford, 18th and 19th centuries.

Detail
1, 6, 13, 14, 15

197 Magdalen College

Address   Oxford OX1 4AU   Located at: High Street

197A The Archives

Telephone   (01865) 276000   *Fax*   (01865) 276103 / 276094

Access   By appointment, restricted to certain days of the week.

Index
Handlist of Maps Group 1, and card indexes for Maps Groups 2 and 3, on site.
Most of the pre-1800 maps are described in the manuscript 10-volume *Catalogue of the estate records of St Mary Magdalen College, Oxford*, on site, copy at NRA.

Summary
The estate maps in the College archives cover 20 counties, evidence of the extensive estates once owned by Magdalen. Many items have not yet been listed but it is estimated that there are about 500 items in the collection, most of which are manuscript maps. (This figure does not include the OS maps.) The earliest dated maps are 1613, but there is an undated sketch-map attributed to the late 16th century. There are three groups of loose maps and three bound volumes; one of the latter contains mainly 20th-century maps. There are also a number of rough sketch plans among the estate papers. The Maps 1 series, in particular, includes fine examples of the cartographer's art. There is a number of pre-enclosure maps. Counties represented are Berks., Beds., Bucks., Essex, Glos., Hants., Kent, Lincs., London, Middx., Norfolk, Northants., Notts., Oxon., Som., Suffolk, Surrey, Sussex, Warwicks., Wilts. There is a large collection of OS maps of college lands.

Detail
10, 11

Publications of maps held
C. M. Woolgar, 'A late 16th-century map of St Clement's, Oxford', *Oxoniensa* **46** (1981), 94–98.

197B The Library

Telephone (01865) 276045   *Fax* (01865) 276103//276094

Access By appointment.

Index
Card index on site.

Summary
Chiefly estate maps and plans of college properties in the counties of Beds., Berks., Bucks., Glos., Hants., Kent, Lincs., Norfolk, Northants., Notts., Oxon., Som., Suffolk, Surrey, Sussex, Warwicks., Isle of Wight, Wilts. and Yorks., dating from 1613 onwards.

Detail
1, 10a,b,c, 11, 12

Publications of maps held
All the estate maps pre-1800 are described in: C. M. Woolgar, *Catalogue of the estate archives of St Mary Magdalen College, Oxford* (1982), reproduced by National Register of Archives.

198 Merton College, The Library

Address Oxford OX1 4JD   Located at: Merton Street

Telephone (01865) 276380   *Fax* (01865) 276361

Access By written appointment.

Index
Handlist on site.

Summary
Mainly manuscript estate maps of college properties in Oxon., Surrey (Maldon, Chessington and Farleigh) and Leicester, dating from 16th century. Copies of the Surrey and Leicester maps are held by the respective County Record Offices.

Detail
11, 12

Reproductions of maps on sale
Reproductions of the Surrey and Leicester maps can be obtained from the respective County Record Offices.

Filmstrips available from Bodleian Library:
Maps of the village centre of Kibworth Harcourt, Leicestershire, 1606, 1635 and 1780. Roll 253.1 (4 frames).

199 New College, The Archives

Address Oxford OX1 3BN Located at: New College Lane

Telephone (01865) 279555 *Fax* (01865) 279590

Access By appointment. NB Some estate maps are held by the Land Agent but access should be arranged through the Archivist.

Index

Maps are noted in the geographical section of F. W. Steer, *The Archives of New College, Oxford*. (Phillimore, 1974), pp.155–486.
Typed handlist to mid-19th century manuscript maps which are kept by the College Land Agent for reference.

Summary

Nearly all the maps are in manuscript. The earliest dates from 1590 and the latest from 1873. They illustrate College estates in Beds., Bucks., Berks., Cambs., Essex, Glos., Hants., Herts., Kent, London, Middx., Norfolk, Oxon., Salop and Wilts. Of particular interest is a group of mid-18th-century maps drawn by Edward John Eye for the College. There are a few interesting draft maps. Some of the estate maps contain drawings of buildings. There are some ground-plans of buildings and plots owned by the College in London and Oxford, the earliest dating from the mid-17th century. There are some thematic maps showing the extent of the College woods, which are thought to have been prepared by Thomas Langdon *c*.1600.
The estate maps of lands in Hornchurch and Bradwell on Sea, Essex, include shorelines, marshes and drawings of ships.
There are some detailed maps of watercourses where these indicate boundaries, for example, between the parishes of Alton Barnes and Alton Priors, Wilts., in the early 17th century.
A large number of the maps illustrate manuscript survey books.

Detail

5, 6b, 10a,b, 11, 12, 15, 17a,c

Publications of maps held

E. M. Elvey, *A handlist of Buckinghamshire estate maps*,

(Buckinghamshire Record Society, 1963), reproduced one New College estate map.

S. A. Bendall, 'Interpreting maps of the rural landscape: an example from late sixteenth-century Buckinghamshire', *Rural History* **4** (1993), 107–21, discusses and reproduces three maps of land in Oakley, Brill and Boarstall in the 1590s.

Actual-size photographs of the College's Oxford estate maps are held at the Centre for Oxfordshire Studies, The City Library, Westgate, Oxford.

200 Oriel College

Address   Oxford OX1 4EW   Located at: Oriel Square

200A The Archives

Telephone   (01865) 276555   *Fax*   (01865) 791823

Access   By appointment. Access restricted to certain days of the week.

Index
Rough card index to estate records on site.
Typed handlist of maps.

Summary
Manuscript maps of estates and individual properties, 1683–1900. Counties represented are Berks., Devon, Essex, Heref., Kent, Lincs., Oxon., Som., Wilts.,
OS maps at 6 and 25 inches to the mile, of College estates. Further maps may be included in uncatalogued material.

Detail
10b, c, 11, 12, 13, 17a

Publications of maps held
C. L. Shadwell and H. E. Salter, 'Oriel College Records', *Oxford Historical Society* **85** (1926) deals with the College site and College lands near Oxford.

200B The Library

Telephone (01865) 276558 *Fax* (01865) 791823

Access By appointment.

Index
Card index on site.

Summary
Printed maps and atlases of counties, regions and towns.
Military maps.

Detail
1, 2, 3, 6a, 7, 9

201 Pembroke College

Address Oxford OX1 1DW Located at: St Aldate's

201A The Archives

Telephone (01865) 276444 *Fax* (01865) 276418

Access By appointment with the Librarian.

Index
Typed handlist of estate maps on site.

Summary
Manuscript and annotated OS maps of College estates from the 18th,
19th and 20th centuries. The estates are located in Berks., Middx, Oxon,
Pembs. and Wilts. Very large scale maps and plans of the College site.

Detail
11

201B The Library

Telephone (01865) 276444 *Fax* (01865) 276418

Access By appointment.

Index
On site.

Summary
There is no map collection as such, but the McGowin Library contains some maps and atlases.

Detail
1

202 The Queen's College

Address Oxford OX1 4AW Located at: High Street

202A The Archives

Telephone (01865) 279120 *Fax* (01865) 790819

Access By appointment.

Index
Typescript calendar of maps and plans relating to Southampton and district (copy in Southampton City Record Office); other maps etc. listed only in typescript general calendar of the archives.

Summary
Manuscript estate maps and plans of the College and its properties mainly in Berks., Hants (especially Southampton), and Oxon., from 17th to 19th centuries.

Detail
7, 10b, 11, 12, 13, 17a,c

Publications of maps held
J. R. Magrath, *The Queen's College* (Oxford, 1921) reproduces a few College plans.
'The Cartulary of God's House', *Southampton Record Series* 1 (1976), reproduces two plans of God's House, Southampton.

202B   The Library

Telephone   (01865) 279130   *Fax*   (01865) 790819

Access   By appointment.

Index
Catalogue cards (by author) on site.

Summary
Some early printed atlases, and antiquarian travel and topography books which include maps, plans and views. A 17th-century manuscript plan for linking the Thames, Avon and Severn to provide a navigable route from London to Bristol.

Detail
1, 2, 3, 4, 6a,b, 7, 8, 10c, 11

203   St Edmund Hall, The Library

Address   Oxford OX1 4AR   Located at: Queen Street

Telephone   (01865) 279000   *Fax*   (01865) 279090

Access   By appointment.

Index
Catalogue on site, but rather rudimentary.

Summary
The Old Library contains a few early printed atlases.

Detail
6b, 7

204   St John's College

Address   Oxford OX1 3JP   Located at: St Giles'

204A The Library

Telephone   (01865) 277300   *Fax* (01865) 277435

Access   By appointment.

Index
No index to maps.

Summary
Early printed atlases. 18th-century map of London in 24 sheets.

Detail
1, 7

204B The Muniment Room

Telephone   (01865) 277300   *Fax* (01865) 277435

Access   By appointment.

Index
H. M. Colvin, 'Manuscript maps belonging to St John's College, Oxford',
   Oxoniensia **40** (1950), 92–102.
Unpublished handlist supplementing Colvin's catalogue on site.

Summary
The map collection covers the period from the late 16th century to the
present day. Manuscript maps are plentiful: extensive tithe award maps
for College estates as well as surveys, and plans of (mainly North Oxford)
suburban developments of the 19th and 20th centuries. There are 127
maps in all, excluding house plans. The counties covered by manuscript
maps and/or annotated OS maps are Beds., Bucks., Essex, Glos., Lancs.,
Northants., Oxon., Surrey, Warwicks., Westmor., Wilts.

Detail
7, 10a,b,c, 11, 12, 13, 14, 15, 17a,b,c,

Publications of maps held
T. Hinchcliffe, *North Oxford* (New Haven, Conn. and London: Yale
   University Press, 1992), traces suburban development on St John's
   College land.

205   Trinity College, The Archives

Address   Oxford OX1 3BH   Located at: Broad Street

Telephone   (01865) 279900   *Fax*   (01865) 279911

Access   By written appointment.

Index
Hand list on site.

Summary
Trinity's collection relates to the College estates, namely Wroxton and Balscot, and Holcombe, Oxon., and Great Waltham, Stoppesley and Abbots Langley in Essex. The College owns manuscript estate plans and some enclosure maps of the 18th and 19th centuries. There are also some annotated OS printed maps.

Detail
11, 12

206   University College Archives

Address   University College, Oxford OX1 4BH
NB These archives are made available at Oxfordshire Archives, County Hall, New Road, through whom enquiries should be made, on their telephone number, (01865) 815203.

Access   By appointment; two weeks' notice is required for maps to be produced.

Index
Shelf-list, with index, available at University College and at Oxfordshire Archives.

Summary
The greater part of the College's maps are connected with its estates in Essex, Hants., Hunts., Monts., Newcastle, Oxford and Oxon., Yorks., including the City of York and Pontefract. One or two predate 1750; the great majority date between 1750 and 1900 and usually show areas which are owned by the College.

Detail
2, 7, 11, 12

207 University College, The Library

Address   Oxford OX1 4BH   Located at: High Street

Telephone   (01865) 276621   *Fax*   (01865) 276790

Access   By appointment.

Index
No index to maps.

Summary
Printed material only, mostly atlases, dating from the late 18th century.

Detail
1, 2, 3, 4, 5, 6,a,b, 7, 15

208 Wadham College

Address   Oxford OX1 3PN   Located at: Parks Road

208A The Archives

Telephone   (01865) 277900   *Fax*   (01865) 277937

Access   By appointment.

Index
Wadham College Muniments, section 35 [nd]. List also held at NRA.

Summary
Manuscript estate maps of College properties in Gloucester, Essex and Oxfordshire, dating from 1740.

Detail
11, 12

208B   The Library

Telephone   (01865) 277900   *Fax*   (01865) 277937

Access   By appointment.

Index
Card index, arranged by author, on site.

Summary
The Old Books Collection contains a few published atlases, dating from the 17th century, and published Oxford town plans.

Detail
1, 7

209   Worcester College, The Library

Address   Oxford OX1 2HB   Located at: Beaumont Street

Telephone   (01865) 278300   *Fax*   (01865) 278387

Access   By appointment; evidence of identity and/or letter of recommendation normally required.

Index
Typed handlist available in the Library.

Summary
(1) Clarke papers (William Clarke 1623–66, George Clarke 1660–1736) include a number of manuscript military maps and plans, relating to Scotland, Ireland, England and the Continent, mostly dating from the late 17th century to the early 18th century, but a few, of Scotland and Ireland, from the Cromwellian period.
(2) George Clarke's collection of books includes some 17–18th century atlases, both English and continental, e.g. Joan Blaeu's *Atlas Maior, sive Cosmographia Blaviana* (Amsterdam 1662, 12 vols.).
(3) Estate maps of College properties in Berks., Bucks., Oxon., Wilts., and Worcs. plus large portfolio of annotated large scale OS maps of the estates.
(4) Important collection of architectural maps, plans and drawings, mainly of Oxford, from 18th and 19th centuries.

Detail
1, 9

Publications of maps held

H. M. Colvin (comp. and introduction by), *A catalogue of architectural drawings of the 18th and 19th centuries in the Library of Worcester College, Oxford* (1964).

C. H. Firth (ed.), *Scotland and the Protectorate*. Publications of the Scottish Historical Society No. 31 (Edinburgh: 1899).

SHROPSHIRE

210   Shropshire Records and Research Unit

NB The Record Office and the Local Studies Library will be brought together under one roof in around 1995.

210A   Shropshire Record Office

Address   Shirehall, Abbey Foregate, Shrewsbury SY2 6ND

Telephone   (01743) 252852   *Fax*   (01743) 360315

Access   By appointment.

Index
Estate map catalogue in preparation.
Card index to many maps, arranged by parish, on site.
Lists for some collections which include maps are held by NRA.

Summary
No special map collection, they occur in general collections. A large number of enclosure and tithe maps for the county are also held. Another collection of particular interest is the set of canal plans which relate to work undertaken by the Ellesmere Canal Depot, the central depot of the Ellesmere and Chester Canal Company and the Shropshire Union Canal Company.

Detail
6a,b, 7, 10a,b,c, 11, 12, 13, 14, 15, 17a,c

Facsimiles and reproductions on sale
Field name maps based on the tithe maps are available for sale.

210B Local Studies Library

Address Castle Gates, Shrewsbury SY1 2AS

Telephone (01743) 361058 *Fax* (01743) 368576

Access Open.

Index
Lists and indexes on site.

Summary
All maps and plans in the collection relate to Shropshire. Holdings of printed maps of the county are virtually complete from 1577 to 1900. A fine series of town plans of Shrewsbury *c.*1590–1882 (1:500 OS) is invaluable for studies of the town's development. Among the manuscript plans is a 3-volume survey of the estates of the Earl of Craven, *c.*1770, many of the plans showing pre-enclosed parishes of the county. Railway plans include manuscript working plans and detailed surveys of established lines.

Detail
5, 6a,b, 7, 10a,b,c, 11, 13, 17a

Publications of maps held
T. Rowley, *Shropshire landscape* (1972) reproduces Craven plans.
B. S. Trinder, *Industrial revolution in Shropshire* (1973) reproduces a plan of The Calcutts, Broseley, *c.*1730.

SOMERSET

211   Somerset Record Office

Address   Obridge Road, Taunton TA2 7PU

Telephone   (01823) 278805 / 337600   *Fax* (01823) 325402

Access   Open.

Index
Somerset Enclosure Acts and Awards (1948).
Handlist of Deposited Plans and Catalogue of Estate and Parish maps, unpublished typescript, on site.
Catalogue of Wells Cathedral Dean and Chapter estates' maps.

Summary
Enclosure maps and awards, from 1720 but mainly 1770–1830, deposited plans and books of reference, from 1791 (both series originally deposited with the Clerk of the Peace), the diocesan set of the tithe apportionment maps and awards for the diocese of Bath and Wells, mainly 1838–44, and manuscript maps of estates or parishes, from c.1600, but mainly 1770–1840, deposited in collections of records by individuals or firms of estate agents, solicitors, etc. The office also has a limited holding of printed county maps, and some out-county maps, especially for Devon, Dorset and Wiltshire.

Detail
6a, 7, 10a,b,c, 11, 12, 13, 14, 15, 17a,b

Publications of maps held
J. B. Harley, 'John Strachey of Somerset: an antiquarian cartographer of the early eighteenth century', *Cartographic Journal* **3** (1966), 2–7.
J. B. Harley and R. W. Dunning (eds), *Somerset maps: Day & Masters 1782, and Greenwood 1822* (Somerset Record Society, **76** 1981). Reprints two county maps at 1 inch to the mile, with introduction.

212   Somerset County Council, Local History Library

Address   The Castle, Castle Green, Taunton TA1 4AD

Telephone   (01823) 288871

Access   Open.

Index
T. Chubb, *A Descriptive List of the Printed Maps of Somersetshire, 1575–1914* (Taunton, 1914) describes most of the maps of which the library holds copies.

Summary
About 120 maps, all printed, nearly all of Somerset or parts of Somerset, dating 1599–1897.

Detail
6a,b, 7, 8, 10a

Facsimiles and reproductions on sale
J. B. Harley and R. W. Dunning (eds.), *Somerset maps: Day & Masters 1782, and Greenwood 1822* (Somerset Record Society, **76**, 1981). Reproduces the two maps at 1 inch to the mile, with introduction.

213   Wells Cathedral Library

Address   West Cloister, Wells Cathedral, Wells BA5 2PA

Telephone   (01749) 674483

Access   To research workers of postgraduate status and above, as a library of last resort. By written appointment.

Index
There is no separate index to maps and plans. Books published before 1701 are listed in *The Cathedral Libraries catalogue*, vol. I (British Isles), (Bibliographical Society, 1984).
For the Archives collection, see the Historical Manuscript Commission, *Calendar of Manuscripts of the Dean and Chapter of Wells*, vols I and II (1907, 1914) covering medieval and early modern records. This is supplemented by typescript catalogues of modern and Almshouse records, which note plans but do not index them separately. Copies of these

catalogues are available at Somerset County Record Office and the Local History Library.

Summary
The Library of the Dean and Chapter was built up by 17th and 18th century scholarly clerics and, in the main, consists of theology, canon law and civil law, history, etc., printed before 1800. It has no map collection as such, but there are some interesting topographical volumes of the 17th century, containing maps and charts. Several have important provenance (William Camden to Thomas James; John Ogilby to the Dean and Chapter of Wells.)
The Archives comprise records of the Cathedral itself, of Dean and Chapter estates and of Wells Old Almshouse. As such, they include some individual property plans, mostly on 19th century deeds, chiefly in and around Wells.
The Somerset County Record Office now holds many of the Dean and Chapter estate records, including maps and plans. There is a separate map catalogue for these at the Record Office.

Detail
1, 2, 3, 11

Facsimiles and reproductions for sale
Reproduction of William Simes 'Plan of Wells' (1735), published by, and available from, Wells Museum, 8 Cathedral Green, Wells BA5 2UE.

214   Hydrographic Office

Address   Ministry of Defence, Taunton TA1 2DN

Telephone   (01823) 337900   *Fax*   (01823) 284077

Access   By written appointment to the Curator, Hydrographic Data Centre.

Index
Admiralty Chart catalogue published annually since 1825, microfilm copies are available in major map libraries.
Manuscript catalogues and graphic indexes on site.

Summary

The Hydrographic Department of the Admiralty was founded in 1795. The principal collections held are:

(1) Record copies of published Admiralty charts, from c.1800. The most extensive known collection of such charts.

(2) Manuscript hydrographic surveys, from the 17th century but principally 19th and 20th centuries.

(3) Historical manuscripts, including views.

Detail

8

Publications of maps held

A. Day, *The Admiralty Hydrographic Service, 1795–1919* (1967), reproduces in colour the Fair Survey of Loch Awe (1861).

Facsimiles and reproductions on sale

'The Admiralty Collection. A selection of reproductions from the archives of the Hydrographic Office', Edition 2, 1993. The Collection contains 18 items illustrating the ports and harbours of Great Britain, 1751 to 1839, and is constantly being enlarged. Catalogue available on request.

215 Somerset Archaeological and Natural History Society

Address   Taunton Castle, Taunton TA1 4AD

Telephone   (01823) 288871

Access   Open.

Index

No index to maps.

Summary

About 80 separate printed maps, nearly all of Somerset, 1607–1882, and about a dozen atlases, mainly of the English counties, 1676–1856. Includes a copy of W. Sanders, 'Map of the Bristol Coal Fields, in 19 sheets, geologically surveyed', (1862). Other material belonging to the Society has been deposited at the Somerset Record Office.

Detail

5, 6a,b, 7, 10a

STAFFORDSHIRE

216   Staffordshire Record Office with William Salt Library

Address   Eastgate Street, Stafford ST16 2LZ

Telephone   Staffs. RO (01785) 223121 ext. 8380/8373
William Salt Lib. (01785) 52276

Access   Open. Staffordshire Archive Service reader's ticket required.

Index
Unpublished indexes and catalogues to collections on site and at NRA. *Staffordshire Estate Maps before 1840* (1980) and *Supplement.*

Summary
The collection comprises: county printed maps, 16th to 19th centuries, mostly of Staffordshire; Enclosure Awards, 18th and 19th centuries, Staffordshire; Tithe Awards, c.1835–50, Staffordshire, Shropshire, and other counties; estate maps, 1600 to 20th century, mostly Staffordshire; OS, c.1830 to date, mostly Staffordshire; printed town maps, 18th and 19th centuries, Staffordshire; a few printed atlases, 17th to 19th centuries.

Detail
5, 6a,b, 7, 9, 10a,b,c, 11, 12, 13, 14, 15, 17a,b,c,

Facsimiles and reproductions on sale
Staffordshire, by William Kip (1609), by Emanuel Bowen (1747), by Smith (1840).

217   Lichfield Joint Record Office

Address   The Friary, Lichfield WS13 6QG

Telephone   (01543) 256787   *Fax*   (01543) 263181

Access   By appointment. Staffordshire Archive Service reader's ticket required.

Index
Staffordshire Archive Service publications:
Handlist of Diocesan, Probate and Church Commissioners Records at Lichfield Joint Record Office (2nd edition, 1978), includes full list of tithe maps.
Handlist of Staffordshire Tithe Maps and Awards (1993).
Staffordshire Estate Maps before 1840 (1980), and *Supplement*.
Unpublished lists, on site and at NRA.

Summary
Tithe maps for the diocese of Lichfield, *c.*1837–1850.
Manuscript and printed maps for the city of Lichfield.
Manuscript estate maps for the diocese of Lichfield and county of Staffordshire.

Detail
7, 11, 13, 14, 15, 17a

218   Burton Library

Address   Riverside, High Street, Burton upon Trent DE14 1AH

Telephone   (01283) 43271

Access   OS maps on open access; appointment necessary for access to other maps.

Index
No index to maps.

Summary
A miscellaneous collection of manuscript and printed maps of Burton and its immediate environment.

Detail
10c, 12, 13

219 Lichfield Library, Local History Section

Address   The Friary, Lichfield WS13 6QE

Telephone   (01543) 262177   *Fax*   (01543) 263181

Access   Open.

Index
No index to maps.

Summary
Many of the maps held are copies of originals in the Lichfield Joint Record Office.
Staffordshire: by J. Speed (1610); by E. Bowen (1749), both copies. Hundred and parish boundaries, engraved by J. Down (1832), original. Lichfield: by John Snape (1766); and area, by W. Yeats (1775); and area, by Greenwood (1819–20); parishes and wards, by Dewhirst and Nichols (1836); and area, by Crompton (1862), all copies. Lichfield tithe maps, 1848, for the parishes of St Michael, St Mary, St Chad. Burntwood enclosure award and map (1860), copy.
OS sheets, Lichfield, 1:500 and 1:2,500 (1884).

Detail
6a,b, 7, 10b,c, 12, 17

Publications of maps held
Lichfield maps (Staffordshire County Council Education Department, 1970).
G. L. King, *The printed maps of Staffordshire 1577–1850, a checklist.* (Staffordshire Libraries, Arts and Archives, 1988).
[Staffs. C.C.], *Staffordshire maps before 1840, a handlist in the County Record Office* (Staffordshire County Council, 1980), with *Supplement* (undated).

220 University of Keele, Department of Geography, Map Library

Address   Keele ST5 5BG

Telephone   (01782) 621111 ext. 7554   *Fax*   (01782) 711553

Access   Open but advance notice to the Map Librarian recommended.

Index
No index to maps.

Summary
Historical collection comprises some county maps of Staffordshire and Cheshire, OS 1st edition sheets of the local area, and a number of town plans. There are also some manuscript maps of the local area.

Detail
5, 6a,b, 7, 10a, 11, 13, 14

SUFFOLK

221A   Suffolk Record Office

Address   Ipswich Branch, Gatacre Road, Ipswich IP1 2LQ

Telephone   (01473) 264541   *Fax*   (01473) 250954

Access   Open. CARN reader's ticket required.

Index
Handlists on site.
Lists of the manuscript maps at both the Ipswich and Bury-St-Edmunds Record Offices were published in *Archive News* (the newsletter of the Suffolk Record Office) as follows:
Part 1 (pre-1700) in No.5, Jan-June 1975; Part 2 (1701–1730) in No.7, Jan–June 1976; Part 3 (1731–1750) in No.9, Jan-June 1977; Part 4 (1751–1770) in No.11, Jan–June 1978; Part 5 (1771–1790) in No.12, July–Dec 1978; Part 6 (1791–1800) in No.17, April–Sept 1981. (*Archive News* is now deposited with the copyright libraries; photocopies of relevant sections from back numbers can be supplied if required.)

Summary
The Ipswich Branch Office collects from the former county of East Suffolk. Material for Waveney District is now held by Lowestoft Branch Office.
The maps date back to the late 16th century. The greater part comprise estate maps, mostly manuscript, but including a wide selection of parish maps and maps illustrating road, canal and railway development. The history of navigation in the River Orwell and the development of the port of Ipswich are contained in the records of the Ipswich Dock Commission.

Detail
6a,b, 7, 8, 10a,b,c, 11, 12, 13, 14, 15, 16, 17a,b,c

Publications of maps held
Seven centuries of surveying in Suffolk, a catalogue of an exhibition held in the Wolsey Art Gallery, Ipswich, Oct-Nov 1954.

Facsimiles and reproductions for sale
Ipswich at different periods.
'Needham Market' by J. Pennington (1772).

221B   Lowestoft Branch, Central Library

Address   Clapham Road, Lowestoft NR32 1DR

Telephone   (01502) 503308   *Fax*   (01502) 503311

Access   Open. CARN reader's ticket required.

Index
Card index of manuscript maps; card index, mainly to non-OS maps, on site. Lists of some deposited collections which contain maps are with the NRA.

Summary
This branch of the Suffolk R.O. collects maps for the northeastern part of the county (the modern Waveney District; part of the former East Suffolk). The dates covered are from *c.*1600 to 1900.
Manuscript maps consist mainly of estate, farm, drainage and survey maps. Some tithe maps are held, but very few enclosure maps. Others show roads and railways, harbour and haven improvements, etc.
The printed map collection consists of OS and county maps, town plans, sea charts and sale catalogue plans for estates, farms, building plots etc.

Detail
6a,b, 7, 8, 10a,b,c, 11, 12, 13, 17a

Facsimiles and reproductions on sale
'Suffolk' by Jan Jansson (1649).

221C   Bury St Edmund's Branch

Address   Raingate Street, Bury St Edmunds, IP33 1RX

Telephone   (01284) 722522

Access   Open. CARN reader's ticket required.

Index
Card index to maps before 1850 on site.
For lists of manuscript maps, see under **221A** for details.

Summary
The Bury St Edmunds Branch collects archival and printed material relating to the former West Suffolk area.

Detail
6a,b, 10a,b,c, 11, 12, 15, 17a

Facsimiles and reproductions on sale
'Suffolk' by Jan Jansson (1649).

SURREY

222A   Surrey Record Office

Address   County Hall, Penrhyn Road, Kingston upon Thames KT1 2DN

Telephone   (0181) 541 9065   *Fax* (0181) 541 9005

Access   Open, but appointment essential for Saturday openings. CARN reader's ticket required.

Index

Card index to original (largely manuscript) maps and plans (groups 3 and 4 below).

Unpublished volumes and handlists on site.

Summary

The collection can be grouped as follows:

(1) maps and plans drawn up by officers of Surrey Court of Quarter Sessions and of Surrey County Council in execution of their official duties, 18th to 20th centuries.

(2) Maps and plans deposited with the Clerk of the Peace for Surrey and the Clerk to the Surrey County Council, 18th to 20th centuries. These have been comprehensively described in a series of volumes on site, with a date index to surveyors, engineers and places.

(3) Original maps, 17th to 20th centuries, among various accumulations of archives deposited in Surrey Record Office, indexed on the card index mentioned above.

(4) Printed maps of Surrey or parts of the county, 17th to 20th centuries.

(5) OS 6 and 25 inch to the mile plans, 1st edition in complete series for area of the present administrative county; 2nd and subsequent editions have some gaps.

NB Groups (1) and (2) are held in certain cases for all parts of the ancient county of Surrey; (3) are in most cases held only for the area of the post-1889 administrative county of Surrey. The western half of the county is dealt with by Guildford Muniments Room.

Maps belonging to the Kingston Borough Archive: a tithe map of 1840 and altered apportionments for the 1850s, are made available in the Surrey Record Office, by appointment.

Detail
5, 6a,b, 7, 10a,b,c, 11, 12, 13, 14, 15, 17a,b,c

Facsimiles and reproductions on sale
Surrey, by John Speed (*c.*1610), by Joan Blaeu (*c.*1645), by Emanuel Bowen (*c.*1760).

222B   Kingston Borough Archives

Access   The records are made available in the Surrey Record Office searchroom, by appointment.

Index
Royal Borough of Kingston upon Thames, Guide to the Borough Archives (1971).

Summary
The only maps in the Borough archives are a parish copy of Kingston tithe map, 1840, and altered apportionments for 1 June 1850, 20 December 1855, 4 December 1856 (includes map), 18 May 1859 (includes map and 22 October 1868 (includes map).

Detail
17a

222C   Guildford Muniment Room

Address   Castle Arch, Guildford GU1 3SX

Telephone   (01483) 573942

Access   By appointment.

Index
Card index arranged by parish on site.
Summary Guide to Guildford Muniment Room (1967) lists briefly the more important private manuscript maps prior to 1810.
Catalogues of the Loseley manuscripts, and the Onslow manuscripts, with estates in Essex and Norfolk, have sections on plans and maps. (Copies at NRA).

Summary
The collection concentrates on the western part of the county (leaving Surrey Record Office as the source for the eastern part) and dates from

the 16th century onwards. It chiefly consists of maps deposited as part of private accumulations of Surrey archives – predominately estate and manorial maps, mostly manuscript but also printed plans attached to sale particulars. Large scale maps of Wey and Godalming Navigations. Incomplete set of tithe maps for Surrey parishes. There are also photocopies of important maps of the area held elsewhere.

Detail
1, 4, 5, 6a,b, 7, 11, 14, 17a

223   Kingston Museum and Heritage Service

Address   North Kingston Centre, Richmond Road, Kingston upon Thames KT2 5PE

Telephone   (0181) 547 6738   *Fax*   (0181) 547 6747

Access   Open.

Index
List of Surrey maps and OS maps, on site.

Summary
Surrey County maps from the 16th to 19th centuries.
Various specialist maps of Kingston Borough area.
OS sheets at $2\frac{1}{2}$, 6 and 25 inches to the mile, covering the present Kingston Borough area from 1860s to 1930s.

Detail
5, 6, 7, 9, 10b,c, 11, 12, 15, 16, 17a,b,c

Publications of maps held
Kingston in Maps: Archive Teaching Unit No. 4 (Royal Borough of Kingston, 1979).

224   Croydon Public Libraries, Museums and Arts

Address   Central Library, Katharine Street, Croydon CR9 1ET

Telephone   (0181) 760 5400   *Fax*   (0181) 253 1004
(0181) 679 5414 (Local Studies Library)

Access   Open.

Index

Index on site.

Sharp's *Historical catalogue*, detailed below, is practically a catalogue of Surrey maps in the collection.

Summary

General reference collection but is reasonably strong in Croydon and Surrey maps, notably Croydon by Jean-Baptiste Say (1785), enclosure map of 1800, W. Robert's tithe map (1847) and his plan of Croydon. Reproductions of local maps by John Speed, Christopher Saxton and John Rocque.

OS one inch to the mile from 1816, 6 and 25 inches to the mile from 1861–71, 2 inches to the mile from 1809–10, half-inch to the mile from 1889. Geological maps of the area from 1868.

Detail

1, 6a,b, 10a,b,c, 11, 13

Publications of maps held

H. A. Sharp, *Historical Catalogue of Surrey maps* (Croydon, 1929).

SUSSEX

225   East Sussex Record Office

Address   The Maltings, Castle Precincts, Lewes BN7 1YT

Telephone   (01273) 482349   *Fax* (01273) 482341

Access   Open. CARN reader's ticket.

Index

K. W. Dickens, *A catalogue of manuscript maps in the custody of the Sussex Archaeological Society* (Sussex Archaeological Society, Occasional paper No. 4, 1981).

F. W. Steer, *A catalogue of Sussex Estate and Tithe Award maps* (Sussex Record Society, **51**, 1962).

F. W. Steer, *A catalogue of Sussex maps*, vol.2. (Sussex Record Society, **66**, 1968).

W. E. Tate, *A Handlist of Sussex Inclosure Acts and Awards* (E. and W. Sussex C.C., 1950).

Catalogue of maps and plans accumulated by W. Figg (n.d.)

Summary

As an archive repository, the Office holds official maps, such as deposited plans of public undertakings, enclosure maps and tithe maps.

There are some thousand private estate maps, mainly manuscript, and dating from the 17th century onwards; also a collection of maps and plans accumulated by William Figg, land surveyor, of Lewes, formerly held by the Sussex Archaeological Trust.

As reference material, the Office holds a large number of OS maps of the county, at various dates and scales.

Detail

10a,b,c, 11, 12, 13, 15, 17a

Publications of maps held

D. J. Butler, *Town plans of Chichester*, (1972). (Reproductions of maps, 1595–1898).

D. Kingsley, *Printed maps of Sussex 1575–1900*, Sussex Record Society **72** (1982).

T. R. Holland, *Sussex Archaeological Collection* **95** (1957), 94–104.

K. C. Leslie and T. J. McCann, *Local history in West Sussex. A guide to sources* (2nd edition, 1975), 35–41.

H. Margary (ed.), *Two hundred and fifty years of map-making in the County of Sussex* (1970). (Reproductions of maps, 1575–1825).

226   West Sussex Record Office

Address   County Hall, Chichester PO19 1RN
Located at: Sherburne House, 3 Orchard Street, Chichester

Telephone   (01243) 533911   *Fax*   (01243) 777952

Access   Open. CARN reader's ticket required. At least two weeks advance notice required for Petworth House Archives maps (in the records of the Percy, Wyndham and Egremont families).

Index

Card index to maps; supplementary card indexes for manuscript maps and deposited plans, on site.

F. W. Steer, *A catalogue of Sussex Estate and Tithe Award maps* (Sussex Record Society **51**, 1962).

F. W. Steer, *A catalogue of Sussex maps*, vol. 2 (Sussex Record Society **66**, 1968).

W. E. Tate, *Sussex Inclosure Acts and Awards* (E. and W. Sussex C.C., 1950).

Catalogue of the Petworth House Archives, vol. 1, F. W. Steer and Osborne (eds.), (1968); vol. 2, T. J. McCann (ed.) (1979).

Summary

There is an extensive collection of county, parish, town and estate maps, printed and manuscript, dating from the late 16th century. This includes a series of county maps by Christopher Saxton, John Norden, John Speed, John Ogilby, Richard Budgen, and Thomas Yeakell and William Gardner. The collection of estate maps includes a superb set of surveys of the Goodwood Estate executed by Yeakell and Gardner in the late 18th century for Charles Lennox, 3rd Duke of Richmond. The Petworth House Archives include a fine series of maps of estates in Yorkshire, and some in Ireland.

Detail

1, 5, 6a,b, 7, 8, 9, 10a,b,c, 11, 12, 13, 14, 15, 17a,b,c

Publications of maps held

D. J. Butler, *Town plans of Chichester* (1972). (Reproductions of maps, 1595–1898).

D. Kingsley, *Printed maps of Sussex 1575–1900, Sussex Record Society* **72** (1982).

T. R. Holland, *Sussex Archaeological Collection* **95** (1957), 94–104.

K. C. Leslie and T. J. McCann, *Local history in West Sussex. A guide to sources* (2nd edition, 1975), 35–41.

H. Margary (ed.), *Two hundred and fifty years of map-making in the County of Sussex* (1970). (Reproductions of maps, 1575–1825).

227 Horsham Museum

Address 9 The Causeway, Horsham RH12 1HE

Telephone (01403) 254959

Access By appointment.

Index

Handlist on site and at West Sussex Record Office.

Summary

500 printed maps, including all editions of OS.

50 manuscript maps, 18th and 19th centuries, mainly of the Horsham area, including estate maps from 1651, railway plans.

Numerous sale particulars from 1777, some including maps of the properties.

Detail

5, 6a,b, 7, 9, 10a,b,c, 11, 12, 13, 14, 15, 17a

TYNE AND WEAR

228   Tyne and Wear Archives Service

Address   Blandford House, Blandford Square, Newcastle upon Tyne NE1 4JA

Telephone   (0191) 232 6789

Access   Open.

Index
Handlists on site. Some lists available at NRA.

Summary
Collection includes manuscript and printed maps, 1723 to date, largely Newcastle area.

Detail
1, 6a,b, 8, 10a,b,c, 11, 13, 17c

229   Newcastle upon Tyne Central Library, Local Studies Section

Address   Princess Square, Newcastle upon Tyne NE99 1DX

Telephone   (0191) 261 0691   *Fax*   (0191) 261 1435

Access   Open.

Index
Local catalogue of material concerning Newcastle and Northumberland
 (Newcastle Public Libraries Committee, 1932) lists maps and plans.
The card catalogue of local reference stock includes maps.

Summary
General collection of maps covering the whole North East area at all periods. It includes printed and manuscript maps; for example, estate plans.

Detail
5, 6a,b, 7, 8, 10a,b,c, 11, 12, 13, 15, 16

Publications of maps held
H. Whitaker, *A descriptive list of the maps of Northumberland, 1576–1900* (Newcastle Society of Antiquaries and Newcastle Public Libraries Committee, 1949).

230   Gateshead Central Library

Address   Prince Consort Road, Gateshead NE8 4LN

Telephone   (0191) 477 3478   *Fax*   (0191) 477 7454

Access   Open.

Index
Card index on site.

Summary
Ward boundary maps, town plans, estate, factory and railway maps and plans at various scales.
Of historical importance is the Bell manuscript collection, compiled by the Bell family of land surveyors between 1800 and 1850. The areas covered are Felling, Gateshead and Whickham (all within the area of the present Gateshead Metropolitan Borough Council).
OS maps: at 1:2500, 1st edition (1858), 2nd edition (1898), covering Gateshead Metropolitan Borough. At 1:500, 1st edition (1858), 2nd edition (1898), covering the central part of the old Gateshead County Borough. At 1:10,560 (1898), covering Gateshead Metropolitan Borough plus some adjoining areas.

Detail
5, 6a,b, 7, 10a,b,c, 11, 12, 13, 15, 17c

231   University of Newcastle upon Tyne

Address   The Robinson Library, Special Collections, Newcastle upon Tyne NE2 4HQ

Telephone   (0191) 222 7671   *Fax*   (0191) 222 6235

Access   Non-members of the University by written appointment.

Index
Handlist of John Speed proofs on site.

Summary

Thirteen proofs of county maps, from John Speed's *Theatre of the Empire of Great Britain* (c.1611).
Plans of the Clarence railway, Co. Durham (1827 and 1829). Town plans of Newcastle upon Tyne by Thomas Oliver (1844 and 1857–58), and a later revision by W. Boyd (1909). Town plans of Newcastle upon Tyne published by Andrew Reid (1878 and 1879). Various maps of Northumberland, 1580 to 1867. John Wood's Northumberland and Durham Town Atlas, 1822–27.
J. T. W. Bell's plans of the great northern coalfield, 1843–1852. William Oliver's map of the Northumberland and Durham coalfield (1851). M. Burleigh's plan of the River Wear (1737). 17th century survey of the River Tyne. J. F. Ure's maps of the River Tyne, 1781, 1881, 1889.
OS maps, 1 inch to 1 mile, 1st edition, full set except for Isle of Man; 6 inches to 1 mile, 1864–7, Northumberland only, incomplete.

Detail
1, 5, 6a, 7, 10a,b, 13, 15

232   The Literary and Philosophical Society

Address   Westgate Road, Newcastle upon Tyne NE1 1SE

Telephone   (0191) 232 0192

Access   Open to members of the Society, and to others on request.

Index

Catalogue of the Library of the Literary and Philosophical Society of Newcastle upon Tyne (Newcastle, 1903).
Unpublished handlist to *Local Maps and Plans* (4 vols).
Complete card catalogue of holdings to date, on site.

Summary

The Society's Library is 200 years old and reflects the Society's early interests in science and technology, in reports of voyages of exploration and discovery, and in literature, history and the arts, and in all these things with particular reference to the North East. The map collection is a general one which includes material of special interest, such as the 6 inch to the mile OS maps of Ireland of c.1840. Local maps and plans, printed and manuscript, relate to topography, road, rail and river transport and the mining industry and date from the early 17th century.

Detail
1, 2, 3, 4, 5, 6a,b, 7, 8, 10a,b,c, 11, 13, 14, 15

WARWICKSHIRE

233   Warwickshire County Record Office

Address   Priory Park, Cape Road, Warwick CV34 4JS

Telephone   (01926) 412735   *Fax*   (01926) 412509

Access   Open. Reader's ticket required, issued on production of adequate identification.

Index
Card Indexes on site.

Summary
Manuscript plans:
Estates of Warwickshire families, 17th century onwards. These include some out-county maps, e.g. estate maps of Buckinghamshire occur among the Throckmorton of Coughton papers.
Tithe, 19th–20th centuries; enclosure, 18th–19th centuries. Deposited plans of public enterprises (deposited with the Clerk of the Peace), late 18th century onwards; highway diversions, late 18th century onwards.
Colliery plans, 18th–20th centuries; non-coal mines (from the Health and Safety Executive), 19th century onwards.
Board of Health town plans, 19th century.
Printed maps:
Extensive range of county maps (mostly 1 inch to 1 mile or less), 16th century onwards.
OS plans, at 6, 25 and 50 inches to 1 mile, from the 1880s. (Extensive but incomplete series).

Detail
6a,b, 7, 10a,b,c, 11, 12, 13, 14, 15, 17a,b,c

Publications of maps held
P. D. A. Harvey and H. Thorpe, *The printed maps of Warwickshire, 1576–1900* (Warwickshire County Council, 1959).
D. Pannett, 'The manuscript maps of Warwickshire', *Warwickshire History* 6 (3) (1985), 69–85.

WILTSHIRE

234   Wiltshire Record Office

Address   County Hall, Trowbridge BA14 8JG

Telephone   (01225) 713138   *Fax*   (01225) 713999

Access   Open. CARN reader's ticket required.

Index

R. E. Sandell (ed.), *Abstracts of Wiltshire inclosure awards and agreements*, Wiltshire Records Society 25 (1952).

R. E. Sandell (ed.), *Abstracts of Wiltshire tithe apportionments*, Wiltshire Records Society 30 (1975). Most of the awards and apportionments are held in the Office.

Unpublished catalogues and indexes to map collection, on site.

Summary

Manuscript maps: Tithe and apportionments for Wiltshire parishes (diocesan copies) c.1840. Enrolled enclosure awards and plans, 18th to early 19th centuries. Estate maps, predominantly but not exclusively of properties in Wiltshire, 16th to 20th centuries.

Printed maps: Extensive coverage of OS county series at 6 and 25 inches to the mile, and town plans at 1:500.

Detail

6a,b, 10a,b,c, 11, 12, 13, 14, 15, 17a,b,c

Publications of maps held

Andrews' and Drury's map of Wiltshire, 1771, a reduced facsimile, in atlas format with introduction by E. Crittall. Wiltshire Record Society **8** (1974).

Gee Langdon (ed.), *The year of the map* (Tisbury: Compton Russell Ltd, 1976) reproduces Bradford on Avon tithe map and apportionment to a reduced scale.

235 Longleat House, Library and Archives of the Marquess of Bath

Address   Warminster, BA12 7NN

Telephone   (01985) 844400   *Fax* (01985) 844885

Access   Open to established scholars by appointment only.

Index

Unpublished computer catalogue of estate papers includes estate maps. Unpublished indexes to the libraries.

Summary

The collection of books and documents has been drawn together by the Thynne family, the owners of Longleat, since the early sixteenth century. The earliest maps are medieval (a TO map in a copy of Higden's *Polychronicon* and 15th century sketch additions to the *Liber rubeus Bathoniae*, a manuscript of the 1420s). Manuscript maps include also a late 16th-century map of Plymouth, two survey books of the manor of Farney in County Monahan in Ireland (Thomas Raven, 1635 and Bernard Scalé, 1777), as well as a series of some 400 maps, interspersed with some printed material, dating between the later 17th century and around 1940, comprising mainly enclosure, tithe and general estate maps, and referring to Thynne property in Glos., Herefs., Shrops., Som., and Wilts.

The earliest printed atlas in the collection is the Rome edition of Ptolemy's *Geographia* (1499): the Strasbourg edition of 1525 is also held. There is a significant collection of 16th and 17th century printed atlases including a coloured Ortelius (Antwerp, 1575), Saxton (London, 1579), a Dutch Blaeu (1664–65), a composite Blaeu/Jansson (Amsterdam, 1647–67), Moses Pitt's *English Atlas* (Oxford, 1680–81), Ogilby's *Britannia* (1698). The small quantity of maritime material includes John Seller's *English Pilot* (1671–72).

General and regional maps of England and Wales: published by Philip Overton and Thomas Bowles (1735), by John Cary (1794). General maps of Ireland include Nathaniel McKinlie's map of 1735. Printed county maps of Surrey (John Senex, 1729), Cornwall (1748), Herefordshire (1754), Hampshire and the Isle of Wight (1759), Hertfordshire (Andrews and Drury, *c.*1760), Wiltshire (Andrews and Drury, 1773), Bedfordshire (1765), Devonshire (1765).

Amongst the estate maps are important early maps of Gurston in Broad Chalke (Wilts.) *c.*1660, surveyed by John Lodge; Walton (Som.) late 17th century; Corsley (Wilts.) 1747, Frome (Som.), 1744, Horningsham

(Wilts.) 1747, Longbridge Deverill (Wilts.) 1748, all by John Ladd; Warminster (Wilts.) c.1760 by Joseph Singer and Buckland (Glos.) c.1780. Mid to late 19th century maps cover railways in Wilts., Som., and Shrops., lead mines at Wagbeach and Snailbeach, near Minsterley in Shropshire and quarries at Box (Wilts.). A number of the enclosure, tithe and general estate maps are supplemented by surveys, terriers and related papers. OS maps include coloured geological surveys of NW Wiltshire and Bath (1817) at 1 inch to 1 mile, and Gloucestershire (the Severn Estuary) (1845 and 1866–67) at 1 inch to 1 mile.

Detail
1, 2, 3, 4, 5, 6a,b, 7, 8, 9, 10a,b,c, 11, 12, 13, 15, 17a

Publications of maps held
Victoria County History of Wiltshire, viii, 14, reproduces the Corsley enclosure map of 1783.

YORKSHIRE

236   North Yorkshire County Record Office

Address   County Hall, Northallerton DL7 8AD   Located at:
             Malpas Road, Northallerton

Telephone   (01609) 777585   *Fax*   (01609) 780447

Access   Open.

Index
North Yorkshire County Record Office Publications:
No. 40: *Guide No. 3. List of North Yorkshire and North Riding Maps and Plans*, revised to March 1993.
No. 41: *Guide No. 4, List of . . . Enclosure awards*, revised to June 1993.
No. 32: *Bilsdale Maps 1781–1857* (February 1983), a companion to *Bilsdale Surveys 1637–81*, edited by M. Y. Ashcroft and A. M. Hill (1980).

Summary
Maps relating to North Yorkshire, i.e. parts of the former counties of North, East and West Ridings of Yorkshire, and those parts of Cleveland and County Durham which formerly lay in the North Riding. They include estate maps from the 16th to the 19th century; maps of manors, pasture, common fields, commons and wastes, of the 18th and 19th centuries.
Plans of public utilities.

Detail
5, 6a,b, 7, 10a,b,c, 11, 12, 13, 14, 15, 17a

Facsimiles and reproductions on sale
Most of the collection has been microfilmed. Microfilm printouts are available.

237   York City Archives

Address   Art Gallery Building, Exhibition Square, York YO1 2EW

Telephone   (01904) 651533

Access   By appointment.

Index
City of York, *Catalogue of the Charters, House Books ... compiled by William Giles* (York, 1908).
Typescript handlists.

Summary
A number of maps, mainly deposited with the Town Clerk as Clerk of the Peace. The earliest is 'A Plott of the Manor farm and lands called Belthorpe Grange' in the East Riding, 1629. Four manuscript maps of the York Strays (substantial tracts of land held by the city in trust for the Freemen of York under the various enclosure acts) by John Lund jnr., 1772: Micklegate Ward Stray from a map of Robert Kershaw (1719), Walmgate Ward Stray from a plan by George Smith (1736), Bootham Ward Stray, from a map by George Smith (1736). Also a manuscript plan of an estate at Carlton Miniot (or Miniott) and Sand Hutton, surveyed in 1766 by John Ward.
Eight of the Enclosure Awards of the 18th and 19th centuries have attached plans.
A chart of the rivers Ouse and Humber by Thomas Survey, 1699, is included in Survey's 'Journal from London to York' (1699).
Printed railway plans from 1840 onwards are also held.

Detail
7, 8, 10b,c, 11, 12, 13, 17c

Publications of maps held
Paul Hughes' article on Thomas Survey's Journal is in preparation for the *Yorkshire Archaeological Journal*, 1994.

238   York Central Library, Local Studies Library

Address   Museum Street, York YO1 2DS

Telephone   (01904) 654144   *Fax*   (01904) 611025

Access   Open.

Index

H. Whitaker (ed.), *A descriptive list of the printed maps of Yorkshire and its Ridings, 1577–1900.* Yorkshire Archaeological Society Record Series 86 (1933).

Summary

The collection, most of which are reproductions, consists of maps of York and maps of Yorkshire as a whole. Their dates range from Christopher Saxton's map of Yorkshire (1577) to the 19th century. There is one manuscript map: 'The plott of the Manor of Dringhouses lying within the City of York' by Samuel Parsons (1624). Also of interest is a set of OS maps at 5 feet to 1 mile, 1852, which have been hand-colourwashed.

Detail

6a, 7, 10b,c, 15

Publications of maps held

H. Murray, 'Nathaniel Whittock's bird's-eye view of the City of York in the 1850s: a commentary' (York: Friends of York City Art Gallery, 1988).

239 York Minster Library and Archives

Address   Dean's Park, York YO1 2JD

Telephone   (01904) 625308

Access   By appointment

Index

No index to maps.

Summary

The collection includes manuscript and printed maps of the properties of the Dean and Chapter and Vicars Choral in Lincs., London, Notts., and Yorks; deposited parliamentary plans from the 17th century onwards; manuscript and printed maps of Yorkshire from the 17th century onwards (mainly from the antiquarian collection of Edward Hailstone); county atlases from the 16th century onwards.

Detail

1, 5, 6a,b, 7, 9, 10a,b,c, 11, 12, 13, 14, 15

240 University of York, Borthwick Institute of Historical Research

Address St Anthony's Hall, York YO1 2PW

Telephone (01904) 642315

Access Open.

Index
Card index, and hand list to the Stewart Collection, on site.

Summary
Tithe maps and awards for the diocese of York.
Enclosure maps for some parishes in the archdeaconry of York and in former ecclesiastical properties.
Estate maps for the archiepiscopal and Minster dignitary lands, 17th to 19th centuries.
Maps and atlases, including OS 1 inch to the mile from 1805 onwards for all Britain, in the Stewart collection of British maps and atlases, donated by M. and D. M. Stewart in 1969.
Miscellaneous estate and parish maps from the late 16th century onwards.

Detail
1, 6a,b, 10a, 11, 12, 13, 14, 17a,b

241 National Railway Museum

Address Leeman Road, York YO2 4XJ

Telephone (01904) 621261 *Fax* (01904) 611112

Access By appointment. Reader's ticket available on written application.

Index
Handlist of maps, and card index to Railway Clearing House maps, on site.

Summary
Almost complete collection of Railway Clearing House (RCH) maps, and railway junction diagrams. Large number of OS 1 inch maps including Ireland. Miscellaneous 19th century British maps including those of the Board of Trade (1846) showing proposed railway schemes.

Detail
1, 2, 3, 4, 5, 6a, 10a, 13

242 Barnsley Archive Service and Local Studies Department

Address   Barnsley Central Library, Shambles Street, Barnsley S70
2JF

Telephone   (01226) 733241   *Fax*   (01226) 285458

Access   Open.

Index
The Library's *Family History Handbook* (Barnsley Library Service, n.d.)
lists enclosure awards.
Indexes to OS maps on site.

Summary
The Archive Service holds:
Some original enclosure maps, 18th–19th centuries, and copies of tithe
maps for Barnsley Metropolitan Borough Council area.
The Local Studies Department holds:
Plans at 1:500 (c.1890) (some are reduced copies) and a plan of Barnsley
town centre (1850) at 5 feet to 1 mile.
Geological maps at 6 inches to 1 mile (c.1870) covering approximately
the present Barnsley Metropolitan Borough.
OS maps: a series at 6 inches to 1 mile (1850).

Detail
1, 2, 3, 4, 5, 7, 10a,b,c, 11, 12, 14, 17a,c

Facsimiles and reproductions on sale
The Alan Godfrey Edition of old OS maps, for Barnsley (SE), Barnsley
South, Barnsley (NE) (1904)

243 Doncaster Metropolitan Borough Council Archives

Address   King Edward Road, Balby, Doncaster DN4 0NA

Telephone   (01302) 859811

Access   Open.

Index
Doncaster Metropolitan Borough Council, guide to the archives, second
edition (1981) has a section on maps and plans.

Summary
Doncaster Archives is the respository for the records of Doncaster
Metropolitan Borough Council, and is also the diocesan record office for
the Archdeaconry of Doncaster in the Diocese of Sheffield.
Within the family and business collections there are maps of estates
falling within the Doncaster area, for the most part of local interest only.
The collections also include maps and plans of railway developments in
the area; some 18th and 19th century maps connected with the River
Don Navigation and the Aire and Calder Navigation; tithe, enclosure
and OS maps.

Detail
1, 5, 6a,b, 7, 10a,b,c, 11, 12, 13, 14, 15, 17a,b

244   Sheffield Archives

Address   52 Shoreham Street, Sheffield S1 4SP

Telephone   (01142) 734756   *Fax*   (01142) 735009

Access   Open. Reader's ticket required.

Index
R. Meredith, *Guide to the manuscript collections in Sheffield City Libraries*
    (1956), and *Supplement* ... (1976).
*Guide to the Fairbank Collection of maps, plans, surveyors' books and
    correspondence in Sheffield Reference Library* (Sheffield City Libraries,
    1936).

Summary
Manuscript and printed maps relating principally to the Sheffield area
and its immediate environs, i.e. the southern part of the former West
Riding of Yorkshire and North Derbyshire, and covering the 18th to
20th centuries.
The Wentworth collection includes maps relating to the family estate at
Wicklow; the Wharncliffe muniments include maps and plans of Lord
Wharncliffe's properties in Cornwall, 18th and 19th centuries, and some
plans of Belmont Castle, etc., in Scotland. Of special interest is the
Fairbank Collection – the archive of the Fairbank family's three gen-
erations of Sheffield Surveyors and map makers, 1688–1848, active in

Sheffield and its surroundings, and elsewhere in Britain. The collection includes more than 4600 plans and maps, and more than 1000 surveyors' books. The plans are in four categories: railways in various parts of England; turnpike roads in Derbys., Notts., and Yorks.; enclosures in Derbys. and Yorks., and maps of parishes, townships, cities and manors in various parts of England.

Detail
4, 6a,b, 7, 10a,b,c, 11, 12, 13, 14, 15, 16, 17a

Publications of maps held
T. W. Hall, *The Fairbanks of Sheffield 1688 to 1848* (Sheffield, 1932), reproduces more than 60 field sketches of properties within the town and its environs.

245   West Yorkshire Archive Service, Bradford

Address   15 Canal Road, Bradford BD1 4AT

Telephone   (01274) 731931   *Fax*   (01274) 734013

Access   By appointment.

Index
Maps in the Bradford District Archives, Handlist 3, duplicated.

Summary
The map collection is principally manuscript, comprising:
(1) Township maps for some townships within the Bradford MDC area.
(2) Maps among family and estate archives.
(3) The Bradford Board of Health plan (1857). 87 of the original 125 sheets covering the whole Borough survive, surveyed at 10 yards to 1 inch; some parts resurveyed in 1876–8; also a Board of Health plan for Baildon (1854) at 60 feet to 1 inch.
(4) Other maps and plans from local authority sources, especially maps transferred from Bradford Borough Surveyors and Engineers' department.
(5) Copies of tithe maps for some parishes in Bradford Diocese and within the Bradford Council area.
(6) OS maps, mainly annotated, from local authority sources.

Detail
5, 7, 10a,b,c, 11, 12, 13, 14, 15, 17b

Publications of maps held
B. English, *Yorkshire Enclosure Awards* (University of Hull, 1980), contains references to enclosure maps held by the Office.

246   Leeds University Library

Address   Leeds LS2 9JT

Telephone   (01132) 335518   *Fax*   (01132) 334381

Access   By appointment.

246A   The Brotherton Collection

Index
No index to maps.

Summary
Maps are a very minor element of the Brotherton Collection, which is a large research collection of printed books and manuscripts chiefly dating from the 15th century to the present. English literature is the central concern but there are many related historical and cultural interests.
Papers relating to the estates of Marrick Priory, Swaledale, 12th to 19th centuries, include four manuscript maps of Marrick in 1592.

Detail
5, 11

246B   The Whitaker Collection

Index
The Harold Whitaker Collection of County Atlases, Road-Books and Maps, presented to the University of Leeds (Leeds, 1947).

Summary
The Whitaker Collection contains some 450 items, about half of which are atlases of England and Wales dating from the 16th to 19th centuries; there are sub-groups containing road-books, maps of Yorkshire, general and foreign atlases and reference works. All items are predominantly printed. The contents of the collection and its origins as the personal collection of Dr Harold Whitaker are fully described in its catalogue.

Detail
1, 6a,b, 7, 10a, 13, 14, 15

247 Yorkshire Archaeological Society

Address   'Claremont', 23 Clarendon Road, Leeds LS2 9NZ

Telephone   (01132) 465362

Access   Open for the Library; by appointment for the Archives

Index

Maps are identified in

F. W. Crossley, *Catalogue of Manuscripts and Deeds in the Library of the Yorkshire Archaeological Society 1867–1931*, 2nd edition, 1931 (Reprinted by the Archive Advisory Council for West Yorkshire, 1986).

S. Thomas, *Guide to the Archive Collections of the Yorkshire Archaeological Society 1931–1983 and to collections deposited with the Society*, (Archive Advisory Council for West Yorkshire, 1985).

Unpublished lists on site.

Summary

The maps held by the Society fall into two groups. Those held in the archives are mainly maps and plans amongst family and estate papers. There are many 19th century estate plans, drawn up for different purposes, a large number of which belong to the records of the manor of Wakefield.

The library holds the first edition 6 inch to the mile OS maps for most of the West Riding but few for the East and North Ridings. It also holds various non-OS maps of Yorkshire which are available through the catalogues.

Detail
1, 6a,b, 10a,b,c, 11, 12

Publications of maps held

G. E. Kirk (comp.), *Catalogue of maps and plans in the library of the Yorkshire Archaeological Society* (Yorkshire Archaeological Society, 1937).

H. Whitaker (ed.), 'Printed maps of Yorkshire', *Yorkshire Archaeological Society Record Series*, 86 (1933). (The Society does not hold an example of every map in this comprehensive list).

CHANNEL ISLANDS & ISLE OF MAN

248   States of Guernsey Archives Service

Address   29 Victoria Road, Saint Peter Port, Guernsey

Telephone   (01481) 724512   *Fax*   (01481) 715814

Access   By appointment.

Index
Greffe Catalogue, vol. 3 (unpublished).

Summary
States Engineer and States Architect's plans, 19th and 20th century.
19th and 20th century plans submitted for conveyancing and licensing purposes.
OS plans of the Island, 1787, 1900 and 1938 editions.
19th century plans of Communes de l'Ancresse, Communes de l'Ile d'Aurigny, and Communes de la Forét.

Detail
5, 7, 10b,c

249   Priaulx Library

Address   Candie Road, St Peter Port, Guernsey

Telephone   (01481) 721998

Access   Open.

Index
No index to maps.

Summary
Maps of the Channel Islands, 1650 to the present, including some maritime charts.

Detail
5, 6a, 7, 8, 9, 10c

250 Jersey Library, Reference and Local History Section

Address Halkett Place, St Helier, Jersey, Channel Islands

Telephone (01534) 59992 *Fax* (01534) 69444

Access Open.

Index
Catalogue on site.

Summary
Large collection of mostly printed maps of Jersey, dating from 1795 onwards.

Detail
1, 2, 3, 4, 6a, 10c, 15

251 Manx National Heritage

Address The Manx Museum, Douglas, Isle of Man

Telephone (01624) 675522 *Fax* (01624) 661899

Access Open.

Index
Card indexes arranged by cartographer and by subject or place name, on site.

Summary
The collection includes printed and manuscript maps.
(1) Topographical sections of the island, town plans from the late 18th century onwards, town improvement scheme plans, elevations of specific buildings, 19th century geological maps of the whole island, facsimiles and photographs of earliest recorded maps, from the 13th century onwards.
(2) Various navigational charts for surrounding seas and harbours, with notes on anchorage, for instance between Calf and Isle of Man in 1835.
(3) Plans and sections of mines, for instance, the Great Laxey mine and wheel. Late 19th century steam and electric railway developments.

(4) Maps showing traditional land divisions including James Woods, *A new atlas and gazetteer of the Isle of Man* (1867) which has accompanying tables naming land owners and acreages.

(5) Disafforesting Commission maps, 1860s.

Detail

1, 5, 6, 7, 8, 10a,b,c, 11, 13, 15, 17c

Publications of maps held

Maps of the Isle of Man 1280–1760 (Limited edition, Shearwater Press, 1975). Representative selection of the most interesting and unusual maps of the Isle of Man; only a few originals are held by the Museum.

A. M. Cubbon, *Early maps of the Isle of Man, a Guide to the Collection in the Manx Museum* (4th edition, 1974). A 48-page non-comprehensive booklet covering the Museum's holdings to 1873.

Facsimiles and reproductions on sale

Reproductions in colour: Isle of Man, by John Speed (1610), by J. Drinkwater (1836).

WALES

252   The National Library of Wales, Department of Pictures and Maps

Address   Aberystwyth, Dyfed SY23 3BU

Telephone   (01970) 623816   *Fax*   (01970) 615709

Access   Admission by reader's ticket.

Index
Card index on site for part of the collection.
Computer catalogue of railway plans.

Summary
Early printed maps and atlases, from 1570, with an emphasis on smaller scale engraved county and other maps of Wales and UK.
Of special interest to historians: (of Wales) Manuscript estate plans, in N.L.W and deposited collections, 1740–1860. Tithe maps, c.1840. Enclosure Awards and Maps – Montgomeryshire and Cardiganshire, 1785–1865. Railway plans and sections, 19th century. Lead mining plans, North Cardiganshire, 1850–1910.

Detail
1, 2, 3, 4, 5, 6a,b, 7, 8, 10a,b,c, 11, 12, 13, 14, 15, 16, 17a,c

Publications of maps held
R. Davies, *Estate Maps of Wales 1600–1836* (Exhibition catalogue, 1982).
R. Davies, *An atlas of the tithe maps of Wales* (1994).
M. G. Lewis, 'The printed maps of Merioneth, 1578–1900, in N.L.W.' *Journal of the Merioneth Historical and Record Society* **1** (1951), 162–79.
M. G. Lewis, 'The printed maps of Cardiganshire, 1578–1900, in N.L.W.' *Ceredigion* **2** (1955), 244–76.
M. G. Lewis, 'The printed maps of Breconshire, 1578–1900, in N.L.W.' *Brycheiniog* **16** (1972), 139–74.
M. Lewis, 'Thomas Taylor's maps of Wales, 1718', *Journal of the Welsh Bibliographical Society* **7** (1953), 193–5.
M. Lewis, 'Some cartographical works in the National Library of Wales', *The National Library of Wales Journal* **5** (1948), 209–14.

Facsimiles and reproductions on sale
N.L.W. reproduction – George Owen's (manuscript) map of Pembrokeshire, 1603 (1973).

253 National Monuments Record for Wales

Address	Royal Commission on the Ancient and Historical Monuments of Wales, Plas Crug, Aberystwyth, Dyfed SY23 2HP
Telephone	(01970) 624381 *Fax* (01970) 627701
Access	Advance notice recommended.

Index
Manual catalogues, soon to be transferred to a computerised system.

Summary
Extensive but incomplete sets of OS maps, at 25 inches to the mile in 1st and 2nd editions, and at 6 inches to the mile. The most important of these are an OS working set of 2nd edition 25 inch maps which carry an earlier survey marked in blue along with the surveyors' and editorial signatures (marked in the borders). One or two of these maps do not appear to have been subsequently published at this scale. There is a basic catalogue of all these maps.

Copies and extracts from early maps relating to specific archaeological and architectural monuments are held but generally these can only be retrieved by site and they are not catalogued as maps. They are virtually all copies of maps held in known collections.

Detail
5, 7, 10b,c

CLWYD

254   Clwyd Record Office, Hawarden Branch

Address   The Old Rectory, Hawarden, Deeside CH5 3NR

Telephone   (01244) 532364   *Fax*   (01244) 538344

Access   Open. CARN reader's ticket required.

Index

A. G. Veysey, *Guide to the Flintshire Record Office* (1974) gives a summary description.

A. G. Veysey, *Guide to the parish records of Clwyd* (1984), Appendix I: Enclosure Awards, Appendix II: Tithe Maps, gives a brief listing.

Unpublished handlists, to Quarter Sessions, estate collections, and OS maps.

Computerised catalogue of estate maps. (Printouts available for a small charge).

Summary

Material relating to the former county of Flintshire. Plans of public undertakings, mostly railways but also roads, canals, etc., 1792–1943 (about 250 schemes), deposited among Flintshire Quarter Sessions Records.

Enclosure awards and maps, 27 from 1777 to 1870.

Highway diversion maps, late 18th to 20th centuries among Quarter Sessions Records. Tithe maps, (either original parish copy, or photograph of diocesan copy in National Library of Wales etc.,) of all Flintshire parishes. Estate maps of Flintshire, 17th to 19th centuries. These maps are mostly manuscript.

OS maps at 1 and 6 inches to the mile and a few 25 inches to the mile town plans of Denbighshire. Selection of county maps of Denbighshire, Flintshire and North Wales, 16th – 19th centuries.

Detail

2. 6a, 7, 10a,b,c, 11, 12, 13, 14, 15, 17a,b,c

Facsimiles and reproductions on sale

John Speed's 'Denbighshire' (1611) and 'Flintshire' (1611).
Wood's 'Wrexham' (1833). 'Rhyl' (1861).

359

Alan Godfrey Edition of old OS maps, at 25 inches to the mile, of 'Flint' (1870), 'Ruthin' (1874) and 'Wrexham' (1872).

255   Clwyd Record Office, Ruthin Branch

Address   46 Clwyd Street, Ruthin LL15 1HP

Telephone   (01824) 703077   *Fax*   (01824) 705180

Access   Open. CARN reader's ticket required.

Index
A. G. Veysey, *Guide to the parish records of Clwyd* (1984), Appendix I:
    Enclosure Awards, Appendix II: Tithe Maps, gives a brief listing.
Unpublished handlists, to Quarter Sessions, estate collections, and OS maps.
Computerised catalogue of estate maps. (Printouts available for a small charge).

Summary
Material relating to the former county of Denbighshire. Plans of public undertakings, mostly railways but also roads, canals, etc., 1792–1943, deposited among Denbighshire Quarter Sessions Records.
Enclosure awards and maps, 30 from 1801 to 1870.
Highway diversion maps, late 18th to 20th centuries among Quarter Sessions Records Tithe maps (either original parish copy, or photograph of diocesan copy in National Library of Wales etc.) of all Denbighshire parishes. Estate maps of Denbighshire, 17th to 19th centuries. These maps are mostly manuscript.
OS maps at 1, 6 and 25 inches to the mile and town plans of Denbighshire in various editions. OS maps at 1, 6 and 25 inches to the mile for parts of Flintshire and Merionethshire.
Selection of county maps of Denbighshire, Flintshire and North Wales, 16–19th centuries.

Detail
2, 6a, 7, 10a,b,c, 11, 12, 13, 14, 15, 17a,b,c

Facsimiles and reproductions on sale
John Speed's 'Denbighshire'(1611) and 'Flintshire' (1611).
Wood's 'Wrexham' (1833). 'Rhyl' (1861).
Alan Godfrey Edition of old OS maps, at 25 inches to the mile, of 'Flint' (1870), 'Ruthin' (1874) and 'Wrexham' (1872).

256 Clwyd Library and Information Service Headquarters

Address   Headquarters Library, County Civic Centre, Mold CH7 6NW

Telephone   (01352) 752121   *Fax*   (01352) 753662

Access   Open.

Index
No index to maps produced before 1900.

Summary
Small collection of OS, including 1 inch to 1 mile, c.1840, reprint for Flintshire and Denbighshire. Other small scale printed maps mainly pertaining to Clwyd.

Detail
6a, 10a

Facsimiles and reproductions on sale
John Speed's 'Denbighshire' and 'Flintshire'.

DYFED

257   Dyfed Archive Service, Carmarthenshire Area Record Office

Address   County Hall, Carmarthen SA31 1JP

Telephone   (01267) 233333 ext. 4182

Access   Open.

Index
Handlists of all material deposited in the RO are available to readers; most of these include maps in a separate section. A 'Topic list' of maps of Carmarthen Town is also available.

Summary
There is no map collection as such. The material mostly relates to the former county of Carmarthenshire. Maps of various types are found within collections consisting mainly of other kinds of documents. These include estate plans (manuscript and printed), town plans (manuscript and printed), railway maps (printed), public utilities maps (water, gas, electricity), roads, canals, harbours, as well as printed OS sheets at $2\frac{1}{2}$ inch, 6 inch and 25 inches to 1 mile (some 1st edition, most 2nd for Carmarthenshire). Tithe maps and enclosure awards for some Carmarthenshire parishes.

Detail
1, 2, 5, 6a,b, 7, 8, 10a,b,c, 11, 12, 13, 14, 15, 17a

258   Dyfed Archive Service, Cardiganshire / Ceredigion Record Office

Address   County Office, Marine Terrace, Aberystwyth SY23 2DE

Telephone   (01970) 617581 ext. 2120

Access   Open.

Index
Handlist, and index of maps in other collections, available on site.

Summary
The map collection is a small one consisting mainly of OS maps of areas and parishes within the former county of Cardiganshire. These include two reprints of the 6 inches to 1 mile (first edition, 1837), some sheets of the 1 inch (first edition, 1889/90) and second edition (1905/06) and an example of the special edition of 1913. There are a few examples of other types of maps.

Detail
2, 5, 6a,b, 7, 10a,b,c, 11, 13, 15, 17a

259 Dyfed Archives Service, Pembrokeshire Area Record Office

Address The Castle, Haverfordwest SA61 2EF

Telephone (01437) 763707

Access Open.

Index
Unpublished brief list of Quarter Sessions maps.
Typed list of the main groups; index of estate, tithe, and Quarter Sessions maps and plans, also OS and sales catalogues.

Summary
There are manuscript and printed maps. The material relates mainly to the former county of Pembrokeshire. The provenance of some items might be of historical interest: those that are in private collections mainly derive from surveys made of landowners' estates, also by surveyors and auctioneers for estate auctions; those among official classes contain manuscript annotations of official undertakings etc. The Quarter Sessions plans are the usual type of plan of proposed railway undertakings etc deposited with the Clerk of the Peace under the Railway Acts etc. Also tithe maps for fifteen Pembrokeshire parishes, a few enclosure maps, some town plans. OS at six inches to the mile, and 1st edition at 25 inches to the mile; moderate coverage.

Detail
1, 2, 5, 6a,b, 7, 10a,b,c, 11, 12, 13, 15, 17a

260 St David's University College

Address   The Old Library, Lampeter SA48 7ED

Telephone   (01570) 422351   *Fax*   (01570) 423423

Access   By appointment.

Index
No index to maps. Card index to Old Library stock.

Summary
Printed maps only. A wide-ranging but random selection of cartographic material from the 16th to the early 19th centuries included in donations made between 1834 and 1851 by Thomas Phillips (1760–1851), a former surgeon with the East India Company. The earliest maps relating to Britain are those in the London edition of Ortelius, *Theatrum orbis terrarum* (1606), containing Humphrey Lhuyd's celebrated map of Wales drawn in 1568 and first published by Ortelius in 1573 and in Philemon Holland's translation of William Camden's *Britannia*, 1610. Other early items relating to Britain are the anonymous maps of Leicestershire and Rutland (1602) and Warwickshire (1603), now known to be by William Smith (*c.*1550–1618), contained in a made-up volume consisting of fifty-four 17th century county and regional maps, 39 of which are by John Speed.

Detail
1, 2, 3, 4, 6a, 7, 8, 10a

Publications of maps held
B. L. James, 'Maps and atlases in the Old Library at St David's University College, Lampeter', *Society of University Cartographers Bulletin*, **10** (1976), 15–24. Contains illustrations and reproductions of maps in the collection.

261 University College of Wales E. G. Bowen Map Library, Institute of Earth Studies

Address   Llandiniam Building, Penglais, Aberystwyth, SY23 3DZ

Telephone   (01970) 622603   *Fax*   (01970) 622659

Access   Appointment advised because of other duties of Curator.

Index
Catalogue of main holdings, on site.

Summary
The collection aims to meet the needs of teaching and research within the Institute of Earth Studies and hence is biased towards these requirements, for example, the coverage of Wales at larger topographical scales.

Detail
1, 2, 3, 4, 5, 6a,b, 7, 8, 10a,b,c

262   Haverfordwest Area Library

Address   Dew Street, Haverfordwest SA61 1SU

Telephone   (01437) 4591

Access   Open.

Index
No index to maps.

Summary
The collection is chiefly a local one, mainly composed of printed maps, plans and charts relating to Pembrokeshire. In addition there are a number of maps relating to Wales, and some referring to other parts of the British Isles.

The local collection contains maps by Christopher Saxton (1578), George Owen (1610), John Speed (1616), Joan Blaeu (1648), Thomas Kitchin (1754), Robert Morden (1701), Thomas Taylor (1718), Jan Jansson (1646), Schenk and Valk (?1683), a plan of the French landing (1797), and various charts of the Pembrokeshire coast by Lewis Morris, 18th century.

The maps of Wales include those by Joan Blaeu (1663), Humphrey Lhuyd (1630) and John Speed (1676).

Detail
1, 2, 5, 6a, 7, 8, 10b,c, 11, 15, 17a,b

263   Llanelli Borough Library

Address   Vaughan Street, Llanelli SA15 3AS

Telephone   (01554) 773538   *Fax*   (01554) 750125

Access   Collection in reserve; appointment required.

Index

Card index on site.

Summary

The maps and local plan collection covers basically OS and other printed maps of the area of the Borough of Llanelli and parts of Carmarthenshire. There are more than 1,100 manuscript maps and plans, chiefly of mine workings, ports and harbours, estates and railways. Many should be described strictly as plans but as topographical detail is also shown – for example in plans of mine-workings where ground detail is often also shown – they are of great importance locally as maps as well as plans. The earliest local maps in the collection date from around the middle of the 18th century, with many estate, mine, dock and railway maps and plans of the 19th century, particularly the latter half.

Detail

1, 2, 5, 6b, 7, 8, 10a,b,c, 11, 12, 13, 14, 15, 17a,c

MID AND SOUTH GLAMORGAN

264   Glamorgan Record Office

Address   County Hall, Cathays Park, Cardiff CF1 3NE

Telephone   (01222) 780282   *Fax*   (01222) 780027

Access   Open.

Index
Unpublished handlists on site.

Summary
Maps and plans of the former county of Glamorgan, manuscript and printed, 17th to 20th centuries, including Manors of Barry, Fonmon, Llancadel, Penmark by Evans Mouse (1622).
Estate surveys include: Plymouth (1766), Dunraven (c.1780), Kemeys-Tynte (1767), Merthyr Mawr (c.1800, 1813), Bute (1824).
Deposited Quarter Sessions plans for roads, canals, railways, 18th to 20th centuries.
Mining surveyors' plans; abandoned mines (non-coal) plans.
Large-scale (1:500 or similar) OS plans of Cardiff, Aberdare, Merthyr Tydfil, late 19th century.

Detail
5, 6a,b, 7, 8, 10a,b,c, 11, 12, 13, 14, 15, 16, 17a

Publications of maps held
H. M. Thomas, *A catalogue of Glamorgan estate maps* (Glamorgan Archives Publication, 1992).

Facsimiles and reproductions on sale
Cardiff, by John Speed (1610), by John Wood (late 1830s), Cardiff centre, OS (1851), Cardiff and district by T. Waring (1869). Merthyr Tydfil, north and south (1898). Swansea centre, OS at 25 inches to 1 mile (1878 and 1897). Glamorgan, by Joan Blaeu (1645), by George Yates, (1799); strip road map by John Ogilby (1675), Glamorgan, Uplands and Vale,

by Emanuel Bowen (1729). From Carmarthen to Margam, by Emanuel Bowen (1729).

265 University of Wales, College of Cardiff, Arts and Social Studies Library

Address   Corbett Road Bridge, Cardiff CF1 1XQ

Telephone   (01222) 874000   *Fax* (01222) 371921

Access   By appointment (for non-resident members of the College).

Index
No index to maps.

Summary
There is a Welsh map collection and the following may be noted:
(1) A collection of 17 scrapbooks of E. G. R. Salisbury (1819–1890) containing prints and printed maps (mostly extracted from topographical works and atlases) of the Welsh counties and adjoining counties of England.
(2) A set of OS maps at 6 inches to the mile, first edition, covering Glamorgan and Monmouthshire.
(3) A few early atlases and topographical works containing maps, by, for example, John Speed (1676), William Camden (various editions), J. Evans, *Map of North Wales* (1795).
(4) Facsimile reprint on microfiche of the OS 1:2500 series of 1880, for the county of Glamorganshire.
(5) A set of OS maps, 6 inches to the mile series, surveyed in 1867–78 (revised 1913–1920) for the counties of Glamorganshire and Monmouthshire.

Detail
2, 6, 10b,c

266 Mid Glamorgan County Library

Address   Coed Park, Park Street, Bridgend CF31 4BA

Telephone   (01656) 767451   *Fax* (01656) 645719

Access   For reference use, on request.

Index
No index to maps.

Summary
No special interest group, but some thematic/historical maps relating to Glamorgan. No manuscript maps. Several photocopies. Principal atlases held.
OS small scale coverage of Wales, and most of British Isles. OS large scale coverage of Glamorgan.

Detail
1, 2, 5, 6a,b, 7, 10a,b, 11, 12, 13, 14, 15, 17a

267 Merthyr Tydfil Public Libraries

Address   Central Library, Merthyr Tydfil, CF47 8AF

Telephone   (01685) 723057   *Fax* (01685) 370690

Access   Open.

Index
No index to maps.

Summary
Speed's county maps of Wales.
Print of OS 2 inches to the mile drawings of this locality, 1813, 1814.
OS maps of this locality, 1832, 1876.
OS maps of some other districts of Wales, 1870–1900.

Detail
5, 6a, 7, 10a,b,c, 11, 13, 14, 17a

268 South Glamorgan Library Headquarters, Central Library

Address   St David's Link, Frederick Street, Cardiff CF1 4DT

Telephone   (01222) 382116   *Fax*   (01222) 238642

Access   Open.

Index
No index to maps.

Summary
A general collection of maps covering in the main, the whole of Wales.
A large part of the collection is of OS maps, all periods and scales being
represented. An effort is made to keep, as far as possible (especially for
the local area) copies of all editions of the larger OS plans. There are
also examples of county and general maps by early cartographers and a
collection is maintained showing the development of Cardiff over the
years. There are some manuscript plans in stock, as well as printed maps.

Detail
1, 2, 3, 4, 5, 6a,b, 7, 8, 10a,b,c, 11, 12, 13, 14, 15, 16, 17a,c

269 National Museum of Wales

Address   Cathays Park, Cardiff CF1 3NP

Telephone   (01222) 397951   *Fax*   (01222) 373219

Access   All applications to see maps should be made through
              the Main Library.

Index
Handlists to geological maps are held in the Geology Department.

Summary
The main map collection is under the charge of the Keeper of Geology
and is held in his department. It consists principally of geological maps
of Wales and its counties, including 1st and 2nd editions. There is also
a collection of Welsh topographical maps of historical interest, e.g.
Humphrey Lhuyd, Christopher Saxton and John Speed.
The Main Library and the Department of Archaeology have a collection
of Welsh OS maps at 6 inches to the mile.

Detail
1, 2, 3, 4, 5, 6a,b, 7, 8, 10a,b,c, 13, 14, 15

Publications of maps held
The following were all published by the National Museum of Wales.
F. J. North, *Geological maps: their history and development; with special reference to Wales* (1928).
F. J. North, *Humphrey Lhuyd's maps of England and Wales* (1928).
F. J. North, *The map of Wales before 1600* (1935).
F. J. North, *Maps, their history and uses, with special reference to Wales ... handbook to a temporary exhibition ... 1933* (1933).

270 Welsh Industrial and Maritime Museum

Address   Bute Street, Cardiff CF1 6AN

Telephone   (01222) 481919

Access   Open.

Index
Handlists and indexes, arranged by subject, on site.

Summary
Thematic maps indicating coal, metal, slate, lead deposits and workings. A proportion of these are plans of the transport system in relation to a particular industry. Transport maps showing railways, roads, canals and tramways. Maritime charts. The majority of these maps are printed and date from the mid-19th century.
OS for the South Wales area, mostly at 6 inches to 1 mile, dated 1870–1890.

Detail
1, 2, 5, 6a,b, 7, 8, 10a,b,c, 11, 13, 14, 15, 16

WEST GLAMORGAN

271   West Glamorgan County Archive Service

Address   County Hall, Oystermouth Road, Swansea SA1 3SN

Telephone   (01782) 471589   *Fax*   (01792) 471340

Access   Open.

Index
Handlist on site.

Summary
(1) Estate maps for the following estates in West Glamorgan: Briton Ferry, Cadoxton Lodge, Cilybebyll, Gnoll, Beaufort, Margam, Neath Abbey, Penrice, Yniscedwyn, 17th–19th centuries, mostly manuscript.
(2) Tithe maps for parishes in West Glamorgan, 1840s–50s. Where originals are not held, copies have been obtained from the National Library of Wales.
(3) 1st edition OS, at 6 and 25 inches to the mile, for West Glamorgan, c.1878 and 1880; some 2nd edition OS at 25 inches to the mile, c.1899.

Detail
6a, 7, 8, 10b,c, 11, 16, 17a

Publications of maps held
Estate maps in the West Glamorgan County Archives are included in H. M. Thomas, *A Catalogue of Glamorgan Estate Maps* (Glamorgan Archives, 1992).

Facsimiles and reproductions on sale
'Glamorgan', by Johannes Blaeu, 1645; as strip road map by John Ogilby, 1675; by Emanuel Bowen, 1729; and by George Yates, 1799.
Two maps of Swansea centre, OS, 25 inches to 1 mile, 1878 and 1897.

272   West Glamorgan County Libraries

Address   Swansea Reference Library, Alexandra Road, Swansea
SA1 5DX

Telephone   (01792) 54065/6   *Fax*   (01792) 645751
(01792) 655521 (Reference Library only)

Access   Open.

Index
Unpublished handlists: 'Early Printed Maps', 'Swansea'.

Summary
Early 17th century printed maps of the Welsh counties, the work of John
Speed, Thomas Kitchin and other noted cartographers. Many maps are
included within the Local History Collection at Swansea Reference
Library.

Many maps and plans of the Swansea area are held, e.g. tithe maps
(photocopy) of the Swansea and Gower area 1835–1840.

Insurance plans, Swansea Town area 1888 and 1897, Swansea Local
Board of Health plans 1852, and many plans relating to the local docks
and railways (itemised on handlist).

Few manuscript maps are held. There are some plans relating to the
Swansea Docks. Many of the maps held, in particular the early printed
maps, are of great historical interest and are valuable primary source
material to the historian.

OS maps, 1 inch to the mile series covering the whole of Wales, 19th
century; 6 inches to the mile series, 1900, covering parts of West
Glamorgan; 25 inches to the mile, 1876–1880, Glamorgan County Series
covering Swansea and the Llw Valley. (Maps from this series covering
other areas of West Glamorgan are held in Neath and Port Talbot
Reference Libraries as appropriate.)

Detail
2, 5, 6a,b, 7, 8, 10a,b,c, 11, 13, 14, 15, 16, 17a

273   University College of Swansea

Address   Singleton Park, Swansea SA2 8PP

273A   University Library

Telephone   (01792) 205678

Access   Open.

Index
No separate catalogue. Material accessible through general library author and subject catalogues.

Summary
The total number of maps and atlases held for this period is small. The majority of the atlases and printed maps are located in the Natural Sciences Sub-Library where they are shelved as a separate collection. However, the older maps and atlases, which fall within the scope of this survey, are mostly located either in the independent Geography map collection, or wherever possible, in the Main Library, Rare Books Room. The collection consists entirely of atlases and printed maps. No manuscript items are held. While the majority of the pre-1900 holdings date from the 19th century, there are various items of 17th and 18th century date. The earliest maps held are those which make up John Speed's *Prospect* ... (1627), supplemented by facsimile editions of earlier maps and atlases.

Detail
1, 2, 4, 5, 6a, 7, 8, 10a

273B   The Map Library, Dept. of Geography

Access   Open.

Index
Card index on site.

Summary
A small collection of manuscript maps of Wales, mostly county sheets, 1600–1800. Local 25-inch OS first edition plans.

Detail
2, 6a, 7, 8, 10a,b,c, 15

274 Swansea Museum

Address   Victoria Road, Swansea SA 1 1SN

Telephone   (01792) 653763   *Fax*   (01792) 652585

Access   By appointment.

As of 1994 the map collection is awaiting conservation. In some cases enquirers will be directed to an alternative local collection.

Index

Handlist on site.

Summary

A number of 18th century maps including a few manuscripts and atlases are held but the collection is concerned mainly with South Wales in the 19th century. A number of surveys of Welsh ports are included.

Good South Wales cover of the early editions of OS at 1, 6, and 25 inches to the mile, together with Swansea Corporation Surveys. Early geological maps of Wales and a number of other thematic maps mainly concerned with early industrialisation.

Detail

1, 2, 5, 6a,b, 7, 8, 10a,b,c, 13

GWENT

275 Gwent County Record Office

Address   County Hall, Cwmbran NP44 2XH

Telephone   (01633) 832266/832217   *Fax*   (01633) 838225

Access   Open. CARN reader's ticket required.

Index
Handlist on site.

Summary
The maps are contained in various collections of archives. They consist of both manuscript and printed maps and date generally from c.1750.

Detail
5, 6a, 8, 10a,b,c, 11, 12, 13, 14, 15, 17a

276 Newport Borough Libraries, Central Library

Address   John Frost Square, Newport NP9 1PA

Telephone   (01633) 265539   *Fax*   (01633) 222615

Access   Open.

Index
No index to maps.

Summary
Some manuscript and printed maps, mostly local to Wales. Special interest in Monmouthshire.

Detail
2, 6a,b, 7, 10a,b,c, 11, 12, 13, 14, 15, 17a

GWYNEDD

277   Gwynedd Archives Service, Caernarfon Area Record Office

Address   Victoria Dock, Caernarfon LL5 1SH

Telephone   (01286) 679095   *Fax*   (01286) 679545

Access   Open. CARN reader's ticket required.

Index
Handlists of all maps and plans on site.

Summary
Mostly 18th to 20th centuries. Estate plans and surveys, and deposited plans of public utilities, railways, roads and harbours. London and Northwestern Railway maps and plans of North Wales lines and stations. Abandoned mine plans. Plans of quarry sections in the quarrying collections.
Nearly comprehensive collection of OS maps for Caernarfonshire.

Detail
1, 2, 6a,b, 7, 10a,b,c, 11, 12, 13, 15, 17a

Facsimiles and reproductions on sale
Reproductions of William Morris sea-charts of the 18th century.

278   Gwynedd Archives Service, Dolgellau Area Record Office

Address   Cae Penarlâg, Dolgellau LL40 2YB

Telephone   (01341) 422341 ext. 261

Access   Open. CARN reader's ticket required.

Index
No index to maps.

Summary
Mostly 19th and early 20th centuries. Plans of quarry sections in the quarrying collections.
Nearly comprehensive collection of OS maps.

Detail
2, 6a, 10a,b,c, 11, 12, 13, 15, 17a

279 Gwynedd Archives Service, Llangefni Area Record Office

Address	Shire Hall, Llangefni LL77 7TW
Telephone	(01248) 750262 ext. 269
Access	Open. CARN reader's ticket required

Index
Maps are incorporated into the Office index.
Catalogues on site.

Summary
With few exceptions the maps are 19th and 20th century.
A few OS maps, at 6 and 25 inches to the mile, first edition. Most of the OS maps covering the County of Anglesey in the second edition (around 1900).
Enclosure awards, deposited and official maps and plans of harbours, roads and bridges, railways etc., (deposited with the Clerk of the Peace); abandoned mine plans.

Detail
10a,b,c, 11, 12, 13, 15, 17a

280 Gwynedd Library Service, Aberconwy Area Library

Address	Mostyn Street, Llandudno LL30 2YG
Telephone	(01492) 860941 *Fax* (01492) 876826
Access	Open.

Index
No index to maps.

Summary
Map prepared for sale of part of the Gloddaeth estate on which present town of Llandudno was built, 1849. OS sheets (25 inches to the mile) for the Town of Llandudno and adjoining Gloddaeth estate, etc. (1888 and 1889 survey).

Detail
10c

281 Gwynedd Library Service, Anglesey Area Library

Address   Lôn-y-Felin, Llangefni LL77 7TW

Telephone   (01248) 750262

Access   Open.

Index
No index to maps.

Summary
The collection comprises material relating to the Isle of Anglesey and the adjoining mainland only. There are no original maps in the collection.

Detail
6a, 8, 10a. 17a

282 Gwynedd Library Service, Meirionnydd Area Library

Address   Fron Serth, Dolgellau, LL40 2YF

Telephone   (01341) 422771

Access   Open.

Index
No index to maps.

Summary
Collection consists of one-inch and six-inch OS maps. One-inch maps of

Wales in general, a reprint of the 1st edition. Complete set of the six-inch maps of Merionethshire, 1901 edition.

Detail
10a,b

POWYS

283   Powys County Archives Office

Address   County Hall, Llandrindod Wells LD1 5LG

Telephone   (01597) 826087   *Fax*   (01597) 826230

Access   By appointment. CARN reader's ticket required.

Index
A guide to the *Powys County Archives Office* (Powys County Archives
Office, 1993).
Indexes and catalogues on site.

Summary
The present county of Powys covers the former counties of Mont-
gomeryshire, Radnorshire and Breconshire.
Extensive collection of OS maps: at 2 inches to 1 mile, c.1817–1825
(photocopies); at 1 inch to 1 mile, c.1833 and c.1865; at 6 inches to 1
mile, c.1888 and later.
Maps in classes such as public records, official records, local authority
records: tithe maps; enclosure awards from the late 18th century.
Deposited Plans which include railway, road and canal projects.
Maps of mines and quarries, etc. Numerous maps of minor estates within
Powys, and some topographical maps of Brecknockshire, Radnorshire
and Montgomeryshire, most notably Thomas Kitchin's maps from
c.1754.

Detail
5, 6a, 7, 9, 10a,b,c, 11, 12, 13, 14, 15, 17a

Publications of maps held
Maps of the old counties are described in, for example:
The Radnorshire Transactions, published annually by the Radnorshire
Society.
Brycheinog, published annually by the Brecknock Society.
The Montgomeryshire Collections, published annually by the Powysland
Club.
J. Booth, *Antique Maps of Wales* (Montacute Bookshop, 1977).

284   Powys County Libraries, Brecon Area Library

Address   Ship Street, Brecon LD3 9AE

Telephone   (01874) 623346

Access   Open.

Index
No index to maps.

Summary
A collection of printed maps, with some reproductions.
All Welsh counties are represented. Some maps are taken from atlases or books. Included are general district maps, showing roads, rivers, railways and canals. Town plan of Brecknock, 1744. County maps include those of Montgomery by W. Kip, 1607 and 1610; J. Speed, 1610 and later; T. Kitchin, 1747; T. Osborne, 1748; J. Roper, 1816; S. Leigh, 1831, and others. Turnpike and railway maps of the 19th century, the River Wye from Chepstow to Monmouth, 1836, and tithe maps for Breconshire. Reprint of the OS 1st edition for England and Wales.

Detail
1, 2, 5, 6a,b, 7, 10a, 13, 14, 15, 17a

285   Powys County Libraries, Newtown Area Library

Address   Park Lane, Newtown SY21 1EJ

Telephone   (01686) 626934

Access   By appointment.

Index
Handlist on site.

Summary
The maps cover areas of Wales, and adjacent parts of England, more particularly the counties of Montgomery, Merioneth, Radnorshire, Denbigh, and Glamorgan. County, road and turnpike maps. Incomplete OS coverage, late 19th century. Photocopies of allotment and tithe maps.

Detail
2, 7, 10a,b, 13, 14, 15, 17a

286   Brecknock Museum

Address   Captain's Walk, Brecon LD3 7DW

Telephone   (01874) 624121

Access   By appointment only.

Index
Handlist on site.

Summary
Printed maps of Wales, 18th century onwards; printed maps of Breconshire, 16th century onwards.
Geological maps of Breconshire and surrounding areas, from 1900.
Miscellaneous enclosure and estate plans relating to Breconshire.
John Ogilby's strip maps; Brecon and Abergavenny Canal plans; tramway plans.

Detail
2, 5, 6a,b, 7, 11, 12, 13, 14, 15

287   The Powysland Club

Address   c/o The Powysland Museum, Canal Wharf, Welshpool SY21 7AQ

Access   By appointment only.

Index
No index to maps.

Summary
Tithe maps for Montgomeryshire. Two local township maps, manuscript.
OS 19th century sheets for the locality.

Detail
10, 11, 17a

288   The Powysland Museum

Address   Canal Wharf, Welshpool SY21 7AQ

Telephone   (01938) 554656

Access   By appointment only.

Index
Typed handlist of maps.

Summary
The collection includes published maps of Wales, particularly the counties of Montgomeryshire and Merionethshire, dating from 1579 onwards, and including 'Montgomery' by Christopher Saxton (1579), John Speed (1610), by Thomas Taylor (1718), 'Merioneth and Montgomery' by John Rocque (1760), 'Flint, Denbigh and Montgomery' by C. and J. Greenwood, and others. Road maps for parts of Wales from John Ogilby's *Britannia* (1675), by Thomas Gardner for Edward Vaughan, and others. 'North Wales' by J. Carey (1809), and by J. Badeslade (1741).

Detail
1, 2, 3, 4, 6a, 7

SCOTLAND

289 Scottish Record Office

Address West Register House, Charlotte Square, Edinburgh EH2 4DF

Telephone (0131) 556 6585 *Fax* (0131) 225 7973

Access Open. Reader's ticket required. Some maps are restricted to authorised researchers.

Index

I. H. Adams (ed.), *Descriptive list of Plans in the Scottish Record Office*, vol. 1 (Edinburgh, 1966), vol. 2 (Edinburgh, 1970), vol. 3 (Edinburgh, 1974), vol. 4 (edited by I. H. Adams and Loretta R. Timperley) (Edinburgh, 1988).

A Repertory of Register House Plans, 56 volumes, can be consulted in typescript. This contains information on provenance, surveyor, engineer or architect and topographical coverage. Topographical card-indexes, limited subject-indexes and limited indexes to surveyors are also maintained.

Summary

About 63,000 maps, manuscript and printed, are held, including a large number of photocopies of plans in private custody in Scotland. Sources include legal disputes in the Court of Session, deposit with sheriff courts throughout Scotland under legislation, records of government departments and nationalised industries, including pre-vesting coal and railway companies, and deposited solicitors' and estate collections. Coverage is strongest from late 18th to early 20th century.

Detail

1, 2, 3, 4, 5, 6a,b, 7, 8, 9, 10b,c, 11, 12, 13, 14, 15

Publications of maps held

Many maps from this extensive collection have been reproduced in publications.

Facsimiles and reproductions on sale

'Plan of Old and New Edinburgh' (1773).

290 National Library of Scotland, Map Library

Address   33 Salisbury Place, Edinburgh EH9 1SL

Telephone   (0131) 226 4531   *Fax*   (0131) 668 3472

Access   Open for research and reference not readily available
elsewhere.
Some manuscript maps are held by the Manuscripts
Division, George IV Bridge, Edinburgh EH1 1EW;
readers ticket required.

Index
Holdings of early maps are entered under NLS in D. G. Moir (ed.), *Early
maps of Scotland to 1850*, vols. 1 and 2, (Edinburgh: Royal Scottish
Geographical Society, 1973 and 1983).
Catalogue of Manuscripts acquired since 1925, vols. 1–8 (Edinburgh,
1938–92), see under 'Maps'; *Summary Catalogue of the Advocates'
Manuscripts* (Edinburgh, 1970), see under 'Geography and Travel'.
Unpublished *Catalogue of Manuscripts acquired since 1925*, vols. 9–19,
with indexes.
Inventories of deposit and uncatalogued accessions.

Summary
The Map Library aims at bibliographical completeness for its record of
maps of the whole or part of Scotland and acquires as much as possible
produced by Scots either as compilers, engravers, publishers or printers,
of maps of all parts of the World. Maps of the British Isles range from
the 15th century in original or facsimile, and include virtually complete
coverage of large scale OS maps of Scotland and good, but incomplete,
coverage of the rest of the UK.
Manuscript maps range in date from a world map of the 12th century
to the present, mostly from the 18th and 19th centuries. They comprise
estate and agricultural maps, engineering plans connected with colliery
and harbour works, and military maps. The maps by Timothy Pont,
Robert and James Gordon, and John Adair are of prime importance for
early Scottish cartography and of interest for their provenance. Mid 18th
century Board of Ordnance maps include plans of military installations
and road surveys. Plans by Messrs Stevenson, civil engineers in the 19th
and 20th centuries, are primarily concerned with sea-works.
Special collections:
Marischal Collection, 137 maps of Scotland collected in France by

Jacobites and their descendants, the earliest being acquired at the Court in exile of James VII and II.

Newman Collection, about 1150 road books, itineraries and related maps of Great Britain mainly from the 18th and 19th centuries.

Graham Brown Collection of mountaineering and travel material (mostly areas outside UK).

Detail
1, 2, 3, 4, 5, 6a,b, 7, 8, 9, 10a,b,c, 11, 12, 13, 14, 15, 16

Publications of maps held
J. C. Stone, *The Pont manuscript maps of Scotland, sixteenth-century origins of a Blaeu atlas* (Tring: Map Collector Publications, 1989).

M. Wilkes, 'He will do well in the beginning to provide a map', *The Map Collector* **56** (1991), 2–7, is an introduction to the NLS collections.

M. Wilkes, *The Scot and his maps* (Motherwell: Scottish Library Association, 1991), describes and illustrates some items from NLS collections.

Facsimiles and reproductions for sale
Georg Braun and Franz Hogenberg, 'Edenburgum: Scotiae Metropolis' (c.1582), from *Civitates orbis terrarum*, vol. 3 (Amsterdam, 1572–1618).

J. Geddy, manuscript, 'St Andrews' (c.1580).

John Speed, 'The Kingdome of Scotland' (London, 1662).

Aleph, 'Scotland', from *Geographical fun: being humorous outlines from various countries* (London, 1869).

BORDERS REGION

291   Borders Region Archive and Local History Centre

Address   St Mary's Mill, Selkirk TD7 5EW

Telephone   (01750) 720842   *Fax*   (01750) 722875

Access   Open.

Index
No index to maps.

Summary
Maps are included in the Local History collection. There is a good holding of OS maps at 25 inches to the mile.
In addition, small collections of Scottish and regional maps are housed in Area Libraries.

Detail
3, 6a,b, 7, 10a,b,c

CENTRAL REGION

292 Central Regional Council Archives Department

Address   Unit 6, Burghmuir Industrial Estate, Stirling FK7 7PY

Telephone   (01786) 50745

Access   Open.

Index

Catalogues of the collection, including maps, to 1976, appendix to 1978, are held by Stirling University, Falkirk Technical College, Callander Park Training College, Stirling Central and District Libraries, Clackmannan District Library, Edinburgh Central Library, National Library of Scotland, HM General Register House and West Register House.

Summary

The Department holds around 1000 maps and plans, mostly pertaining to local government in the area now known as Central Region. Many are annotated OS maps. There are a few 18th century plans of Stirling Burgh lands and property but the bulk of the collection belongs to the 19th and 20th centuries.

Detail

3, 5, 6a,b, 7, 10a,b,c, 13, 15, 17c

293 Stirling District Library Headquarters

Address   Barrowmeadow Road, Stirling FK7 7TN

Telephone   (01786) 432380   *Fax*   (01786) 432395

Access   Appointment advised as some material is outhoused.

Index
Handlist on site.

Summary
The area covered is that of the former Clackmannan, Falkirk and

Stirling Districts. Local estate plans, 19th century. Plans of the Field of Bannockburn.

Detail
7, 9, 11, 15, 17c

DUMFRIES AND GALLOWAY

294   Dumfries Archive Centre

Address   33 Burns Street, Dumfries DG1 2PS

Telephone   (01387) 69254

Access   By appointment.

Index
Handlist and card index for all maps held, on site.

Summary
Printed, manuscript and photostat maps, including:
(1) Timothy Pont's maps of Dumfries and Galloway, from W. and J. Blaeu, *Theatrum orbis terrarum*, vol. 5 (1654).
(2) Manuscript maps by the architect Walter Newall of River Nith and his schemes (1811–49) for railways, waterworks, etc.
(3) OS maps at various scales, of Dumfries and other towns in the region.
(4) Miscellaneous estate plans, 18th and 19th centuries.
(5) Miscellaneous plans of Dumfries Burgh, 18th to 20th centuries.
(6) Chart of the Solway Firth (1742) with photostats of later Solway charts in the Scottish Record Office.
(7) William Crawford's map of Dumfriesshire (1804).

Detail
3, 5, 6a,b, 7, 8, 10b,c, 11, 13, 15

295   Ewart Library, Dumfries and Galloway Collection

Address   Catherine Street, Dumfries DG1 1JB

Telephone   (01387) 53820/52070   *Fax*   (01387) 60294

Access   Open.

Index
No index to maps.

Summary
There is a small number of OS sheets at 1 and 6 inches to the mile, published before 1900. Coverage is of the former counties of Dumfries, Kircudbright and Wigtown. Many of the maps are reproductions of originals in national or private collections. There are no manuscript maps and no provenances of particular interest.

Detail
3, 5, 6a,b, 7, 8, 9, 10a,b, 11, 12, 13, 15

296   Dumfries Museum

Address   The Observatory, Dumfries DG2 7SW

Telephone   (01387) 53374   *Fax*   (01387) 65081

Access   By appointment.

Index
Unpublished handlist, on site.

Summary
The collection includes the Pont-Gordon maps from the Blaeu atlas, 1654.
A number of estate maps and a good manuscript plan of the George Street development of 1806. William Crawford's map of Dumfriesshire, 1804. John Wood's map of Dumfries, 1819.
A set of maps of the 1820s by Thompson and others. Plan of lands of Drummore by H. Stitt, 1873.
OS sheets at 25 inches to 1 mile for Dumfriesshire.

Detail
1, 6a,b, 7, 9, 10a,b,c, 11, 13, 15

FIFE

297   Dunfermline Central Library, Local History Collection

Address   1 Abbot Street, Dunfermline KY12 7NW

Telephone   (01383) 723661   *Fax*   (01383) 620761

Access   Open.

Index
Dunfermline Central Libraries, *A guide to local maps and plans held in Dunfermline Central Library's Local History Collection* (Dunfermline, 1978). (Available free to enquirers).

Summary
Local maps, a few manuscript but mostly printed. Blaeu's Atlas and a few other early maps. The majority of the collection is 19th century. Firth of Forth maritime surveys.

Detail
3, 5, 6a, 7, 8, 10a,b,c, 11, 12, 15

298   Kirkcaldy District Libraries, Central Library

Address   War Memorial Gardens, Kirkcaldy KY1 1YG

Telephone   (01592) 260707

Access   Open.

Index
No index to maps.

Summary
The map collection relates mainly to Kirkcaldy District.
General maps of the county of Fife, street maps, geological and OS maps, and maps showing parish boundaries and rights of way.

Detail
1, 6a,b, 7, 10a,b,c, 11,

Facsimiles and reproductions on sale
'The Sherifdome of Fyfe' by Blaeu (Amsterdam, 1654).
'The Counties of Fife and Kinross' by Sharp, Greenwood and Fowler (1828).

299   University of St Andrews Library

Address   North Street, St Andrews KY16 9TR

Telephone   (01334) 62281   *Fax*   (01334) 62282

Access   Open.

Index
Catalogue on site, includes place-name entries.

Summary
About 3000 maps, mainly OS, from the 19th century to the present. Most are at 1 inch to the mile, with larger scale coverage for Fife. There is a number of 18th and 19th century Scottish maps (in addition to 17th century maps in atlases). The collection is mostly miscellaneous.

Detail
1, 2, 3, 4, 5, 6a,b, 7, 8, 9, 10a,b,c

GRAMPIAN REGION

300   Grampian Regional Archives

Address   Old Aberdeen House, Dunbar Street, Aberdeen AB2 1UE

Telephone   (01224) 481775

Access   By appointment.

Index
No separate index to maps.

Summary
A few unrelated manuscripts and maps, some uncatalogued, including OS maps recently acquired.

Detail
6b, 11, 15

301   Moray District Record Office

Address   Tolbooth, High Street, Forres IV36 0AB

Telephone   (01309) 73617   *Fax*   (01309) 74166

Access   Open.

Index
Unpublished handlist on site.

Summary
96,000 plans, relating to local government activities, *c.*1790–1975, and privately deposited plans of houses, schools etc., *c.*1825–1960.

Detail
1, 3, 6a,b, 7, 10a,b,c, 11, 13

302 North East of Scotland Library Service, Local History Department

Address   Meldrum Meg Way, The Meadows Industrial Estate, Oldmeldrum AB51 0GN

Telephone   (01651) 872707   *Fax*   (01651) 872142

Access   Open.

Index
No index to maps.

Summary
Volume of estate plans of Strichen Estate, Aberdeenshire, 1768–1774; later plans of this estate, by John Boulton, 1846–49. Other local plans of lands in Strichen and Fraserburgh parishes by John Boulton, c.1850. Town plan of Stonehaven, 1823. Plan of Aberdeen-Inverurie canal. Incomplete set of OS maps at 25 inches to the mile, 1870, for Aberdeenshire and Banffshire.

Detail
7, 10c, 11, 14

303 Aberdeen City Libraries

Address   Rosemount Viaduct, Aberdeen AB9 1GO

Telephone   (01224) 634622   *Fax*   (01224) 641985

Access   Open.

Index
Maps included in the alphabetical sequence of *Catalogue of the local collection* (1914).
Handlist, *Key to Aberdeen maps*, continuously updated.

Summary
The historical map collection relates mainly to Aberdeen with a smaller number of maps of Aberdeenshire, and some historical maps of Scotland. Town plans of Aberdeen from 1661 to present. Feuing and estate plans. Aberdeen Harbour plans. Aberdeenshire railway and canal maps. Sketches and elevations for outstanding buildings in the City.
OS maps at 6 inches to 1 mile, 19th century, for several Scottish counties including the whole area north of the Tay.

Detail
3, 6b, 7, 9, 10,a,b,c, 11, 13, 14, 15

304 University of Aberdeen

Access Departments are open to members of the University, otherwise by appointment.

304A Queen Mother Library

Address Meston Walk, Old Aberdeen AB9 2UE

Telephone (01224) 272579 *Fax* (01224) 487048

Index
No index to maps.

Summary
The holdings include many reprints of early maps, particularly those in W. and J. Blaeu, *Theatrum orbis terrarum*.
For Scotland, the 6 inch to 1 mile county series, the microfilm of the military survey and BL copies on paper.
OS first edition at 1 inch to 1 mile for Britain.

Detail
1, 2, 3, 4, 9, 10a

Publications of maps held
Jeffrey Stone, 'The cartographic treasures of Aberdeen University Library', *The Map Collector*, **36** (1986), 30–4.

304B Special Collections and Archives

Address King's College, Aberdeen AB9 2UB

Telephone (01224) 272588 *Fax* (01224) 487048

Index
No separate index to maps. The majority of printed maps and atlases are entered on the computerised catalogue. Handlists on site to the major collections of estate papers.

Summary
Sizeable collection of 16th to 19th century atlases (e.g., those of Blaeu, Ortelius, Ptolemy, and the Society for the Diffusion of Useful Knowledge, some of which are also available in facsimile). This collection has a good coverage of Scotland, including for example maps by John Adair, Herman Moll, Sir Robert Sibbald, John Wood.
The O'Dell Railway Collection contains a significant collection of large-scale 19th century railway maps and charts of Scotland, especially the north-east region. The collection also has a number of 18th century travellers' companions, for example, Cary's.
The Local Collection has a small number of printed maps and estate plans from the mid-18th century.
Many of the Department's major estate archives (predominately from the north-east) contain plans, mostly 18th and 19th century (e.g., Duff House papers).
The Department also has a collection of manuscript plans of local towns and buildings, collected by Dr W. D. Simpson, past Librarian.

Detail
1, 3, 6a,b, 7, 10a, 11, 13, 14, 15

304C   Department of Geography, Map Library

Address   Elphinstone Road, Aberdeen AB9 2UF

Telephone   (01224) 272328   *Fax*   (01224) 487048

Access   Open only during Departmental hours.

Index
Alphabetical list on site. The Aberdeen section of the McDonald Maps is fully card indexed, the rest being sorted chronologically.

Summary
The historical section is part of a large collection covering the entire world and consists of 2000–3000 items of general interest. In addition, the McDonald Maps consist of some 6000 items ranging from c.1740–1920, of local interest, the majority pertaining to North East Scotland.

Detail
1, 2, 3, 4, 5, 6a,b, 7, 8, 9, 10a,b,c, 11, 12, 13, 14, 15, 17c

Facsimiles and reproductions on sale
Several historical maps have been reproduced by the Department for the benefit of its students.

LOTHIAN

305   City of Edinburgh District Council Archives

Address   City Chambers, High Street, Edinburgh EH1 1YJ

Telephone   (0131) 225 2424   *Fax*   (0131) 529 7477
                 (0131) 529 4016

Access   By appointment only.

Index
Unpublished handlist on site.

Summary
The collection consists essentially of the various maps and plans used by Edinburgh Corporation for its own practical purposes. The vast bulk of the collection comprises maps dated from about 1750 onwards, most of which relate to the area of the city at the time in question.

Detail
7, 10c

306   Edinburgh City Libraries, Central Public Library

Address   George IV Bridge, Edinburgh EH1 1EG

Telephone   (0131) 225 5584   *Fax*   (0131) 225 8783

Access   Open.

306A   The Edinburgh Room

Index
William Cowan, *The maps of Edinburgh, 1544–1929*, 2nd edition, revised, with census of copies in Edinburgh Libraries, by C. B. B. Watson (Edinburgh, 1932).

Summary
Map collection numbers some 2600 items, the bulk of the collection deriving from the 20th century Cowan, Sanderson, and Boog Watson Bequests.

Imaginary and reconstructed views of the Edinburgh area, the collecting area being governed by the City boundary, from medieval times to 1900; other maps from the 16th century, e.g. the Siege of Leith, 1560, to the present. Printed maps, originals and facsimiles. The collection also includes, from the 18th century, plans of individual buildings and streets, feuing plans, and from the 19th century, improvement plans and boundary extension maps, Edinburgh Water Company plans etc. Post Office Directory plans, 1828 onwards.

OS plans, at 5 feet to 1 mile for 1852–55 and 1877; at 6 inches to 1 mile for 1855 (parts of Midlothian sheets 2 and 6) and 1892–3; at 10 feet to 1 mile for 1892–3; at 25 inches to 1 mile for 1894–6 (part of the City only).

Detail
7, 10a,b,c, 11, 13, 14, 15

306B   Scottish Department

Index
Maps are indexed very generally under county or town in the main card catalogue. Some parts of the collection have their own index, e.g. a card index to town plans. A project to index the maps in more detail is under way at present (1994).

Summary
A collection of almost 4000 maps dealing only with Scotland. The collection includes original and facsimile maps from mid-16th century onwards, as well as several 19th century county atlases, and town plans from the 19th and 20th centuries.

OS sheets, at 1 inch to 1 mile, for the Lothians area, 1890s; Single sheets of some 1 inch to 1 mile, 1st edition.

Detail
3, 6a,b, 7, 10a,b,c, 11, 14, 15

306C   Reference Department

Index
No special index to pre-1900 maps or atlases. All pre-1900 stock catalogued in main card catalogue.

Summary
Some pre-1900 atlases, including facsimiles of important British maps.
Small number of pre-1900 OS maps of England, Wales and Ireland, and
town plans of England and Wales.

Detail
1, 4, 6a

307   Edinburgh University, Map Library

Address	George Square, Edinburgh EH8 9LJ
Telephone	(0131) 650 3969 / 3376 *Fax* (0131) 667 9780
Access	Non-members of Edinburgh University should apply beforehand in writing to the Librarian, Edinburgh University Library

Index
The Map Collection in the Main Library; a descriptive guide, Library
    Guides 5.
Unpublished catalogue/handlist, *Preliminary checklist of atlases, published
    before about 1870, held in the Main Library* (1971).

Summary
The collection of maps and atlases dates back to the Library's foundation
in 1580. In the early years most of the maps were presented, often by
members or associates of the University. Most of the early maps are
printed and concerned with Scotland and its parts. The atlas collection
is primarily of world, or general, atlases. Current acquisition concentrates
on completing coverage of south-east Scotland.

Detail
1, 2, 3, 4, 5, 6a,b, 7, 8, 9, 10a,b,c, 13, 14, 15

308 Huntly House Museum

Address Canongate, Edinburgh EH8 8DD

Telephone (0131) 225 2424

Access Appointment essential for stored items.

Index
E. Cumming (comp.), *Catalogue of the City of Edinburgh Art Collection*, 2 vols. (Edinburgh, 1979). Maps and views are listed by artist.

Summary
About 20 printed and manuscript maps, dating from c.1742, also two charts of the Firth of Forth (1681 and 1682). About 180 items dating from c.1740, comprising plans, bird's-eye views and perspective views, of the city and its environs.

Detail
3, 5, 7, 8, 17c

309 National Museums of Scotland Library

309A Chambers Street Library (Royal Museum of Scotland)

Address Chambers Street, Edinburgh EH1 1JF

Telephone (0131) 225 7534 ext. 142 *Fax* (0131) 220 4819

Access By written appointment.

Index
Map section in general card index, arranged by county and by author/publisher.

Summary
A collection of atlases, printed maps and photocopies of early maps, including George Taylor and Andrew Skinner's survey and maps of the roads of Scotland, editions of 1776 and 1805. Bathymetrical survey of the Fresh-water lochs of Scotland, (1896–1908): 8 hand coloured maps of lochs in Perthshire and Stirlingshire based on OS sheets.

Detail
1, 2, 3, 4, 5, 6a, b, 7

309B Department of Science, Technology and Working Life

Address   Royal Museum of Scotland, Chambers Street, Edinburgh EH1 1JF

Telephone   (0131) 225 7534   *Fax*   (0131) 220 4819

Access   By appointment.

Index
Card index on site. Maps on inventory can be retrieved from the Museum database.

Summary
About 75 historical maps and charts of Scotland, relating to the development of surveying, including sheets by John Adair, the Blaeu family, Thomas Kitchin and John Barber, James Kirkwood, John Senex, John Speed, Gerard Mercator and Timothy Pont. Plan of the battle of Culloden, attributed to John Finlayson, 1745.
Also a few maps of Britain collected in 1906 for a proposed geographical exhibition.

Detail
1, 3, 4, 5, 6a, 8, 9, 13, 14, 15

Publications of maps held
G. Dalgleish and D. Mechan, 'Finlayson's Map', in *'I am come home':
Treasures of Prince Charles Edward Stuart* (Edinburgh, National Museum of Antiquities of Scotland, 1985), pp.19–20.
A. D. C. Simpson, 'John Adair, cartographer and Sir Robert Sibbald's "Scottish Atlas"', *Map Collector* **62** (1993), 32–36.

309C Queen Street Library (Museum of Antiquities)

Address   Queen Street, Edinburgh EH2 1JD

Telephone   (0131) 225 7534 ext. 369   *Fax*   (0131) 557 9498

Access   Open.

Index
Indexed through NMS database.

Summary
Bound early atlases (originally in the collection of the Society of Antiquaries of Scotland): Ptolemy's *Geographia* (Venice, 1561, 1562, Amsterdam 1730); Blaeu's *Theatrum orbis terrarum* (Amsterdam, 1648–1655);
Ortelius' *Theatrum orbis terrarum* (Antwerp, 1570).
Approximately 60 printed maps, almost entirely Scottish 18th century,
by John Adair and others. Counties represented include Western Isles,
1688 and 1822, Angus (Montrose) 1693, Peeblesshire, 1741, Lothians,
1735 and 1744, Stirlingshire 1745, Perthshire 1770, Bute 1814, Ayrshire,
1773 and 1807, Edinburgh 1780, Galway 1610, Battle of Prestonpans,
1745.
Manuscript map of St Kilda, 1860, showing holdings.

Detail
1, 3, 4, 5, 6a, 7, 11, 14, 17c

309D Scottish United Services Museum Library

Address   The Castle, Edinburgh EH1 2NG

Telephone   (0131) 225 7534 ext. 404   *Fax*   (0131) 225 3848

Access   By appointment.

Index
Indexed through NMS database.

Summary
Small collection of maps from the Department of Armed Forces History,
including General Wade's roads, the march of the Royal Army, 1745–6,
Edinburgh 1765, Great Britain, showing campaigns of 1745–48, and a
manuscript map of Jersey, 1819, by Captain John Ford, 79th Regiment.

Detail
7, 9, 15

310 East Lothian District Libraries, Local History Centre

Address   Library Headquarters, Lodge Street, Haddington EH41 3DX

Telephone   (0162) 082 4161   *Fax* (0162) 082 5735

Access   Open access, telephone to confirm opening hours.
The map collection is available on microfilm aperture cards; the original maps are now stored elsewhere and cannot be produced immediately.

Index
Card catalogue on site.

Summary
The collection is limited to maps of East Lothian District, i.e. the former East Lothian County plus the parish of Inveresk and the Burgh of Musselburgh, but includes a few general maps acquired for their local content. The main collection covers the period 1799 to date, though there are a few earlier general maps. In addition to maps acquired by the local authority, the Centre houses the map collection of the East Lothian Antiquarian and Field Naturalists Society.

Detail
3, 6a,b, 7, 10a,b, 15

ORKNEY

311 The Orkney Library

Address   Laing Street, Kirkwall KW15 1NW

Telephone   (01856) 873166/875260

311A Orkney Archives

Access   By appointment.

Index
No index to maps.

Summary
The bulk of the collection consists of estate plans from 1830–1880, the provenance being either Orkney Sheriff Court or local solicitors' offices. Some Earldom estate plans from the 1770s.

Detail
11

311B Library

Access   Open.

Summary
A few 6 inch and 25 inch OS pre-1900 maps.

Detail
10b,c

SHETLAND

312   Shetland Museum

Address   Lower Hillhead, Lerwick ZE1 0EL

Telephone   (01595) 5057   *Fax*   (01595) 6729

Access   Appointment needed as maps are in an external store.

Index
Computer printout available.

Summary
There are about 144 printed maps and published marine charts which show or have a specific reference to Shetland and the surrounding seas, 1605 to the present day.

Detail
5, 6a,b, 8, 10a,b,c, 15

Publications of maps held
T. Henderson, *Shetland maps and charts: descriptive catalogue of an exhibition in the Picture Gallery of Zetland County Museum* (Lerwick: Zetland County Library, early 1970s.)

STRATHCLYDE

313   Strathclyde Regional Archives

Address   Mitchell Library, North Street, Glasgow G3 7DN

Telephone   (0141) 227 2405   *Fax*   (0141) 248 5027

Access   Open.

Index
Catalogue on site.

Summary
Printed and manuscript maps classed as follows, with approximate number of holdings in each group:
(1) City of Glasgow administrative maps and plans, 18th to 20th centuries, (800).
(2) Clyde Port Authority maps and plans, harbours, navigation, lighthouses, shipping, installations, 18th to 20th centuries, (600).
(3) Merchants House of Glasgow, plans of properties, cemeteries, world atlases etc, 17th to 20th centuries (*c.*500).
(4) Solicitors' collections deposited, mainly estates, minerals, urban properties, 18th to 20th centuries, (3000).
(5) Ardgowan Estate (Inverclyde area), 18th to 20th centuries, (500).
(6) Other family and estate collections, many including territorial plans.
(7) Insurance company maps; building control plans of buildings, (80,000).

Detail
3, 5, 6a,b, 7, 8, 10a,b,c, 11, 13, 14, 15, 16

314   Glasgow City Libraries Headquarters

Address   The Mitchell Library, North Street, Glasgow G3 7DN

Telephone   (0141) 221 7030   *Fax*   (0141) 204 4824

Access   Open.

Index
Hand-lists:
Maps in the Cairns Mitchell Collection, 1564–1892.
Maps of Scotland, 1536–1950. Pre-1940 Scottish town plans.
Pre-1900 county maps of Scotland. Glasgow early maps.
Description of portolan chart from Manuscripts Catalogue.
Holdings of pre-1850 maps are entered under MLG in Part II of
   D. G. Moir (ed.), *Early maps of Scotland to 1850*, vols. 1 and 2
   (Edinburgh: Royal Scottish Geographical Society, 1973 and 1983).

Summary
General collection of maps of Scotland from 1536; the Cairns Mitchell
collection of maps of Scotland from 1564; OS maps of UK and Ireland
from 1832; Glasgow maps issued prior to the OS of 1857–63; Glasgow
PO Directory street maps at 4 inches to 1 mile, 1847 to 1977.
Manuscript portolan chart of the coasts of England, Wales and Scotland,
together with the adjoining coasts of western Europe to southern Spain,
mid-16th century, evidently by a French chartmaker.
Partial set (sheets 13–31) of Murdock Mackenzie's Maritime Survey of
Ireland and the West of Great Britain, 1775–6, covering the west coast
of Scotland and the Isle of Man. Sets of Blaeu's *Atlas Major* in French,
Latin and Spanish.

Detail
1, 2, 3, 4, 6a, 8, 9, 10a,b,c

315 Hamilton Central Library, Reference and Local Studies Department

Address   98 Cadzow Street, Hamilton ML3 6HQ

Telephone   (01698) 282323 ext. 2403   *Fax*   (01698) 286334

Access   Open for Library Collection.
              By appointment for Hamilton Estates maps.

Index
Maps included in Library catalogue on site, but some collections unlisted.
Separate listing of Hamilton Estates items.
Map information leaflet available.

Summary
Maps of Hamilton and surrounding area from late 18th century.
Hamilton Estates maps, some manuscript, others annotated OS sheets,

of lands belonging to the Dukes of Hamilton in Lanarkshire.

Historical maps of Hamilton, including town plans by Thomas Burns (1781), Thomas Richardson (1807), John Wood (1819), Thomas Boyd (1848 and c.1855) and a large scale OS edition of 1861 at a scale of 10 feet to 1 mile.

OS maps at 6 and 25 inches to the mile, first edition of 1859–64, 2nd edition of 1896–99, for Hamilton District and parts of Lanarkshire (incomplete coverage).

Detail
6a,b, 7, 10a,b,c, 11, 12, 13, 15

316 Renfrew District Libraries, Local History Collection

Address   Central Library, High Street, Paisley PA1 2BB

Telephone   (0141) 889 2360 / 887 3672

Access   Open.

Index
Unpublished handlist on site.

Summary
Small collection of local maps, with some reproductions of maps held elsewhere, dating from that of Joan Blaeu (1654).

Town plans, railway and Parliamentary maps for Paisley and Renfrewshire.

OS maps, at 25 inches to the mile, for the centre area of Paisley, at 6 inches to the mile, 1st edition, sections 3, 6, 8, 11, and 12 only.

Other published maps are available in the Library's Reference Department.

Detail
6a,b, 7, 10a,b,c, 13, 15, 17c

317 Glasgow University Library

Address	Hillhead Street, Glasgow G12 8QE
Telephone	(0141) 339 8855 *Fax* (0141) 330 4952
Access	Open but appointment preferred for earlier material. For non-members of the university, a vistors ticket will be issued before entry to the collections.

Index

Holdings for pre-1850 Scottish maps and plans are recorded in D. G. Moir (ed.), *The early maps of Scotland to 1850* (Edinburgh: Royal Scottish Geographical Society, 1983).
Sheaf catalogue to loose map sheets and atlases, arranged geographically. This catalogue also lists maps entered in books but is not comprehensive and many atlases and maps can only be traced in the General Catalogue of Books or in Special Collections Department Catalogues.

Summary

A general university library collection supplemented by specialist local collections strong on Scottish, particularly Glasgow and West of Scotland, maps. The Special Collections Department has several important early atlases including a complete set of *Geographia Blauiana* of 1662 and several unique city plans of Glasgow.

Detail

1, 3, 5, 7, 8, 9, 10a,b,c, 14, 15

Publications of maps held

J. N. Moore, 'Manuscript charts by John Adair: a further discovery', *Scottish Geographical Magazine* **101** (1985), 105–110.

J. N. Moore, *Maps for a small country: an exhibition of historical maps and atlases of Scotland held in Glasgow University Library, 1991* (Glasgow, 1991).

J. N. Moore, 'Early printed county maps of Scotland in Glasgow University Library', *The College Courant* **73** (1984), 16–27.

318 Royal Scottish Geographical Society

Address	40 George Street, Glasgow G1 1QE
Telephone	(0141) 552 3330
Access	Open, advance notice required.

Index

Index in preparation (1994). See as a guide, D. G. Moir (ed.), *The early maps of Scotland to 1850* (1973–83).

Summary

General maps of Scotland c.1700 to 1900; county maps 1654 to 19th century. See D. G. Moir (ed.), *The early maps of Scotland*, vol. 1 (1973). Some of the Society's maps have been deposited at the National Library of Scotland.

Detail

3, 6a,b, 7, 8, 9, 10a,b, 11, 13, 14, 15

Publications of maps held

D. G. Moir (ed.), *The early maps of Scotland to 1850*, vol. 1 (Edinburgh: Royal Scottish Geographical Society, 1973), vol. 2 (1983).

TAYSIDE

319   Dundee District Archive and Record Centre, Administration Division

Address   21 City Square, Dundee DD1 3BY   Located at: 1 Shore Terrace, Dundee

Telephone   (01382) 23141 ext. 4494   *Fax*   (01382) 203302

Access   By appointment.

Index
Unpublished handlist on site.

Summary
Duplicates of deposited Parliamentary plans relating to Forfarshire/Angus and Dundee, 1842–1946; Contour survey of Dundee by James Collie, 1851–2, at approx 25 inches to 1 mile; Insurance plan register of Dundee, 1891; Estate plans of property in ownership of Council: Scotscraig, 1769, 1838 and Craigie, 1860; Dundee Port Authority, plans of Harbour, 1816–1926.

Detail
5, 6b, 7, 8, 10a,b,c, 11, 13, 15, 16

320   Dundee University Library, Archives and Manuscripts Department

Address   Perth Road, Dundee DD1 4HN

Telephone   (01382) 344095   *Fax*   (01382) 29190

Access   Open.

Index
Descriptive list, card index, and database (part), on site.

Summary
The collection relates mainly to Dundee, Angus and Perthshire. It comprises almost 3000 sheets, a proportion of which is made up of

architectural and technical drawings; manuscript and printed plans are included. The earliest plan is dated 1743 and the majority of the collection is of the 19th century, particularly the latter half.

Detail
3, 5, 6, 7, 8, 10a,b,c, 11, 12, 13, 15, 16

321   Perth and Kinross District Archives

Address   Sandeman Library, 16 Kinnoull Street, Perth PH1 5ET
NB The Sandeman Library will be moving to York Place, Perth, in 1994.

Telephone   (01738) 23329   *Fax*   (01738) 36364

Access   By appointment only.

Index
Handlist on site.

Summary
Collection relates to Perth, Kinross and Fife. Survey of the Counties of Perth and Clackmannan by James Stobie (1783). Plans of Perth, Crieff etc., with various 19th century improvements entered.
OS maps, many marked with local estates, borough features. Railway plans and sections for Fife & Kinross, and North British Railways, from 1854.

Detail
7, 10, 11, 13, 15

322   Perthshire Map Collection

Address   Sandeman Library, 16 Kinnoull Street, Perth PH1 5ET
NB The Sandeman Library will be moving to York Place, Perth, in 1994.

Telephone   (01738) 23329   *Fax*   (01738) 36364

Access   Open.

Index
Incomplete handlist on site.
List of maps and plans of Perth and Perthshire (Perth and Kinross District Libraries, c.1970).

Summary
Relates mainly to Perthshire and Kinross-shire. Town plans of Perth, from 1715, showing fortifications of 1715–6 (photocopies of originals held elsewhere). Surveys of the River Tay and its estuary, by James Knox (1831), by James Ritson (1833). Road, tram and railway maps from 1850.
OS large-scale maps of the district.
A large number of photocopies, e.g. of the Pont and Gordon maps of the earlier 17th century, have been acquired from the National Library of Scotland, the Scottish Record Office, the House of Lords Record Office, etc.

Detail
5, 6, 7, 9, 10, 13, 15

323 Angus District Libraries and Museums Service

Address   County Buildings, Forfar, DD8 3LG
NB Correspondence should be sent to the above address.

Telephone   (01307) 465101   *Fax*   (01307) 464834
Address   Forfar Library, 50 West High Street, Forfar DD8 1BA

Access   Open.

Index
Handlist, *List of all maps and plans in the collection of Angus District Museums at Arbroath, Brechin, Forfar and Montrose* (1979–80), on site.

Summary
This Library holds the most extensive collection of maps for Forfarshire and Angus. Branch libraries at Arbroath, Montrose, Brechin, Carnoustie and Kirriemuir hold only maps covering their localities.
Original early maps of Scotland, from 1640 to 1867, by John Ainslie, Robert Edward, Timothy Pont and Robert Gordon. Maps of Angus by Herman Moll (1725) and John Blackadder (1823.)
John Wood's plans of Brechin, Arbroath, Forfar and Montrose.
All series of OS maps for Forfarshire and Angus, 1865–1938.

Detail
3, 6b, 10a,b,c, 11, 14

WESTERN ISLES

324   Western Isles Libraries Headquarters

Address   Keith Street, Stornoway, Isle of Lewis PA87 2QG

Telephone   (01851) 703064   *Fax*   (01851) 705657

Access   Prior notice advised for early local maps.

Index
No index to maps.

Summary
Photocopies of OS sheets, 1848–52 and 1895, for whole of the Western Isles. Maps of local interest include estate and demesne, 1785, 1850; town plans, 1785, 1812, 1900; survey maps for the Stornoway to Carloway railway, 1890.

Detail
7, 10b,c, 11, 12, 13, 15

NORTHERN IRELAND

325   Public Record Office of Northern Ireland

Address   66 Balmoral Avenue, Belfast BT9 6NY

Telephone   (01232) 661621 / 663286   *Fax*   (01232) 665718

Access   Open. Reader's ticket required. First-time visitors are advised to send for the *Guide to the Public Record Office of Northern Ireland* (1991).

Index

Maps are catalogued according to their provenance. There are series of catalogues of OS maps and Valuation maps, but estate maps, county maps, etc., are scattered throughout our private archives and collections. In the series of *How to use the Record Office* leaflets, Nos. 11 to 18 deal with Maps and Plans, for the counties of Antrim, Armagh, Down, Fermanagh, Londonderry, Tyrone, Belfast (dates vary with the county, but broadly *c.*1600–1830) and of General Maps of Ireland and Ulster, *c.*1538–*c.*1830, also 'A catalogue of large scale town plans prepared by the Ordnance Survey' which contains OS and Valuation maps.

Summary

A large collection of estate maps for every big estate in Northern Ireland and for a large number of smaller estates, mainly from 1750. OS maps and town plans, from the 1830s to the present. Valuation maps and town plans from the 1830s. Railway plans, *c.*1870–1940. Photocopies of early maps relating to Ulster in other collections.

Detail

4, 5, 6a,b, 7, 8, 10a,b,c, 11, 13

326   Geological Survey of Northern Ireland

Address   20 College Gardens, Belfast BT9 6BS

Telephone   (01232) 666595   *Fax*   (01232) 662835

Access   Open, but appointment advised if professional guidance is required.

Index
No index to maps.

Summary
A map collection covering all of Ireland at 1 inch to 1 mile exists as bound copies published as hand coloured maps showing geological lines and boundaries. Similar small scale documents at 6 inches to 1 mile. The GSNI holds a full set of published memoirs pertinent to specific sheets covering all of Ireland. 'The County Series' dating from the 1850s onwards cover only the six counties of Northern Ireland, the remainder of the set being held by the Geological Survey of Ireland.
Plans of coal mining operations in Northern Ireland dating from the late 1880s.
GSNI acts as principal curator for all borehole logs from drilling operations within the province.

Detail
4, 5, 6a,b

327   Ordnance Survey of Northern Ireland

Address   Colby House, Stranmillis Court, Belfast BT9 5BJ

Telephone   (01232) 661244   *Fax*   (01232) 683211

Access   Open for inspection and purchase of copies. Study facilities are only available by appointment through the Director.

Index
Reference system on site.

Summary
Bound volumes of complete sets of OS sheets at 6 inches to 1 mile for each of the six counties of Northern Ireland from the 1830s survey and the 1850s revision. (Approximately 640 maps). NB maps from these

volumes may not be copied; some two-thirds of the sheets are also available loose, which can be copied.

Other pre-1900 sheets: at 1 inch to 1 mile (loose); at 5 feet to 1 mile (1:1056) of Belfast City; depicting parish and barony boundaries.

Detail
4, 6b, 7, 10a,b, 13, 17c

ARMAGH

328   Armagh County Museum

Address   The Mall East, Armagh BT61 9BE

Telephone   (01861) 523070   *Fax*   (01861) 522631

Access   By appointment.

Index
No index to maps.

Summary
Manuscript maps include:
Griffith's Valuation town plans (1839), 15 sheets covering 20 County Armagh towns: 15 sheets covering 20 County Armagh towns. Reproductions of eleven Ulster escheated counties Barony maps of 1609. Copy of the 1837 map of Armagh, geological map of County Armagh etc., Davidson's Lough Neagh flint sites. Sundry rail and 19th century Grand Jury maps of roads and Upper Bann Navigation Trust maps. Charts of Carlingford and Neagh Loughs. Estate maps in Tyrone, Armagh.
OS sheets, at 25 inches to 1 mile for Armagh, Down, Louth and Tyrone. OS 6 inches to 1 mile, sets and parts for Armagh, Down, Louth and Tyrone, 1835, 1864. OS 1 inch to 1 mile, various Irish counties. OS 5 feet to 1 mile, Armagh towns.

Detail
6a,b, 7, 8, 10a,b,c, 11, 13, 14, 15

BELFAST

329   Central Library, Irish and Local Studies Department

Address   Royal Avenue, Belfast BT1 1EA

Telephone   (01232) 243233   *Fax*   (01232) 332819

Access   By appointment.

Index
Unpublished guides include *Irish Antiquarian Maps* and *Guide to maps.*

Summary
The library holds approximately 5,000 maps of Ireland. These include about 500 antiquarian maps, with a small number of manuscript items. The earliest maps held are 16th century. Major holdings of more modern maps include much of the 1834 OS survey of Ireland at 6 inches to the mile, and complete holdings of more modern series.

Detail
4, 6a,b, 7, 8, 10a,b,c, 11, 13, 14, 15, 17c

330   Linen Hall Library

Address   17 Donegall Square North, Belfast BT1 5GD

Telephone   (01232) 321707   *Fax*   (01232) 438586

Access   By appointment.

Index
Published list in 'Atlases and Maps' in Linen Hall Library, *Catalogue of the books in the Irish Section* (Belfast, 1917).
Manuscript list for other parts of the UK, on site.

Summary
The collection includes World, European and British Isles maps, but its strength is in its Irish maps.
The Irish maps collection is divided into sections: Ireland; Provinces;

Counties; Towns. Many of these maps are very rare. There are also town plans, charts, and a few estate maps.

Detail
2, 3, 4, 7, 8, 10a,b, 11, 13, 14, 15

Publications of maps held
J. H. Andrews, note accompanying the facsimile reproduction of 'Hyberniae novissima descriptio, 1591, by Jodocus Hondius' (Belfast: Linen Hall Library, 1983).
J. H. Andrews, note accompanying the facsimile reproduction of 'James Williamson's map of County Down, 1810' (Belfast: Linen Hall Library, 1986).

Facsimiles and reproductions on sale
James Williamson's 'Belfast' (1792). Facsimile with descriptive commentary by W. Maguire (Belfast: Linen Hall Library, 1989). John Rocque's 'County Armagh' (1760).'County Down' by Oliver Sloane (1739), facsimile with commentary by R. H. Buchanan. 'Belfast', town plan (1685). 'Belfast' (1757). 'James Lemdrick's map of Antrim, 1780, engraved by Stephen Pyle' (London, 1782), facsimile with note by J. H. Andrews (Belfast: Linen Hall Library, 1987). 'Queen's Elms, Lower malone Road' by C. Langan, 1845.

331   Queen's University of Belfast

Address   Belfast BT7 1NN

331A   Main Library, Special Collections Department

Telephone   (01232) 335020   *Fax*   (01232) 323340

Access   By appointment.

Index
Unpublished typescript handlist.

Summary
The Ewart Map Collection comprises 140 original printed maps and facsimiles of printed and manuscript maps of Ireland; provinces and counties of Ireland; individual places in Ireland, *c.*1573–1900 (facsimiles

from 1567). About 50 of the maps are of Belfast or parts of Belfast, c.1570–1900.

Detail
4, 6a,b, 7, 8, 9, 10b, 13, 14, 15

331B   Department of Geography, Map Library

Telephone   (01232) 245133 ext. 3449

Access   By written appointment.

Index
Catalogue cards, by area, on site.

Summary
OS sheets at 6 inches to the mile, 1830s–1840s. (All other maps are modern.)

Detail
4, 10b

332   Ulster Museum, Department of History

Address   Botanic Gardens, Belfast BT9 5AB

Telephone   (01232) 381251 ext. 240   *Fax*   (01232) 665510

Access   By written appointment.

Index
Card catalogue on site.

Summary
The local history collection comprises approximately 250 maps of Ireland and parts thereof dating from the mid 16th to the late 19th century (including one or two editions of earlier maps, e.g. Ptolemy).
A few manuscript maps are included, also some charts of the sea coast, for example, the complete Irish set by Greenvile Collins. The range covers a representative selection of the work of the English, Dutch, French and Italian cartographers of the 17th and 18th centuries.
Groups of special interest to historians include:
(a) Two facsimiles of contemporary plans entitled 'The taking of Enni-

skillen, 4 Feb. 1592' and 'The Battle of Ballyshannon, 17 Oct. 1593' (both in BL Mss, Cott.Aug.1,ii, 38, 39).

(b) Petrus Bertius's set of seven maps (including Media, i.e. Meath), 1618 Latin text.

(c) Mercator's five Irish maps from the 1619 (French) edition of his *Atlas*.

(d) Jansson's set of five Irish maps, 1646 French text.

(e) Speed's five Irish maps from the 1676 edition of his *Theatre*.

(f) Petty's five map set (Ireland and the four provinces) published by Berry (c.1689).

(g) Petty's *Hiberniae Delineato* (facsimile edition, 1969).

Named collections include (1) Dean King Collection, purchased 1946, ten maps, mostly late 17th and 18th centuries; (2) Sir David Reid Bequest, acquired 1951, five maps including Stangford Lough (1755); (3) Hugh Maude Collection, donated 1963, seventeen maps including items by Mercator, Speed, Blaeu, and Ridge's large maps of County Down (1767).

Detail
4, 5, 6a,b, 7, 8, 9, 10b,c, 11, 13, 14, 15

DOWN

333   North Down Heritage Centre

Address   Town Hall, Bangor, County Down BT20 4BT

Telephone   (01247) 271200

Access   By appointment.

Index
No index to maps.

Summary
Folio of 64 maps by Thomas Raven (1626–7) of lands in Co. Down granted to Sir James Hamilton (later Viscount Claneboye) in 1625 by James I.

Detail
11

Publications of maps held
Raymond Gillespie, 'Thomas Raven and the mapping of the Claneboy estates', *Journal of the Bangor Historical Society* **2** (1981), 6–9.
Sandra A. Millsopp, 'Bangor from the Raven maps', *Journal of the Bangor Historical Society* **2** (1982–3), 30–4.

334   Down County Museum

Address   Downpatrick BT30 6AH

Telephone   (01396) 615218

Access   By appointment.

Index
Maps are listed in computer catalogue.

Summary

Holdings include some 17th century maps of Ireland, and maps relating to County Down.

Detail

4, 6a, 7, 10a,b,c, 11

IRELAND

335   National Archives

Address   Bishop Street, Dublin 8

Telephone   (01) 478 3711   *Fax*   (01) 478 3650

Access   By appointment. Researchers wishing to consult Ordnance Survey material are advised to check on the current position during the transfer of this archive.

Index

Maps are listed in the archive series to which they belong. Some maps from private sources are listed in an index to maps and plans.

Summary

In many cases the series of maps relate to all 32 counties of the island of Ireland. The main classes are as follows:

Ordnance Survey: All 32 counties. The records of the Ordnance Survey between 1824 and the 1960s, currently being transferred to the National Archives, a process expected to take several years.

(1) Six-inch map and revisions. Archives of the survey and calculation work of the six-inch map, 1824–46, are now available. Maps relating to the six-inch map are in transfer and will become available in stages between 1994 and mid-1995. They include diagrams of trigonometrical points; field examination traces; levelling traces; common plots showing boundaries of adjacent counties; plots of the lines surveyed in the surveyors' notebooks on the trigonometrical skeleton; content plots used to calculate square area; fair plans of the final manuscript before engraving; proof impressions; copperplates and printed six-inch maps. Similar archives and maps relating to revisions are due for transfer.

(2) Copperplates and lithographic stones. All the copperplates for maps other than the six-inch described above and a small number of lithographic stones, for one-inch maps, are now available for inspection by prior arrangement. The plates include town plans at various scales, six-inch geological maps, one-inch and half-inch maps and miscellaneous maps.

(3) Other maps due for transfer include unpublished manuscript town plans; manuscript and published town plans; working maps and published

428

maps at one-inch scale; survey documents, plots and maps at 25-inch scale; maps made for the Incumbered Estates Court, Landed Estates Court and Chancery Land Judges Court and miscellaneous maps made for various purposes.

Office of Public Works: All 32 counties. Manuscript and printed maps, 1840s to 1962, relating to projects administered by the Board of Works. These include land improvement, inland navigation, drainage, fisheries, piers and harbours, waterworks, railways and tramways, barracks, post offices, custom houses, coastguard stations, schools, working class and labourers' housing etc. Building projects include the National Library, National Museum, Royal College of Science, Royal University etc.

Maps deposited with the Clerk of the Crown and the Clerk of the Peace: Late 19th to early 20th centuries, for each county. Includes maps, plans and awards of railways, tramways, canals, roads, court houses, lunatic asylums, piers and harbours, bridges, drainage, waterworks, gas and electricity supply, public lighting, borough improvements.

Valuation Office: Boundary Survey traces: All 32 counties. Coloured traces, 1826–44, which show the boundaries of townlands, parishes, baronies and counties as set by the Boundary Survey in preparation for the work of the Ordnance Survey.

Privy Council Office: Includes counties in Northern Ireland. Maps relating to boundary revisions, unions and divisions of parishes, railways, tramways, drainage etc., 1811–88.

Quit Rent Office: Includes counties in Northern Ireland. Maps of the Down Survey, 17th century and later copies; maps of crown lands in Ireland made for the Crown Lands Commissioners, 1820–26; printed Grand Jury maps of Counties Clare, Cork, Donegal, Kildare, Leitrim, Louth, Queen's, Roscommon and Waterford, 1752–1819; set of OS six-inch maps with markings showing boundaries taken from Down Survey parish maps, Land Commission sale maps etc., late 19th to early 20th centuries; miscellaneous maps, 18th to 20th centuries.

Rentals of Incumbered Estates Court, Landed Estates Court and Chancery Land Judges Court: All 32 counties. The rentals of estates sold through these courts contain maps of the estates made by the Ordnance Survey, 1850–1900.

Maps in private archives: Maps covering a wide range of subject matter from various sources including private papers, estate papers and solicitors' collections.

Detail
4, 5, 6a,b, 7, 8, 9, 10a,b,c, 11, 13, 14, 17, 17a

336   National Library of Ireland

Address   Kildare Street, Dublin 2

Telephone   (01) 661 8811   *Fax*   (01) 676 6690

Access   Open. Reader's ticket required and additional Manuscripts reader's ticket for manuscript maps. Appointment recommended as much of the map collection is currently withdrawn for conservation.

Index

Good card catalogue on site.

Manuscript maps and surveys listed in R. Hayes, *Manuscript sources for the history of Irish civilisation* (Boston, 1965), and *Supplement* (Boston, 1979).

Summary

By far the most important collection of Irish maps in Ireland. Its nucleus was the Library of the Royal Dublin Society (founded 1732) and since the establishment of the Library in 1877 it has been continuously and massively augmented by gifts and bequests (notably the Joly collection, perhaps the most important private collection of Irish maps ever formed), by purchase, and by the extensive photostatting and microfilming of maps in other collections. In the absence of a system of county record offices in the Irish Republic, the National Library is especially rich in estate maps and other local surveys.

The most important categories are:

1. Map of Western Europe in a 13th century manuscript of *Topographia Hibernica* by Geraldus Cambrensis.

2. Military surveys of Ulster, late 16th and early 17th century, including those of Richard Bartlett (c.1602); Isle of Lewis and Harris (early 17th century).

3. The Reeves Collection of Down Survey parish maps, late 18th century copies of William Petty's mid-17th century survey covering parishes in the counties of Dublin, Eastmeath, Kilkenny, Leitrim, Limerick, Longford, Laois, Offaly, Tipperary, Waterford, Westmeath, Wexford, Wicklow and Carlow.

4. Manuscript estate maps including the earliest known Irish estate map of parts of the lands of Sir Walter Raleigh at Mogeely, County Cork; many 18th century examples by J. Rocque and Bernard Scalé, and a collection of about 4000 working maps by the surveyor John Longfield of the firm of Brownrigg, Longfield and Murray (c.1775–1833).

5. Printed city and Grand Jury county maps from the 18th and 19th centuries.

6. Manuscript road maps of mail coach routes, surveyed 1805–16.

7. The most complete collection in Ireland of Irish OS maps, especially important for town plans.

Detail
4, 5, 6a,b, 7, 8, 9, 10a,b,c, 11, 13, 15, 17c

Publications of maps held
J. H. Andrews, 'The Longfield Maps in the National Library of Ireland: an agenda for research', *Irish Geography* **24** (1991), 24–34.

G. R. Crone, *Early maps of the British Isles, AD 1000–1579* (Royal Geographical Society, 1958) (facsimile of Ms 700 Western Europe in a copy of Giraldus Cambrensis' *Topography of Ireland, AD 1200*, with commentary).

G. A. Hayes McCoy, *Ulster and other Irish maps, c.1600* (Irish Mss Commission, 1964) (facsimiles of Ms 2656 with introduction and commentary).

Facsimiles and reproductions for sale
National Library of Ireland, *Ireland from Maps* (Dublin, 1980), reproductions of maps with explanatory booklet.

337   Ordnance Survey of Ireland

Address   Phoenix Park, Dublin
NB This archive is in process of being transferred to the National Archive, Bishop Street, Dublin.

Telephone   (8) 206100   *Fax*   (8) 204156

Access   By written application to Director of Operations, showing that OS is a 'library of last resort'. A search fee may be charged.

Index
Various manuscript lists of different parts of the collection but none up-to-date.

Summary
1. 'Raw materials' of almost all Irish OS maps from the 1820s onwards, both the regular series and the *ad hoc* maps produced for other government departments or for use in official reports, i.e., field books, tri-

angulation diagrams, line plots, content plots, fair plans, examination trials, proofs.

2. Copies of most published OS maps of Ireland, but there is no comprehensive collection of 'record copies' and there are some surprising gaps. There are a few OS maps of Britain, mainly at 1 inch to 1 mile.

3. A small but varied collection of non-OS maps, most of them probably acquired in the early years of the Irish Survey as sources of evidence on placenames; others acquired by gift, including (in 1985) Charles Vallancey's 'Royal map of Ireland'. Numerous maps of Irish estates sold through the Lord Judges Court from 1862.

Detail
1, 4, 5, 6b, 7, 8, 9, 10a,b,c, 11, 14, 17c

Publications of maps held
J. H. Andrews, 'Charles Vallancey and the map of Ireland', *Geographical Journal* **132** (1966), 48–61.

J. H. Andrews, *History in the Ordnance map, an introduction for Irish readers* (1974, 2nd edition 1993).

338   Valuation Office

Address   6 Ely Place, Dublin 2

Telephone   (01) 676 3211   *Fax*   (01) 678 9646

Access   Open.

Index
No index to maps.

Summary
Map coverage for the 26 Counties in two categories:

(1) Maps from 1840 to 1850 showing the results of the original perambulatory survey for the valuation of heriditaments and tenements in Ireland.

(2) Maps from 1850–1900 (and later) which follow administrative boundaries of baronies, unions, parishes and townlands, and show the properties therein.

Detail
4, 6b, 7, 10b,c

CAVAN

339   Cavan County Library, Local History Collection

Address   Farnham Street, Cavan

Telephone   (049) 31799   *Fax*   (049) 31384

Access   Open.

Index
No index to maps.

Summary
Manuscript maps of the Farnham Estate and of the Alexander Sanderson Estate. County Cavan from William Petty's *Hibernia Delineatio* and facsimiles of Down Survey barony maps. Maps of the proposed Ballinamore / Ballyconnell Canal, from Lough Erne to the River Shannon (1846) and other 19th century printed maps of County Cavan.
OS at 6 inches to 1 mile for County Cavan (1840).

Detail
6a, 7, 10b, 11, 13, 14

CLARE

340   Clare County Library, Local Studies Centre

Address   The Manse, Harmony Row, Ennis

Telephone   (065) 21616 ext. 271

Access   Open.

Index
No index to maps.

Summary
A small collection of local cover, incomplete.
Barony maps of Clare by William Petty (1685). Henry Pelham's Grand Jury map, 1787, of Clare. Griffith valuation maps (1855) of Clare.
Bound volume of OS sheets, 1840s. OS 1840/41, 1879, and later, of Clare.

Detail
4, 6b, 7, 10a,b,c, 13, 15, 17a

CORK

341   Cork City Library, The Cork Collection

Address   57 Grand Parade, Cork

Telephone   (21) 277100   *Fax*   (21) 275684

Access   Open.

Index
Card catalogue on site. Most of the maps are included in the typewritten select list of holdings in the local history collection.

Summary
The collection consists of maps of Cork City from possibly 1545 (this is a reproduction of 1837 of an original said to be in London) to the present day. Most of these are copies of originals. These maps are invaluable for researchers who are tracing the development of Cork City. The centre of the city is built on a number of small islands, the channels between which have been arched over to form some of its principal streets. The old maps enable us to correlate the modern streets with the old waterways in tracing the growth of the city from the 16th century onwards.
The collection also includes OS and geological maps of the entire county, harbour charts, and reproductions of some old maps of Ireland.
Other notables:
'Cork County Surveyed, by order of the Jury of the County' by Neville Bath (1818). Scale 3/4 inch to 1 mile. Original impression, in six sections, showing roads, seats of nobility, etc.
'Map of the proposed railway from Passage to Cork' (1836) at 20 inches to 1 mile. Original, in eleven sections in leather case.
Charles Goad's Insurance Maps of Cork City, 1st to 7th editions, 1897–1961. Scale 1 inch to 40 feet.
'Atlas to accompany 2nd Report of the Railway Commissioners of Ireland, 1836.' Shows existing and proposed railway lines, density of population, quantities of traffic and passengers in different directions etc. Scale approx 1 inch to 10 miles.

Detail
1, 4, 5, 6a,b, 7, 8, 9, 10a,b,c, 13, 16

Publications of maps held
Eugene Carberry, 'The development of Cork City', *Journal of the Cork Historical and Archaeological Society* **48** (1943), 67–81 (Article based on original maps; copies of most of these are in the Cork Collection.)

342   University College Cork, Boole Library

Address   University College, Cork

Telephone   (021) 276871   *Fax*   (021) 273428

Access   By appointment for non-members of the University.

Index
Card index on site.

Summary
(1) Ireland general.
Full set of OS Ireland, 1st edition. 1st edition and two facsimile reproductions of William Petty's *Hiberniae Delineatio* and *Barony Maps*, and of escheated counties maps, 1609, by OS Southampton, 1861. 19th century travelling, bankers and railroad maps. Reproductions of early maps of Ireland by Boazio, Morden, Norden.
(2) Special interest manuscripts.
(a) Survey of the estate of Rt. Hon. Thomas, Lord Baron of Kerry anno 1697, by Henry Pratt, 66 sheets. PRO Ireland certified copies of portions of records in the Public Record Office, copied by H. Wood, 1916.
(b) Four estate maps: three of Cooleduff, County Cork, for 1805, 1839, 1891, and one of Broomadera, County Kerry, 1796.
(c) Agricultural Statistics Maps and diagrams for County Cork for 1847 to 1930. 29 sheets.
(3) Other manuscript maps.
Folio containing nine estate maps showing townlands of County Kerry in the estate of Samuel Julian Esq., 1865.
(4) Printed maps and charts.
(a) Chart of Kinsale Harbour by Captain Greenvile Collins (undated, *c*.1690) showing plan of outer defences to Charles' Fort, though these were never constructed.
(b) A new chart, being an actual survey of the harbours of Rineshark and Waterford to the confluence of the Rivers Sure and Barrow and sea

coast adjacent. Published by Act of Parliament, January 1737/8.

(c) Chart of River Shannon by John Cowan (*c*.1794) (Stamped Ex libris et mappis Edward Lynam 1945).

(d) Collection of maps and picture plans of Cork City compiled by Rev. J. O'Leary (Mostly xerox copies, dated 1560, 1590, 1600, 1690, 1714, 1759, 1773, 1774, 1801 (1st edition of Beauford's map), 1832, c.1834, 1893).

(e) Maps accompanying 1st to 4th Reports of the Commissioners on the Nature and Extent of the Bogs in Ireland, 1810–14. 54 plates.

Detail

1, 4, 5, 6a, 7, 8, 9, 10b, 11, 13, 15

Publications of maps held

J. H. Andrews, 'Henry Pratt, surveyor of Kerry estates', *Journal of the Kerry Archaeological and Historical Society* **13** (1980), 5–38.

DUBLIN

343   Dublin City Archives

Address   City Hall, Cork Hill, Dublin 2

Telephone   (01) 6796 111 ext. 2818   *Fax*   (01) 679 8159

Access   By appointment.

Index

M. Clark, *The book of maps of the Dublin City Surveyors, 1695–1827, an annotated list with biographical notes and an introduction* (Dublin, 1983).

Lists of maps are included in John P. McEvoy, 'Handlist of holdings of the Corporation of Dublin' (unpublished, 1901).

Summary

For the period 1700–1840 the maps are mainly manuscript and have their provenance in the City Surveyor's Office, Dublin Corporation, and in the Dublin Wide Streets Commissioners. For the period 1840–1900 maps are mainly printed and come from the archives of Dublin Corporation; Rathmines and Rathgar Improvement Commissioners; Pembroke Township Commissioners (the last two were Urban District Councils from 1898.)

Detail

4, 7, 11, 13, 15

Publications of maps held

Mary Clark, 'Dublin surveyors and their maps', *Dublin Historical Record* **29** (1985–6), 140–8.

Niall McCullough, *Dublin: an urban history* (Dublin, 1989).

Niall McCullough (ed.), *A vision of the city: Dublin and the Wide Streets Commissioners* (Dublin, 1991).

344 Gilbert Library, Dublin and Irish Collections

Address   138–141 Pearse Street, Dublin 2

Telephone (01) 677 7662

Access   Open.

Index

D. Hyde and D. J. O'Donoghue, *Catalogue of the Books and Manuscripts comprising the Library of the late Sir John T. Gilbert* (Dublin, 1918). Alphabetical typescript list on site.

Summary

Maps of Dublin City and County. John Rocque's maps for the City and County (1756); H. Moll's map of Ireland with city plans; Speed's maps of Ireland. Maps accompanying *Wilson's Dublin Directory* and later directories (1761-c.1870).

Some manuscript maps such as Robert Lewis's book of maps from the Down Survey.

OS, 6 inches to 1 mile, 1st edition for the whole country on microfiche, and originals for County Dublin, and at 1 inch to the mile.

Detail
4, 5, 6b, 7, 10a,b, 15

Facsimiles or reproductions on sale
A series of maps at reduced scale for sale as postcards.

345 Trinity College

Address   Dublin 2

345A The Library

Telephone (01) 702 2087   *Fax* (01) 679 1003

Access   Open.

Index

There is no separate map catalogue. Manuscript maps are listed in a card catalogue in the Manuscripts Department. Some maps are in the published catalogue of books acquired before 1872. Sheet maps in the collection of Hendrik Fagel (acquired 1802) are listed in T. K. Abbot, *Catalogue of the manuscripts in the Library of Trinity College Dublin* (Dublin, 1900). OS and other 19th century maps are retrieved via the original OS catalogues and by series finding aids and graphic indexes. Some large scale county maps listed in Rodger (2nd edition, 1972).

Summary

This is the largest collection of maps in Ireland; while the majority of printed maps are in the Map Library (established in 1987) many others are in the Department of Manuscripts and the Department of Early Printed Books. Many major atlases and a few (mainly Irish) printed sheet maps have been acquired by purchase or gift since the early 17th century including Ptolemy, Ortelius, Braun and Hogenburg, Mercator, Blaeu, Pitt, Sanson, Jaillot, Saxton, Waghenaer, Speed, Ogilby, Mackenzie. 19th century OS maps of Ireland and Great Britain, geological maps, Admiralty charts and the maps of the larger commercial publishers were acquired on legal deposit after 1801.

A major special collection of printed maps and atlases is that of Hendrik Fagel, chief minister of the Netherlands at the end of the 18th century. A minor one is an incomplete set of John Rocque's maps, apparently acquired at the time of Rocque's visit to Dublin in the 1750s. General and regional printed maps of Ireland are less fully represented than the general size and importance of the library would suggest.

Chief manuscript collections are 'Hardiman' maps (see below): 16th and 17th century maps of Ireland, associated with Sir George Carew; maps of Trinity College estates, 17th-19th centuries, and two volumes of maps by John Rocque of the Manors of Kildare and Rathangan.

A large collection of Irish OS maps at all scales. Also early 6 inches to 1 mile of Lancashire and Yorkshire, and a large number of early British 1:2500 maps.

Detail

4, 5, 6a,b, 7, 8, 9, 10a,b,c, 11, 13, 15, 16

Publications of maps held

F. H. A. Aalen and R. J. Hunter, 'The estate maps of Trinity College', *Hermathena* **98** (1964), 85–96.

J. H. Andrews, 'Baptiste Boazio's map of Ireland', *Long Room* **1** (1970), 29–36.

J. H. Andrews, 'Maps and atlases', in Peter Fox (ed.), *Treasures of the Library, Trinity College, Dublin* (Dublin, 1986), pp.170–82.

J. H. Andrews, 'An early map of Inishower', *Long Room* **7** (1973), 19–25.

J. Hardiman, 'Catalogue of Ms maps of Ireland and parts of Ireland acquired before 1824', *Transactions of the Royal Irish Academy* **14** (1824), 55–7.

R. Dunlop, '16th century maps of Ireland', *English Historical Review* **20** (1905), 309–337.

W. O'Sullivan, 'George Carew's Irish maps', *Long Room* **26/27** (1983), 15–25.

345B Department of Geography, Freeman Library

Telephone	(01) 702 1454
Access	By appointment.

Index
Unpublished catalogue on site.

Summary
Photostat collection of 16th and 17th century maps in other libraries. Various world, British and Irish 19th century maps. OS at 6 inches to 1 mile for most counties.

Detail
1, 4, 9, 10a,b

345C Department of Geology

Telephone	(01) 702 1074
Access	By appointment.

Index
Rough draft catalogue on site.

Summary
Geological maps, global coverage with emphasis on the British Isles. The collection includes a complete set of the Geological Survey of Ireland (1856–90) at 1 inch to 1 mile. Several geological maps at 1 inch to 4 miles by Sir Richard Griffith, 1839–55.

Detail
4, 6a, 5, 10a

346 University College Dublin, Department of Geography, Map Library

Address   Belfield, Dublin 4

Telephone   (01) 269 3244

Access   By written appointment.

Index
Card catalogue in Map Library.

Summary
This is a teaching and reference collection, mostly of modern OS maps. The historical collection includes a near-complete set of reprinted (OS) Down Survey barony maps, and microfilm and partial photostat coverage of Down Survey parish maps. Many 18th and 19th century maps are available, mainly as photostats or published facsimiles.
The small number of manuscript maps relate mainly to (1) surveys of parts of the estate of Francis Synge, near Ashford, County Wicklow, between 1754 and 1813, and (2) a volume of maps, enlarged from the OS by Hodges Smith & Co., showing the estates of Thomas Boyce, Bannow, County Wexford, in Wexford, Kilkenny and Galway in 1843.

Detail
4, 5, 6b, 7, 10a,b,c, 11

Publications of maps held
A. A. Horner, 'Lord Walter Fitzgerald's Ordnance Survey maps of Kilkea and district', *Kildare Archaeological and Historical Society Journal* **17** (Centenary Edition, 1987–91), 8–12.

347 Archbishop Marsh's Library

Address   St Patrick's Close, Dublin 8

Telephone   (01) 54 3511

Access   By written appointment.

Index
Maps and atlases are listed in the general catalogue.

Summary
Manuscript maps of the Liberty of St Patrick's Cathedral, Dublin, 1741–1825 (45 fols).

Printed maps include John Rocque's map of the city and suburbs of Dublin (1756), and the 1773 revision by Bernard Scalé. Survey of the County of Dublin (1802) and of County Monaghan by W. McCrea (1802).

Murdoch Mackenzie, *A maritime survey of Ireland and the west of Great Britain*, 2 vols. (London, 1776). Includes 'nautical descriptions of the North Coast of Ireland from Tory Island to Rachlin Island'.

Atlases, 17th and 18th century, of the World, of Great Britain, of Ireland, including Abraham Ortelius, *Theatrum orbis terrarum* (probably the 1590 or 1598 edition), Sebastian Münster, *Cosmographis universalis* (Basle, 1634), and Joan Blaeu's *Grand Atlas* (Amsterdam, 1662), Visscher, Morden, Blaeu, W. Petty, C. Price, M. Pitt, H. Moll, T. Jefferys, T. Kitchen, and others.

The Library holds a complete set of OS first edition 6 inches to 1 mile for most if not all of the 32 counties (1833–46).

Detail
1, 4, 6b, 7, 8, 10a,b

348   Dublin Port Board Map and Chart Collection

Address   Port Centre, Alexandra Road, Dublin 1

Telephone   (01) 872 2777   *Fax*   (01) 874 1241 / 873 5946

Access   By appointment.

Index
No index to maps.

Summary
Various manuscript charts of the coast of Wicklow, Wexford and Waterford, with Dublin Bay and Harbour, from *c*.1700, which include six manuscript charts of Dublin Harbour and Bay, one of Dun Leary, by George Semple, 1762. Maps of the City of Dublin showing river, port and canal features, from early 18th to early 19th centuries. Charts by Murdoch Mackenzie the elder, of the East Coast of Ireland, and the volumes of his *Natural Description of the West Coast of Great Britain* ... and *Natural Description of the Coast of Ireland* (both dated 1776).

Detail
1, 2, 3, 4, 6a,b, 7, 8, 11

Publications of maps held
An article on the manuscript charts by George Semple will be published
in the *Proceedings of the Royal Irish Academy*.

349   Irish Railway Record Society

Address   Heuston Station, Dublin 8

Telephone   (0238) 528248

Access   By written appointment.

Index
J. Leckey and P. Rigney, *IRRS archival collections D1–D10*. (Dublin,
1976).

Summary
Approximately 5000 manuscript maps and drawings of docks, tramways,
reservoirs, etc. Most complete collection of Parliamentary plans of Irish
railways outside the House of Lords Record Office. OS maps covering
Irish railways.

Detail
5, 10, 13

350   The King's Hospital Archive

Address   Palmerstown, Dublin 20

Telephone   (01) 626 5933   *Fax*   (01) 626 5933 ext. 236

Access   By appointment.

Index
No index to maps.

Summary
All maps are manuscript. Rental maps of the estates of the Hospital and
Free School of King Charles II, Dublin, mostly Dublin property, 1729–
1832. The most interesting are the bound 1832 maps by Joseph Bryne of
the Oxmantown Green and St Stephen's Green areas.
Noddstown, Co. Tipperary, maps of King's Hospital estate, 1783–1881.
Mary Mercer's (of Mercer's Hospital and Mercer's School) Dublin city
estate and in Rathcode, C. Dublin – many maps attached to deeds, 1683–
1826. The Dublin property was part of the lands of old St Mary's Abbey.

Thomas Ivory's map of Oxmantown Green, 1775. (Ivory was the architect of the second King's Hospital, erected in Blackhall Place in the 1770s and 1780s. The plans are in the BL).

Detail
11

Publications of maps held
Ivory's map of Oxmantown Green (1775) is reproduced in Lesley Whiteside, *A History of the King's Hospital, Dublin* (Dublin, 1975; 2nd edition, Dublin, 1985).

351   Library of the King's Inns

Address   Henrietta Street, Dublin 1

Telephone   (01) 874 7134   *Fax*   (01) 872 6048

Access   By advance written application to the Librarian, stating purpose of research.

Index
None. Some maps listed by author in unpublished catalogue of books relating to Ireland.

Summary
A range of printed maps of Ireland and parts of Ireland that is fairly predictable for a large Dublin library of the 18th and 19th centuries. The rare *Memorial Atlas of Ireland* (Philadelphia, 1901). The surprising feature is the large number of non-Irish 19th century atlases, including historical, historical geography, and natural history atlases, and a few facsimiles of early atlases.
County Wexford, copies of Down Survey parish maps 1777–8.
Large collection of Irish Encumbered Estates Court rental maps, from 1850.
Irish Railway Commission maps and sections, 1837–8.
Unique 19th century copies by J. P. Prendergast of 17th century Irish plantation maps.

Detail
4, 6a,b, 7, 8, 10a,b,c, 11, 13, 15, 17a

352 Land Commission

Address   National Archives Building, Bishop Street, Dublin 8

Telephone   (01) 475 0766

Access   By appointment, access only granted to tenants needing to see records of Land Commission allocation. The Land Commission is not a Public Office but a working section of the Department of Agriculture. Records are restricted until they are passed to the National Archives.

Index
List of estates (not maps) held at the National Library, Kildare Street.

Summary
Printed maps, 1881 to 1900, related to land sold by landlords to statutory bodies under Land Acts. The records are listed by landlord's name, county, record number, and townland.

Detail
10b,c, 11

353 Representative Church Body Library

Address   Braemor Park, Churchtown, Dublin 14

Telephone   (01) 92 3979

Access   Open.

Index
Handlists available on site.

Summary
Diocese of Clogher, Co. Fermanagh and Co. Monaghan: maps of parishes and glebes, 23 items, 1824–1904.
Diocese of Cashel and Emley, Co. Tipperary and Co. Limerick: maps of glebes, 15 items, 1787–1876.
Diocese of Dublin, Co. Dublin, Co. Wicklow, Co. Cork: maps of the estates of the archbishops, 63 items, 1654–1813.
Christ Church cathedral, Dublin, Co. Dublin and Co. Kildare: maps of the estates of the Dean and Chapter, 30 items, 1638–1814.
Incorporated Society for promoting Protestant Schools in Ireland: 2 vols. of maps of estates in Co. Roscommon, 1784, and Co. Wexford, 1868.

Detail
11, 17a,c

Publications of maps held
F. H. A. Aalen and Kevin Whelan (eds), *Dublin City and County* (Dublin, 1992) reproduced 'The Lordship of Tallaght ... belonging to the Bishop of Dublin' *c.*1654, from the estate maps of the archbishops of Dublin as a dust jacket.
Irish Historic Towns Atlas series (Royal Irish Academy, forthcoming) will include two maps of the town of Athlone from the Incorporated Society's volume of Co. Roscommon estates.

354   Royal Irish Academy

Address   19 Dawson Street, Dublin 2

Telephone   (01) 676 2570/4222   *Fax*   (01) 676 2346

Access   Open to non-members of the Academy on recommendation of a member or on production of a letter of introduction from a faculty etc.

Index
Good card index catalogue on site.

Summary
Small miscellaneous collection of mainly Irish maps acquired principally by gift at various times since the Academy's foundation in 1785. 'Ireland', by C. Browne (1690) and H. Pratt (1732). Irish atlases by Petty, Lamb, Moll, Grierson. Town plans: Brooking's 'Dublin' (1728); Beauford's 'Cork' (1801). Maritime surveys by Mackenzie (1776), Drury (1789). First part of C. Vallancey's military survey of Ireland, 1776, manuscript. Geological map of Ireland. J. Brownrigg's printed map of Grand Canal (1788). George Taylor and Andrew Skinner, 'Roads of Ireland' (1778). OS, 1 inch to 1 mile, complete 1st edition.

Detail
4, 5, 6a,b, 7,8, 9, 10a,b, 11, 14, 15

355   Royal Society of Antiquaries of Ireland

Address   63 Merrion Square, Dublin 2

Telephone   (01) 676 1749

Access   By appointment.

Index
None published, list in preparation by librarian.

Summary
Small miscellaneous collection, mainly acquired by donation, mainly printed, some manuscript. Especially rich in maps of County Kilkenny (the Society originated as the Kilkenny Archaeological Society), and of some interest in the history of thematic maps.
Historical maps: Ptolemy's Ireland corrected by the aid of Bardic history. Charles O'Conor, 'Ortelius improved' (?1795) 3 copies; more than one state represented. Manuscript antiquarian map of Kilkenny by John G. A. Prim, 1840. 'Antient map of Ireland' (Victorian fake based on Ortelius, with advertisement for same). Numerous plans of archaeological sites.
Maritime surveys include J. Malton's 'Dublin Bay' (1795), S. Carter and N. St Leger's 'Waterford Harbour' (1835), Admiralty Chart, 'Sound of Iona' (1857).
Estate maps by Thomas Reading (1748 and 1765), Brassington and Gale (1840). Canal maps of Kilkenny (1761, printed) and J. Killaly's 'Canals connecting Rivers Barrow, Sure and Shannon' (1811, printed.)

Detail
4, 5, 6a,b, 7, 8, 10a,b, 11, 14, 15

KILDARE

356   St Patrick's College Library

Address   Maynooth, County Kildare

Telephone   (01) 628 5222   *Fax*   (01) 628 6008

Access   By written appointment.

Index
No index to maps.

Summary
The collection includes maps and atlases by Blaeu (1654), Jansson, Speed (1610), F. Halma, H. Moll, Taylor and Skinner, and others, and an early map of the Castle of Maynooth.
The Library has a complete set of the OS 6 inch to 1 mile 19th century maps of Ireland. John Rocque's manuscript survey of the manor of Maynooth, 1757.

Detail
10b, 11

LIMERICK

357   Limerick City Library

Address   The Granary, Michael Street, Limerick

Telephone   (061) 314668 / 415799   *Fax*   (Limerick Corporation)
               (061) 415266

Access   Open.

Index
Roisin Nash, *Bibliography of Limerick History and Antiquities* (*c*.1961–2), pp.43–6.

Summary
1850 edition of 'Limerick' (*c*.1602) from original in Trinity College; 'Limerick' (1786) by John Ferrar; 1820 edition of 'Limerick in 1633' from Thomas Stafford's *Pacata Hibernia*. 19th century maps: 1827 map of Limerick City and County in Fitzgerald and McGregor, *History of Limerick*; Limerick in 1865 in Lenihan, *History of Limerick*; early 19th century map by T. Larcom; map showing the boundary of the several fishery in the River Shannon called Fishers Stent (1861). 17th and 18th century maps of Ireland: by Hondius (1693), by Sanson (1714), by Moll (1714), and by Morden, early 18th century. John Speed's maps of Leinster, Ulster and Connaught. Maps of River Shannon in *Shannon Navigation Reports* (1837). Military maps of battle of the Boyne, Aughrim and Athlone. Town maps of Cork, Cork Harbour (18th century), Londonderry and Enniskillen.

Detail
4, 6a,b, 7, 9, 10b, 15

358   Limerick Museum

Address   1 John's Square North, Limerick

Telephone   (061) 417826   *Fax*   (061) 415266

Access   By appointment.

Index

No index to maps.

Summary

Maps principally of Limerick City, County Limerick, County Clare and Munster, dating from the 17th to 20th centuries.

Collection of reproduction maps of sieges of Limerick, 1690–91. Henry Pelham's Grand Jury map, 1787, of Clare. Hydrological survey of the Shannon Estuary (1794). Atlas of the Earl of Limerick's estate in Limerick City (1823).

OS 5 feet to 1 mile survey of Limerick City (1840).

Detail

1, 4, 6a,b, 7, 8, 10b, 11, 13, 16

ROSCOMMON

359   Strokestown Park

Address   Co. Roscommon

Telephone   (078) 33013   *Fax*   (078) 33454

Access   By appointment.

Index
No index to maps.

Summary
Most maps have been transferred to the National Library, Dublin.
One book of survey of Sandford estate (about 20,000 acres), Castlerea,
Co. Roscommon, 1819–27, the estate of Baron Mount Sandford. Used
for the first OS survey of Ireland in 1829. John Longfield, cartographer.
Approx. 30 maps with index of tenants and holdings.

Detail
4, 11

SLIGO

360   Sligo County Library

Address   The Courthouse, Sligo

Telephone   (071) 42212   *Fax*   (071) 44779

Access   Open.

Index

J. C. McTernan, *Sligo sources of local history* (Sligo County Library, 1988), pp.104–16 covers maps and charts.

Summary

(1) Maps of Sligo County, including: from the Down Survey (1654–57), the county map from William Petty's Atlas *Hiberniae Delineato, 1685*, the Sligo Barony maps of Carbury, Corran, Leyney, Tireragh and Tirerrill, and certified copies of the parish maps for the county; Co. Sligo by John Rocque (1794), by Grierson (1816), by William Larkin, for the Grand Jury (1819), and OS maps from 1837.

(2) Maps of the Town and Borough of Sligo, including: 'Plan of the Town and Forts of Sligo as it was retrenched by Col. Henry Luttrell ... 1689' (reconstructed by Charles Boooth Jones).

(3) Large collection of estates maps, dating from the 18th century onwards.

(3) Charts of Sligo Bay: Admiralty chart (1775) with land features; map of bay and harbour of Sligo by Alexander Nimmo (1821) for the Port Commissioners.

Detail

6a, 7, 8, 10a,b,c, 11, 17c

TIPPERARY

361   Tipperary Joint Libraries Committee, Local Studies Department

Address   Castle Avenue, Thurles

Telephone   (0504) 21555   *Fax*   (0504) 23442

Access   Open.

Index
No index to maps.

Summary
Down Survey maps of Baronies of Clanwilliam, Eliogarty, Ileagh, Ikerrin, Lower Ormond, Upper Ormond, Kilnemanagh, Slieveardagh, Owney and Arra and Kilnelongurty (1908). Extracts from some Tipperary estates, eg, W. Poe Estate, Donnybrook, Ballymackey, Nenagh (1810).
Garrykennedy Demesne (1857); Photocopies of Thurles Estate (1819) and of Thurles and Thomastown Estate (1859). Map constructed by government order for the specific purposes of The Railway Commission (no date) at 1 inch to 4 statute miles.
Clonmel, 24 sheets coloured (1874), Nenagh, 16 sheets (1879), Carrick-on-Suir, 15 sheets (1886), Tipperary, 14 sheets (1880), all at $10\frac{1}{2}$ inches to 1 statute mile.
OS 1st edition at 6 inches to 1 mile for County Tipperary.

Detail
4, 5, 7, 10b, 11

WESTMEATH

362   Westmeath County Library, Local History Collection

Address   County Library Headquarters, Dublin Road, Mullingar

Telephone   (044) 40781 / 2 / 3

Access   Open.

Index
No index to maps.

Summary
Collection includes a selection of maps relating to other parts of Ireland and Britain; estate maps for County Westmeath; navigation charts of the River Shannon; geological maps at 1 inch to 1 mile.
OS 1st edition at 6 inches to 1 mile for Westmeath, and OS town plans for Mulingar and Athlone.

Detail
1, 4, 5, 6a,b, 7, 10b, 11, 14

Publications of maps held
Marian Keaney, *Westmeath local studies: a guide to sources* (Mullingar: Longford-Westmeath Joint Library Committee, 1982).

INDEX

HOYLE, Fred
Our place in the cosmos

CLASS NO. 523.1 HOY

TO AVOID FINES THIS BOOK SHOULD BE RETURNED ON
OR BEFORE THE LAST DATE STAMPED ABOVE, IF NOT
REQUIRED BY ANOTHER READER IT MAY BE RENEWED BY
PERSONAL CALL, TELEPHONE OR POST, QUOTING THE
DETAILS DISPLAYED.